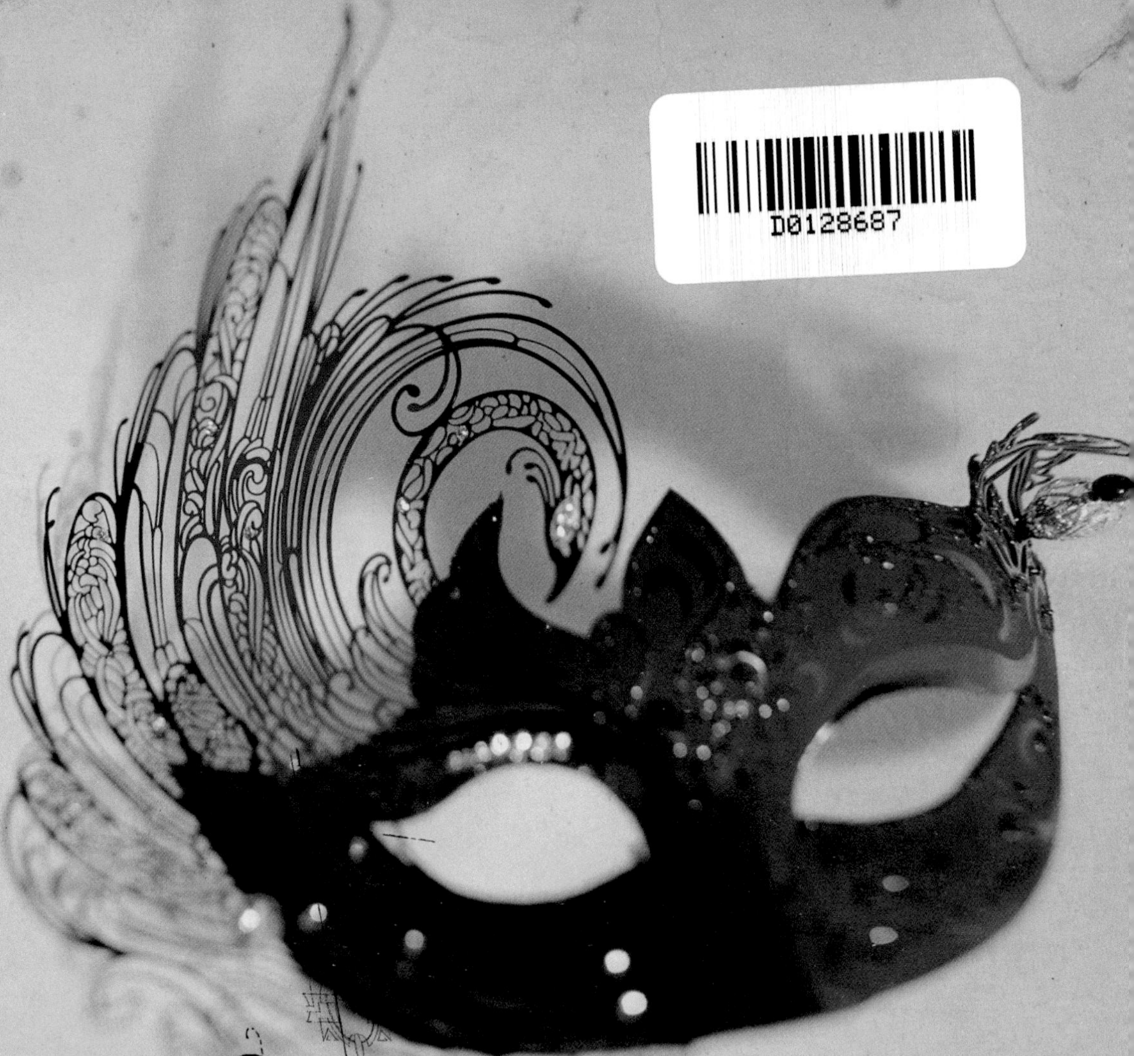

ENDLESS NIGHTS

THE SANDMAN

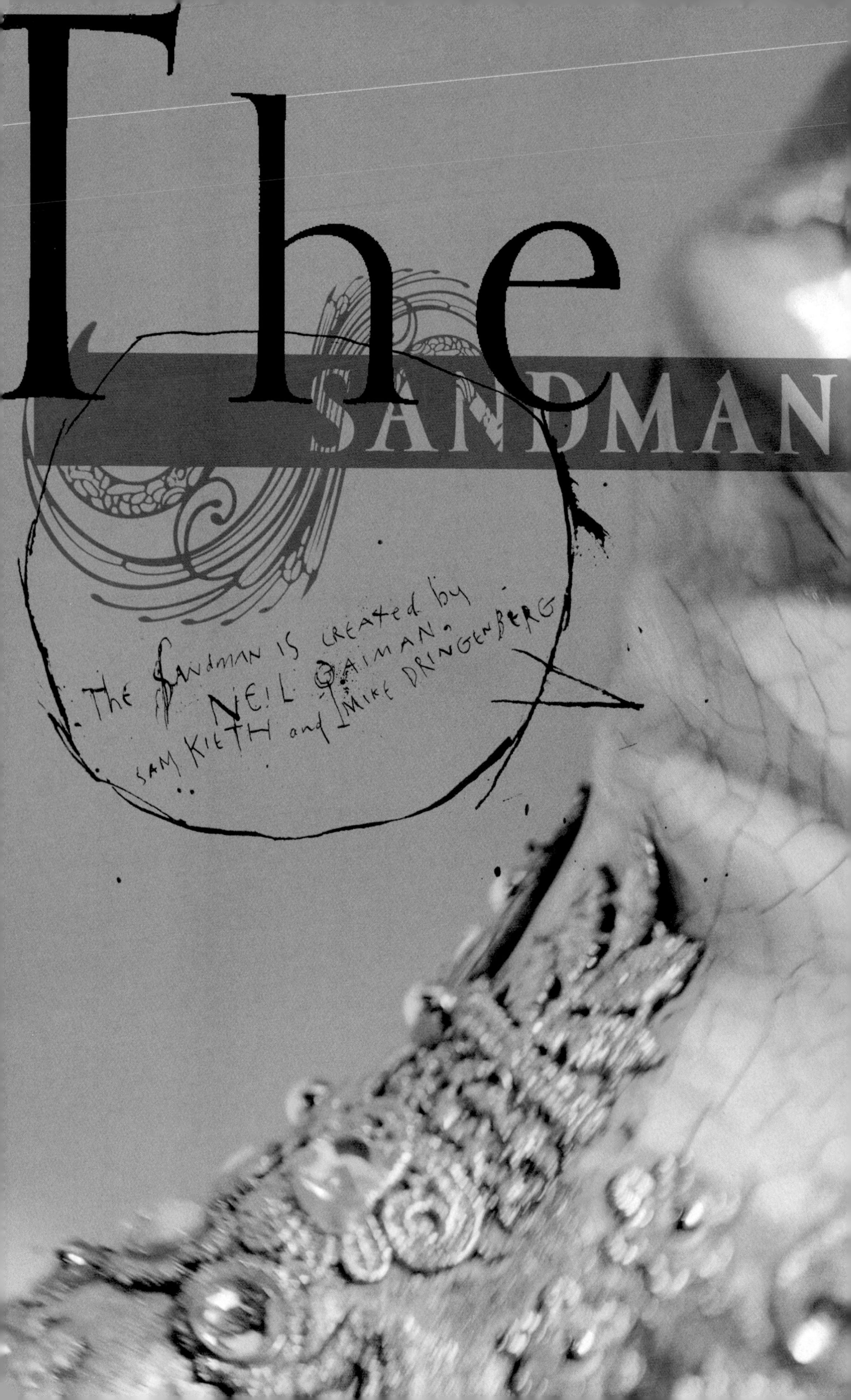
The
SANDMAN
The Sandman is created by
Neil Gaiman,
Sam Kieth and Mike Dringenberg

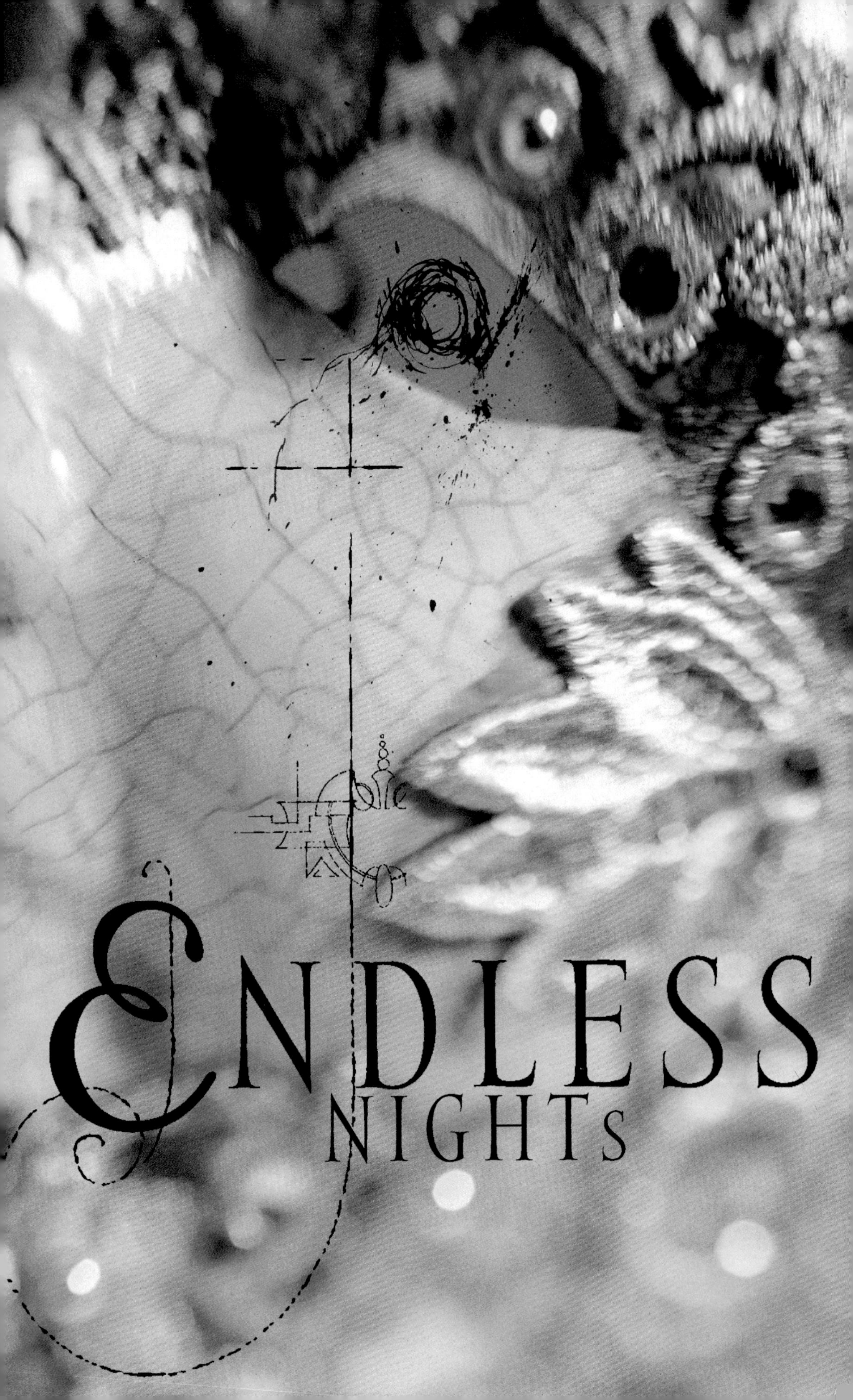
ENDLESS
NIGHTS

Shelly Bond
Executive Editor – Vertigo
Mariah Huehner
Assistant Editor
Robbin Brosterman
Design Director – Books

Hank Kanalz
Senior VP – Vertigo & Integrated Publishing

Diane Nelson
President
Dan DiDio *and* **Jim Lee**
Co-Publishers
Geoff Johns
Chief Creative Officer
John Rood
Executive VP – Sales, Marketing & Business Development
Amy Genkins
Senior VP – Business & Legal Affairs
Nairi Gardiner
Senior VP – Finance
Jeff Boison
VP – Publishing Planning
Mark Chiarello
VP – Art Direction & Design
John Cunningham
VP – Marketing
Terri Cunningham
VP – Editorial Administration
Alison Gill
Senior VP – Manufacturing & Operations
Jay Kogan
VP – Business & Legal Affairs, Publishing
Jack Mahan
VP – Business Affairs, Talent
Nick Napolitano
VP – Manufacturing Administration
Sue Pohja
VP – Book Sales
Courtney Simmons
Senior VP – Publicity
Bob Wayne
Senior VP – Sales

Cover, logo and book design by **Dave McKean**

For Jenette, for Paul, and especially for Karen
for trusting me.
—Neil

THE SANDMAN: ENDLESS NIGHTS
Published by DC Comics. Copyright © 2003 DC Comics.
All Rights Reserved. Vertigo and all characters, their
distinctive likenesses and related elements featured in this
publication are trademarks of DC Comics. The stories,
characters and incidents featured in this publication
are entirely fictional. DC Comics does not read or accept
unsolicited submissions of ideas, stories or artwork.

DC Comics
1700 Broadway, New York, NY 10019
A Warner Bros. Entertainment Company.
Printed in the USA. First Printing.
ISBN: 978-1-4012-4233-6

Library of Congress Cataloging-in-Publication Data

Gaiman, Neil.
   The sandman : endless nights (new edition) / Neil Gaiman.
      pages cm
   "Originally published as Sandman Endless Nights."
   ISBN 978-1-4012-4233-6
   1. Graphic novels. I. Title. II. Title: Endless Nights.
   PN6728.S26G373 2013
   741.5'973—dc23
                                                 2013020544

CONTENTS

All stories written by
Neil Gaiman.
All stories lettered by
Todd Klein.

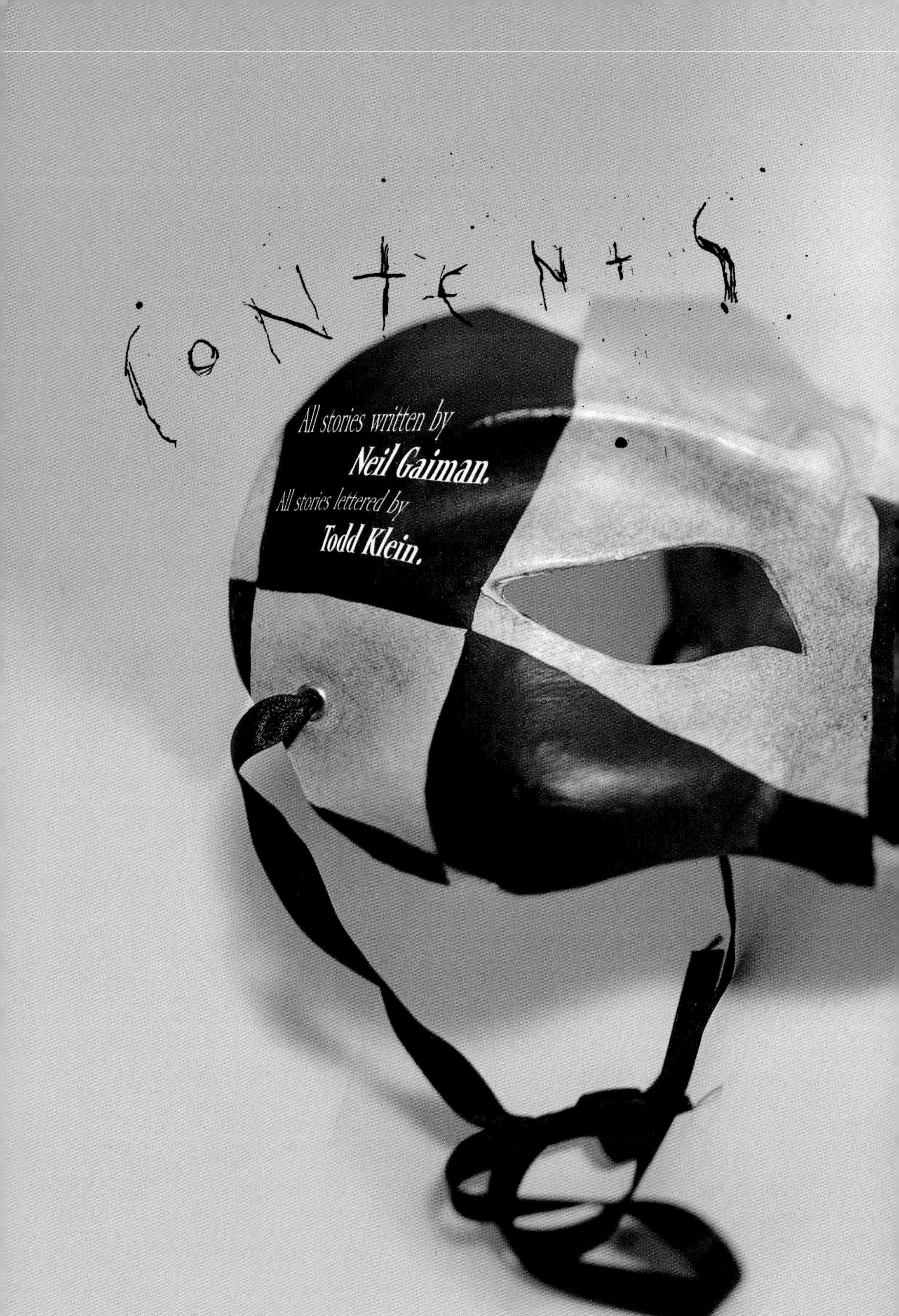

INTRODUCTION by Neil Gaiman

I.

Between 1987 and 1996 most of my working moments, and all of my sleeping ones, were given to telling one story, that of *The Sandman.*

Sandman came out more or less monthly, starting at the end of 1988. The story is collected in ten volumes, and two or three peripheral volumes, and an illustrated book which contained a retelling of an old Japanese folktale I completely made up. The story also spawned a Companion, and, more recently, an illustrated guide. Yesterday, in a hotel lobby in Turin I was asked if I could tell the story of the Sandman in twenty-five words or less. I pondered for a moment:

"The Lord of Dreams learns that one must change or die, and makes his decision," I said.

It's true, as far as it goes, although it leaves out quite a lot. Introductions always do.

II.

When I was done with *Sandman*, people asked if I would ever come back to those characters. Would I ever tell more stories about Morpheus, the King of Stories, or about his family, the Endless?

Sure, I said. One day.

This volume exists because there were artists I wanted to work with, and stories I wanted to tell, and because sometimes you look up and realize that one day is now.

III.

I've only worked with one of the artists in this book before: P. Craig Russell. Our *Sandman* story "Ramadan" was one of my favourites of the individual *Sandman* issues, and it gained a peculiar notoriety by being discussed and mentioned in newspapers around the world when Baghdad fell once more in 2003.

Craig's story is the first one I wrote for this book. I was alone in Venice, the week after September 11th 2001, the day the towers fell, and I found myself pondering the nature of time and of death.

Death is the second oldest of the Endless. It's hard not to love her. She loves you, after all.

Milo Manara has been an artist whose work in comics I've admired for many years: his graphic novel *Indian Summer*, written by Hugo Pratt, is one of the high points of the comics medium. The notion that Manara would draw me a tale of Desire was one of the things that carried me into the book you are now holding.

The story itself was loosely inspired by a historical anecdote mentioned by George MacDonald Fraser.

I met Miguelanxo Prado in 1996, in the Andalusian town of Gijon (graffitied by the locals, on road signs, to Xixon). In Gijon, or Xixon, the mists come off the Atlantic in the morning rendering the town entirely imaginary. When I saw Prado's art I knew I wanted to write something for him to draw.

Chronologically, this is the earliest Sandman story I've ever told. While it is true that I am someone who prefers mysteries to explanations, I found it pleasurable here to explain a number of things.

It would be several hundred million years before Death would cheer up, and longer than that before Delight became Delirium.

The Despair we meet in this story is the first Despair.

Barron Storey is a San Franciscan, an artist, a teacher, an illustrator, and a member of the Brotherhood of the Black Dog. His influence in the world of art has been enormous. I met him through Dave McKean, and soon found myself proposing that we create a big story of small stories together, to be called 25 Portraits of Despair.

I think, on reflection, that it is probably a good thing that we only created 15 Portraits of Despair.

Barron and I would both like to thank Dave McKean for his astonishing design and typographical work on the portraits.

Bill Sienkiewicz is someone I have known for at least sixteen years, and I've admired his work for longer than that. Many, many years ago we plotted a story together: a book of full-page images, which we would call *Obsessional*, in which the entire population of Manhattan, consumed by their own madnesses and desires and obsessions, joined a glorious carnival parade through New York and were eventually swallowed by the East River. The story would have been written by a man obsessed with the parade.

It's one of the best stories we've never told.

Delirium's story in this book is also fed by madnesses although Delirium inhabits the center of it, and not the periphery. The man in white is sometimes called Daniel, although he is more properly Dream. The dog is called Barnabas.

Delirium is the youngest of the Endless.

Glenn Fabry gained international renown for his cover paintings to Garth Ennis and Steve Dillon's *Preacher*, and I was delighted when he was able to make the time to draw the Destruction tale.

When R.A. Lafferty (who wrote like an angel, and, like most things angelic, may not be to everyone's taste) died in March 2002, he proved himself a poor predictive science fiction writer by several weeks, having already listed his year of death, in a 1983 essay, as being 2001. When I heard he had died I sat and read an old interview with him, in which he mentioned an idea that he had never managed to make into a story, and which he offered to the world. I thought it might be a fine memorial to a fine writer to see what I could do with that idea, and I named the peninsula San Raphael after Lafferty as well.

Destruction walked away from his family over four hundred years ago. Still, family ties are hard to break.

While the stories in this book can be read in any order (or none), Destruction's story follows Delirium's.

Finally, Frank Quitely concludes the Endless Nights with an eight-page tale about Destiny, which, it seemed to me when I had finished writing these stories, was a theme they had in common.

I've never met Frank Quitely. I always knew he was good. I didn't know he was this good.

IV.

I have spent the last month travelling across Europe on behalf of a book, being interviewed. In some countries they ask me how I feel about always being known primarily as the author of *Sandman*. (They only ask this in countries where I am known primarily as the creator of *Sandman*. There are countries where they ask me how I feel to be known primarily as a children's book author, or a fantasy writer. In Poland the first question always seemed to be how it felt to be known primarily as a post-modernist...)

And when they ask me that question, I tell them that Sandman is the biggest thing I've ever written, somewhere in excess of two thousand pages. That nothing I've ever written, or, I expect, ever shall write, matches it for scale.

I tell them it's nine years of my life. I tell them I'm proud. Not proud of myself, but proud of what I, and all the artists, and Todd Klein, and Danny Vozzo and the editors managed to bring into the world. People remember big things.

V.

If this is your first encounter with the world of the Sandman, it is worth bearing in mind that the Endless are not gods, for when people cease to believe in gods they cease to exist. But as long as there are people to live and dream and destroy, to desire, to despair, to delight or go mad, to live lives and affect each other, then the Endless will be there, performing their functions. They do not care a jot whether or not you believe in them.

The days are short, and are too soon over.

The nights, for good or bad, can seem endless.

Writing these stories was like coming home.

Neil Gaiman
Torino/Paris May 24, 2003

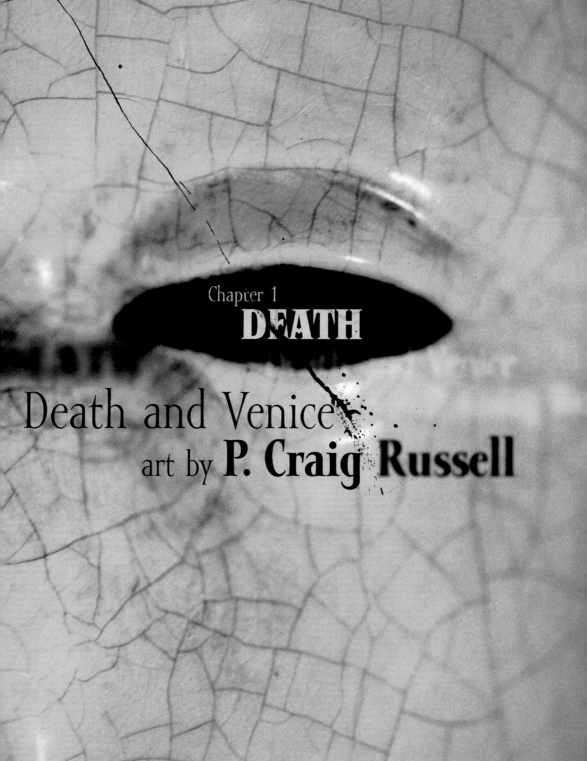

Chapter 1
DEATH

Death and Venice
art by **P. Craig Russell**

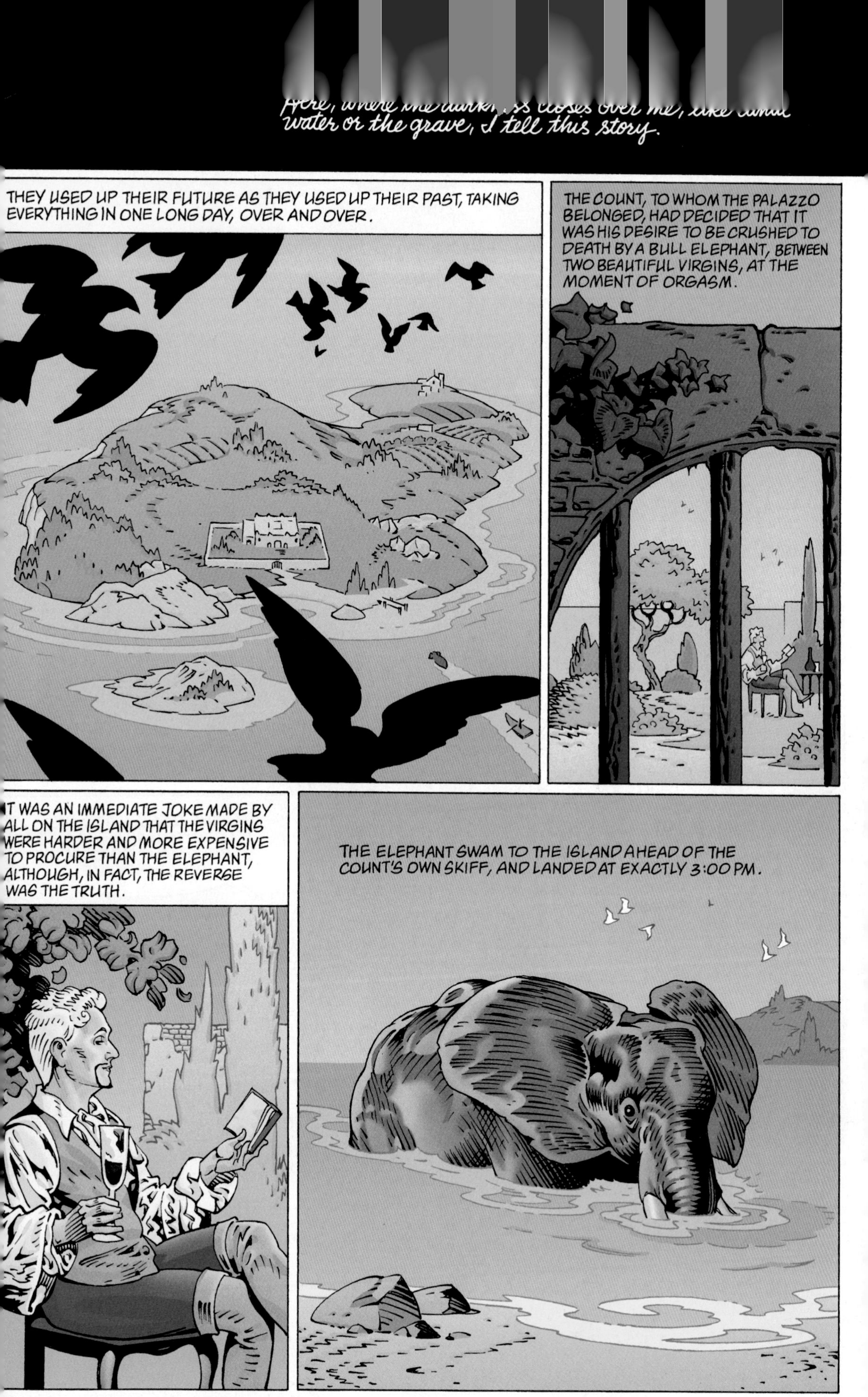

Here, where the … closes over me, like …
water or the grave, I tell this story.
THEY USED UP THEIR FUTURE AS THEY USED UP THEIR PAST, TAKING EVERYTHING IN ONE LONG DAY, OVER AND OVER.
THE COUNT, TO WHOM THE PALAZZO BELONGED, HAD DECIDED THAT IT WAS HIS DESIRE TO BE CRUSHED TO DEATH BY A BULL ELEPHANT, BETWEEN TWO BEAUTIFUL VIRGINS, AT THE MOMENT OF ORGASM.
IT WAS AN IMMEDIATE JOKE MADE BY ALL ON THE ISLAND THAT THE VIRGINS WERE HARDER AND MORE EXPENSIVE TO PROCURE THAN THE ELEPHANT, ALTHOUGH, IN FACT, THE REVERSE WAS THE TRUTH.
THE ELEPHANT SWAM TO THE ISLAND AHEAD OF THE COUNT'S OWN SKIFF, AND LANDED AT EXACTLY 3:00 PM.

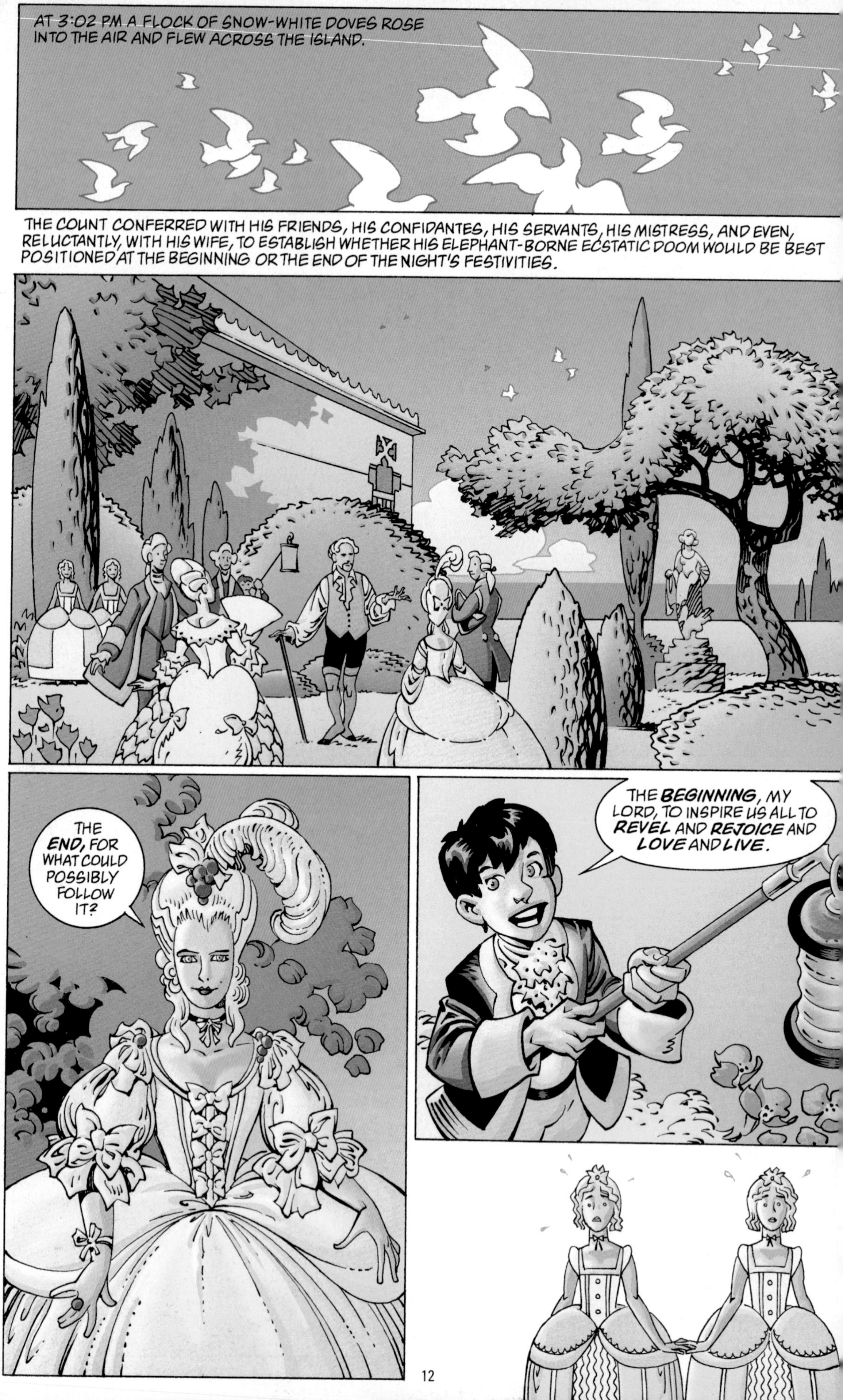
AT 3:02 PM A FLOCK OF SNOW-WHITE DOVES ROSE INTO THE AIR AND FLEW ACROSS THE ISLAND.
THE COUNT CONFERRED WITH HIS FRIENDS, HIS CONFIDANTES, HIS SERVANTS, HIS MISTRESS, AND EVEN, RELUCTANTLY, WITH HIS WIFE, TO ESTABLISH WHETHER HIS ELEPHANT-BORNE ECSTATIC DOOM WOULD BE BEST POSITIONED AT THE BEGINNING OR THE END OF THE NIGHT'S FESTIVITIES.
THE **END,** FOR WHAT COULD POSSIBLY FOLLOW IT?
THE **BEGINNING**, MY LORD, TO INSPIRE US ALL TO **REVEL** AND **REJOICE** AND **LOVE** AND **LIVE**.

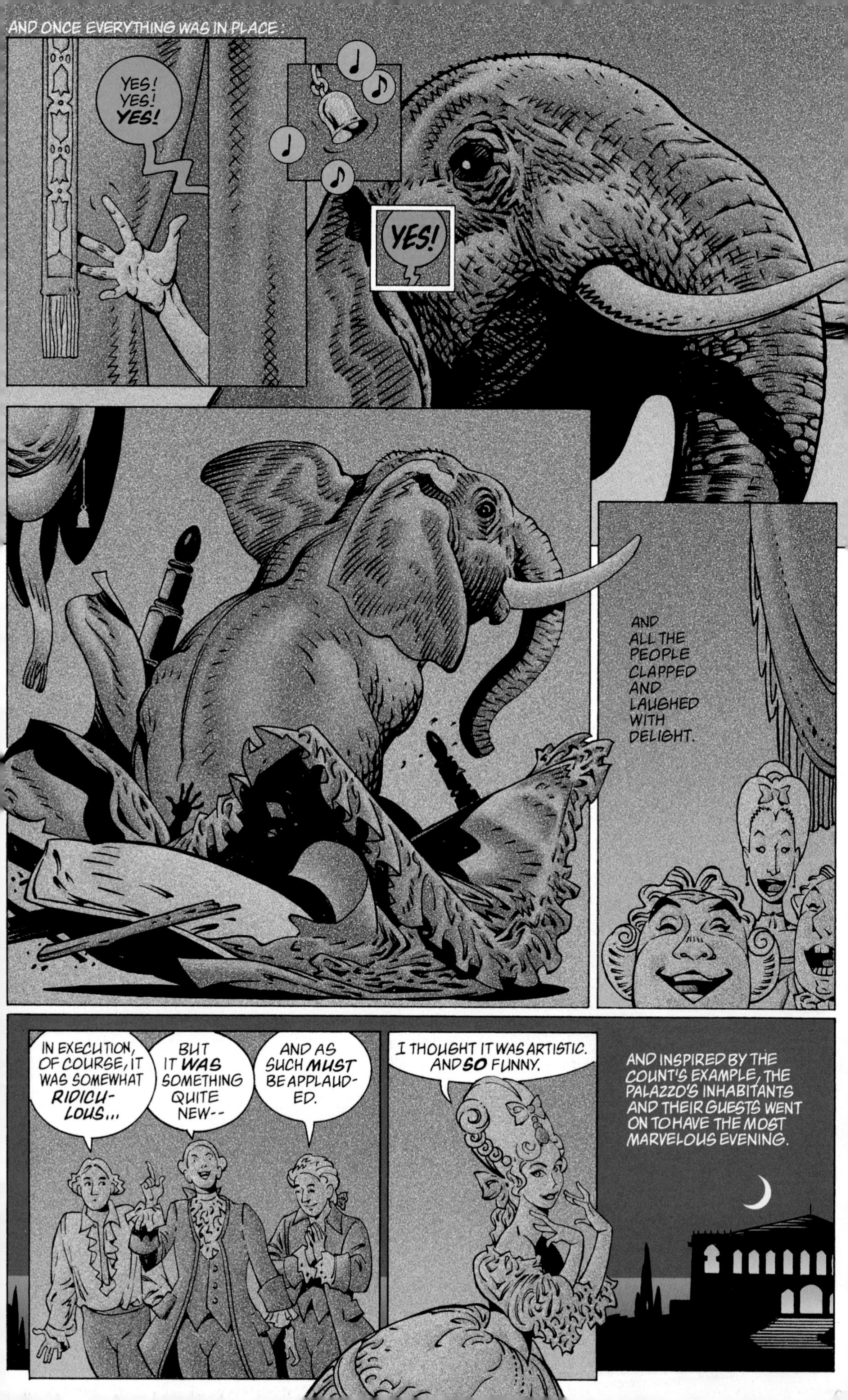
AND ONCE EVERYTHING WAS IN PLACE:
YES! YES! YES!
YES!
AND ALL THE PEOPLE CLAPPED AND LAUGHED WITH DELIGHT.
IN EXECUTION, OF COURSE, IT WAS SOMEWHAT RIDICULOUS...
BUT IT WAS SOMETHING QUITE NEW--
AND AS SUCH MUST BE APPLAUDED.
I THOUGHT IT WAS ARTISTIC. AND SO FUNNY.
AND INSPIRED BY THE COUNT'S EXAMPLE, THE PALAZZO'S INHABITANTS AND THEIR GUESTS WENT ON TO HAVE THE MOST MARVELOUS EVENING.

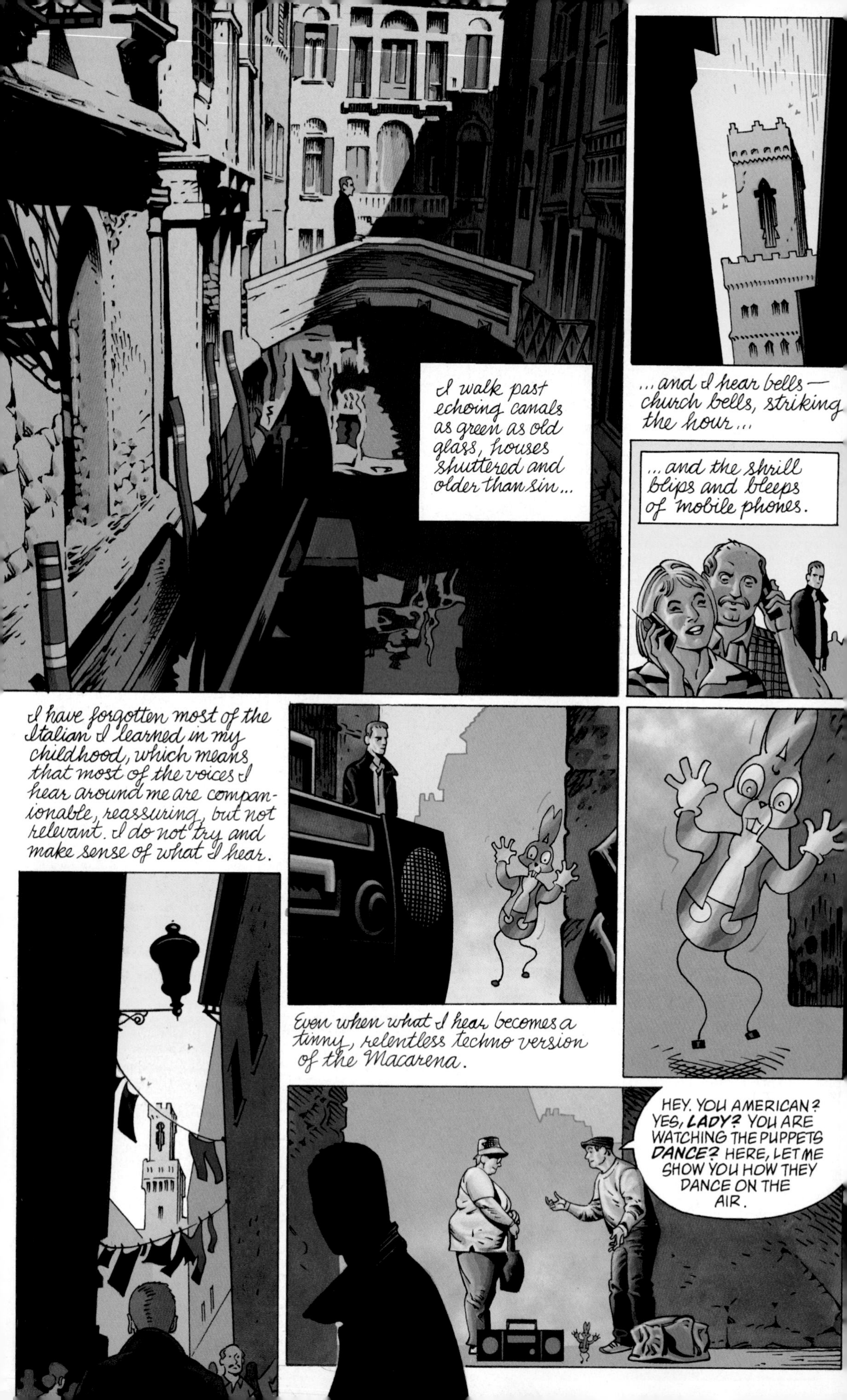
I walk past echoing canals as green as old glass, houses shuttered and older than sin...
...and I hear bells—church bells, striking the hour...
...and the shrill blips and bleeps of mobile phones.
I have forgotten most of the Italian I learned in my childhood, which means that most of the voices I hear around me are companionable, reassuring, but not relevant. I do not try and make sense of what I hear.
Even when what I hear becomes a tinny, relentless techno version of the Macarena.
HEY. YOU AMERICAN? YES, LADY? YOU ARE WATCHING THE PUPPETS DANCE? HERE, LET ME SHOW YOU HOW THEY DANCE ON THE AIR.

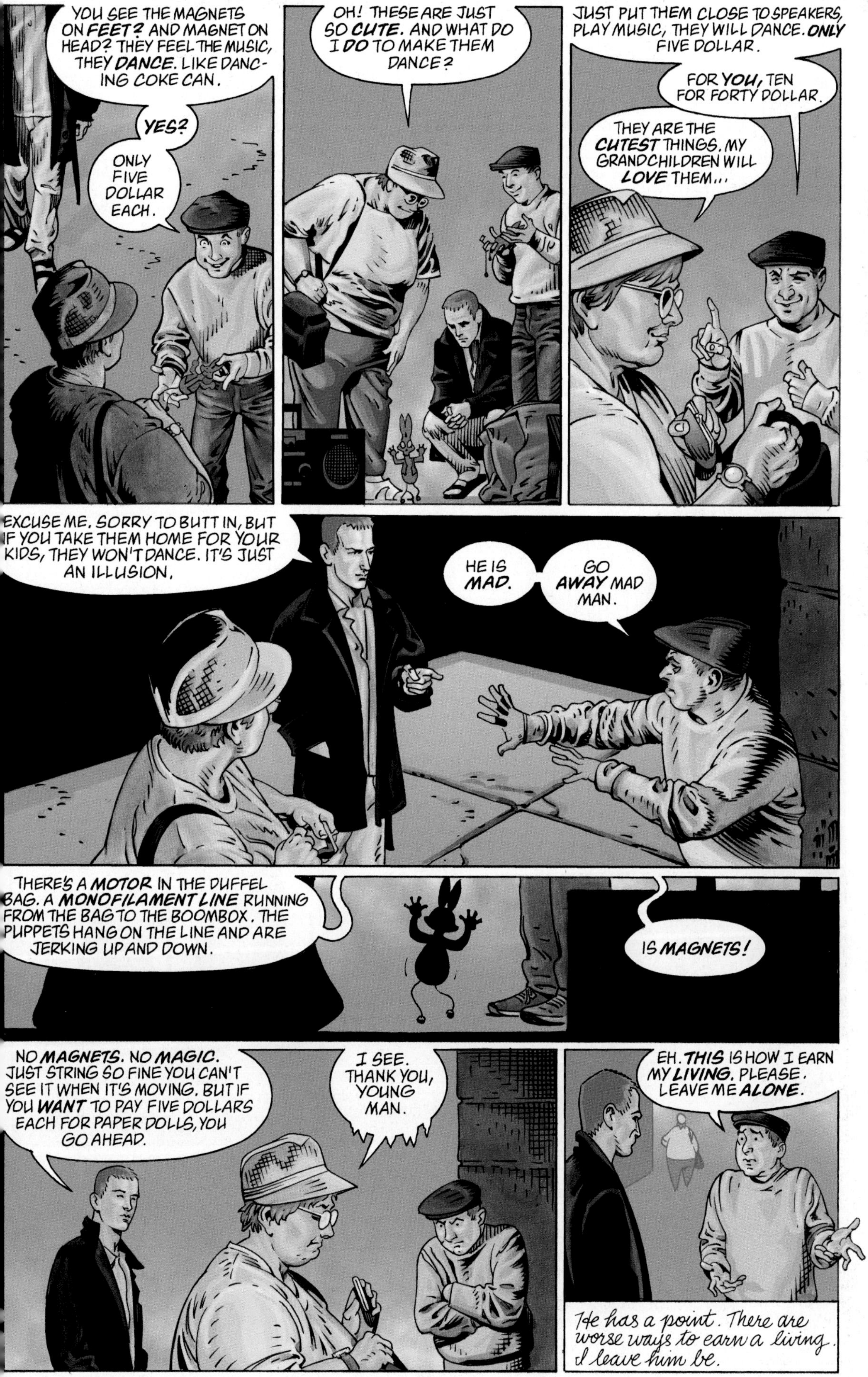
YOU SEE THE MAGNETS ON FEET? AND MAGNET ON HEAD? THEY FEEL THE MUSIC, THEY DANCE. LIKE DANCING COKE CAN.
YES?
ONLY FIVE DOLLAR EACH.
OH! THESE ARE JUST SO CUTE. AND WHAT DO I DO TO MAKE THEM DANCE?
JUST PUT THEM CLOSE TO SPEAKERS, PLAY MUSIC, THEY WILL DANCE. ONLY FIVE DOLLAR.
FOR YOU, TEN FOR FORTY DOLLAR.
THEY ARE THE CUTEST THINGS. MY GRANDCHILDREN WILL LOVE THEM...
EXCUSE ME. SORRY TO BUTT IN, BUT IF YOU TAKE THEM HOME FOR YOUR KIDS, THEY WON'T DANCE. IT'S JUST AN ILLUSION.
HE IS MAD.
GO AWAY MAD MAN.
THERE'S A MOTOR IN THE DUFFEL BAG. A MONOFILAMENT LINE RUNNING FROM THE BAG TO THE BOOMBOX. THE PUPPETS HANG ON THE LINE AND ARE JERKING UP AND DOWN.
IS MAGNETS!
NO MAGNETS. NO MAGIC. JUST STRING SO FINE YOU CAN'T SEE IT WHEN IT'S MOVING. BUT IF YOU WANT TO PAY FIVE DOLLARS EACH FOR PAPER DOLLS, YOU GO AHEAD.
I SEE. THANK YOU, YOUNG MAN.
EH. THIS IS HOW I EARN MY LIVING. PLEASE. LEAVE ME ALONE.
He has a point. There are worse ways to earn a living. I leave him be.

THE COUNT ROSE AT NINE, AND ANNOUNCED A DAY OF PENITENCE AND MORTIFICATION.

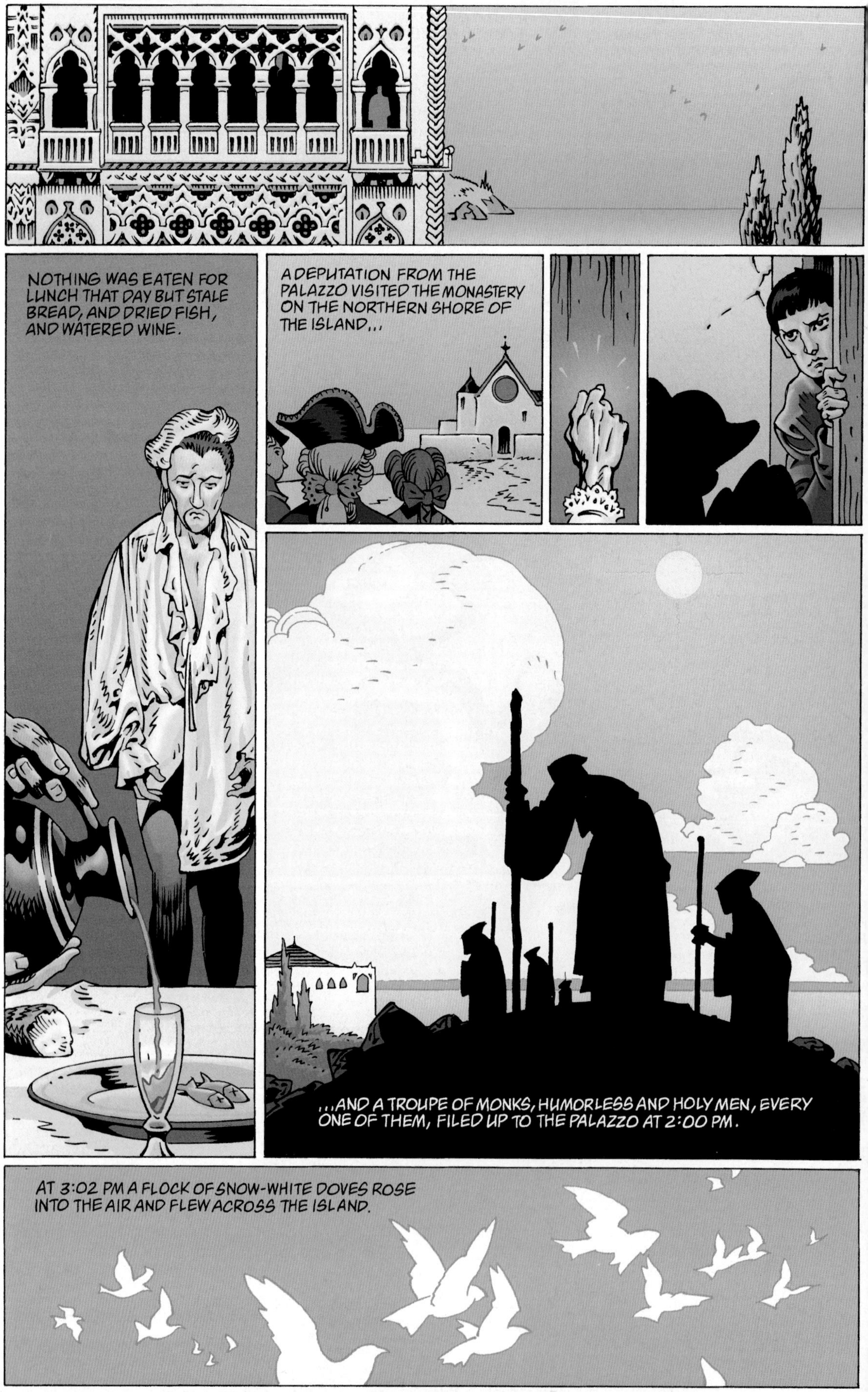
NOTHING WAS EATEN FOR LUNCH THAT DAY BUT STALE BREAD, AND DRIED FISH, AND WATERED WINE.
A DEPUTATION FROM THE PALAZZO VISITED THE MONASTERY ON THE NORTHERN SHORE OF THE ISLAND...
...AND A TROUPE OF MONKS, HUMORLESS AND HOLY MEN, EVERY ONE OF THEM, FILED UP TO THE PALAZZO AT 2:00 PM.
AT 3:02 PM A FLOCK OF SNOW-WHITE DOVES ROSE INTO THE AIR AND FLEW ACROSS THE ISLAND.

THE CONFESSIONS WERE HEARTFELT,
AND ACCOMPANIED BY TEARS.

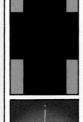

AND ONCE CONFESSED, THE PENITENTS KNELT, TO BE SCOURGED UPON THEIR NAKED BACKS, FLOGGED UNTIL THEIR SKIN WAS LACERATED AND BLOOD RAN ACROSS THE PALAZZO'S MOSAIC FLOOR.

AND NO MAN THERE,
AND NO WOMAN WAS
MORE PENITENT...

...MORE HONEST,
SHED SO MANY
TEARS...

...OR SO
MUCH
BLOOD,...

...AS THE COUNT HIMSELF.

THEY
PRAYED...

...AND
THEY
WAILED,...

...AND THEY
REPENTED,...

...AND THEY BLED
UNTIL MIDNIGHT.

A MARVELOUS
END TO A PERFECT
DAY.

They've been parting visitors from their money for so long here in Venice that they can't help but be good at it. Normally, they give value for money. That last encounter left a sour taste in my mouth. They didn't cheat the tourists when I came here as a boy.

And that starts me remembering once again.

I have remembered this too much; so now I can no longer be sure whether it is the event that I am remembering, or my memory of the event.

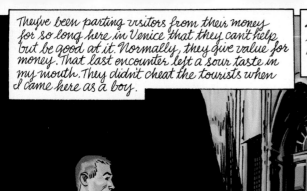

A hot, still day. Lizards on the side of a brick wall, watch me warily.

You could catch them, if you were fast enough. But if you grabbed them by the tail it would break off, wriggling in your hand, while the lizard ran away.

I had been staying with my aunt and uncle, with my cousins. My Italia was not good, but I could make myself understood, and we all spoke som English.

We loaded the picnic food and the bottles of fruit-juice and the wine into my Uncle's vaporetto, the water-taxi he drove, and we travelled out into the lagoon until we reached the island.

There are many islands in the Venice Lagoon. Over the years they have all been inhabited, my Uncle told me as I proudly steered the boat. But times change. He pointed out the islands that hold factories, barracks, munitions, convents, as we passed.

I remember the slosh, slosh, slosh of the water against the side of the motorboat.

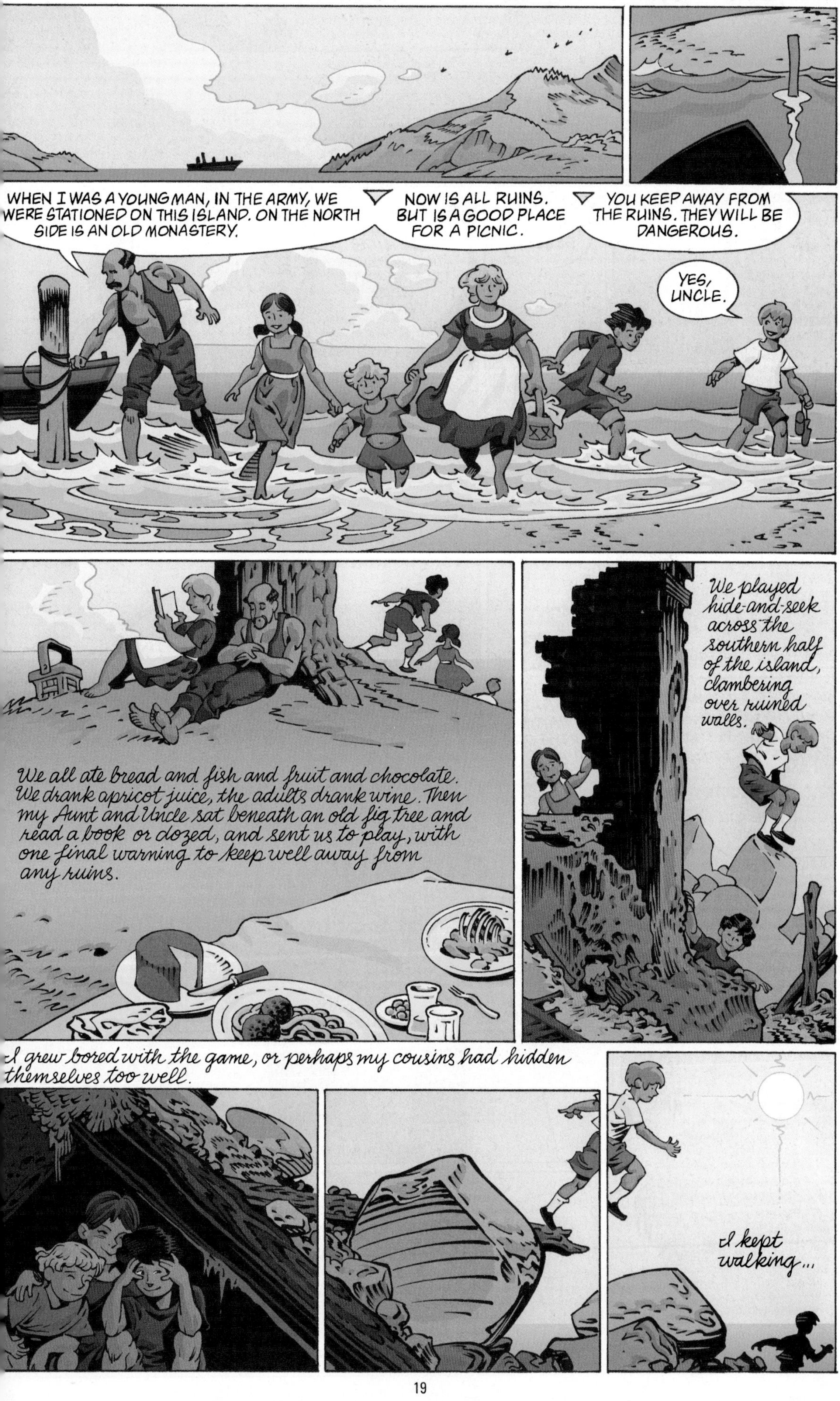
WHEN I WAS A YOUNG MAN, IN THE ARMY, WE WERE STATIONED ON THIS ISLAND. ON THE NORTH SIDE IS AN OLD MONASTERY.
NOW IS ALL RUINS. BUT IS A GOOD PLACE FOR A PICNIC.
YOU KEEP AWAY FROM THE RUINS. THEY WILL BE DANGEROUS.
YES, UNCLE.
We all ate bread and fish and fruit and chocolate. We drank apricot juice, the adults drank wine. Then my Aunt and Uncle sat beneath an old fig tree and read a book or dozed, and sent us to play, with one final warning to keep well away from any ruins.
We played hide-and-seek across the southern half of the island, clambering over ruined walls.
I grew bored with the game, or perhaps my cousins had hidden themselves too well.
I kept walking...

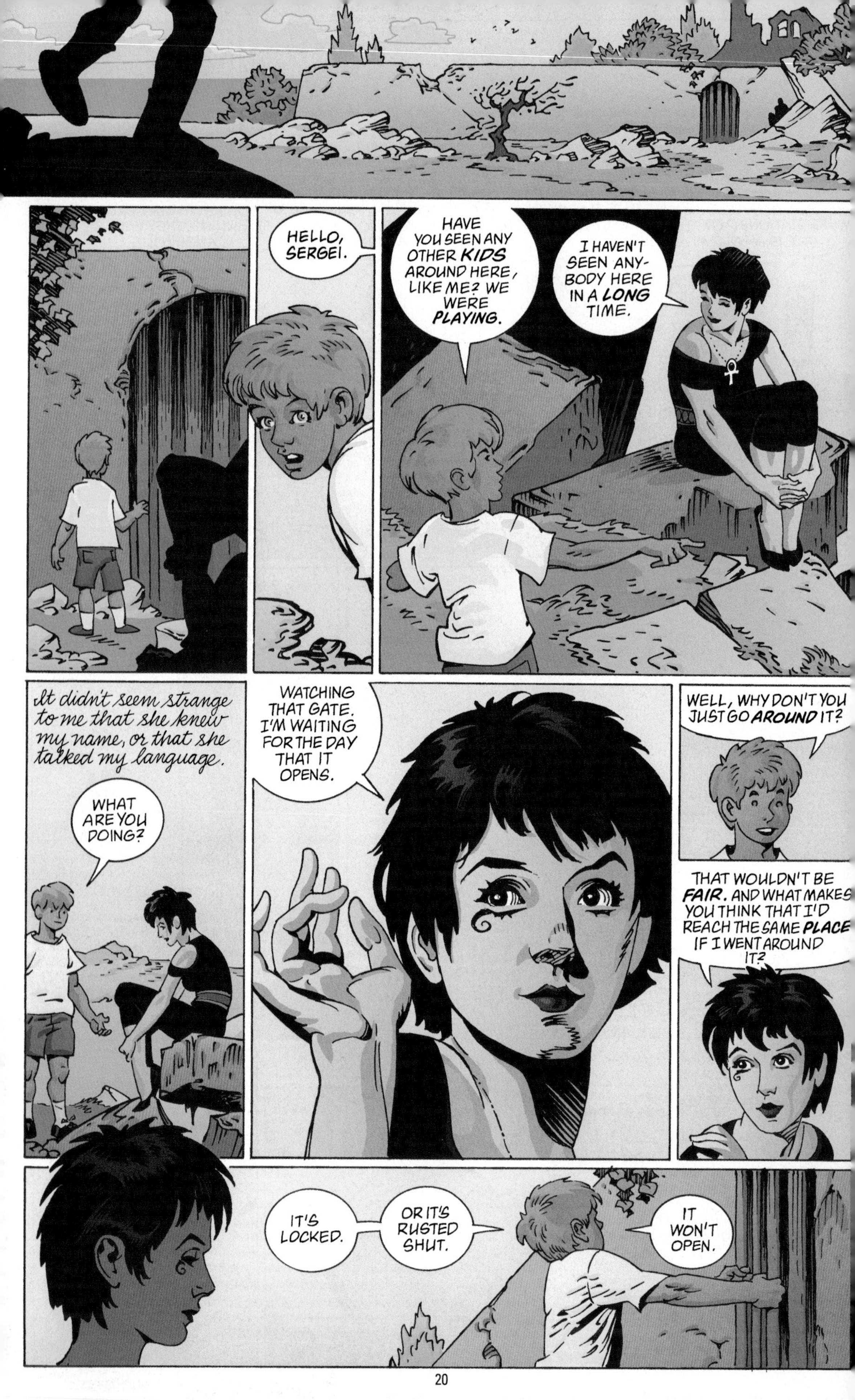
HELLO, SERGEI.
HAVE YOU SEEN ANY OTHER KIDS AROUND HERE, LIKE ME? WE WERE PLAYING.
I HAVEN'T SEEN ANYBODY HERE IN A LONG TIME.
It didn't seem strange to me that she knew my name, or that she talked my language.
WHAT ARE YOU DOING?
WATCHING THAT GATE. I'M WAITING FOR THE DAY THAT IT OPENS.
WELL, WHY DON'T YOU JUST GO AROUND IT?
THAT WOULDN'T BE FAIR. AND WHAT MAKES YOU THINK THAT I'D REACH THE SAME PLACE IF I WENT AROUND IT?
IT WON'T OPEN.
IT'S LOCKED.
OR IT'S RUSTED SHUT.

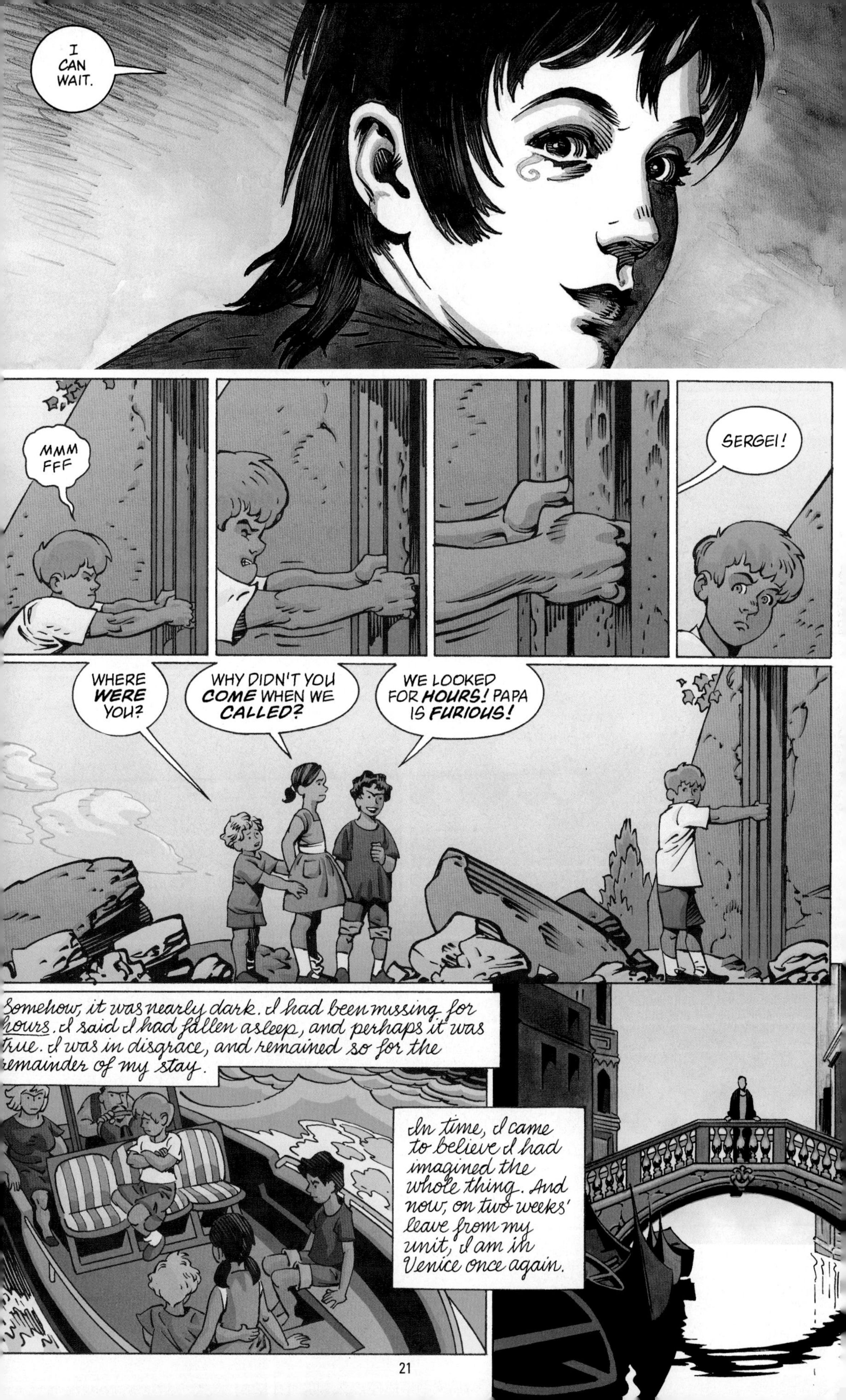
I CAN WAIT.
MMM FFF
SERGEI!
WHERE WERE YOU?
WHY DIDN'T YOU COME WHEN WE CALLED?
WE LOOKED FOR HOURS! PAPA IS FURIOUS!
Somehow, it was nearly dark. I had been missing for hours. I said I had fallen asleep, and perhaps it was true. I was in disgrace, and remained so for the remainder of my stay.
In time, I came to believe I had imagined the whole thing. And now, on two weeks' leave from my unit, I am in Venice once again.

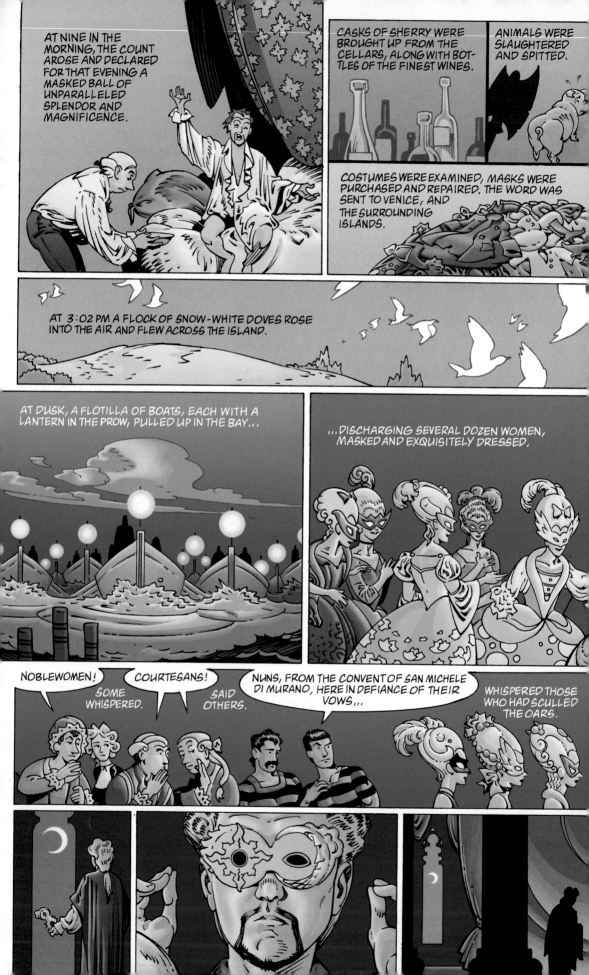

AT NINE IN THE MORNING, THE COUNT AROSE AND DECLARED FOR THAT EVENING A MASKED BALL OF UNPARALLELED SPLENDOR AND MAGNIFICENCE.

CASKS OF SHERRY WERE BROUGHT UP FROM THE CELLARS, ALONG WITH BOTTLES OF THE FINEST WINES.

ANIMALS WERE SLAUGHTERED AND SPITTED.

COSTUMES WERE EXAMINED, MASKS WERE PURCHASED AND REPAIRED. THE WORD WAS SENT TO VENICE, AND THE SURROUNDING ISLANDS.

AT 3:02 PM A FLOCK OF SNOW-WHITE DOVES ROSE INTO THE AIR AND FLEW ACROSS THE ISLAND.

AT DUSK, A FLOTILLA OF BOATS, EACH WITH A LANTERN IN THE PROW, PULLED UP IN THE BAY...

...DISCHARGING SEVERAL DOZEN WOMEN, MASKED AND EXQUISITELY DRESSED.

NOBLEWOMEN!

SOME WHISPERED.

COURTESANS!

SAID OTHERS.

NUNS, FROM THE CONVENT OF SAN MICHELE DI MURANO, HERE IN DEFIANCE OF THEIR VOWS,...

WHISPERED THOSE WHO HAD SCULLED THE OARS.

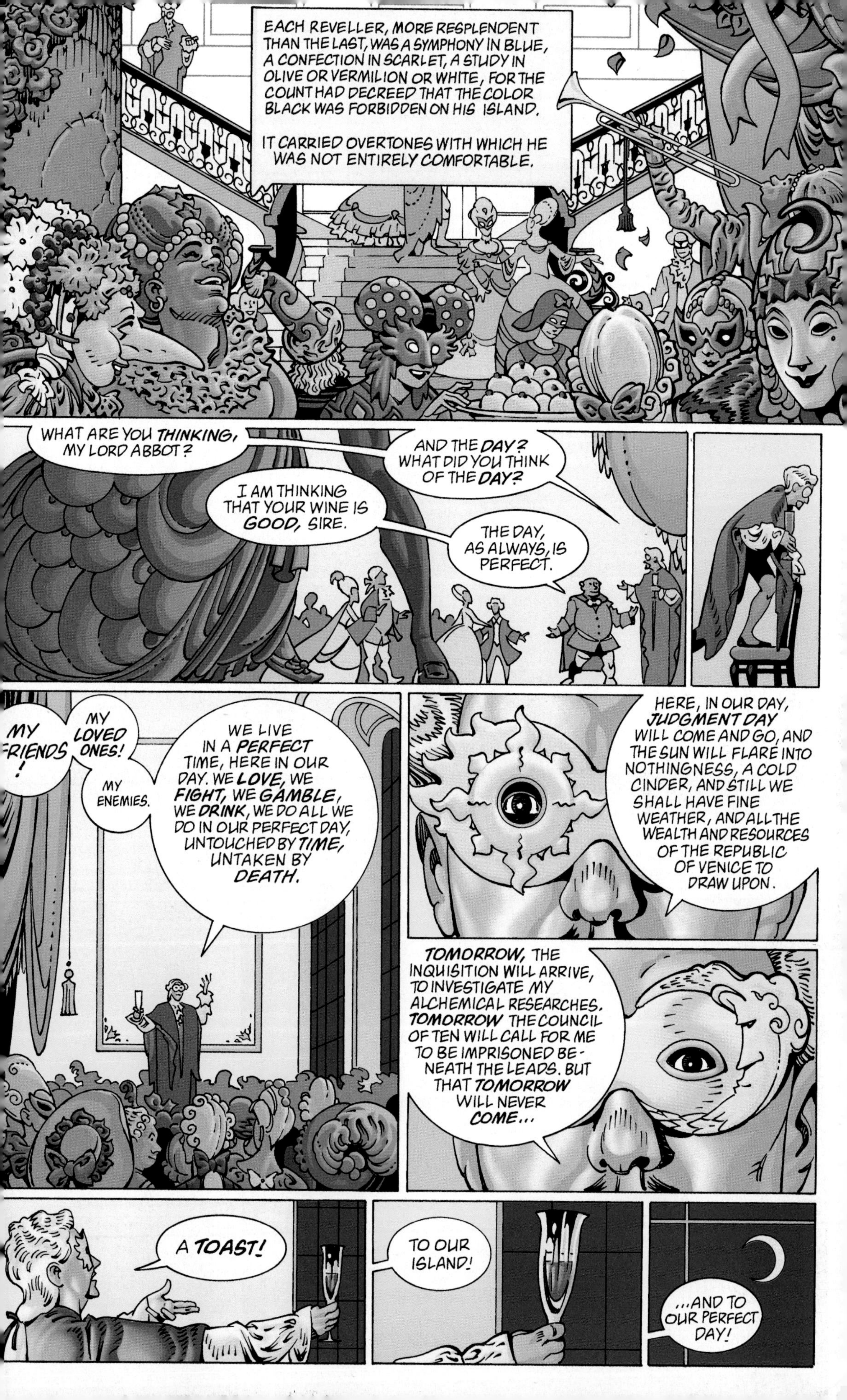
EACH REVELLER, MORE RESPLENDENT THAN THE LAST, WAS A SYMPHONY IN BLUE, A CONFECTION IN SCARLET, A STUDY IN OLIVE OR VERMILION OR WHITE, FOR THE COUNT HAD DECREED THAT THE COLOR BLACK WAS FORBIDDEN ON HIS ISLAND.
IT CARRIED OVERTONES WITH WHICH HE WAS NOT ENTIRELY COMFORTABLE.
WHAT ARE YOU THINKING, MY LORD ABBOT?
I AM THINKING THAT YOUR WINE IS GOOD, SIRE.
AND THE DAY? WHAT DID YOU THINK OF THE DAY?
THE DAY, AS ALWAYS, IS PERFECT.
MY FRIENDS!
MY LOVED ONES!
MY ENEMIES.
WE LIVE IN A PERFECT TIME, HERE IN OUR DAY. WE LOVE, WE FIGHT, WE GAMBLE, WE DRINK, WE DO ALL WE DO IN OUR PERFECT DAY, UNTOUCHED BY TIME, UNTAKEN BY DEATH.
HERE, IN OUR DAY, JUDGMENT DAY WILL COME AND GO, AND THE SUN WILL FLARE INTO NOTHINGNESS, A COLD CINDER, AND STILL WE SHALL HAVE FINE WEATHER, AND ALL THE WEALTH AND RESOURCES OF THE REPUBLIC OF VENICE TO DRAW UPON.
TOMORROW, THE INQUISITION WILL ARRIVE, TO INVESTIGATE MY ALCHEMICAL RESEARCHES. TOMORROW THE COUNCIL OF TEN WILL CALL FOR ME TO BE IMPRISONED BENEATH THE LEADS. BUT THAT TOMORROW WILL NEVER COME...
A TOAST!
TO OUR ISLAND!
...AND TO OUR PERFECT DAY!

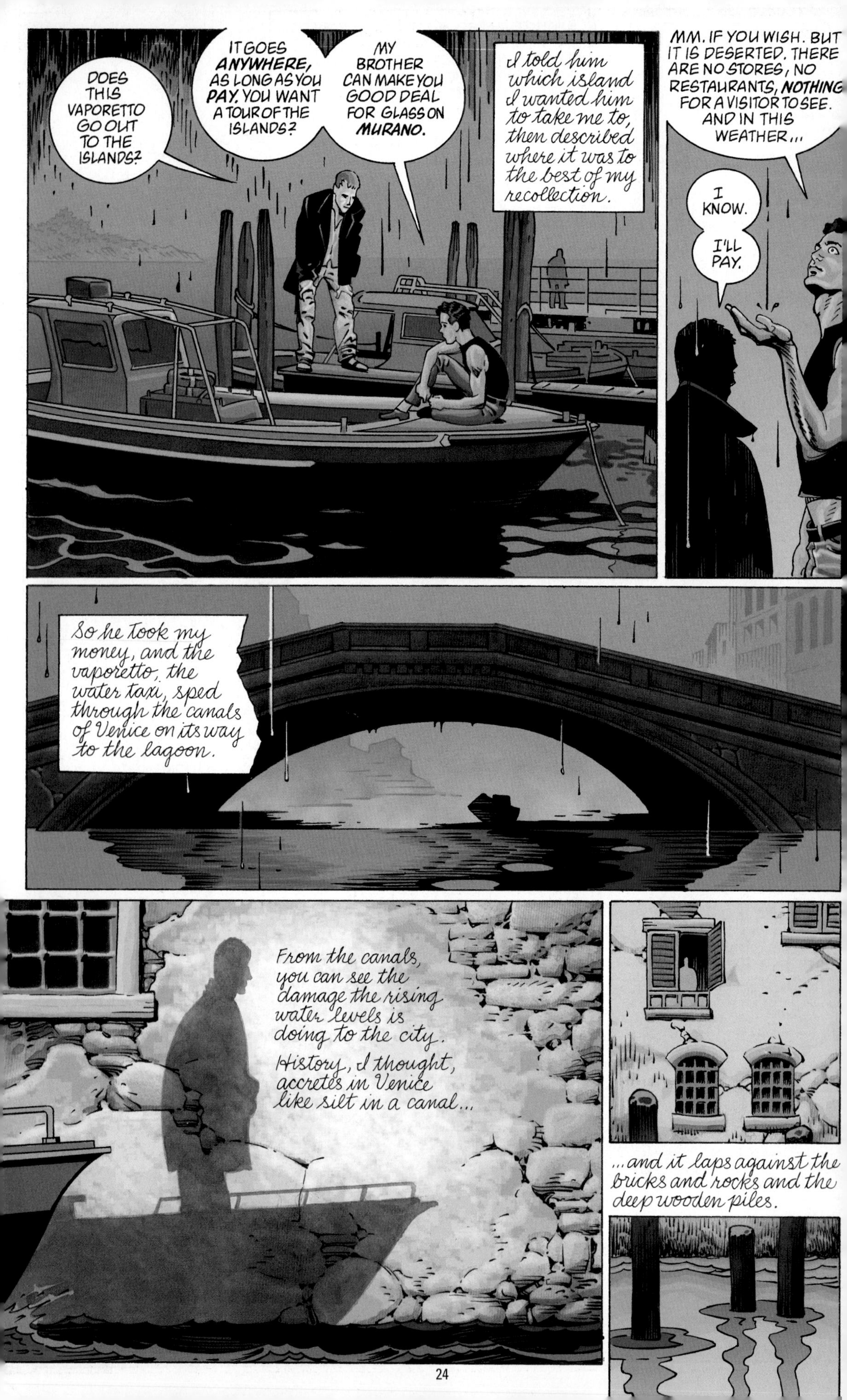
DOES THIS VAPORETTO GO OUT TO THE ISLANDS?
IT GOES ANYWHERE, AS LONG AS YOU PAY. YOU WANT A TOUR OF THE ISLANDS?
MY BROTHER CAN MAKE YOU GOOD DEAL FOR GLASS ON MURANO.
I told him which island I wanted him to take me to, then described where it was to the best of my recollection.
MM. IF YOU WISH. BUT IT IS DESERTED. THERE ARE NO STORES, NO RESTAURANTS, NOTHING FOR A VISITOR TO SEE. AND IN THIS WEATHER...
I KNOW.
I'LL PAY.
So he took my money, and the vaporetto, the water taxi, sped through the canals of Venice on its way to the lagoon.
From the canals, you can see the damage the rising water levels is doing to the city.
History, I thought, accretes in Venice like silt in a canal...
...and it laps against the bricks and rocks and the deep wooden piles.

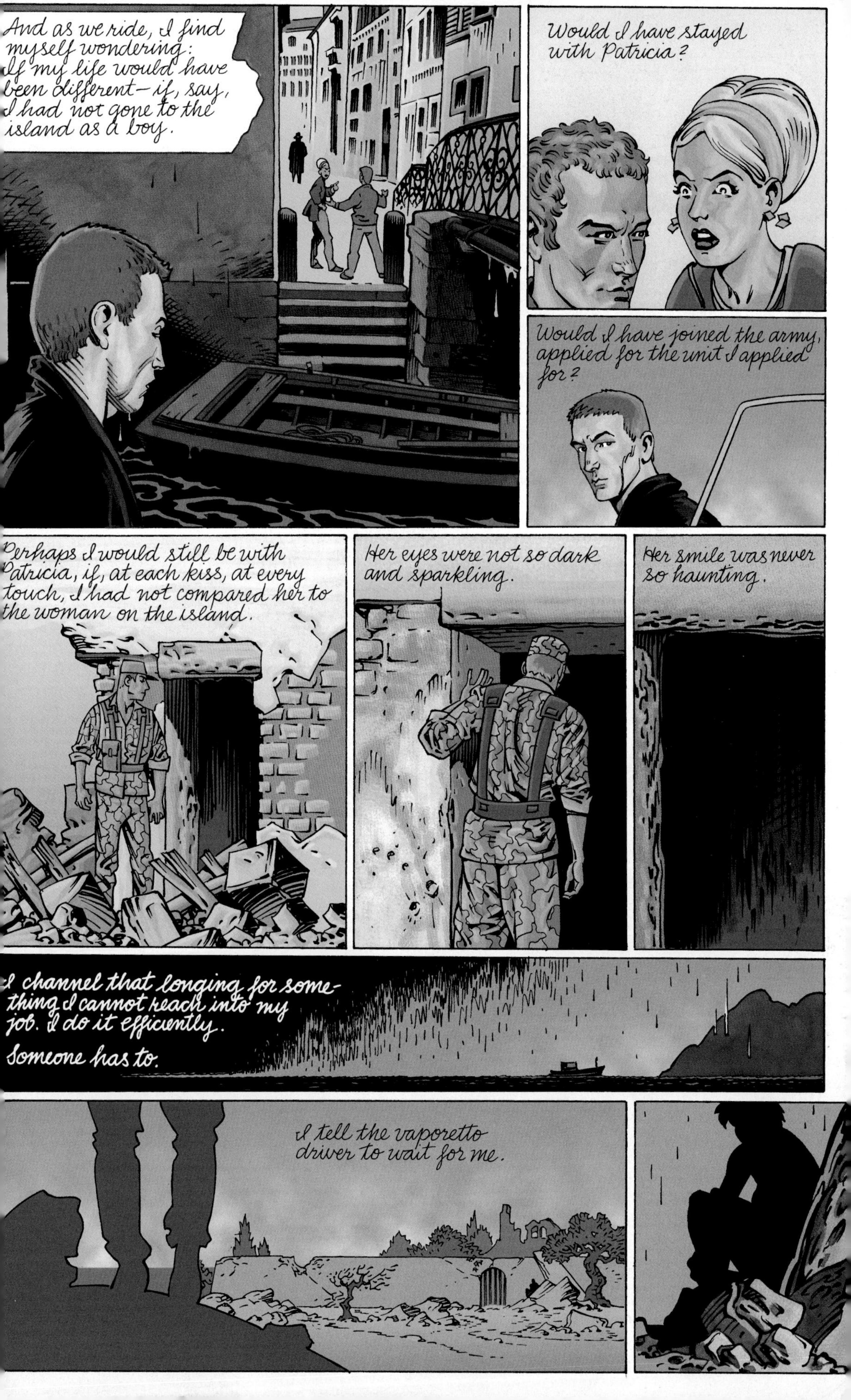
And as we ride, I find myself wondering: If my life would have been different—if, say, I had not gone to the island as a boy.
Would I have stayed with Patricia?
Would I have joined the army, applied for the unit I applied for?
Perhaps I would still be with Patricia, if, at each kiss, at every touch, I had not compared her to the woman on the island.
Her eyes were not so dark and sparkling.
Her smile was never so haunting.
I channel that longing for something I cannot reach into my job. I do it efficiently.
Someone has to.
I tell the vaporetto driver to wait for me.

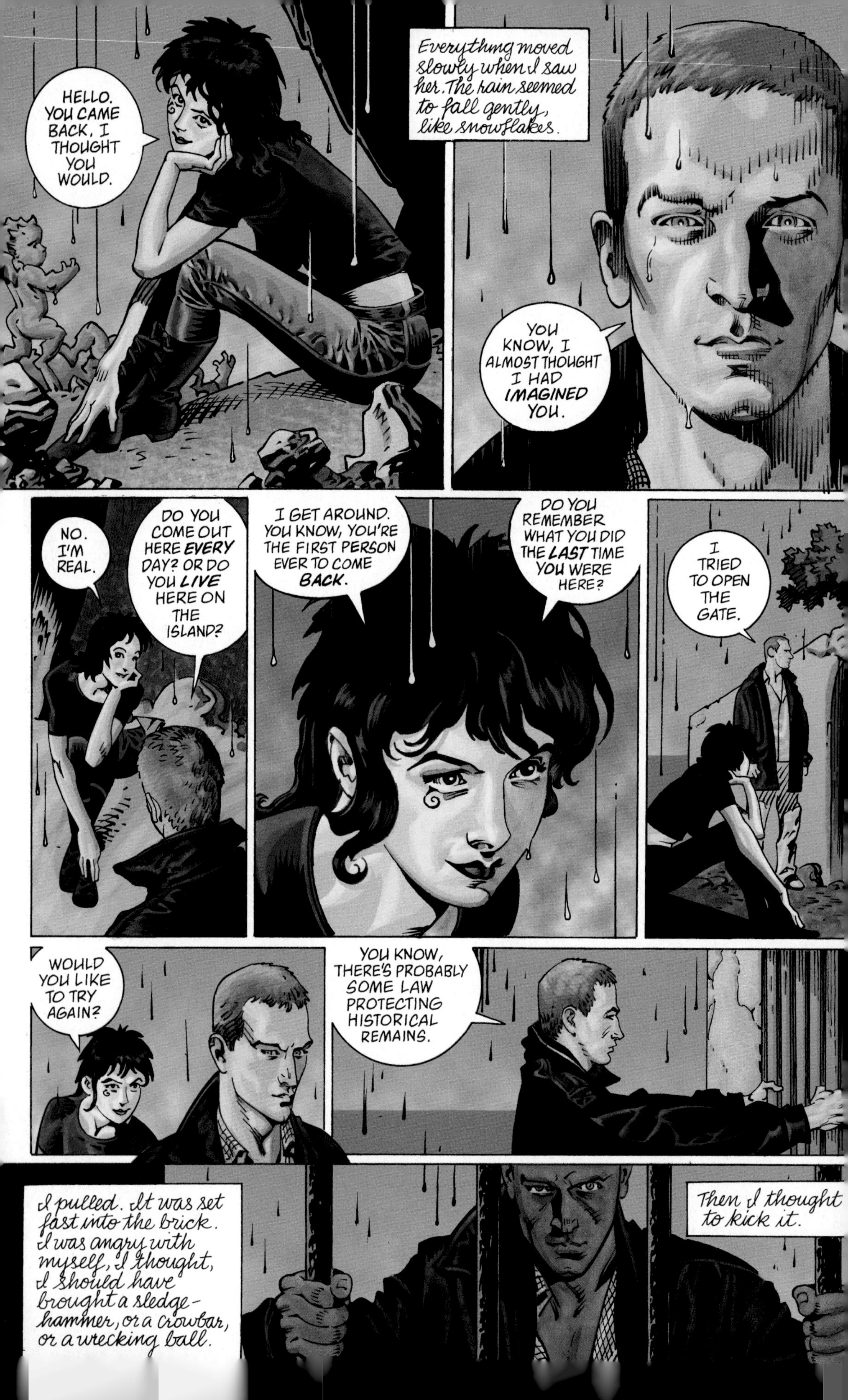
HELLO. YOU CAME BACK, I THOUGHT YOU WOULD.
Everything moved slowly when I saw her. The rain seemed to fall gently, like snowflakes.
YOU KNOW, I ALMOST THOUGHT I HAD IMAGINED YOU.
NO. I'M REAL.
DO YOU COME OUT HERE EVERY DAY? OR DO YOU LIVE HERE ON THE ISLAND?
I GET AROUND. YOU KNOW, YOU'RE THE FIRST PERSON EVER TO COME BACK.
DO YOU REMEMBER WHAT YOU DID THE LAST TIME YOU WERE HERE?
I TRIED TO OPEN THE GATE.
WOULD YOU LIKE TO TRY AGAIN?
YOU KNOW, THERE'S PROBABLY SOME LAW PROTECTING HISTORICAL REMAINS.
I pulled. It was set fast into the brick. I was angry with myself, I thought, I should have brought a sledge-hammer, or a crowbar, or a wrecking ball.
Then I thought to kick it.

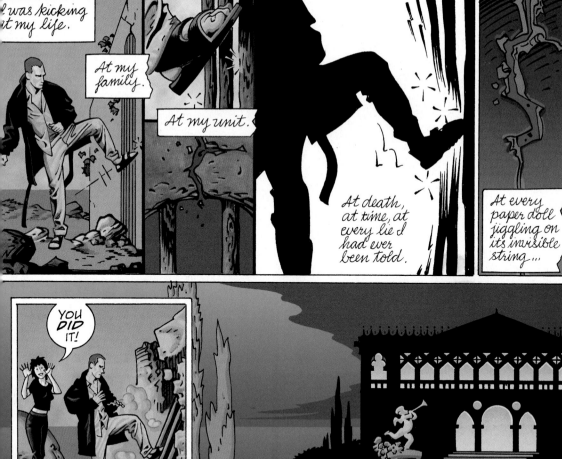

And kicking that damned gate seemed suddenly to be the most satisfying thing I could do.

I was kicking at my life.

At my family.

At my unit.

At death, at time, at every lie I had ever been told.

At every paper doll jiggling on its invisible string...

YOU *DID* IT!

WHERE ARE WE?

MAY THE 23rd, 1751.

THAT'S A *WHEN,* NOT A *WHERE.*

HERE, IT'S A *WHERE.*

CAN YOU WAIT HERE?

I HAVE BUSINESS INSIDE.

I WANT TO COME *WITH* YOU.

OKAY, I GUESS.

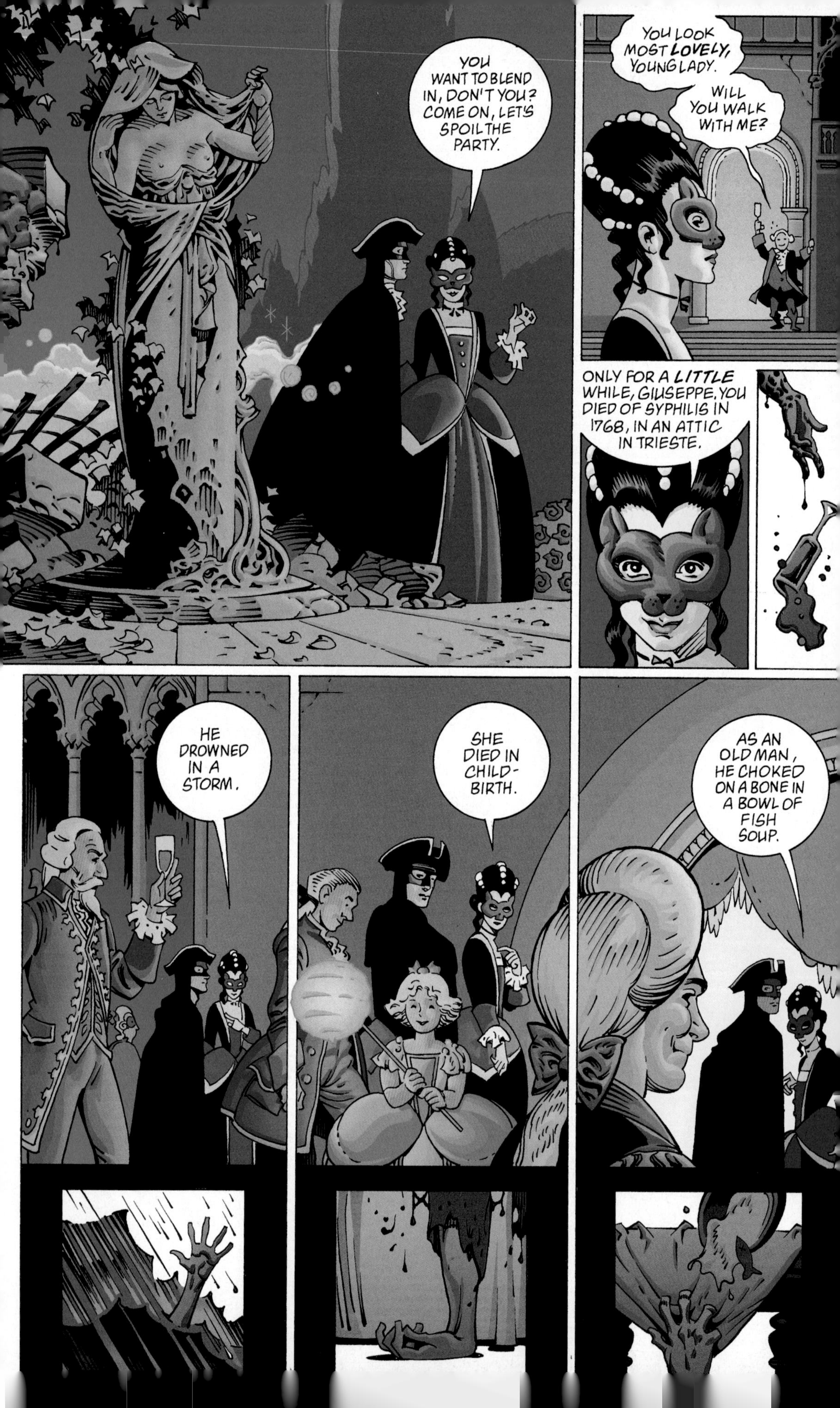
YOU WANT TO BLEND IN, DON'T YOU? COME ON, LET'S SPOIL THE PARTY.
YOU LOOK MOST LOVELY, YOUNG LADY.
WILL YOU WALK WITH ME?
ONLY FOR A LITTLE WHILE, GIUSEPPE. YOU DIED OF SYPHILIS IN 1768, IN AN ATTIC IN TRIESTE.
HE DROWNED IN A STORM.
SHE DIED IN CHILD-BIRTH.
AS AN OLD MAN, HE CHOKED ON A BONE IN A BOWL OF FISH SOUP.

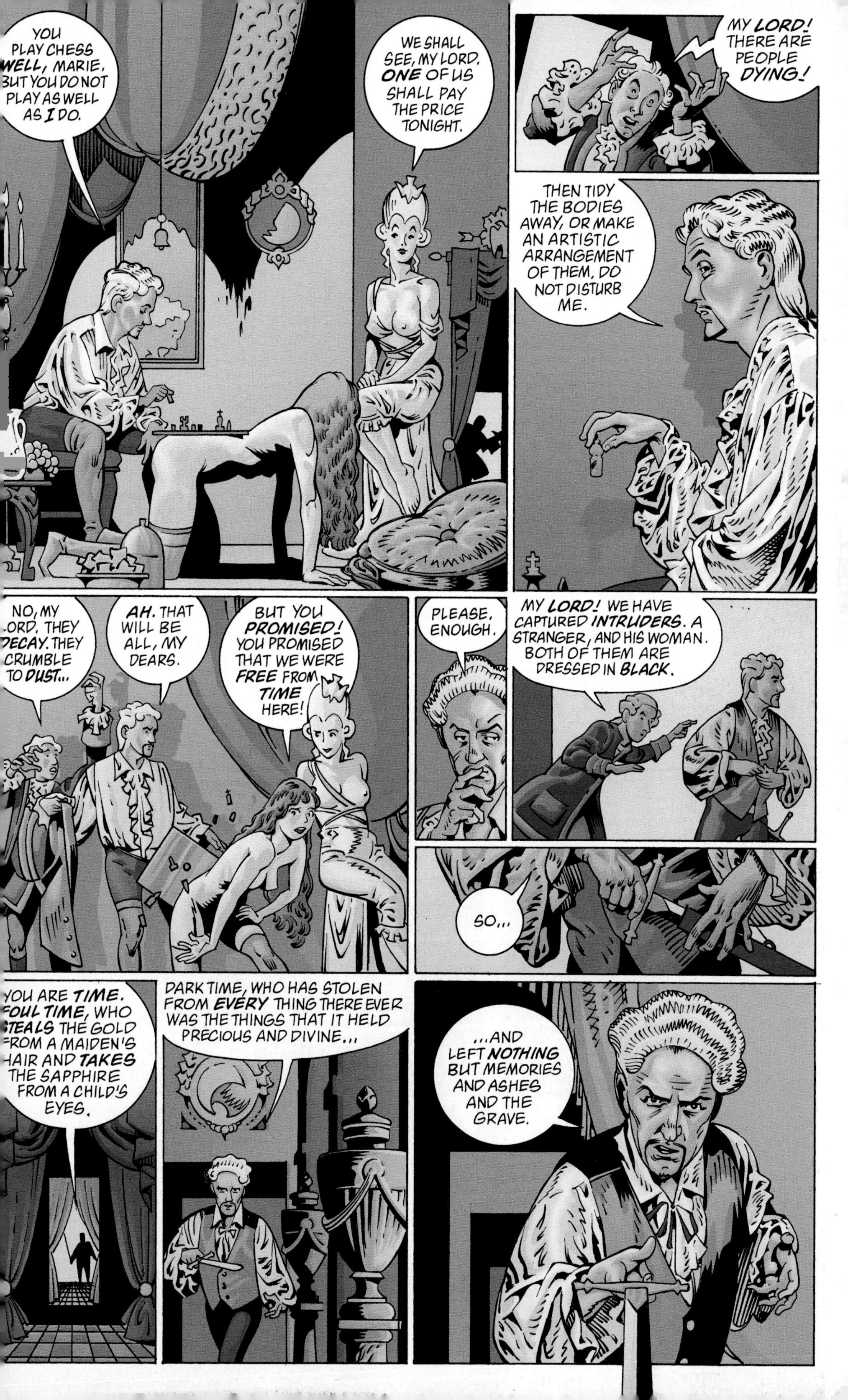

YOU PLAY CHESS WELL, MARIE, BUT YOU DO NOT PLAY AS WELL AS I DO.
WE SHALL SEE, MY LORD. ONE OF US SHALL PAY THE PRICE TONIGHT.
MY LORD! THERE ARE PEOPLE DYING!
THEN TIDY THE BODIES AWAY, OR MAKE AN ARTISTIC ARRANGEMENT OF THEM. DO NOT DISTURB ME.
NO, MY LORD. THEY DECAY. THEY CRUMBLE TO DUST...
AH. THAT WILL BE ALL, MY DEARS.
BUT YOU PROMISED! YOU PROMISED THAT WE WERE FREE FROM TIME HERE!
PLEASE. ENOUGH.
MY LORD! WE HAVE CAPTURED INTRUDERS. A STRANGER, AND HIS WOMAN. BOTH OF THEM ARE DRESSED IN BLACK.
SO...
YOU ARE TIME. FOUL TIME, WHO STEALS THE GOLD FROM A MAIDEN'S HAIR AND TAKES THE SAPPHIRE FROM A CHILD'S EYES.
DARK TIME, WHO HAS STOLEN FROM EVERY THING THERE EVER WAS THE THINGS THAT IT HELD PRECIOUS AND DIVINE...
...AND LEFT NOTHING BUT MEMORIES AND ASHES AND THE GRAVE.

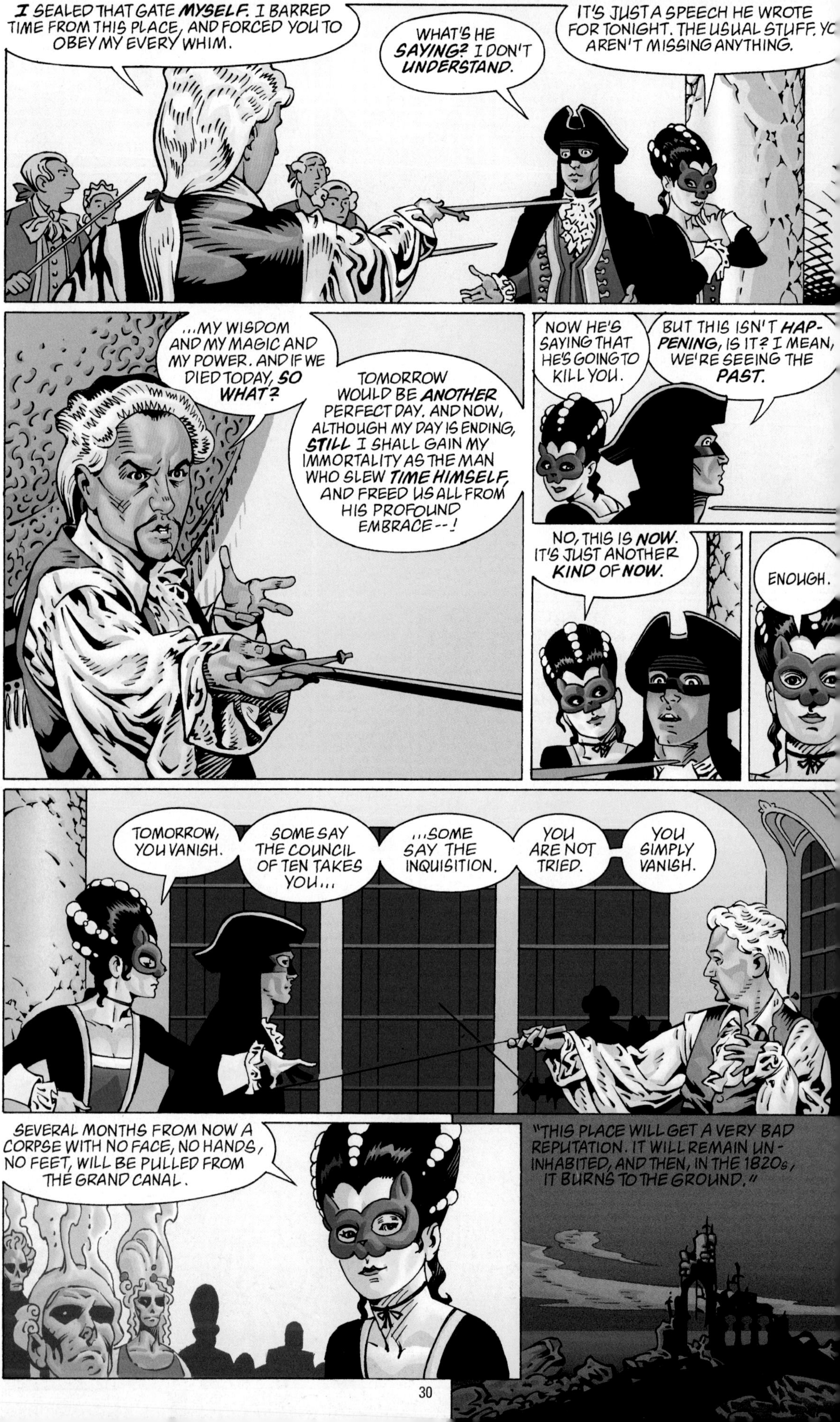

I SEALED THAT GATE MYSELF. I BARRED TIME FROM THIS PLACE, AND FORCED YOU TO OBEY MY EVERY WHIM.
WHAT'S HE SAYING? I DON'T UNDERSTAND.
IT'S JUST A SPEECH HE WROTE FOR TONIGHT. THE USUAL STUFF. YO AREN'T MISSING ANYTHING.
...MY WISDOM AND MY MAGIC AND MY POWER. AND IF WE DIED TODAY, SO WHAT?
TOMORROW WOULD BE ANOTHER PERFECT DAY. AND NOW, ALTHOUGH MY DAY IS ENDING, STILL I SHALL GAIN MY IMMORTALITY AS THE MAN WHO SLEW TIME HIMSELF, AND FREED US ALL FROM HIS PROFOUND EMBRACE--!
NOW HE'S SAYING THAT HE'S GOING TO KILL YOU.
BUT THIS ISN'T HAPPENING, IS IT? I MEAN, WE'RE SEEING THE PAST.
NO, THIS IS NOW. IT'S JUST ANOTHER KIND OF NOW.
ENOUGH.
TOMORROW, YOU VANISH.
SOME SAY THE COUNCIL OF TEN TAKES YOU...
...SOME SAY THE INQUISITION.
YOU ARE NOT TRIED.
YOU SIMPLY VANISH.
SEVERAL MONTHS FROM NOW A CORPSE WITH NO FACE, NO HANDS, NO FEET, WILL BE PULLED FROM THE GRAND CANAL.
"THIS PLACE WILL GET A VERY BAD REPUTATION. IT WILL REMAIN UN-INHABITED, AND THEN, IN THE 1820s, IT BURNS TO THE GROUND."

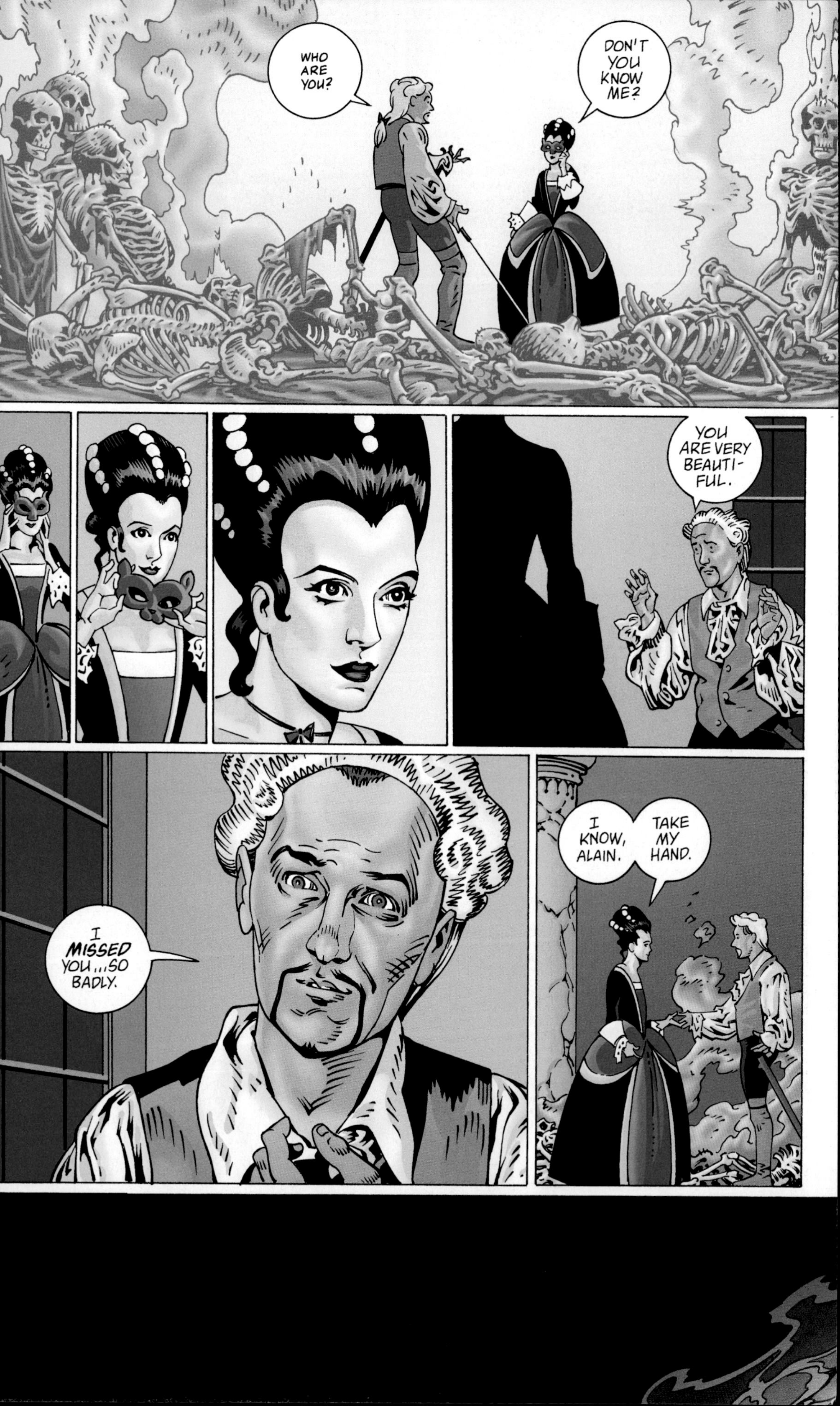
WHO ARE YOU?
DON'T YOU KNOW ME?
YOU ARE VERY BEAUTI-FUL.
I MISSED YOU...SO BADLY.
I KNOW, ALAIN.
TAKE MY HAND.

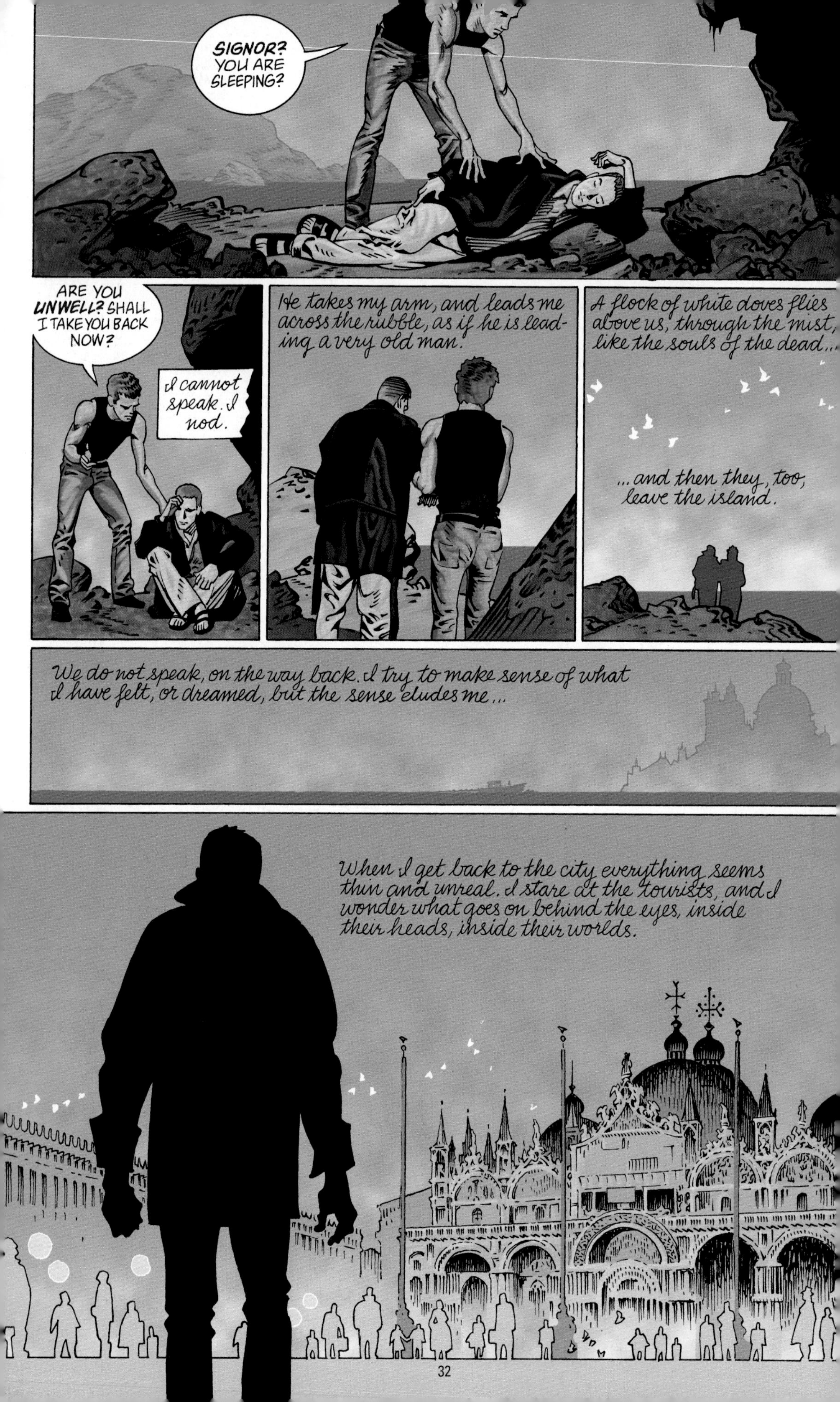
SIGNOR? YOU ARE SLEEPING?
ARE YOU UNWELL? SHALL I TAKE YOU BACK NOW?
I cannot speak. I nod.
He takes my arm, and leads me across the rubble, as if he is leading a very old man.
A flock of white doves flies above us, through the mist, like the souls of the dead...
...and then they, too, leave the island.
We do not speak, on the way back. I try to make sense of what I have felt, or dreamed, but the sense eludes me...
When I get back to the city everything seems thin and unreal. I stare at the tourists, and I wonder what goes on behind the eyes, inside their heads, inside their worlds.

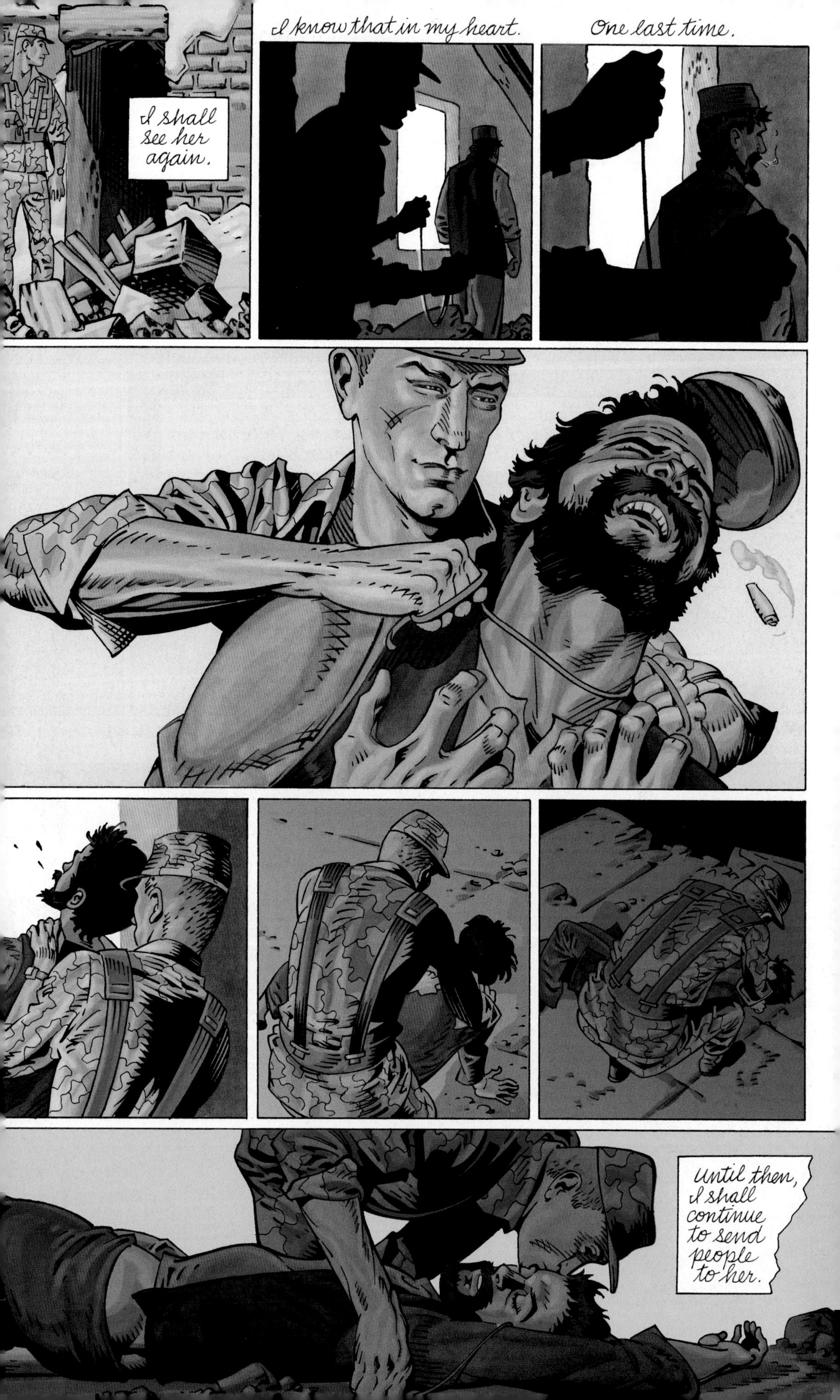
I shall see her again.
I know that in my heart.
One last time.
Until then, I shall continue to send people to her.

Next week, I return to my unit.

The people in the city seem paper thin in the mist.

They believe they are dancing to the music of their lives...

But, I think, like the puppets, each of us is pulled upon invisible strings, until the night comes, and we are put away.

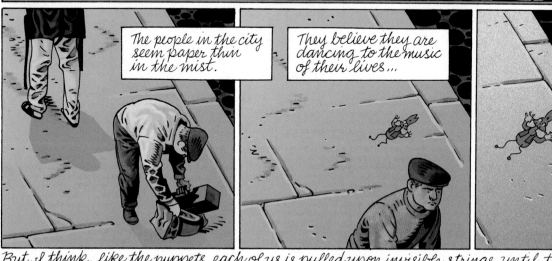

I shiver, and hurry from the square, as the darkness of the city closes over me like canal water or the grave.

Chapter 2
DESIRE
What I've Heard of Desire

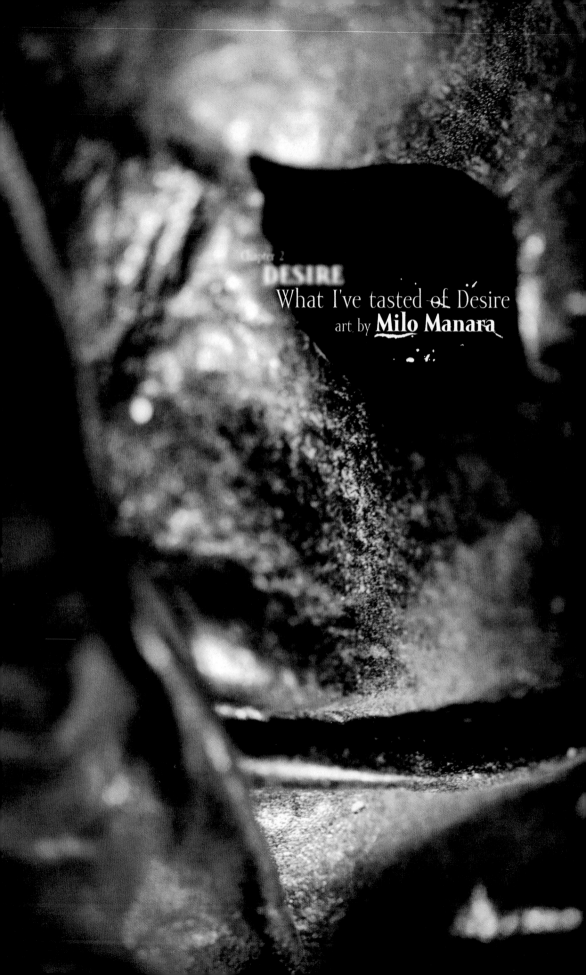

Chapter 2
DESIRE
What I've tasted of Desire
art by **Milo Manara**

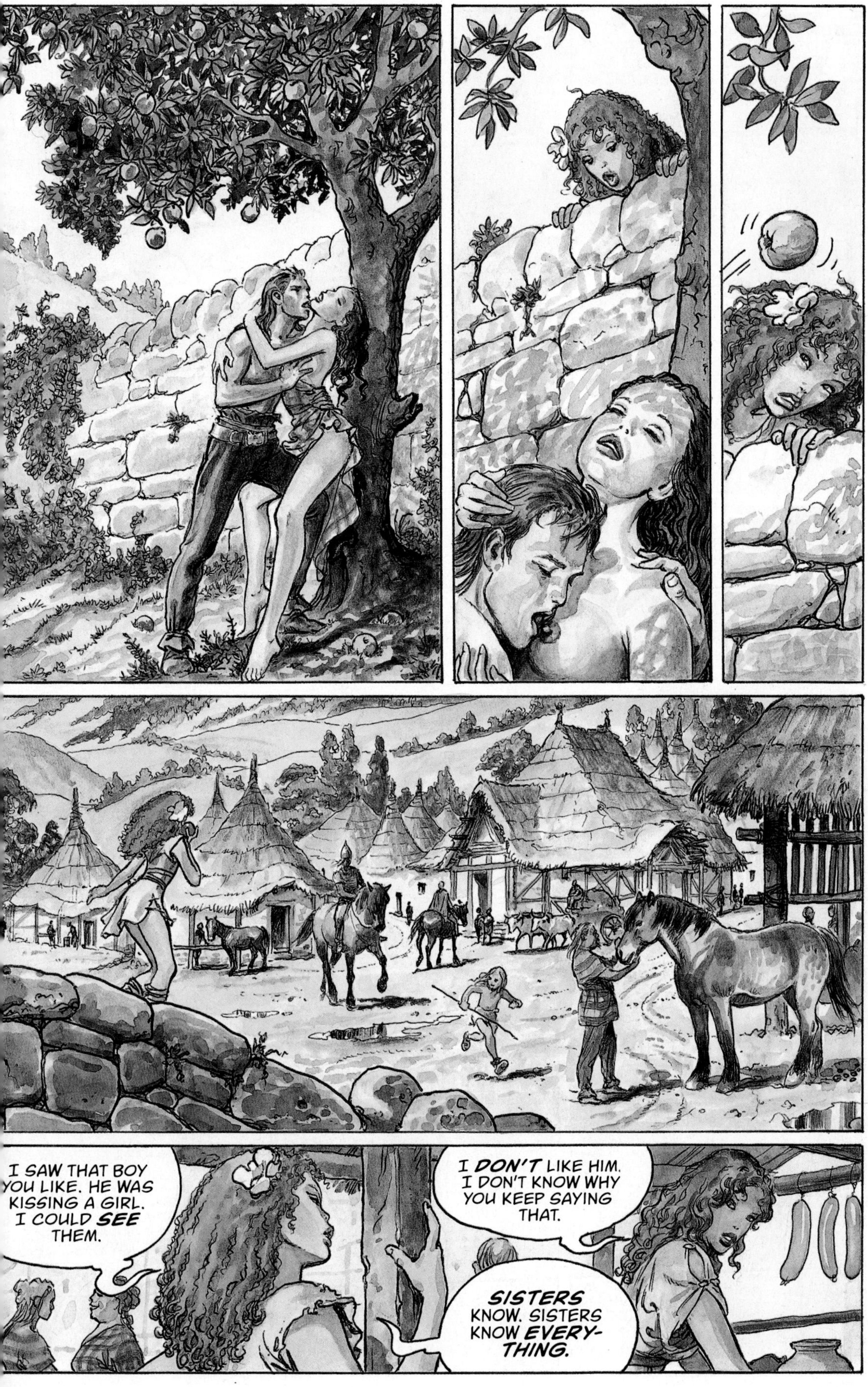

I SAW THAT BOY YOU LIKE. HE WAS KISSING A GIRL. I COULD SEE THEM.
I DON'T LIKE HIM. I DON'T KNOW WHY YOU KEEP SAYING THAT.
SISTERS KNOW. SISTERS KNOW EVERY-THING.

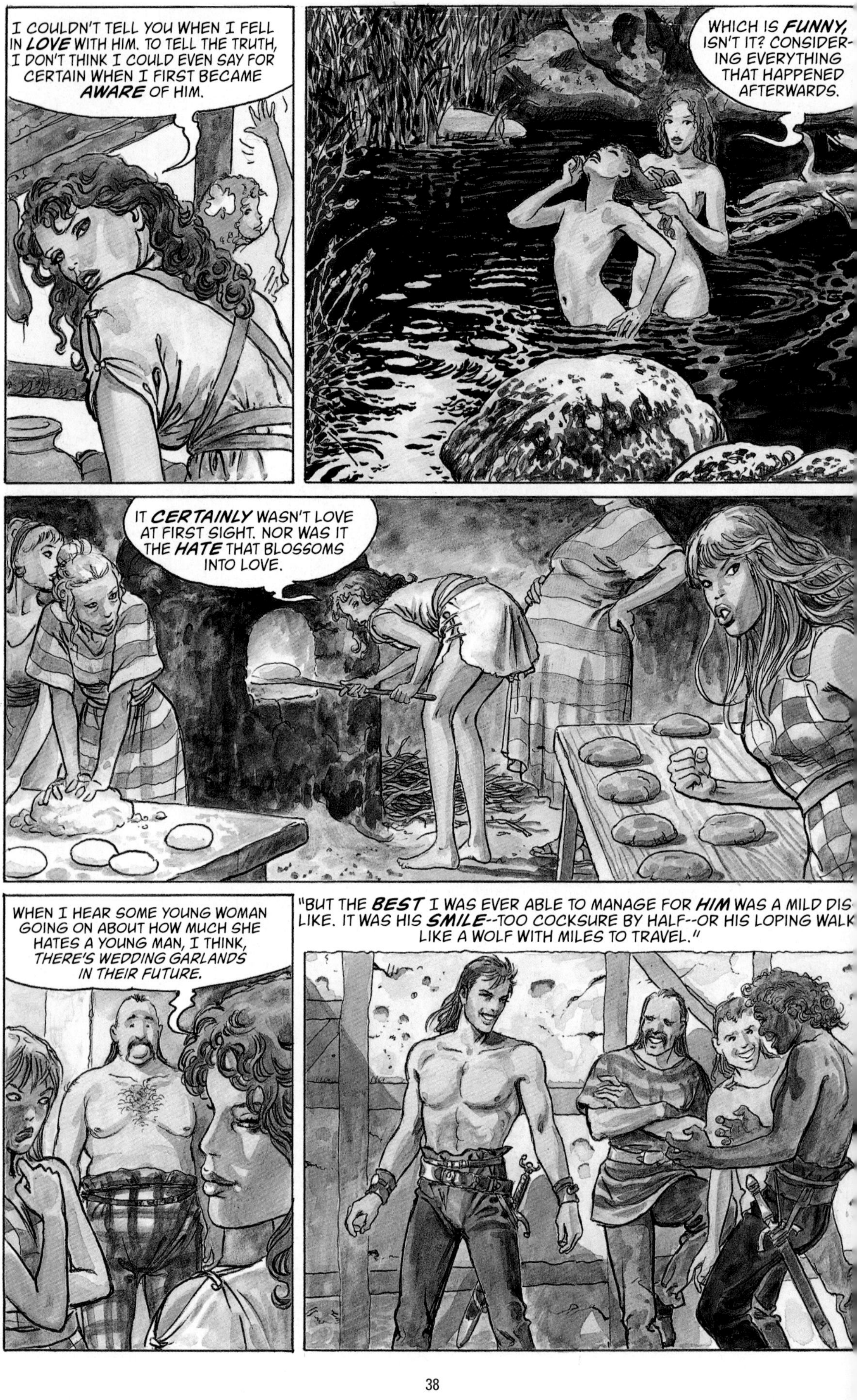
I COULDN'T TELL YOU WHEN I FELL IN LOVE WITH HIM. TO TELL THE TRUTH, I DON'T THINK I COULD EVEN SAY FOR CERTAIN WHEN I FIRST BECAME AWARE OF HIM.
WHICH IS FUNNY, ISN'T IT? CONSIDERING EVERYTHING THAT HAPPENED AFTERWARDS.
IT CERTAINLY WASN'T LOVE AT FIRST SIGHT. NOR WAS IT THE HATE THAT BLOSSOMS INTO LOVE.
WHEN I HEAR SOME YOUNG WOMAN GOING ON ABOUT HOW MUCH SHE HATES A YOUNG MAN, I THINK, THERE'S WEDDING GARLANDS IN THEIR FUTURE.
"BUT THE BEST I WAS EVER ABLE TO MANAGE FOR HIM WAS A MILD DISLIKE. IT WAS HIS SMILE--TOO COCKSURE BY HALF--OR HIS LOPING WALK LIKE A WOLF WITH MILES TO TRAVEL."

...ND MOST IRRITATING OF ALL WAS THE WAY THE OTHER GIRLS THOUGHT HE WAS--"

SWEET!

GORGEOUS!

TASTY!

FUNNY!

--THAT LEFT ME FEELING NOTHING FOR HIM AT ALL.

"SOME OF THEM DESIRED HIM FOR HIS SKILL IN BATTLE--FOR IN THOSE DAYS THERE WERE ALWAYS BORDER SKIR-MISHES, AND WOLVES ATTACKING IN THE WINTER--AND HE TOOK HEADS AND PELTS AS EASILY AS HE TOOK HEARTS."

WE'D MEET, OF COURSE, AND TALK, IN THE WAY YOU DO, AS IT WAS NOT A BIG VILLAGE--A FEAST HALL, AND HOUSES THAT SURROUND-ED IT, INSIDE A WALL. YOU COULDN'T HELP MEET-ING PEOPLE.

"THERE WAS ONE MORNING WE WALKED TOGETHER, HIM ON HIS WAY DOWN TO THE BROOK TO FISH, ME TO SEE TO THE GOATS, AND THE MIST WAS THICK, SO WE WALKED CLOSE, AND WE TALKED-- NOT ABOUT MUCH.

"HE TOLD ME HIS FATHER, OUR CHIEF, SAID THAT THE GODS DID NOT COUNT TIME SPENT FISHING IN THE HOURS OF A MAN'S LIFE...AND I SAID THAT WAS VERY INTERESTING, ALTHOUGH I THOUGHT IT WAS UNLIKELY, ALL THINGS CONSIDERED."

AND WHEN WE CAME TO SAY GOOD MORN-ING AND FARE-THEE-WELL, I COULD THINK OF NOTHING I WANTED MORE THAN TO SPEND THE REST OF MY LIFE WITH THAT INFURIAT-ING YOUNG MAN...

...WITH HIS COCKSURE SMILE AND HIS WOLFISH WALK.

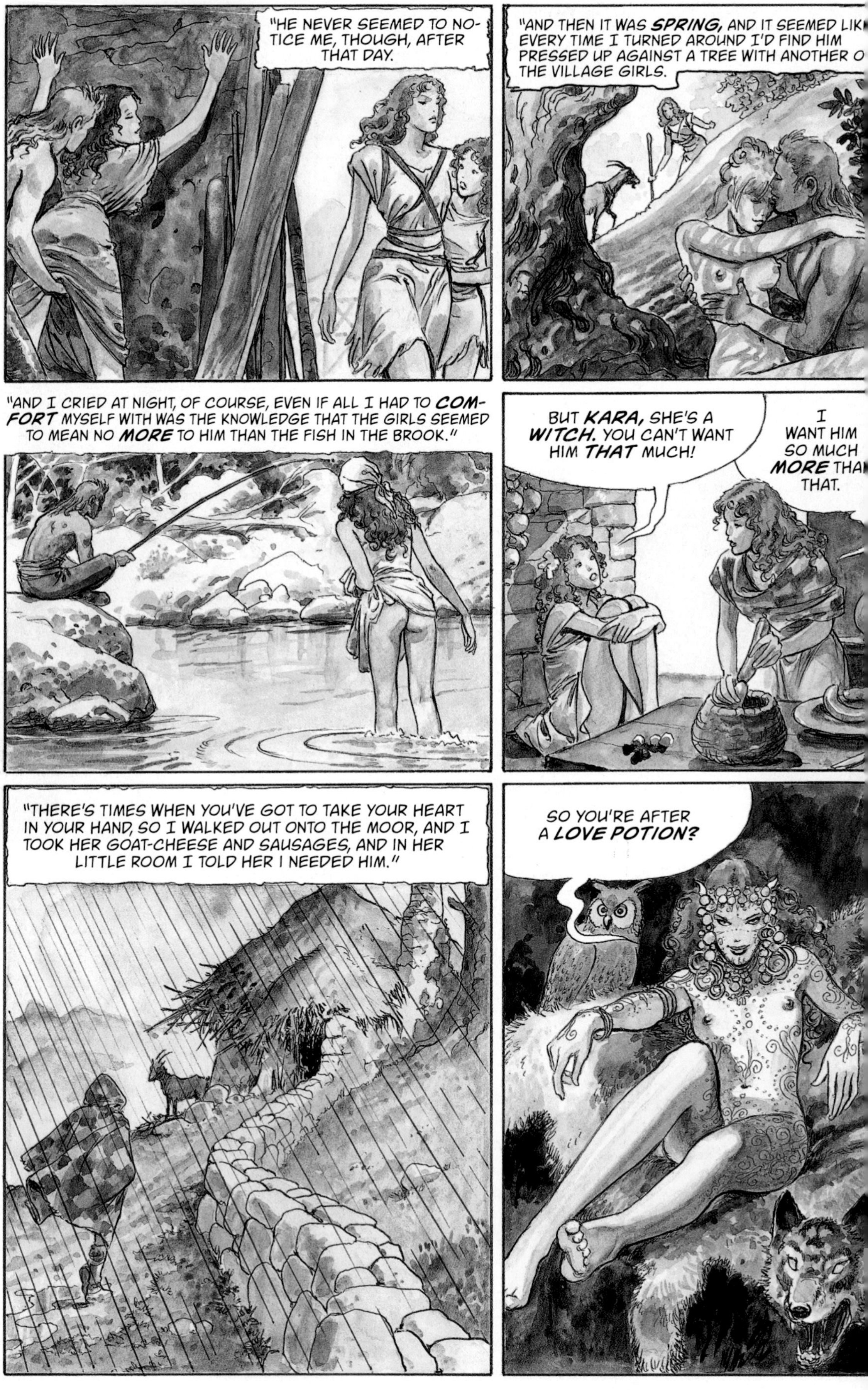
"HE NEVER SEEMED TO NOTICE ME, THOUGH, AFTER THAT DAY.
"AND THEN IT WAS SPRING, AND IT SEEMED LIK EVERY TIME I TURNED AROUND I'D FIND HIM PRESSED UP AGAINST A TREE WITH ANOTHER O THE VILLAGE GIRLS.
"AND I CRIED AT NIGHT, OF COURSE, EVEN IF ALL I HAD TO COMFORT MYSELF WITH WAS THE KNOWLEDGE THAT THE GIRLS SEEMED TO MEAN NO MORE TO HIM THAN THE FISH IN THE BROOK."
BUT KARA, SHE'S A WITCH. YOU CAN'T WANT HIM THAT MUCH!
I WANT HIM SO MUCH MORE THA THAT.
"THERE'S TIMES WHEN YOU'VE GOT TO TAKE YOUR HEART IN YOUR HAND, SO I WALKED OUT ONTO THE MOOR, AND I TOOK HER GOAT-CHEESE AND SAUSAGES, AND IN HER LITTLE ROOM I TOLD HER I NEEDED HIM."
SO YOU'RE AFTER A LOVE POTION?

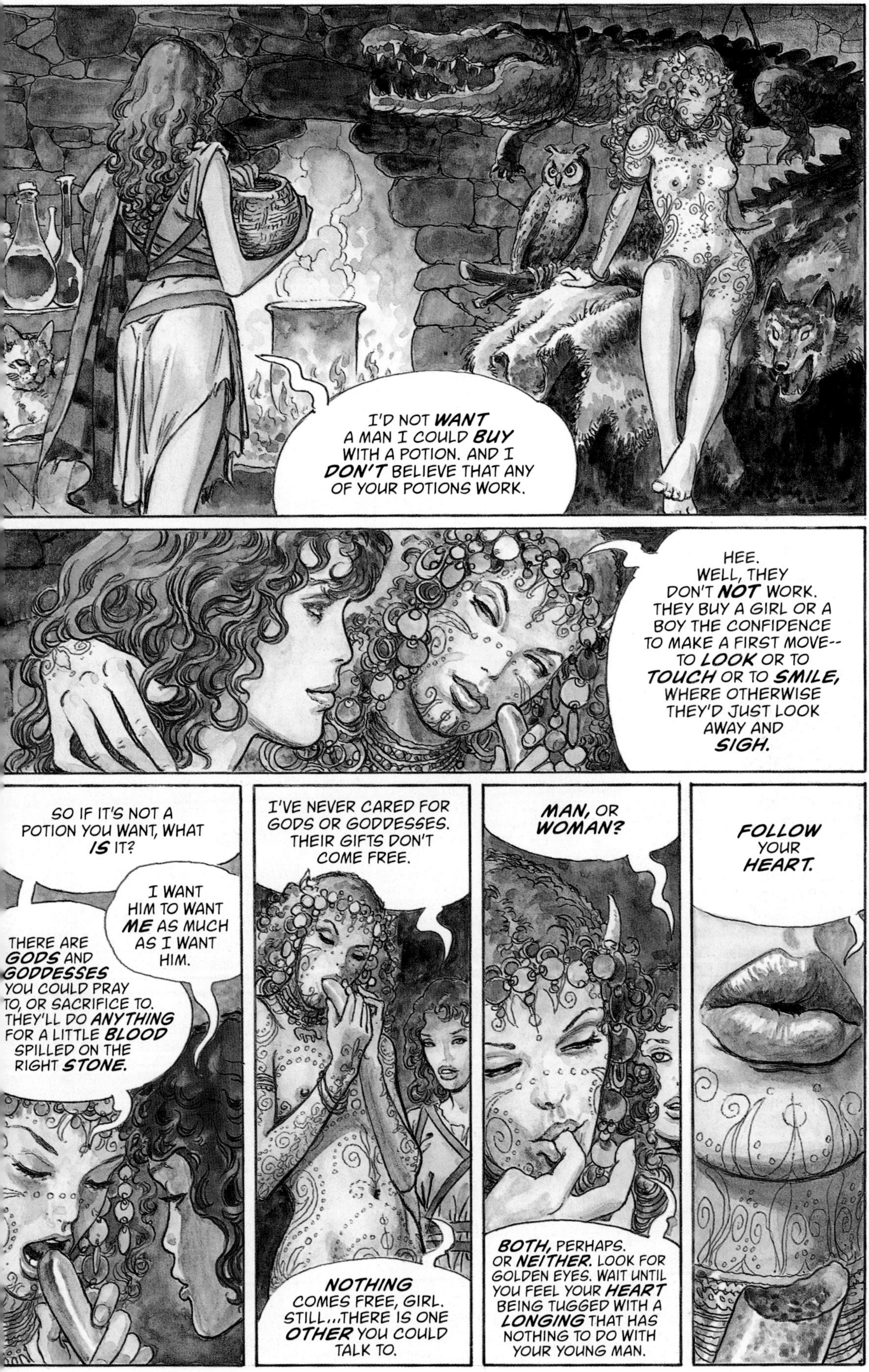
I'D NOT WANT A MAN I COULD BUY WITH A POTION. AND I DON'T BELIEVE THAT ANY OF YOUR POTIONS WORK.
HEE. WELL, THEY DON'T NOT WORK. THEY BUY A GIRL OR A BOY THE CONFIDENCE TO MAKE A FIRST MOVE-- TO LOOK OR TO TOUCH OR TO SMILE, WHERE OTHERWISE THEY'D JUST LOOK AWAY AND SIGH.
SO IF IT'S NOT A POTION YOU WANT, WHAT IS IT?
I WANT HIM TO WANT ME AS MUCH AS I WANT HIM.
THERE ARE GODS AND GODDESSES YOU COULD PRAY TO, OR SACRIFICE TO. THEY'LL DO ANYTHING FOR A LITTLE BLOOD SPILLED ON THE RIGHT STONE.
I'VE NEVER CARED FOR GODS OR GODDESSES. THEIR GIFTS DON'T COME FREE.
NOTHING COMES FREE, GIRL. STILL...THERE IS ONE OTHER YOU COULD TALK TO.
MAN, OR WOMAN?
BOTH, PERHAPS. OR NEITHER. LOOK FOR GOLDEN EYES. WAIT UNTIL YOU FEEL YOUR HEART BEING TUGGED WITH A LONGING THAT HAS NOTHING TO DO WITH YOUR YOUNG MAN.
FOLLOW YOUR HEART.

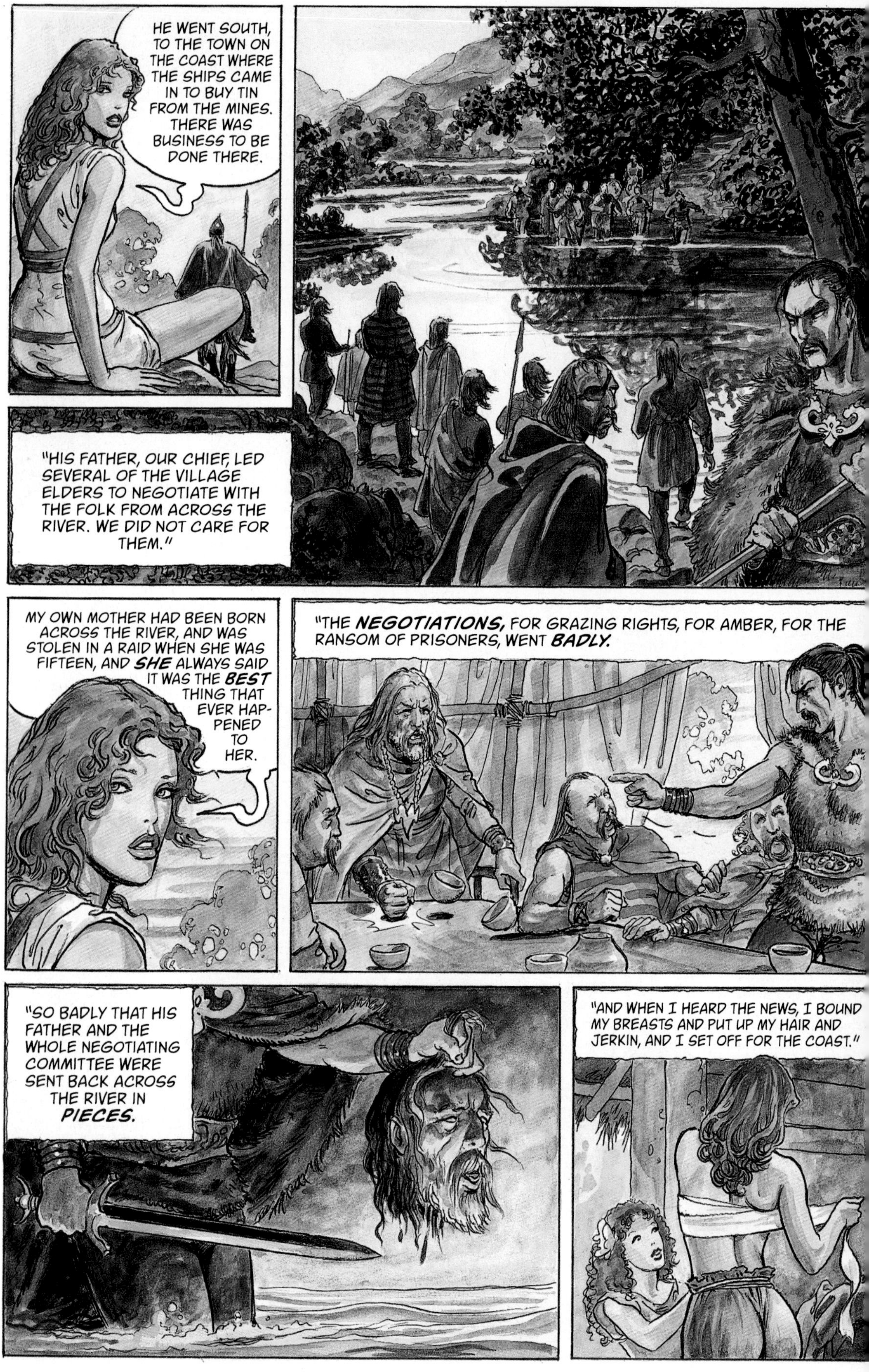
HE WENT SOUTH, TO THE TOWN ON THE COAST WHERE THE SHIPS CAME IN TO BUY TIN FROM THE MINES. THERE WAS BUSINESS TO BE DONE THERE.
"HIS FATHER, OUR CHIEF, LED SEVERAL OF THE VILLAGE ELDERS TO NEGOTIATE WITH THE FOLK FROM ACROSS THE RIVER. WE DID NOT CARE FOR THEM."
MY OWN MOTHER HAD BEEN BORN ACROSS THE RIVER, AND WAS STOLEN IN A RAID WHEN SHE WAS FIFTEEN, AND SHE ALWAYS SAID IT WAS THE BEST THING THAT EVER HAPPENED TO HER.
"THE NEGOTIATIONS, FOR GRAZING RIGHTS, FOR AMBER, FOR THE RANSOM OF PRISONERS, WENT BADLY.
"SO BADLY THAT HIS FATHER AND THE WHOLE NEGOTIATING COMMITTEE WERE SENT BACK ACROSS THE RIVER IN PIECES.
"AND WHEN I HEARD THE NEWS, I BOUND MY BREASTS AND PUT UP MY HAIR AND JERKIN, AND I SET OFF FOR THE COAST."

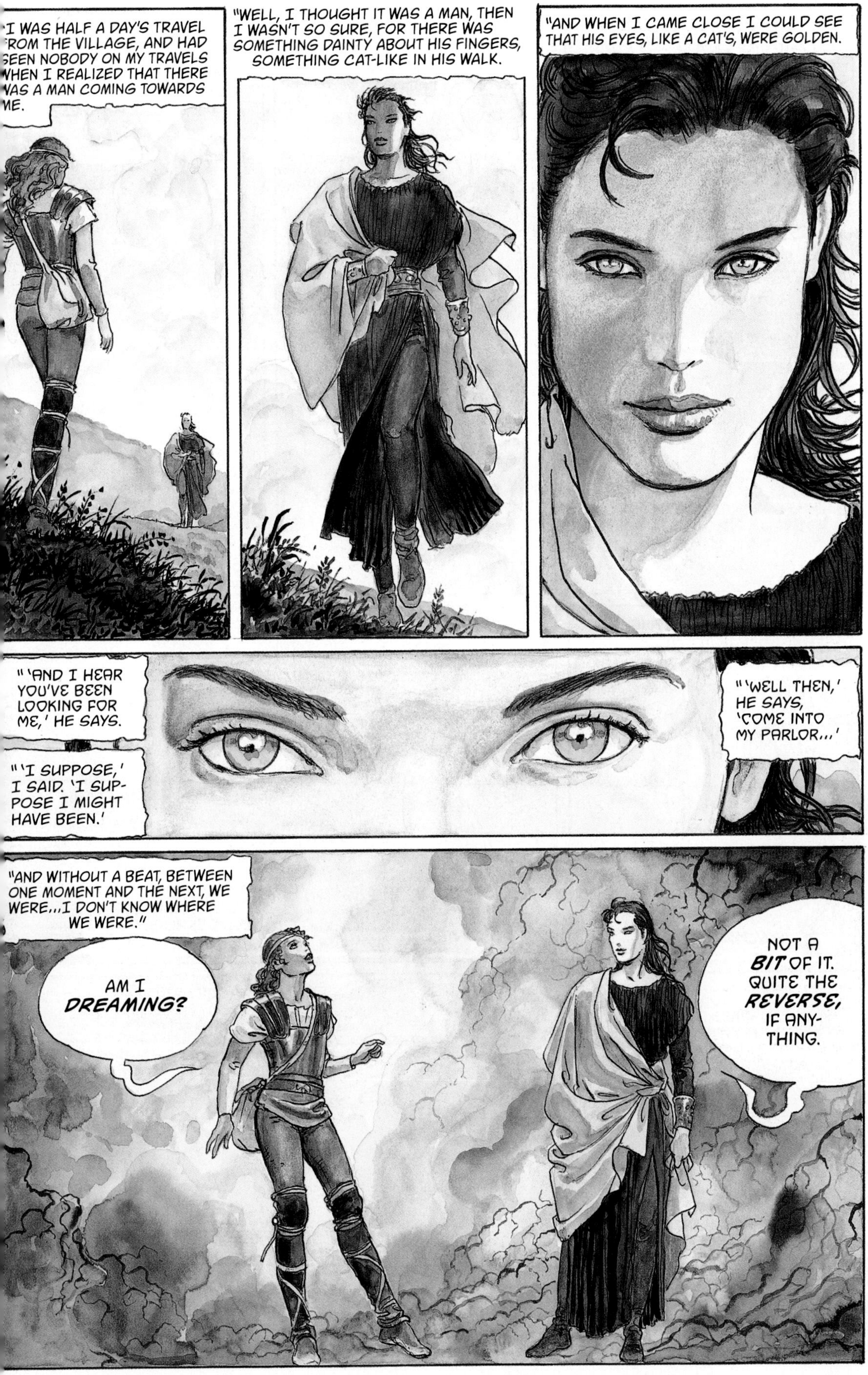
"I WAS HALF A DAY'S TRAVEL FROM THE VILLAGE, AND HAD SEEN NOBODY ON MY TRAVELS WHEN I REALIZED THAT THERE WAS A MAN COMING TOWARDS ME.
"WELL, I THOUGHT IT WAS A MAN, THEN I WASN'T SO SURE, FOR THERE WAS SOMETHING DAINTY ABOUT HIS FINGERS, SOMETHING CAT-LIKE IN HIS WALK.
"AND WHEN I CAME CLOSE I COULD SEE THAT HIS EYES, LIKE A CAT'S, WERE GOLDEN.
"'AND I HEAR YOU'VE BEEN LOOKING FOR ME,' HE SAYS.
"'I SUPPOSE,' I SAID. 'I SUPPOSE I MIGHT HAVE BEEN.'
"'WELL THEN,' HE SAYS, 'COME INTO MY PARLOR...'
"AND WITHOUT A BEAT, BETWEEN ONE MOMENT AND THE NEXT, WE WERE...I DON'T KNOW WHERE WE WERE."
AM I DREAMING?
NOT A BIT OF IT. QUITE THE REVERSE, IF ANYTHING.

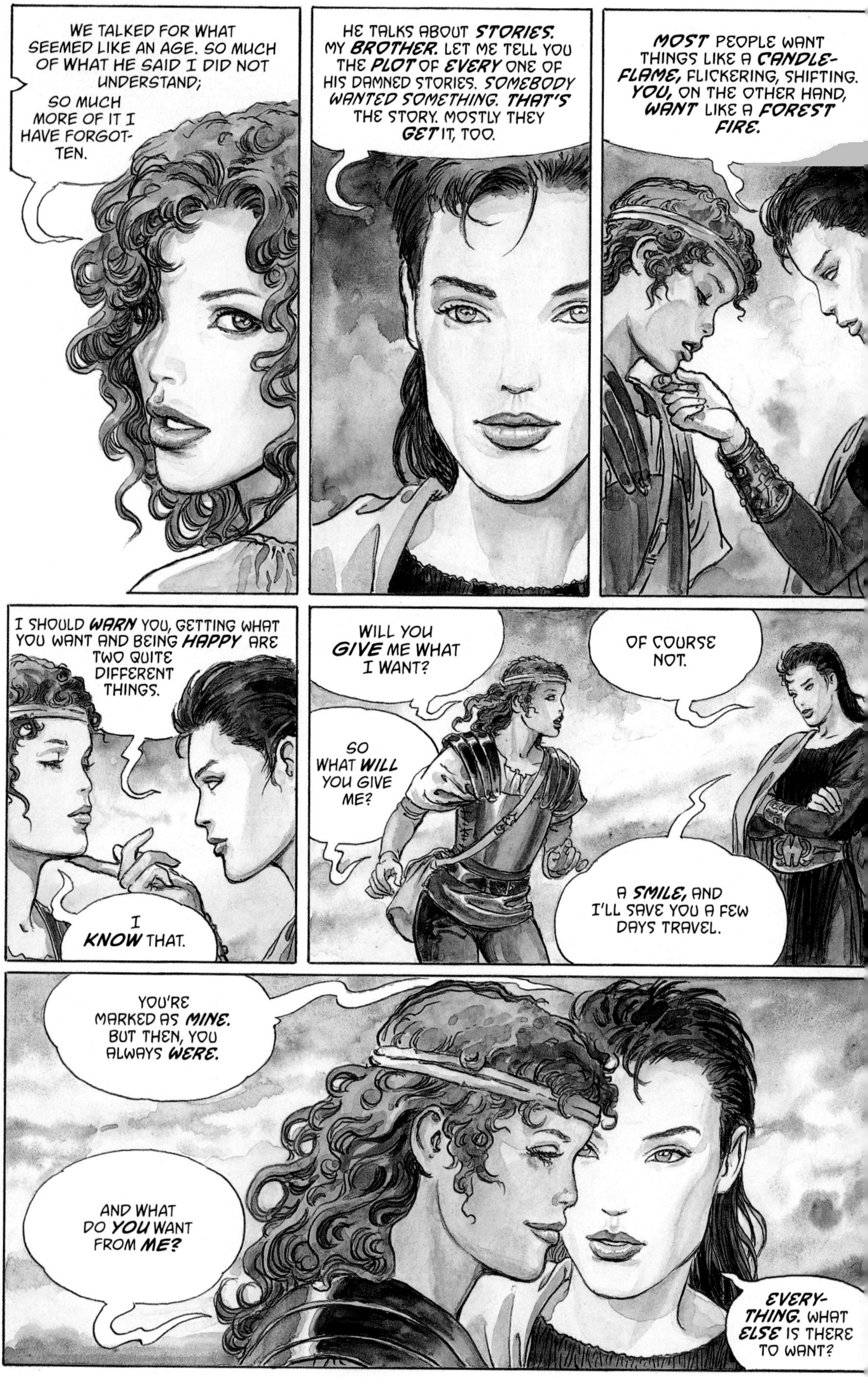
WE TALKED FOR WHAT SEEMED LIKE AN AGE. SO MUCH OF WHAT HE SAID I DID NOT UNDERSTAND;
SO MUCH MORE OF IT I HAVE FORGOTTEN.
HE TALKS ABOUT STORIES. MY BROTHER. LET ME TELL YOU THE PLOT OF EVERY ONE OF HIS DAMNED STORIES. SOMEBODY WANTED SOMETHING. THAT'S THE STORY. MOSTLY THEY GET IT, TOO.
MOST PEOPLE WANT THINGS LIKE A CANDLE-FLAME, FLICKERING, SHIFTING. YOU, ON THE OTHER HAND, WANT LIKE A FOREST FIRE.
I SHOULD WARN YOU, GETTING WHAT YOU WANT AND BEING HAPPY ARE TWO QUITE DIFFERENT THINGS.
I KNOW THAT.
WILL YOU GIVE ME WHAT I WANT?
OF COURSE NOT.
SO WHAT WILL YOU GIVE ME?
A SMILE, AND I'LL SAVE YOU A FEW DAYS TRAVEL.
YOU'RE MARKED AS MINE. BUT THEN, YOU ALWAYS WERE.
AND WHAT DO YOU WANT FROM ME?
EVERYTHING. WHAT ELSE IS THERE TO WANT?

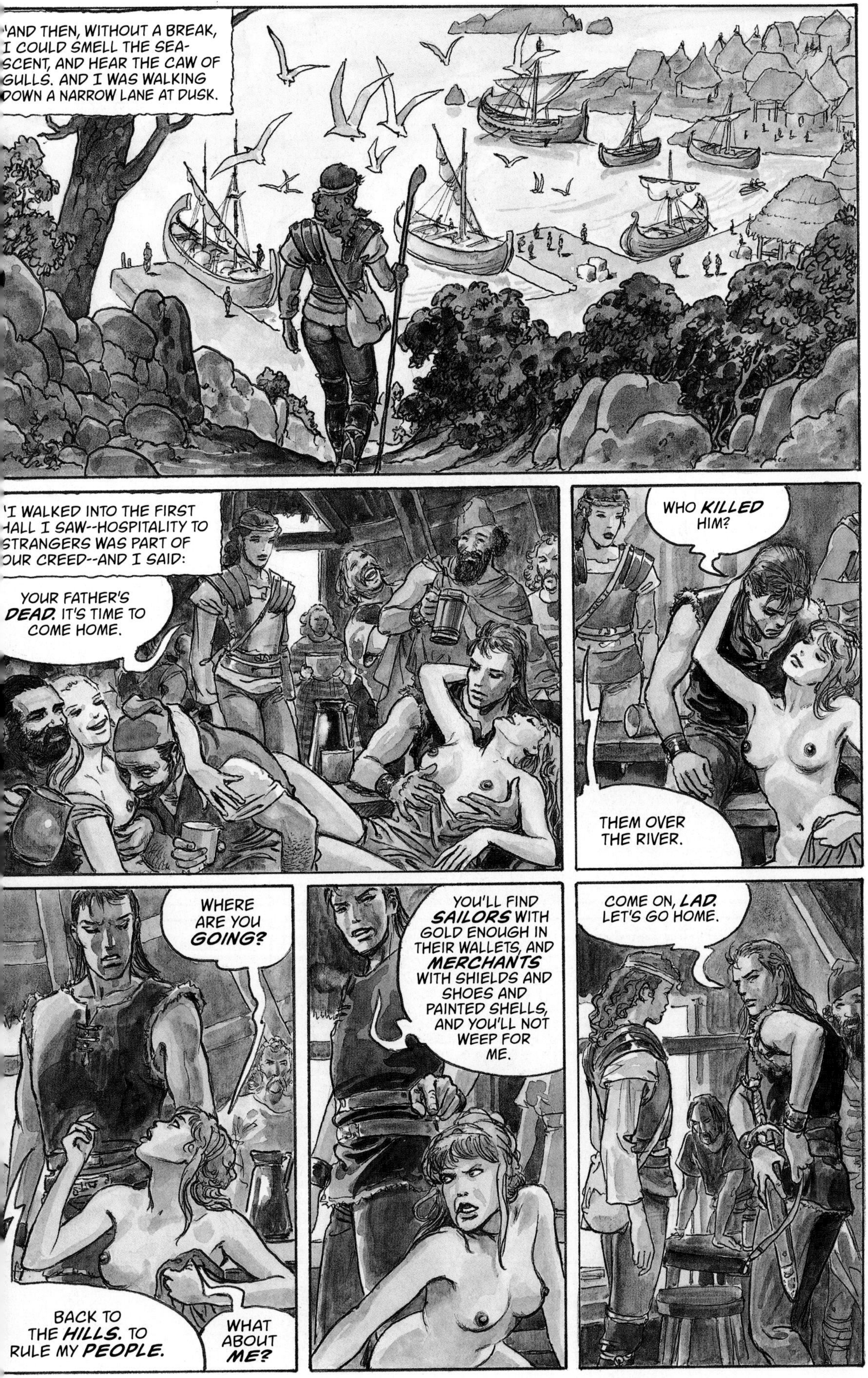
'AND THEN, WITHOUT A BREAK, I COULD SMELL THE SEA-SCENT, AND HEAR THE CAW OF GULLS. AND I WAS WALKING DOWN A NARROW LANE AT DUSK.
'I WALKED INTO THE FIRST HALL I SAW--HOSPITALITY TO STRANGERS WAS PART OF OUR CREED--AND I SAID:
YOUR FATHER'S DEAD. IT'S TIME TO COME HOME.
WHO KILLED HIM?
THEM OVER THE RIVER.
WHERE ARE YOU GOING?
BACK TO THE HILLS. TO RULE MY PEOPLE.
WHAT ABOUT ME?
YOU'LL FIND SAILORS WITH GOLD ENOUGH IN THEIR WALLETS, AND MERCHANTS WITH SHIELDS AND SHOES AND PAINTED SHELLS, AND YOU'LL NOT WEEP FOR ME.
COME ON, LAD. LET'S GO HOME.

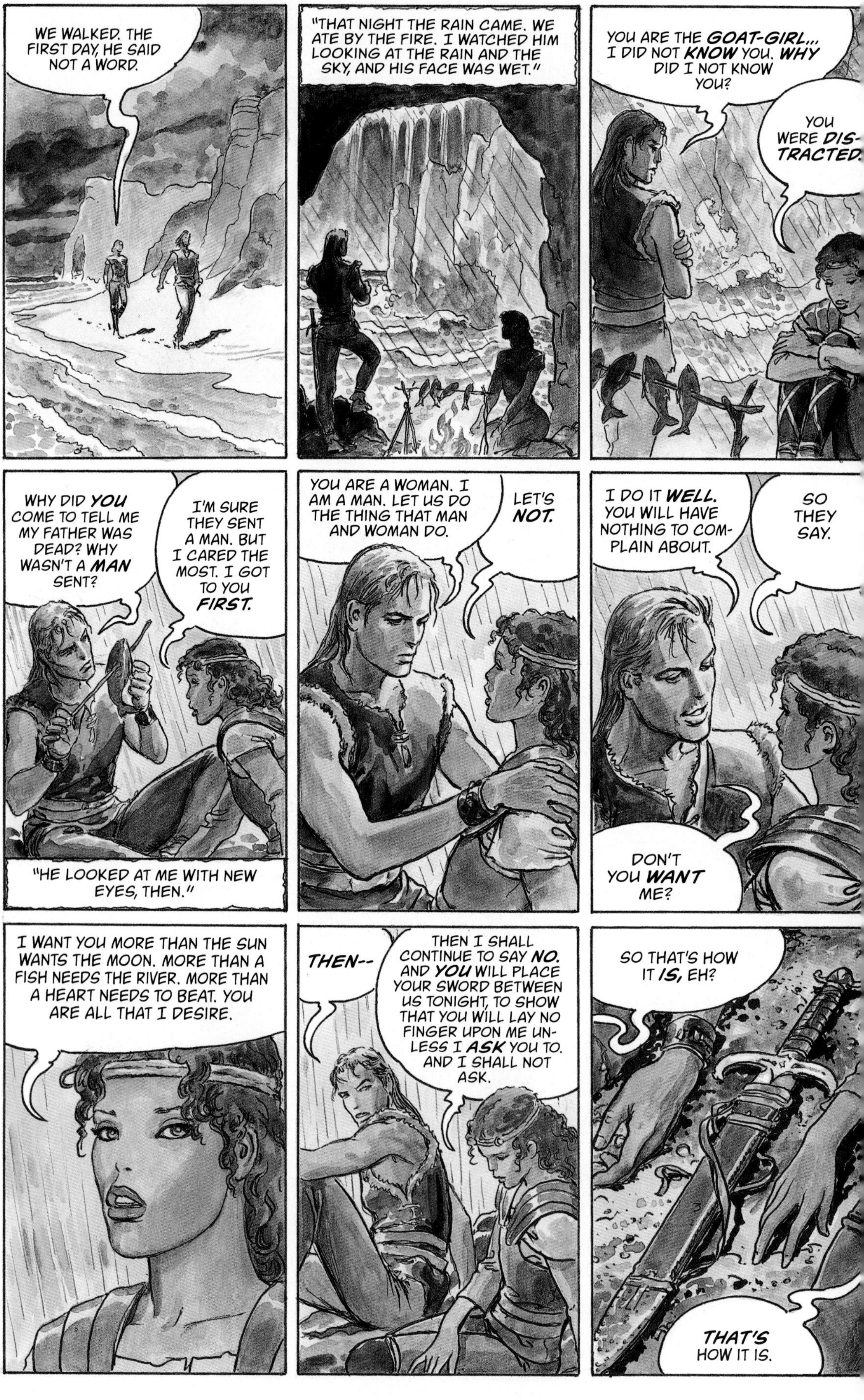
WE WALKED. THE FIRST DAY, HE SAID NOT A WORD.
"THAT NIGHT THE RAIN CAME. WE ATE BY THE FIRE. I WATCHED HIM LOOKING AT THE RAIN AND THE SKY, AND HIS FACE WAS WET."
YOU ARE THE GOAT-GIRL... I DID NOT KNOW YOU. WHY DID I NOT KNOW YOU?
YOU WERE DIS-TRACTED.
WHY DID YOU COME TO TELL ME MY FATHER WAS DEAD? WHY WASN'T A MAN SENT?
I'M SURE THEY SENT A MAN. BUT I CARED THE MOST. I GOT TO YOU FIRST.
"HE LOOKED AT ME WITH NEW EYES, THEN."
YOU ARE A WOMAN. I AM A MAN. LET US DO THE THING THAT MAN AND WOMAN DO.
LET'S NOT.
I DO IT WELL. YOU WILL HAVE NOTHING TO COM-PLAIN ABOUT.
SO THEY SAY.
DON'T YOU WANT ME?
I WANT YOU MORE THAN THE SUN WANTS THE MOON. MORE THAN A FISH NEEDS THE RIVER. MORE THAN A HEART NEEDS TO BEAT. YOU ARE ALL THAT I DESIRE.
THEN--
THEN I SHALL CONTINUE TO SAY NO. AND YOU WILL PLACE YOUR SWORD BETWEEN US TONIGHT, TO SHOW THAT YOU WILL LAY NO FINGER UPON ME UN-LESS I ASK YOU TO. AND I SHALL NOT ASK.
SO THAT'S HOW IT IS, EH?
THAT'S HOW IT IS.

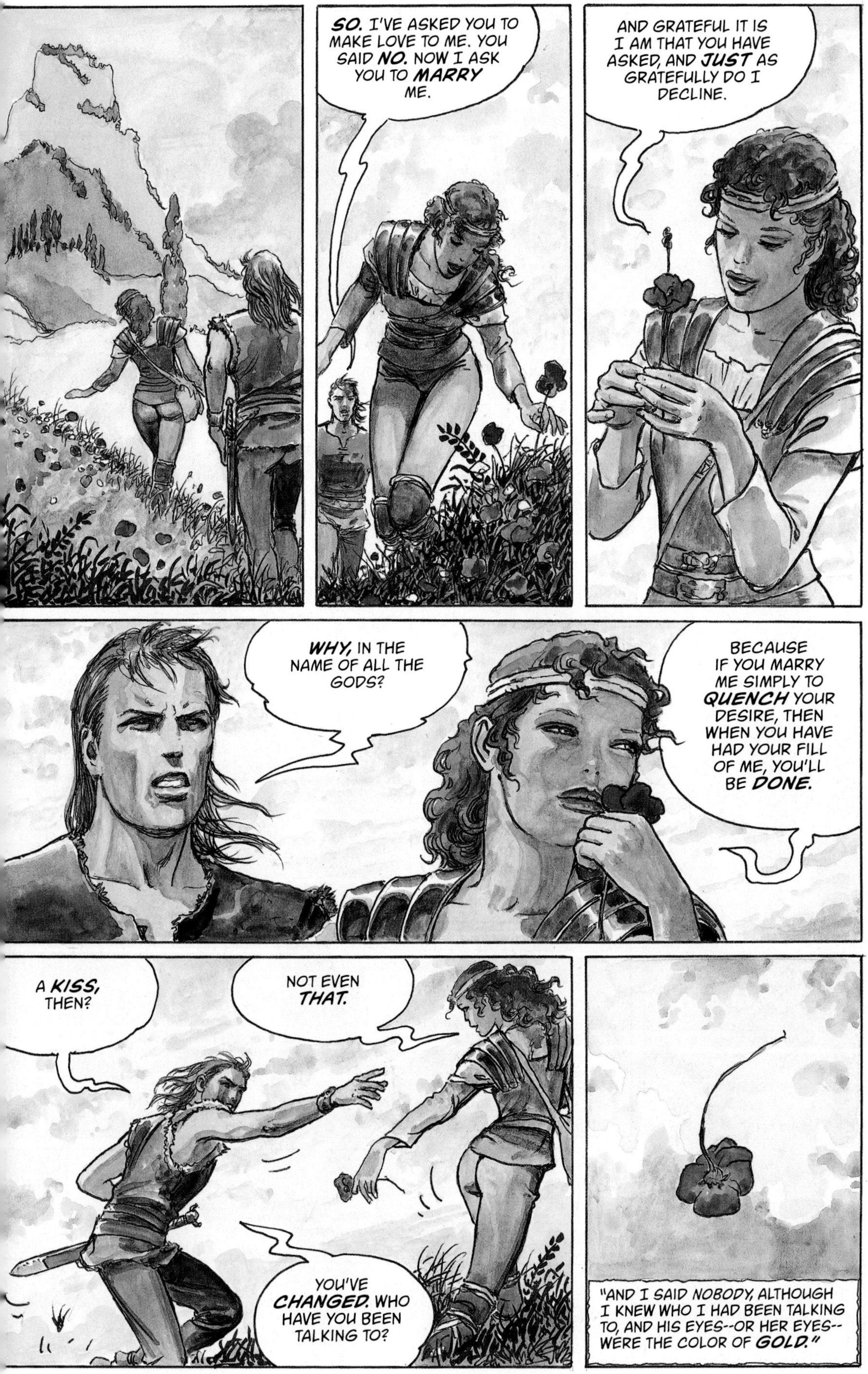
SO. I'VE ASKED YOU TO MAKE LOVE TO ME. YOU SAID NO. NOW I ASK YOU TO MARRY ME.
AND GRATEFUL IT IS I AM THAT YOU HAVE ASKED, AND JUST AS GRATEFULLY DO I DECLINE.
WHY, IN THE NAME OF ALL THE GODS?
BECAUSE IF YOU MARRY ME SIMPLY TO QUENCH YOUR DESIRE, THEN WHEN YOU HAVE HAD YOUR FILL OF ME, YOU'LL BE DONE.
A KISS, THEN?
NOT EVEN THAT.
YOU'VE CHANGED. WHO HAVE YOU BEEN TALKING TO?
"AND I SAID NOBODY, ALTHOUGH I KNEW WHO I HAD BEEN TALKING TO, AND HIS EYES--OR HER EYES--WERE THE COLOR OF GOLD."

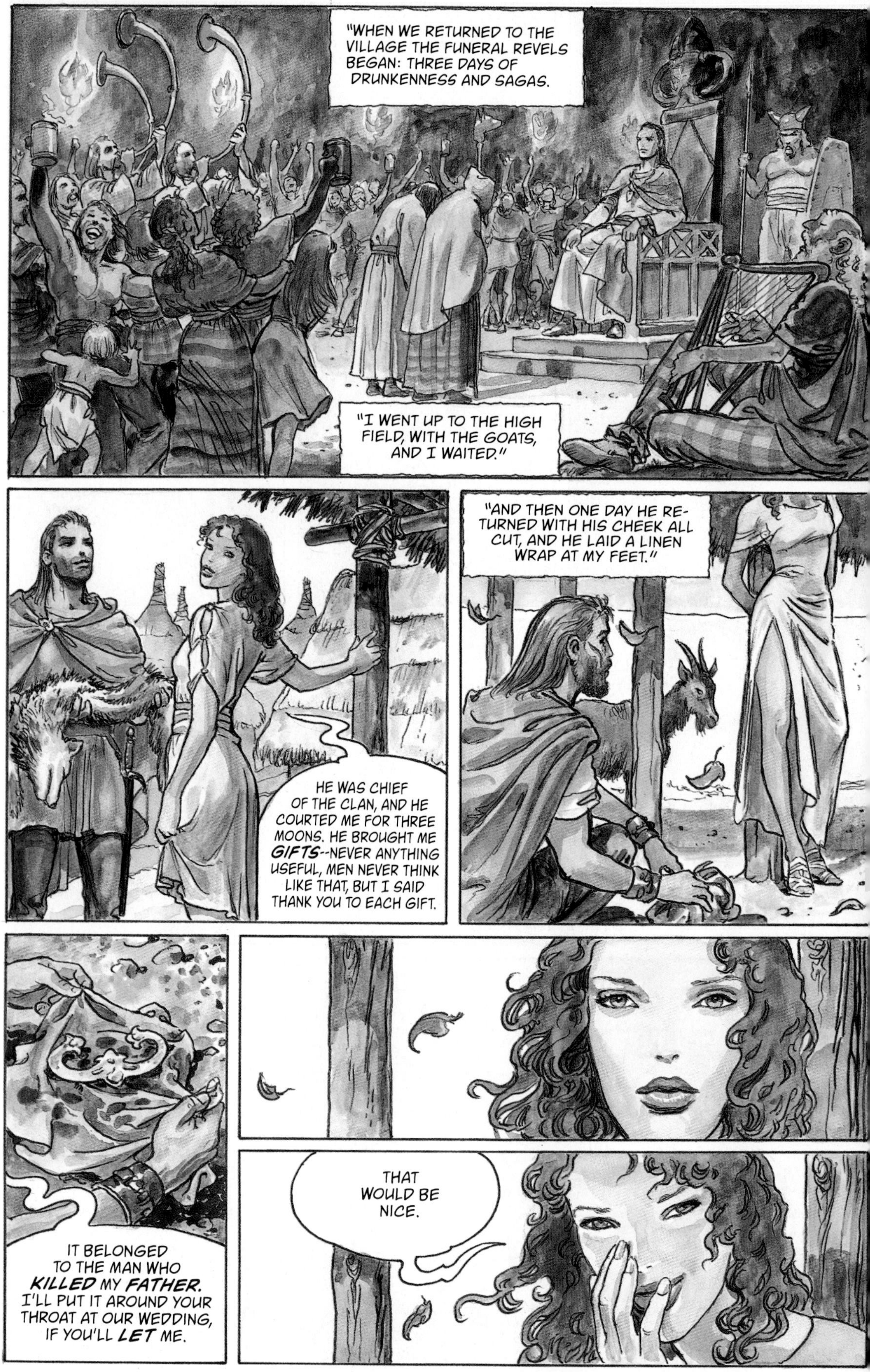
"WHEN WE RETURNED TO THE VILLAGE THE FUNERAL REVELS BEGAN: THREE DAYS OF DRUNKENNESS AND SAGAS.
"I WENT UP TO THE HIGH FIELD, WITH THE GOATS, AND I WAITED."
HE WAS CHIEF OF THE CLAN, AND HE COURTED ME FOR THREE MOONS. HE BROUGHT ME GIFTS--NEVER ANYTHING USEFUL, MEN NEVER THINK LIKE THAT, BUT I SAID THANK YOU TO EACH GIFT.
"AND THEN ONE DAY HE RETURNED WITH HIS CHEEK ALL CUT, AND HE LAID A LINEN WRAP AT MY FEET."
IT BELONGED TO THE MAN WHO KILLED MY FATHER. I'LL PUT IT AROUND YOUR THROAT AT OUR WEDDING, IF YOU'LL LET ME.
THAT WOULD BE NICE.

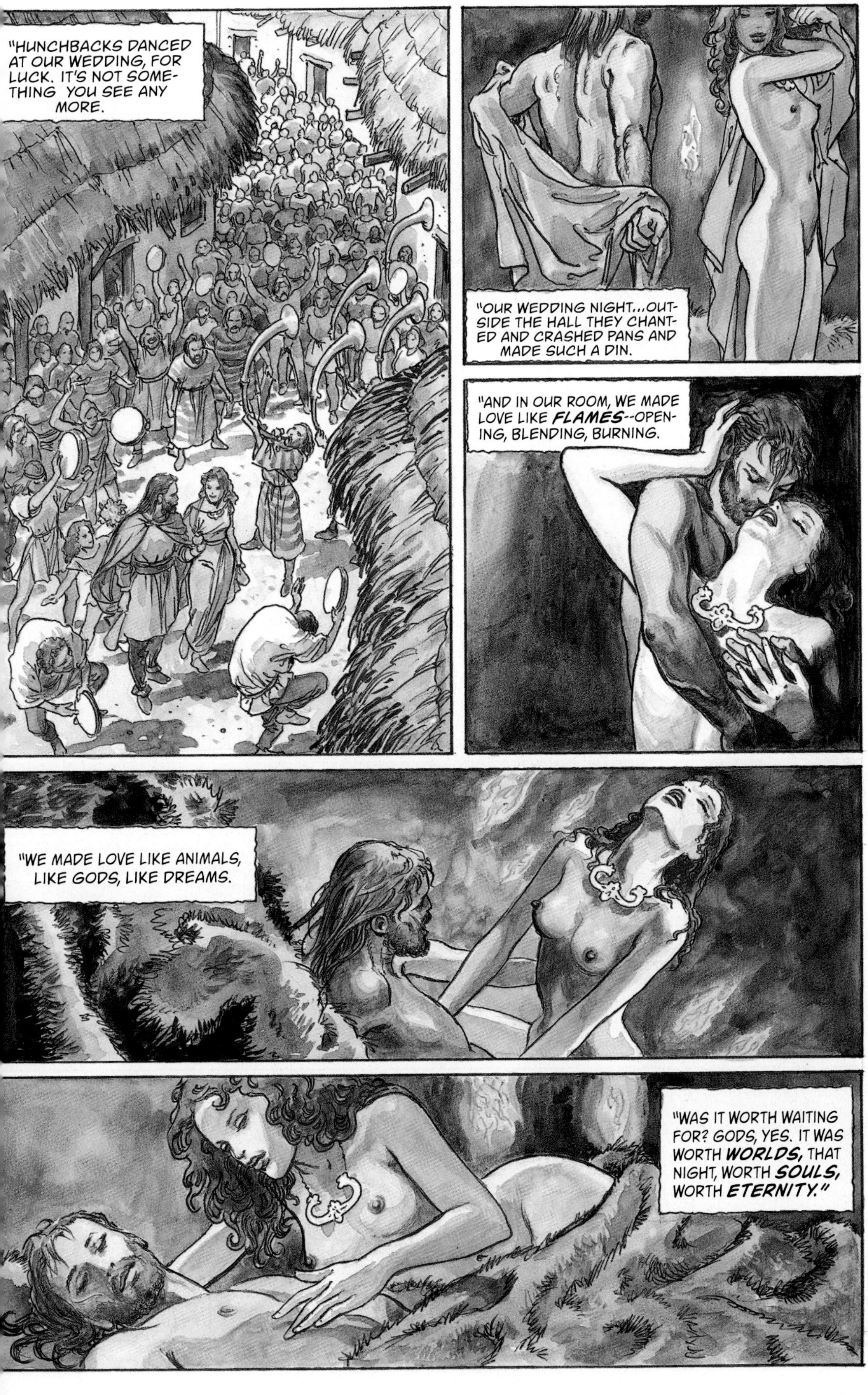
"HUNCHBACKS DANCED AT OUR WEDDING, FOR LUCK. IT'S NOT SOMETHING YOU SEE ANY MORE.
"OUR WEDDING NIGHT...OUTSIDE THE HALL THEY CHANTED AND CRASHED PANS AND MADE SUCH A DIN.
"AND IN OUR ROOM, WE MADE LOVE LIKE FLAMES--OPENING, BLENDING, BURNING.
"WE MADE LOVE LIKE ANIMALS, LIKE GODS, LIKE DREAMS.
"WAS IT WORTH WAITING FOR? GODS, YES. IT WAS WORTH WORLDS, THAT NIGHT, WORTH SOULS, WORTH ETERNITY."

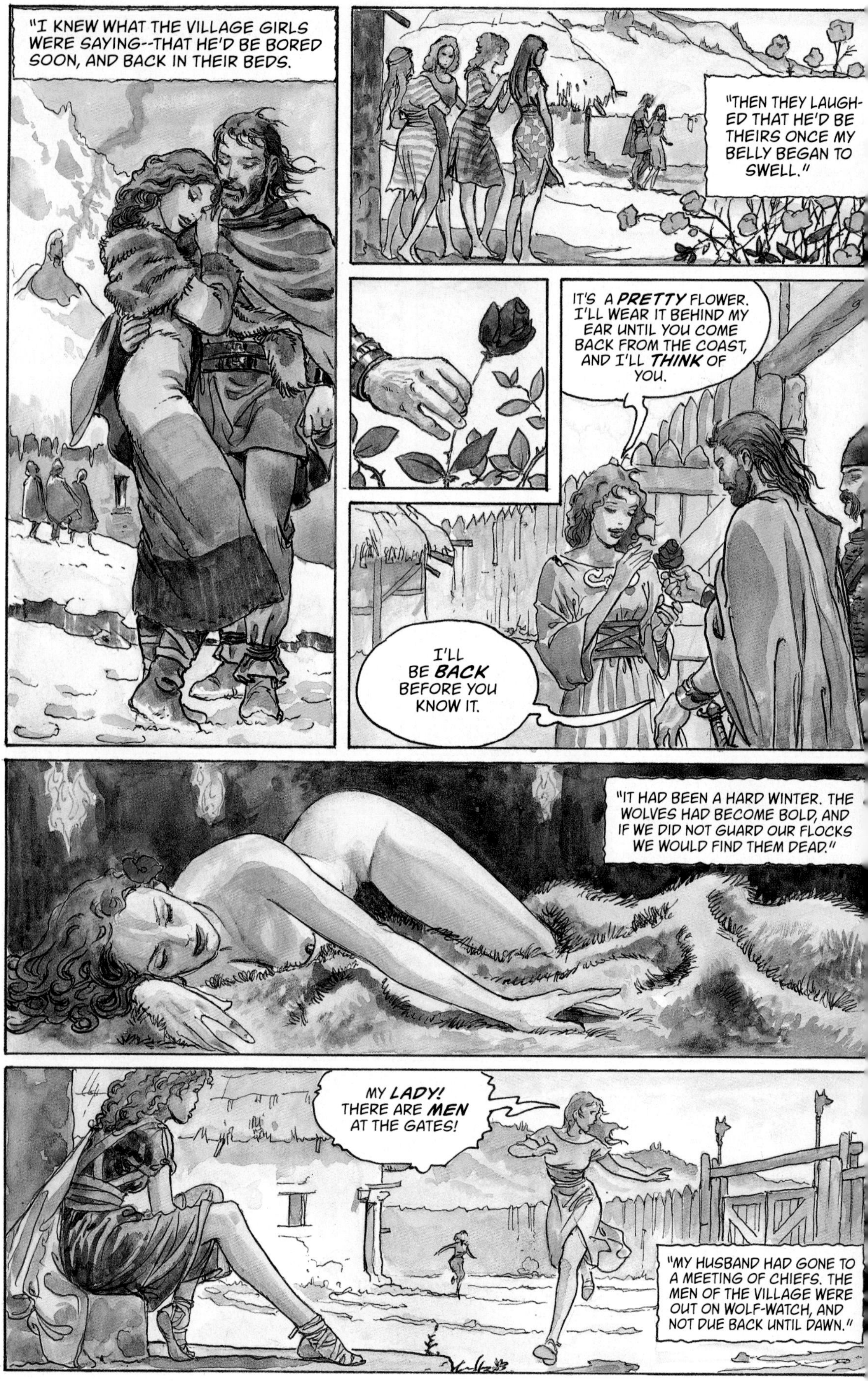
"I KNEW WHAT THE VILLAGE GIRLS WERE SAYING--THAT HE'D BE BORED SOON, AND BACK IN THEIR BEDS.
"THEN THEY LAUGHED THAT HE'D BE THEIRS ONCE MY BELLY BEGAN TO SWELL."
IT'S A PRETTY FLOWER. I'LL WEAR IT BEHIND MY EAR UNTIL YOU COME BACK FROM THE COAST, AND I'LL THINK OF YOU.
I'LL BE BACK BEFORE YOU KNOW IT.
"IT HAD BEEN A HARD WINTER. THE WOLVES HAD BECOME BOLD, AND IF WE DID NOT GUARD OUR FLOCKS WE WOULD FIND THEM DEAD."
MY LADY! THERE ARE MEN AT THE GATES!
"MY HUSBAND HAD GONE TO A MEETING OF CHIEFS. THE MEN OF THE VILLAGE WERE OUT ON WOLF-WATCH, AND NOT DUE BACK UNTIL DAWN."

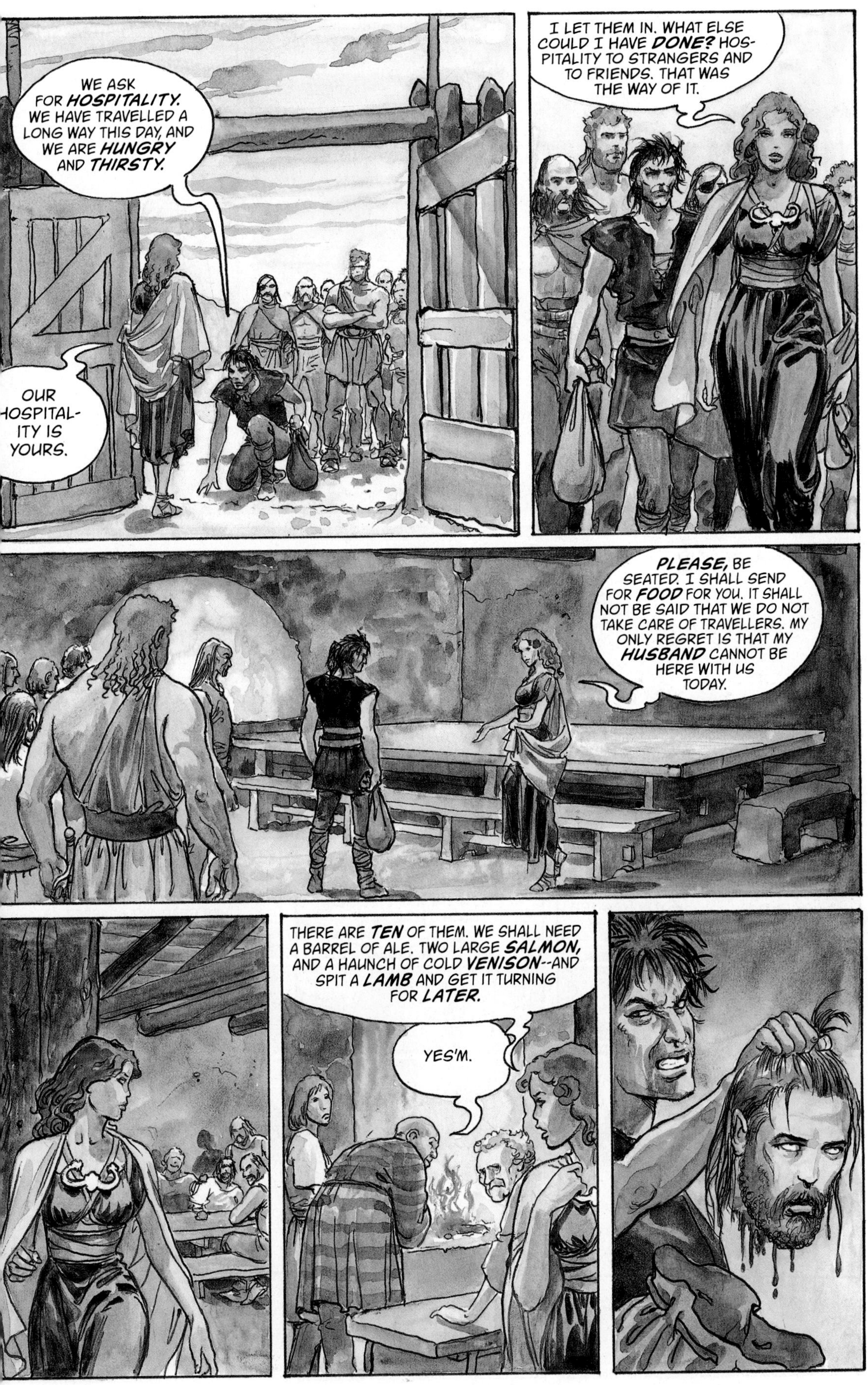

WE ASK FOR HOSPITALITY. WE HAVE TRAVELLED A LONG WAY THIS DAY, AND WE ARE HUNGRY AND THIRSTY.
OUR HOSPITALITY IS YOURS.
I LET THEM IN. WHAT ELSE COULD I HAVE DONE? HOSPITALITY TO STRANGERS AND TO FRIENDS. THAT WAS THE WAY OF IT.
PLEASE, BE SEATED. I SHALL SEND FOR FOOD FOR YOU. IT SHALL NOT BE SAID THAT WE DO NOT TAKE CARE OF TRAVELLERS. MY ONLY REGRET IS THAT MY HUSBAND CANNOT BE HERE WITH US TODAY.
THERE ARE TEN OF THEM. WE SHALL NEED A BARREL OF ALE. TWO LARGE SALMON, AND A HAUNCH OF COLD VENISON--AND SPIT A LAMB AND GET IT TURNING FOR LATER.
YES'M.

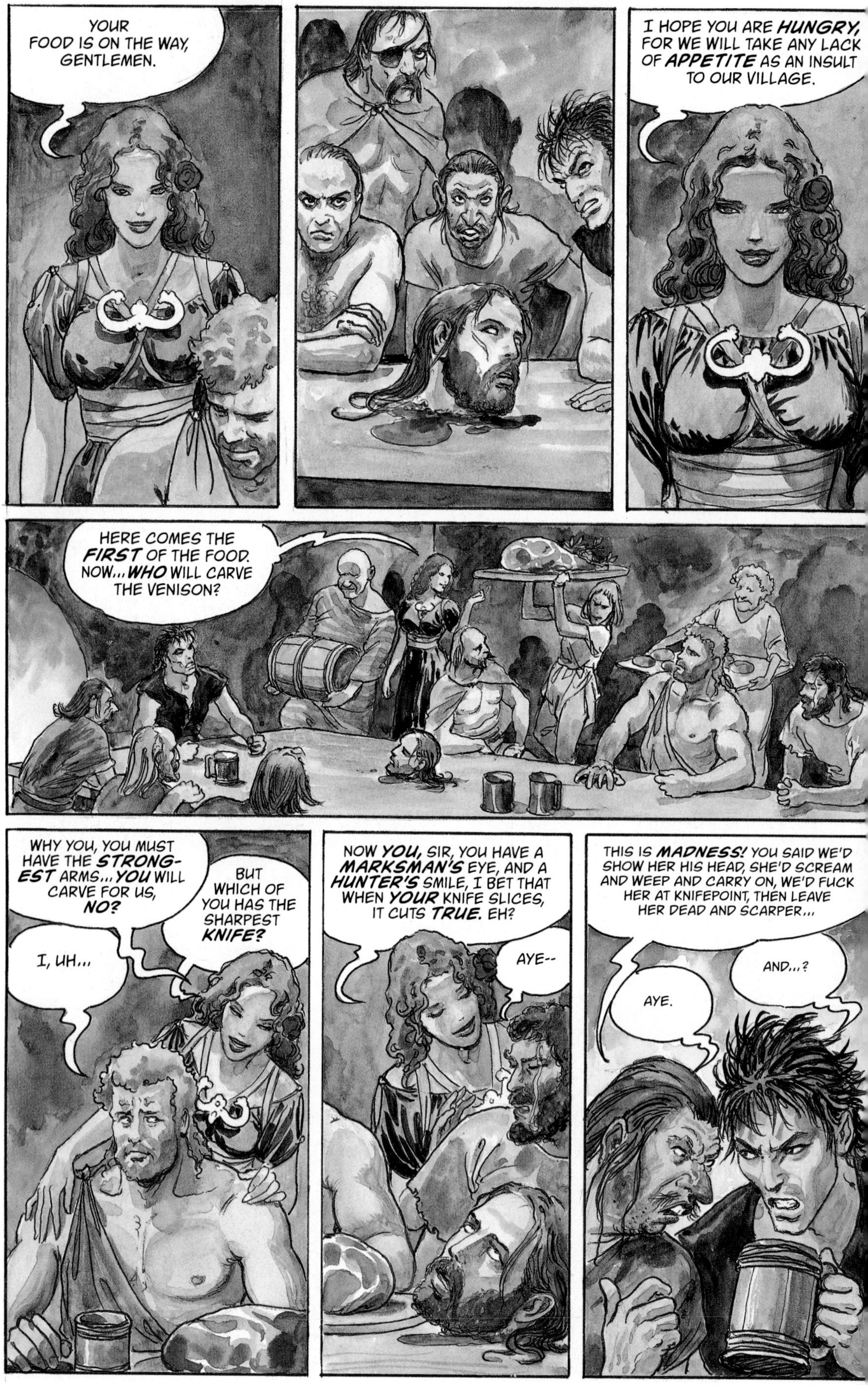
YOUR FOOD IS ON THE WAY, GENTLEMEN.
I HOPE YOU ARE HUNGRY, FOR WE WILL TAKE ANY LACK OF APPETITE AS AN INSULT TO OUR VILLAGE.
HERE COMES THE FIRST OF THE FOOD. NOW... WHO WILL CARVE THE VENISON?
WHY YOU, YOU MUST HAVE THE STRONGEST ARMS... YOU WILL CARVE FOR US, NO?
I, UH...
BUT WHICH OF YOU HAS THE SHARPEST KNIFE?
NOW YOU, SIR, YOU HAVE A MARKSMAN'S EYE, AND A HUNTER'S SMILE, I BET THAT WHEN YOUR KNIFE SLICES, IT CUTS TRUE. EH?
AYE--
THIS IS MADNESS! YOU SAID WE'D SHOW HER HIS HEAD, SHE'D SCREAM AND WEEP AND CARRY ON, WE'D FUCK HER AT KNIFEPOINT, THEN LEAVE HER DEAD AND SCARPER...
AYE.
AND...?

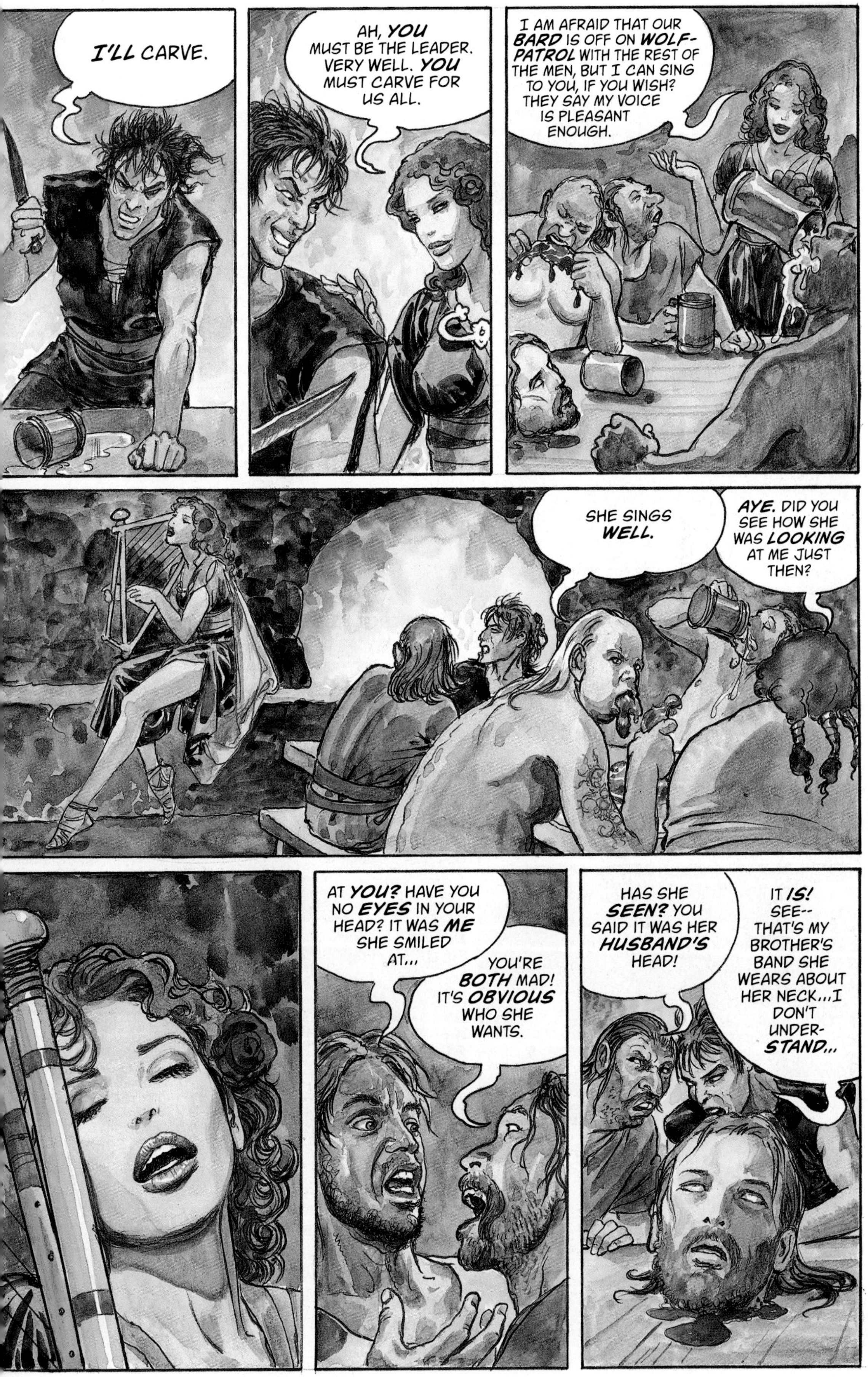
I'LL CARVE.
AH, YOU MUST BE THE LEADER. VERY WELL. YOU MUST CARVE FOR US ALL.
I AM AFRAID THAT OUR BARD IS OFF ON WOLF-PATROL WITH THE REST OF THE MEN, BUT I CAN SING TO YOU, IF YOU WISH? THEY SAY MY VOICE IS PLEASANT ENOUGH.
SHE SINGS WELL.
AYE. DID YOU SEE HOW SHE WAS LOOKING AT ME JUST THEN?
AT YOU? HAVE YOU NO EYES IN YOUR HEAD? IT WAS ME SHE SMILED AT...
YOU'RE BOTH MAD! IT'S OBVIOUS WHO SHE WANTS.
HAS SHE SEEN? YOU SAID IT WAS HER HUSBAND'S HEAD!
IT IS! SEE-- THAT'S MY BROTHER'S BAND SHE WEARS ABOUT HER NECK...I DON'T UNDER-STAND...

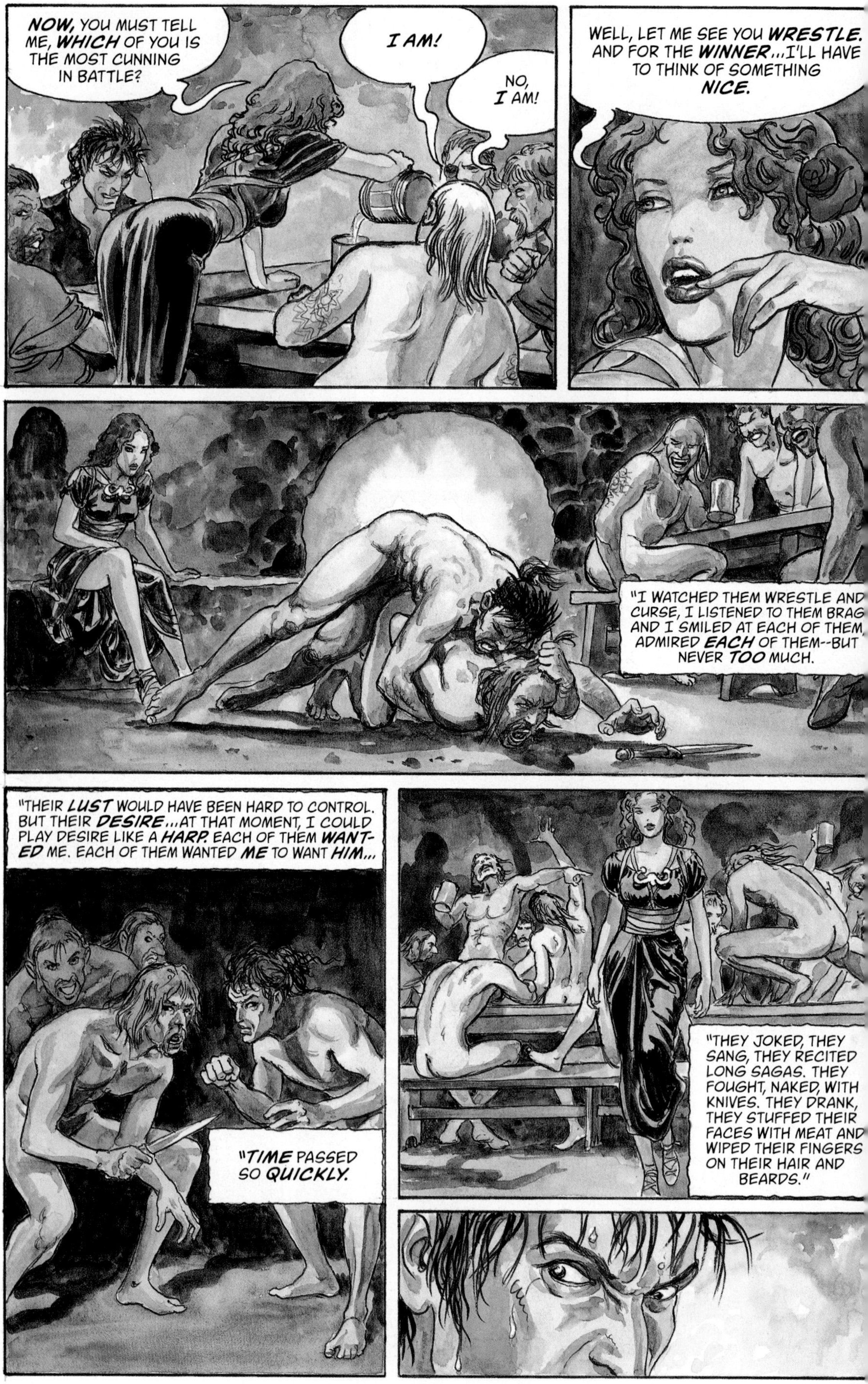

NOW, YOU MUST TELL ME, WHICH OF YOU IS THE MOST CUNNING IN BATTLE?
I AM!
NO, I AM!
WELL, LET ME SEE YOU WRESTLE. AND FOR THE WINNER...I'LL HAVE TO THINK OF SOMETHING NICE.
"I WATCHED THEM WRESTLE AND CURSE, I LISTENED TO THEM BRAG AND I SMILED AT EACH OF THEM, ADMIRED EACH OF THEM--BUT NEVER TOO MUCH.
"THEIR LUST WOULD HAVE BEEN HARD TO CONTROL. BUT THEIR DESIRE...AT THAT MOMENT, I COULD PLAY DESIRE LIKE A HARP. EACH OF THEM WANTED ME. EACH OF THEM WANTED ME TO WANT HIM...
"TIME PASSED SO QUICKLY.
"THEY JOKED, THEY SANG, THEY RECITED LONG SAGAS. THEY FOUGHT, NAKED, WITH KNIVES. THEY DRANK, THEY STUFFED THEIR FACES WITH MEAT AND WIPED THEIR FINGERS ON THEIR HAIR AND BEARDS."

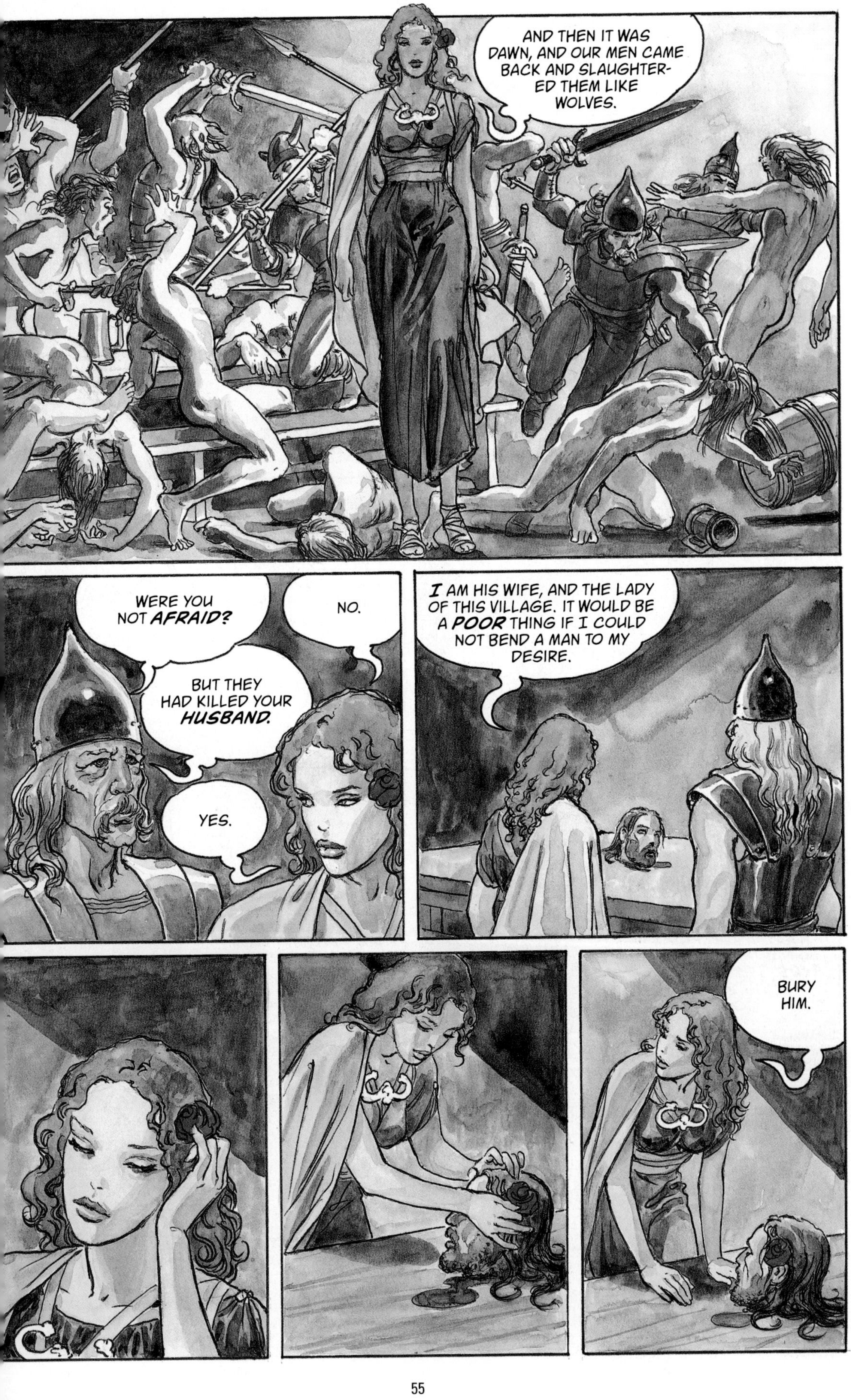

AND THEN IT WAS DAWN, AND OUR MEN CAME BACK AND SLAUGHTERED THEM LIKE WOLVES.
WERE YOU NOT AFRAID?
NO.
BUT THEY HAD KILLED YOUR HUSBAND.
YES.
I AM HIS WIFE, AND THE LADY OF THIS VILLAGE. IT WOULD BE A POOR THING IF I COULD NOT BEND A MAN TO MY DESIRE.
BURY HIM.

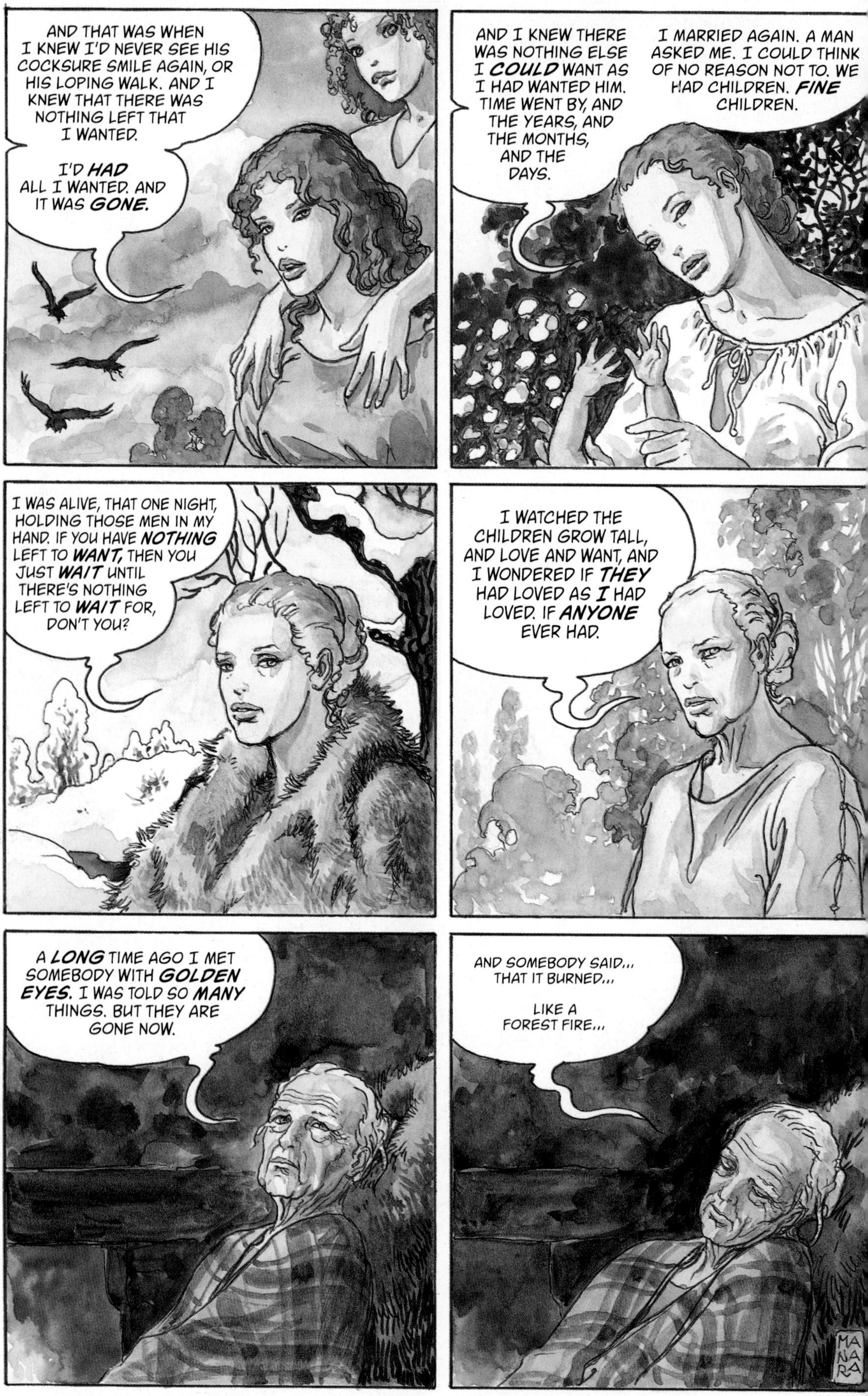
AND THAT WAS WHEN I KNEW I'D NEVER SEE HIS COCKSURE SMILE AGAIN, OR HIS LOPING WALK. AND I KNEW THAT THERE WAS NOTHING LEFT THAT I WANTED.
I'D HAD ALL I WANTED. AND IT WAS GONE.
AND I KNEW THERE WAS NOTHING ELSE I COULD WANT AS I HAD WANTED HIM. TIME WENT BY, AND THE YEARS, AND THE MONTHS, AND THE DAYS.
I MARRIED AGAIN. A MAN ASKED ME. I COULD THINK OF NO REASON NOT TO. WE HAD CHILDREN. FINE CHILDREN.
I WAS ALIVE, THAT ONE NIGHT, HOLDING THOSE MEN IN MY HAND. IF YOU HAVE NOTHING LEFT TO WANT, THEN YOU JUST WAIT UNTIL THERE'S NOTHING LEFT TO WAIT FOR, DON'T YOU?
I WATCHED THE CHILDREN GROW TALL, AND LOVE AND WANT, AND I WONDERED IF THEY HAD LOVED AS I HAD LOVED. IF ANYONE EVER HAD.
A LONG TIME AGO I MET SOMEBODY WITH GOLDEN EYES. I WAS TOLD SO MANY THINGS. BUT THEY ARE GONE NOW.
AND SOMEBODY SAID... THAT IT BURNED...
LIKE A FOREST FIRE...
MANARA

Chapter 3

DREAM

The Heart of a Star

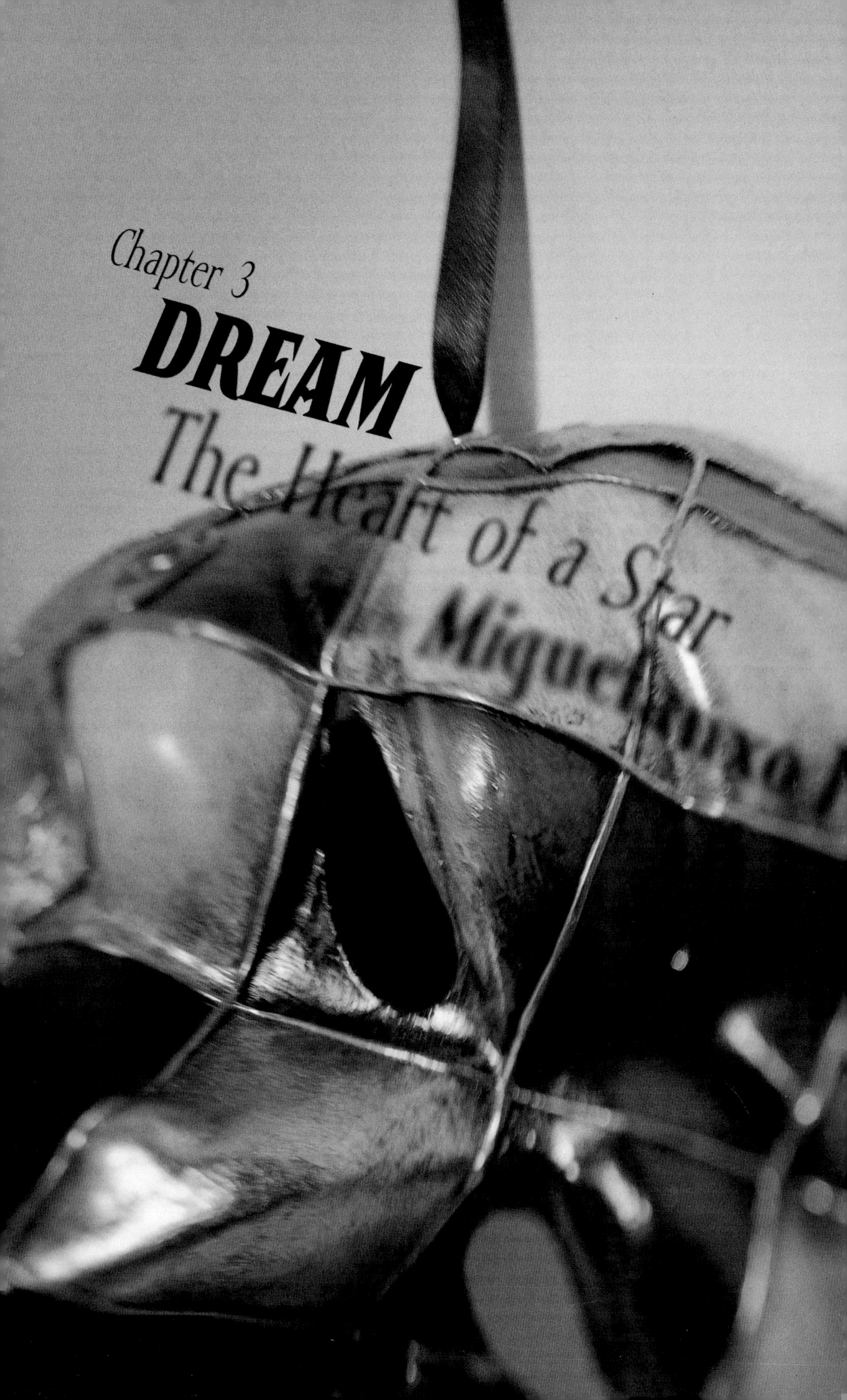

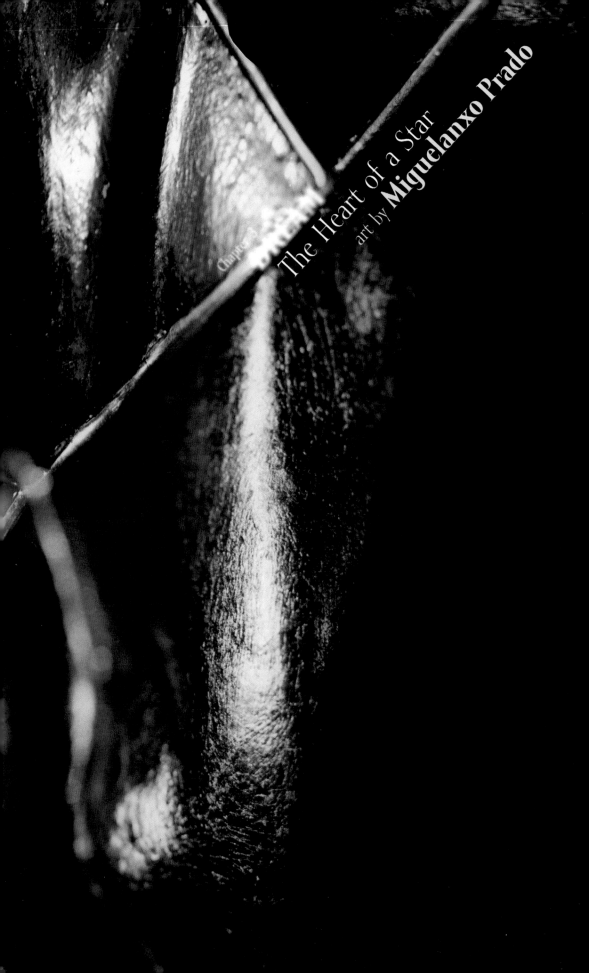

Chapter 3

The Heart of a Star

art by **Miguelanxo Prado**

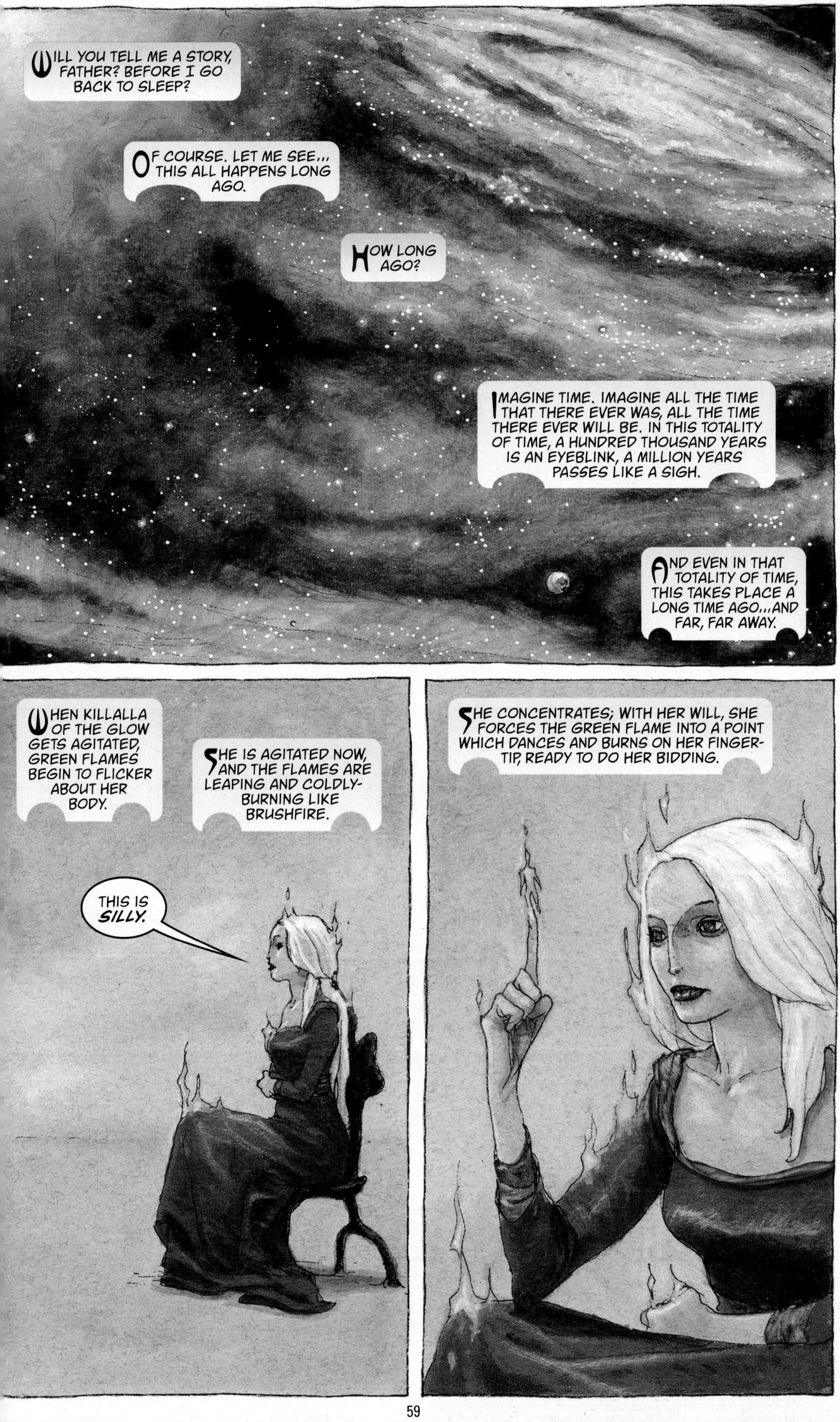
WILL YOU TELL ME A STORY, FATHER? BEFORE I GO BACK TO SLEEP?
OF COURSE. LET ME SEE... THIS ALL HAPPENS LONG AGO.
HOW LONG AGO?
IMAGINE TIME. IMAGINE ALL THE TIME THAT THERE EVER WAS, ALL THE TIME THERE EVER WILL BE. IN THIS TOTALITY OF TIME, A HUNDRED THOUSAND YEARS IS AN EYEBLINK, A MILLION YEARS PASSES LIKE A SIGH.
AND EVEN IN THAT TOTALITY OF TIME, THIS TAKES PLACE A LONG TIME AGO...AND FAR, FAR AWAY.
WHEN KILLALLA OF THE GLOW GETS AGITATED, GREEN FLAMES BEGIN TO FLICKER ABOUT HER BODY.
SHE IS AGITATED NOW, AND THE FLAMES ARE LEAPING AND COLDLY-BURNING LIKE BRUSHFIRE.
THIS IS SILLY.
SHE CONCENTRATES; WITH HER WILL, SHE FORCES THE GREEN FLAME INTO A POINT WHICH DANCES AND BURNS ON HER FINGER-TIP, READY TO DO HER BIDDING.

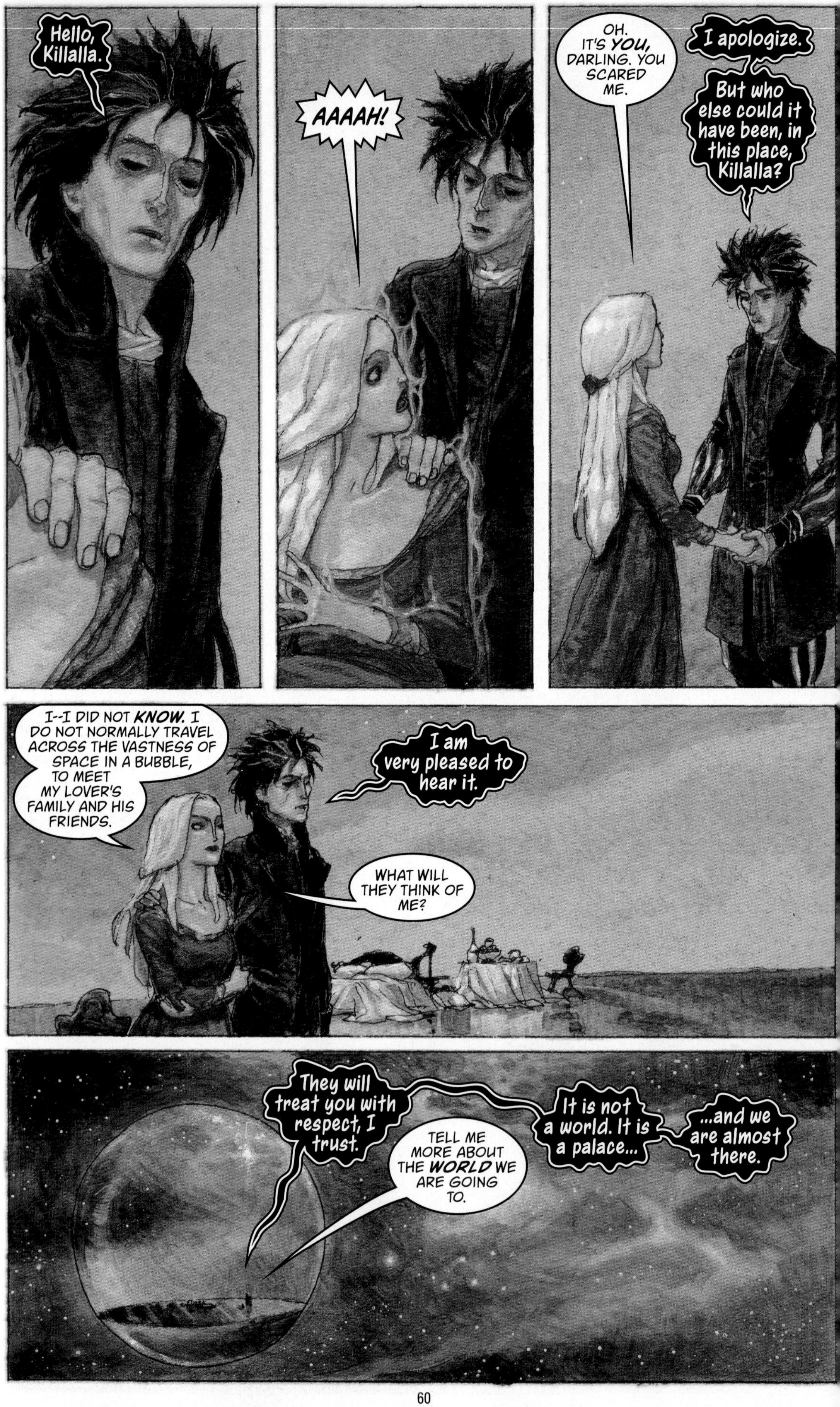
Hello, Killalla.
AAAAH!
OH. IT'S YOU, DARLING. YOU SCARED ME.
I apologize.
But who else could it have been, in this place, Killalla?
I--I DID NOT KNOW. I DO NOT NORMALLY TRAVEL ACROSS THE VASTNESS OF SPACE IN A BUBBLE, TO MEET MY LOVER'S FAMILY AND HIS FRIENDS.
I am very pleased to hear it.
WHAT WILL THEY THINK OF ME?
They will treat you with respect, I trust.
TELL ME MORE ABOUT THE WORLD WE ARE GOING TO.
It is not a world. It is a palace...
...and we are almost there.

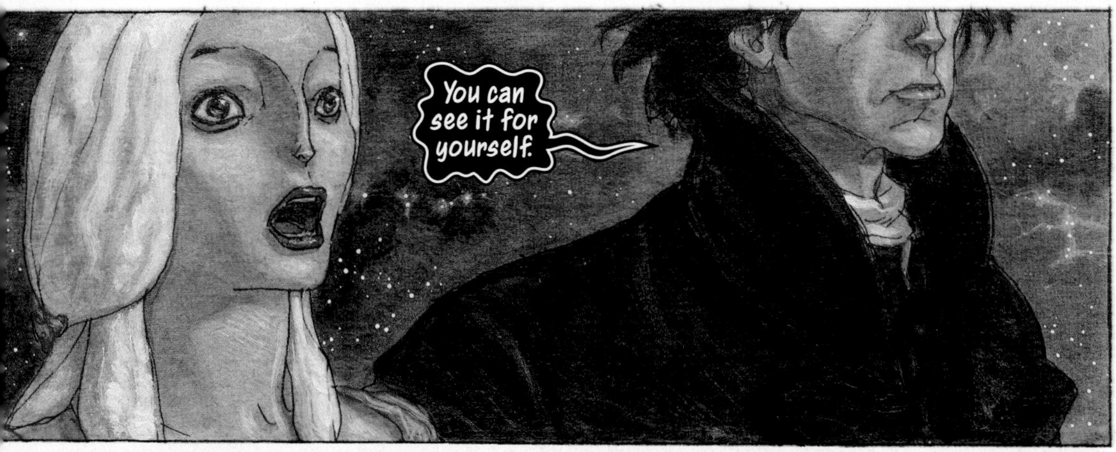
You can see it for yourself.

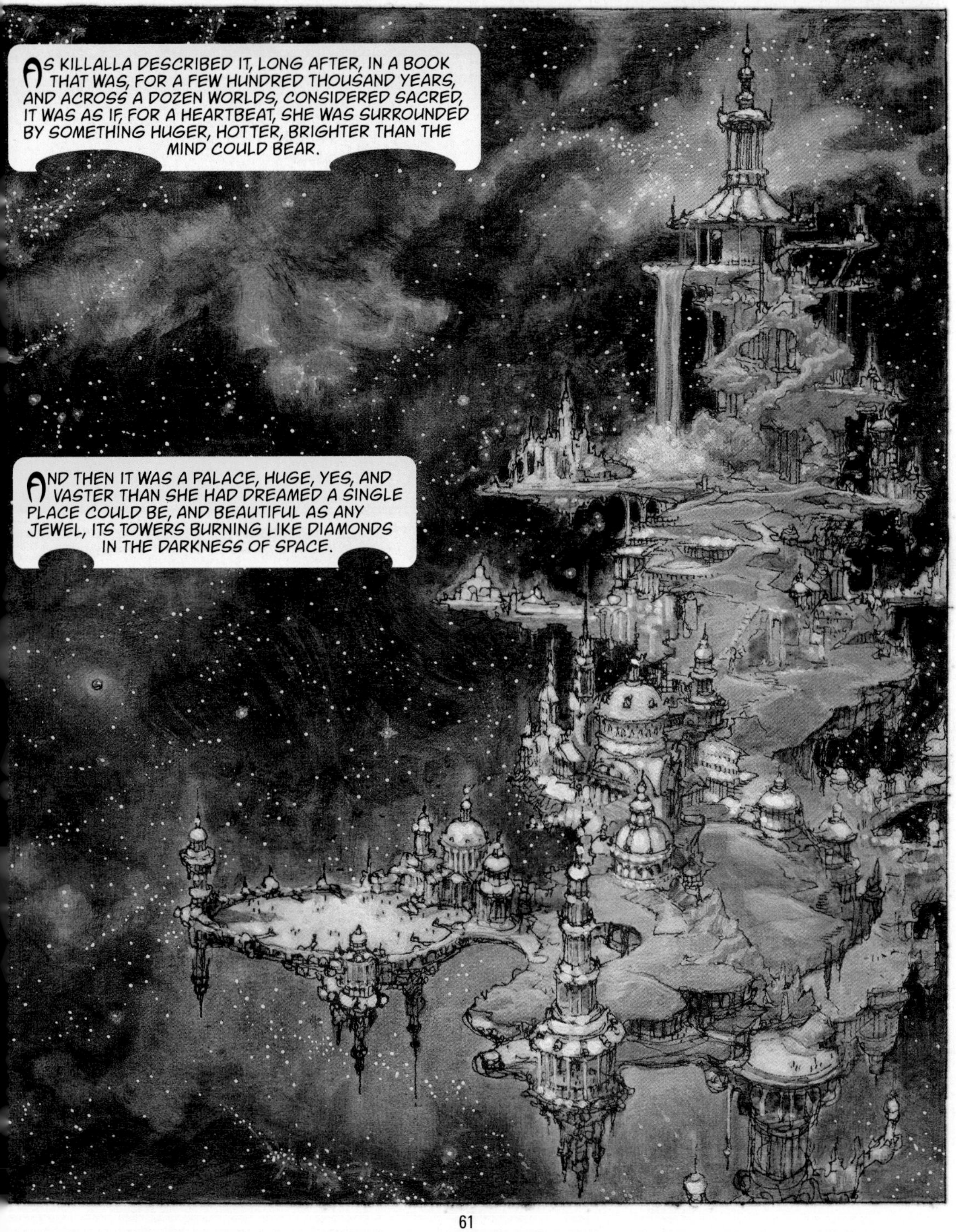
AS KILLALLA DESCRIBED IT, LONG AFTER, IN A BOOK THAT WAS, FOR A FEW HUNDRED THOUSAND YEARS, AND ACROSS A DOZEN WORLDS, CONSIDERED SACRED, IT WAS AS IF, FOR A HEARTBEAT, SHE WAS SURROUNDED BY SOMETHING HUGER, HOTTER, BRIGHTER THAN THE MIND COULD BEAR.
AND THEN IT WAS A PALACE, HUGE, YES, AND VASTER THAN SHE HAD DREAMED A SINGLE PLACE COULD BE, AND BEAUTIFUL AS ANY JEWEL, ITS TOWERS BURNING LIKE DIAMONDS IN THE DARKNESS OF SPACE.

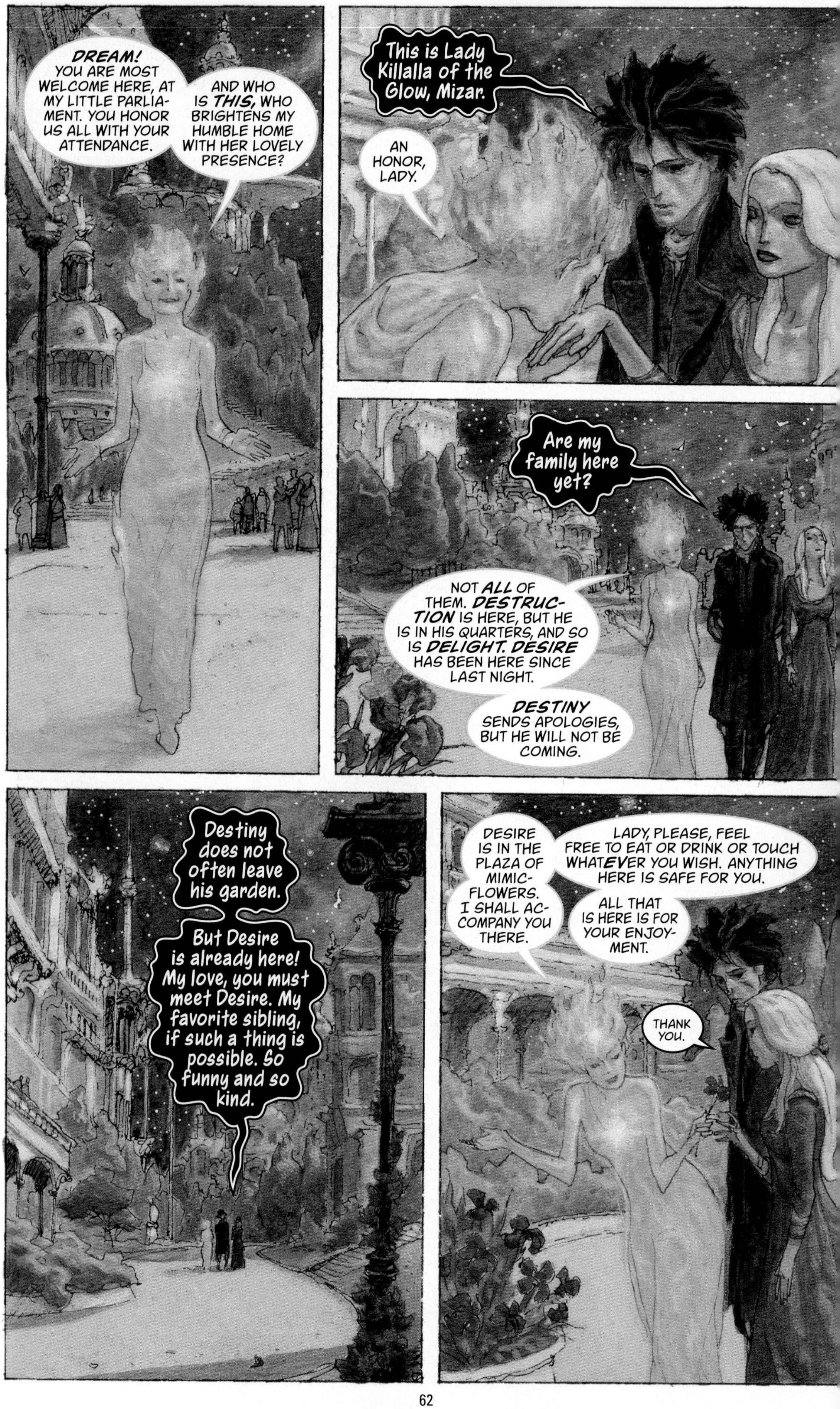
DREAM! YOU ARE MOST WELCOME HERE, AT MY LITTLE PARLIAMENT. YOU HONOR US ALL WITH YOUR ATTENDANCE.
AND WHO IS THIS, WHO BRIGHTENS MY HUMBLE HOME WITH HER LOVELY PRESENCE?
This is Lady Killalla of the Glow, Mizar.
AN HONOR, LADY.
Are my family here yet?
NOT ALL OF THEM. DESTRUCTION IS HERE, BUT HE IS IN HIS QUARTERS, AND SO IS DELIGHT. DESIRE HAS BEEN HERE SINCE LAST NIGHT.
DESTINY SENDS APOLOGIES, BUT HE WILL NOT BE COMING.
Destiny does not often leave his garden.
But Desire is already here! My love, you must meet Desire. My favorite sibling, if such a thing is possible. So funny and so kind.
DESIRE IS IN THE PLAZA OF MIMIC-FLOWERS. I SHALL ACCOMPANY YOU THERE.
LADY, PLEASE, FEEL FREE TO EAT OR DRINK OR TOUCH WHATEVER YOU WISH. ANYTHING HERE IS SAFE FOR YOU.
ALL THAT IS HERE IS FOR YOUR ENJOYMENT.
THANK YOU.

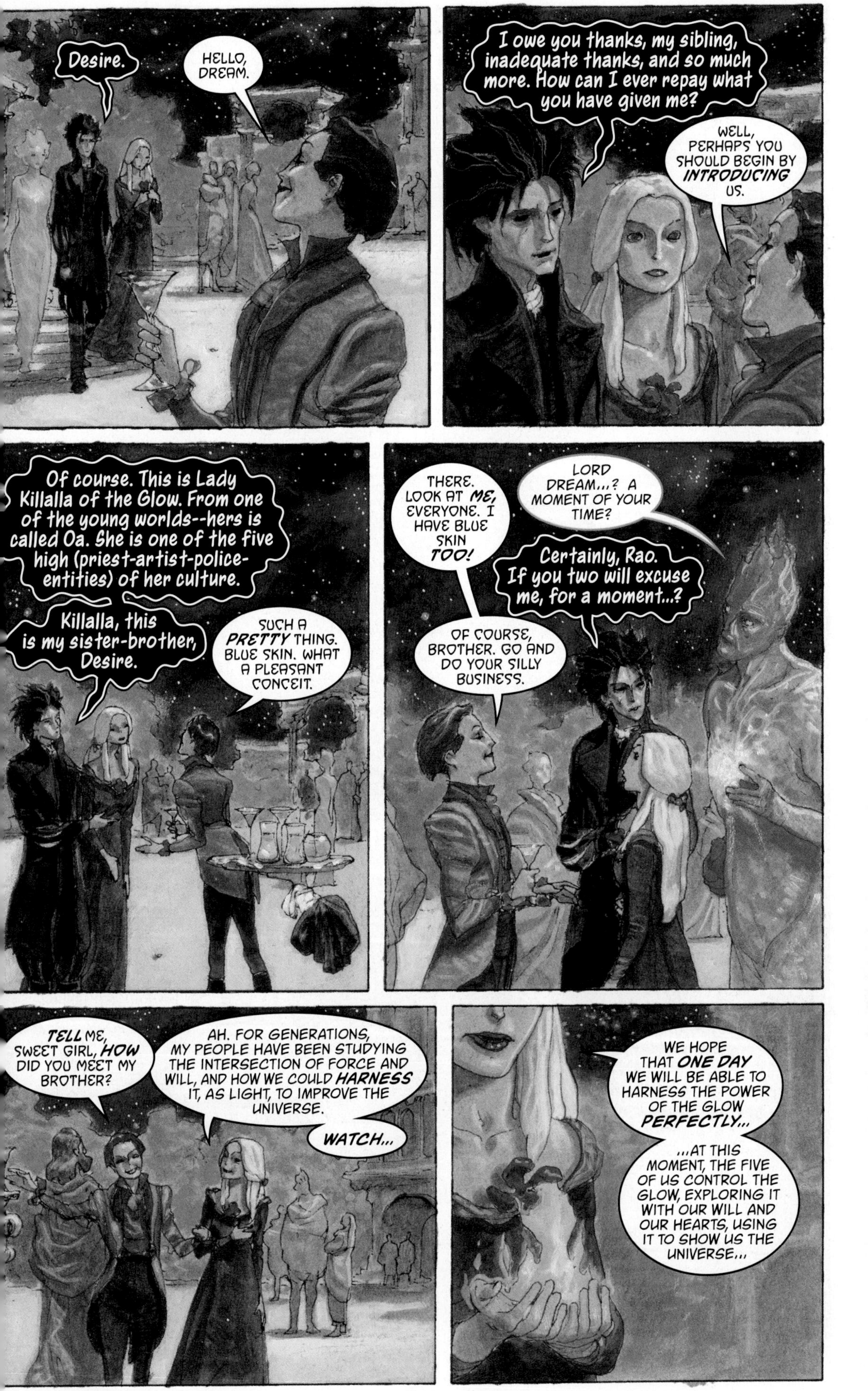
Desire.
HELLO, DREAM.
I owe you thanks, my sibling, inadequate thanks, and so much more. How can I ever repay what you have given me?
WELL, PERHAPS YOU SHOULD BEGIN BY INTRODUCING US.
Of course. This is Lady Killalla of the Glow. From one of the young worlds--hers is called Oa. She is one of the five high (priest-artist-police-entities) of her culture.
Killalla, this is my sister-brother, Desire.
SUCH A PRETTY THING. BLUE SKIN. WHAT A PLEASANT CONCEIT.
THERE. LOOK AT ME, EVERYONE. I HAVE BLUE SKIN TOO!
LORD DREAM...? A MOMENT OF YOUR TIME?
Certainly, Rao. If you two will excuse me, for a moment...?
OF COURSE, BROTHER. GO AND DO YOUR SILLY BUSINESS.
TELL ME, SWEET GIRL, HOW DID YOU MEET MY BROTHER?
AH. FOR GENERATIONS, MY PEOPLE HAVE BEEN STUDYING THE INTERSECTION OF FORCE AND WILL, AND HOW WE COULD HARNESS IT, AS LIGHT, TO IMPROVE THE UNIVERSE.
WATCH...
WE HOPE THAT ONE DAY WE WILL BE ABLE TO HARNESS THE POWER OF THE GLOW PERFECTLY...
...AT THIS MOMENT, THE FIVE OF US CONTROL THE GLOW, EXPLORING IT WITH OUR WILL AND OUR HEARTS, USING IT TO SHOW US THE UNIVERSE...

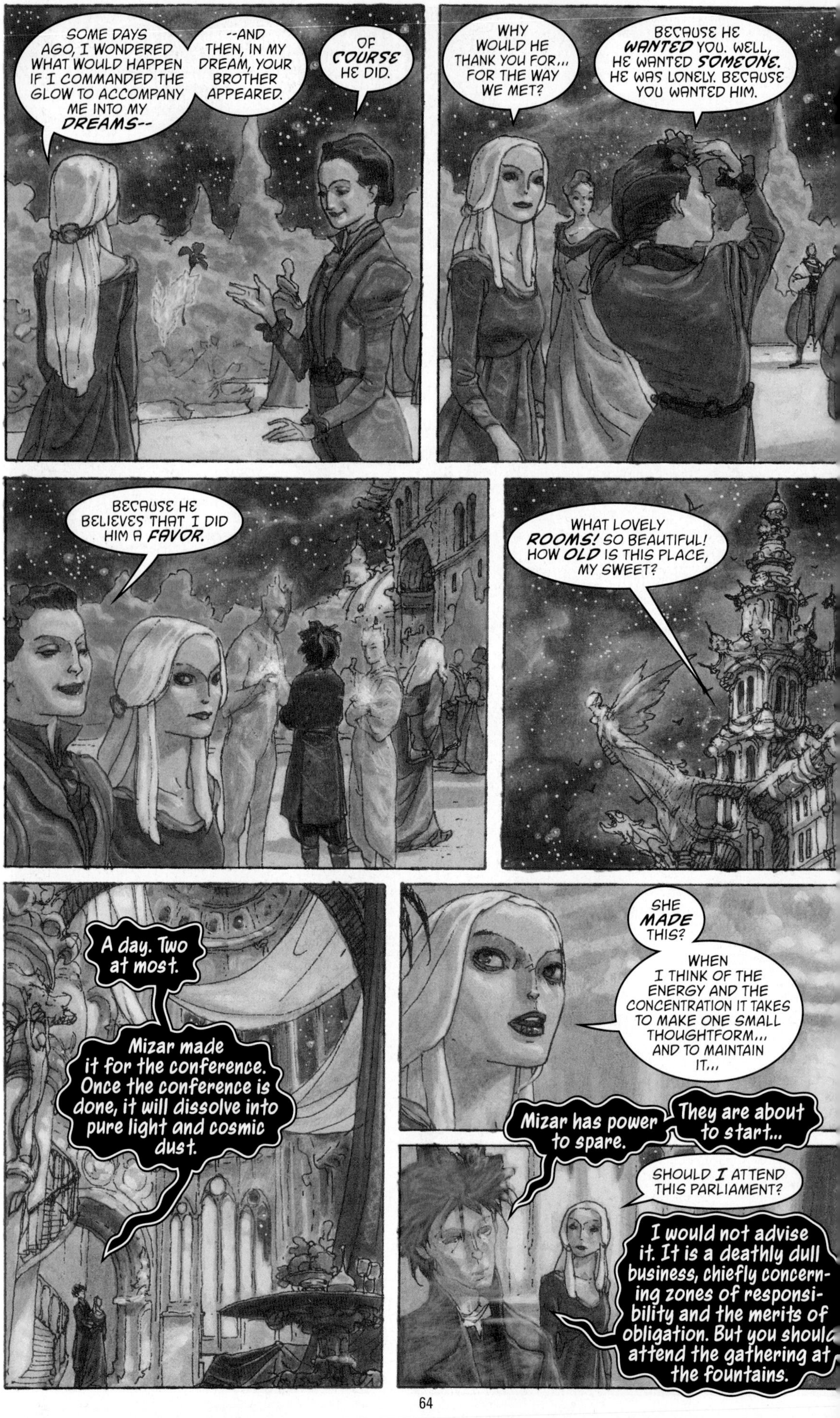

SOME DAYS AGO, I WONDERED WHAT WOULD HAPPEN IF I COMMANDED THE GLOW TO ACCOMPANY ME INTO MY DREAMS--
--AND THEN, IN MY DREAM, YOUR BROTHER APPEARED.
OF COURSE HE DID.
WHY WOULD HE THANK YOU FOR... FOR THE WAY WE MET?
BECAUSE HE WANTED YOU. WELL, HE WANTED SOMEONE. HE WAS LONELY. BECAUSE YOU WANTED HIM.
BECAUSE HE BELIEVES THAT I DID HIM A FAVOR.
WHAT LOVELY ROOMS! SO BEAUTIFUL! HOW OLD IS THIS PLACE, MY SWEET?
A day. Two at most.
Mizar made it for the conference. Once the conference is done, it will dissolve into pure light and cosmic dust.
SHE MADE THIS?
WHEN I THINK OF THE ENERGY AND THE CONCENTRATION IT TAKES TO MAKE ONE SMALL THOUGHTFORM... AND TO MAINTAIN IT...
Mizar has power to spare.
They are about to start...
SHOULD I ATTEND THIS PARLIAMENT?
I would not advise it. It is a deathly dull business, chiefly concerning zones of responsibility and the merits of obligation. But you should attend the gathering at the fountains.

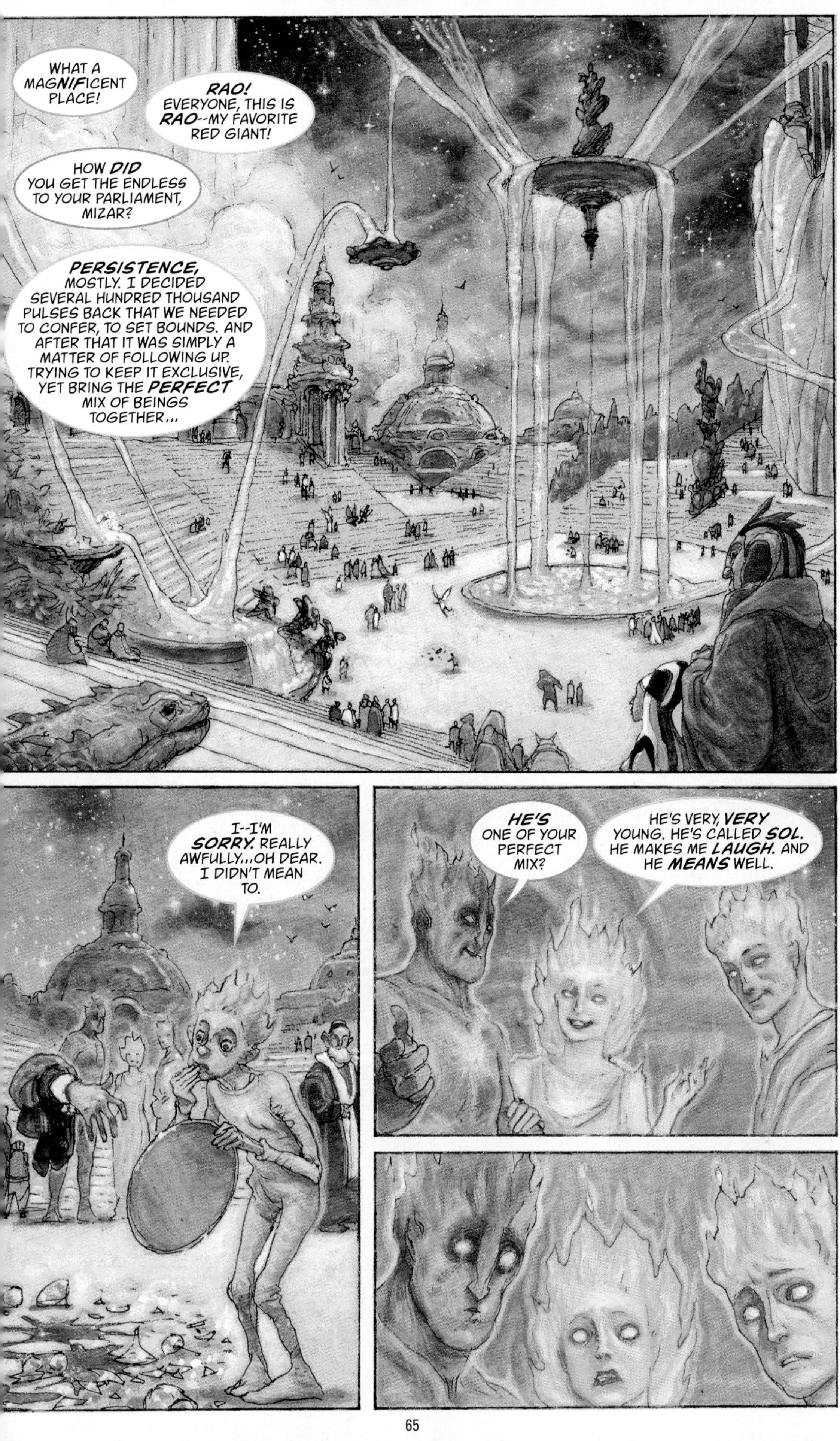
WHAT A MAGNIFICENT PLACE!
RAO! EVERYONE, THIS IS RAO--MY FAVORITE RED GIANT!
HOW DID YOU GET THE ENDLESS TO YOUR PARLIAMENT, MIZAR?
PERSISTENCE, MOSTLY. I DECIDED SEVERAL HUNDRED THOUSAND PULSES BACK THAT WE NEEDED TO CONFER, TO SET BOUNDS. AND AFTER THAT IT WAS SIMPLY A MATTER OF FOLLOWING UP. TRYING TO KEEP IT EXCLUSIVE, YET BRING THE PERFECT MIX OF BEINGS TOGETHER...
I--I'M SORRY. REALLY AWFULLY...OH DEAR. I DIDN'T MEAN TO.
HE'S ONE OF YOUR PERFECT MIX?
HE'S VERY, VERY YOUNG. HE'S CALLED SOL. HE MAKES ME LAUGH. AND HE MEANS WELL.

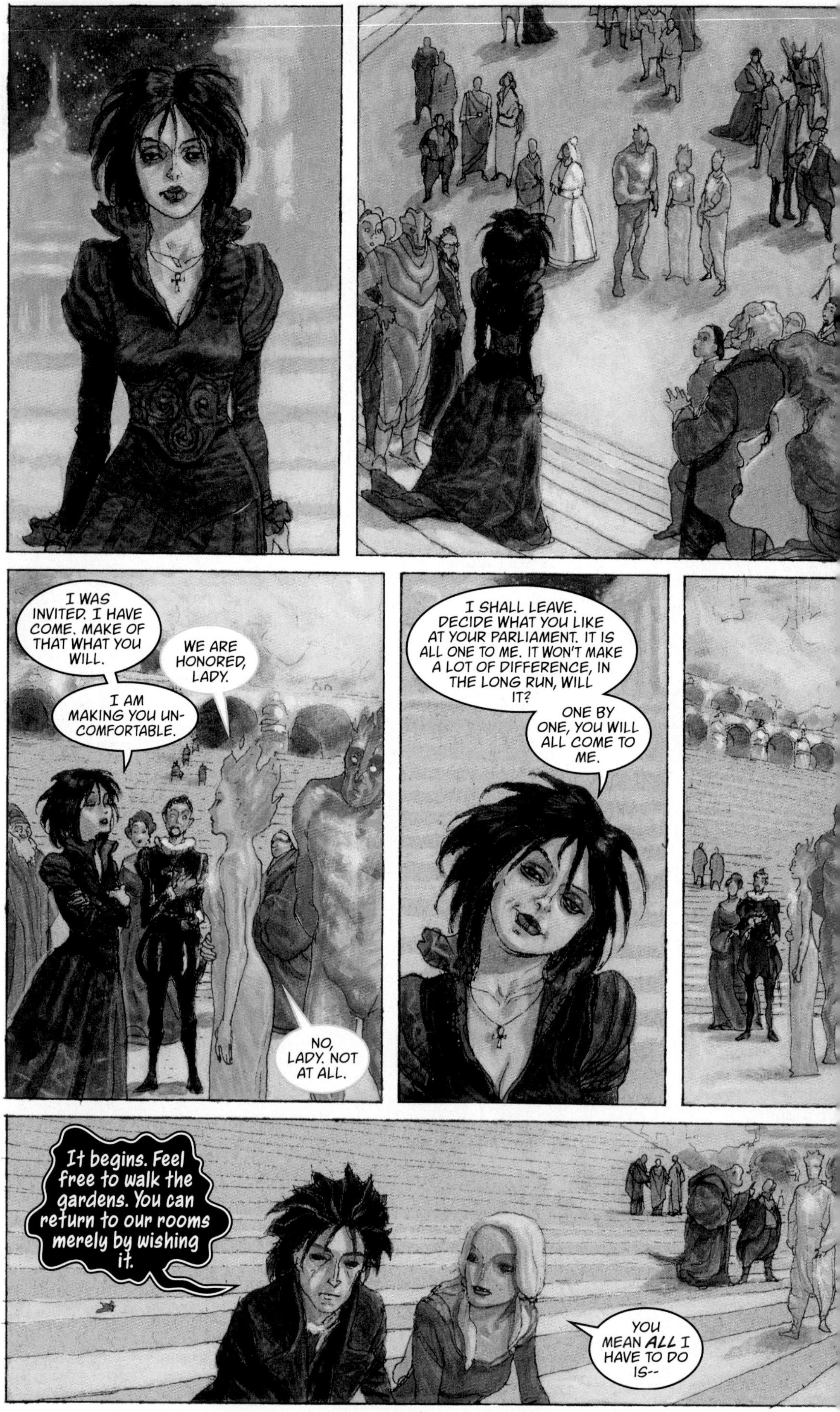
I WAS INVITED. I HAVE COME. MAKE OF THAT WHAT YOU WILL.
WE ARE HONORED, LADY.
I AM MAKING YOU UN-COMFORTABLE.
NO, LADY. NOT AT ALL.
I SHALL LEAVE. DECIDE WHAT YOU LIKE AT YOUR PARLIAMENT. IT IS ALL ONE TO ME. IT WON'T MAKE A LOT OF DIFFERENCE, IN THE LONG RUN, WILL IT?
ONE BY ONE, YOU WILL ALL COME TO ME.
It begins. Feel free to walk the gardens. You can return to our rooms merely by wishing it.
YOU MEAN ***ALL*** I HAVE TO DO IS--

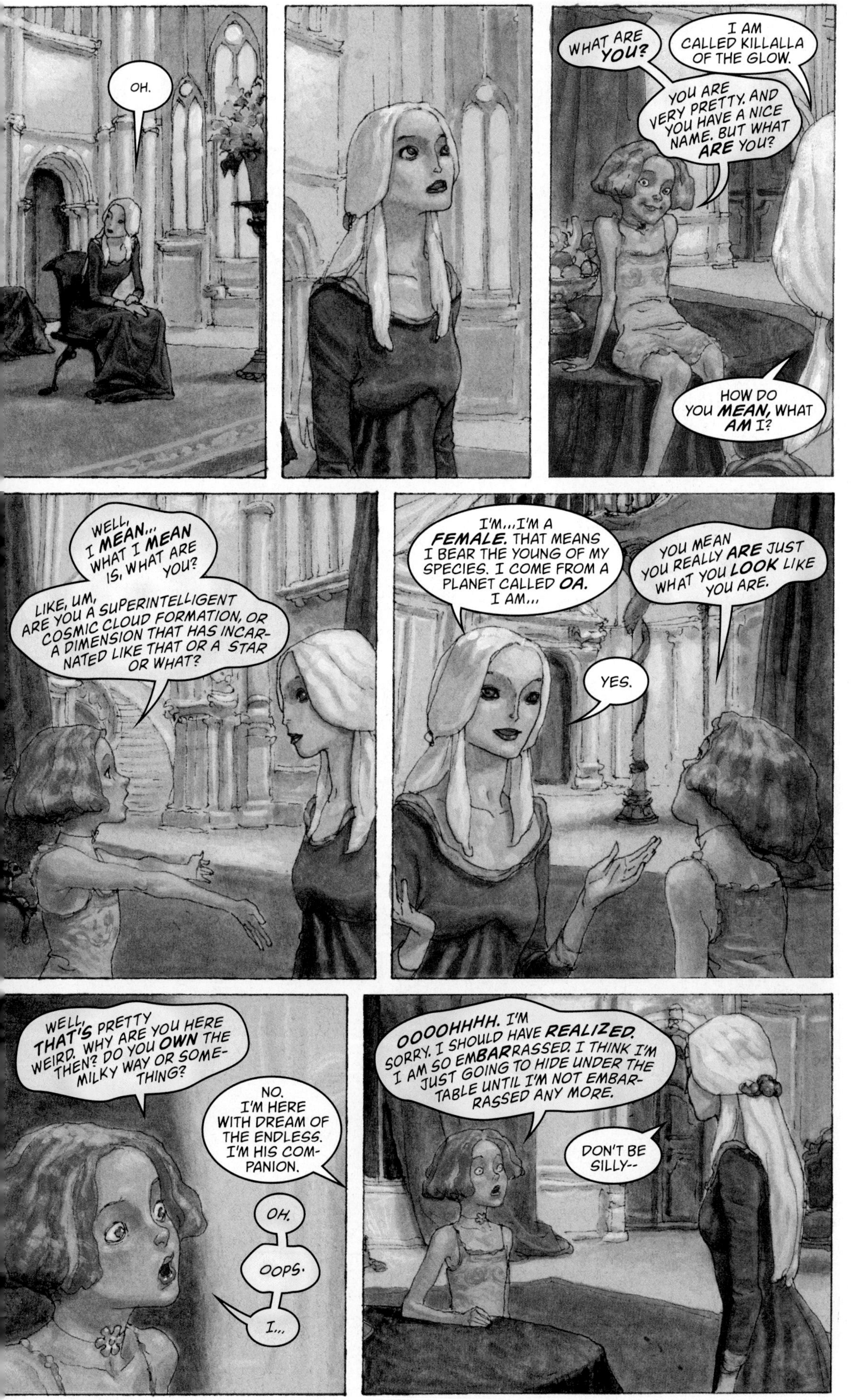
OH.
WHAT ARE YOU?
I AM CALLED KILLALLA OF THE GLOW.
YOU ARE VERY PRETTY. AND YOU HAVE A NICE NAME. BUT WHAT ARE YOU?
HOW DO YOU MEAN, WHAT AM I?
WELL, I MEAN... WHAT I MEAN IS, WHAT ARE YOU?
LIKE, UM, ARE YOU A SUPERINTELLIGENT COSMIC CLOUD FORMATION, OR A DIMENSION THAT HAS INCARNATED LIKE THAT OR A STAR OR WHAT?
I'M...I'M A FEMALE. THAT MEANS I BEAR THE YOUNG OF MY SPECIES. I COME FROM A PLANET CALLED OA. I AM...
YOU MEAN YOU REALLY ARE JUST WHAT YOU LOOK LIKE YOU ARE.
YES.
WELL, THAT'S PRETTY WEIRD. WHY ARE YOU HERE THEN? DO YOU OWN THE MILKY WAY OR SOMETHING?
NO. I'M HERE WITH DREAM OF THE ENDLESS. I'M HIS COMPANION.
OH.
OOPS.
I...
OOOOHHHH. I'M SORRY. I SHOULD HAVE REALIZED. I AM SO EMBARRASSED. I THINK I'M JUST GOING TO HIDE UNDER THE TABLE UNTIL I'M NOT EMBARRASSED ANY MORE.
DON'T BE SILLY--

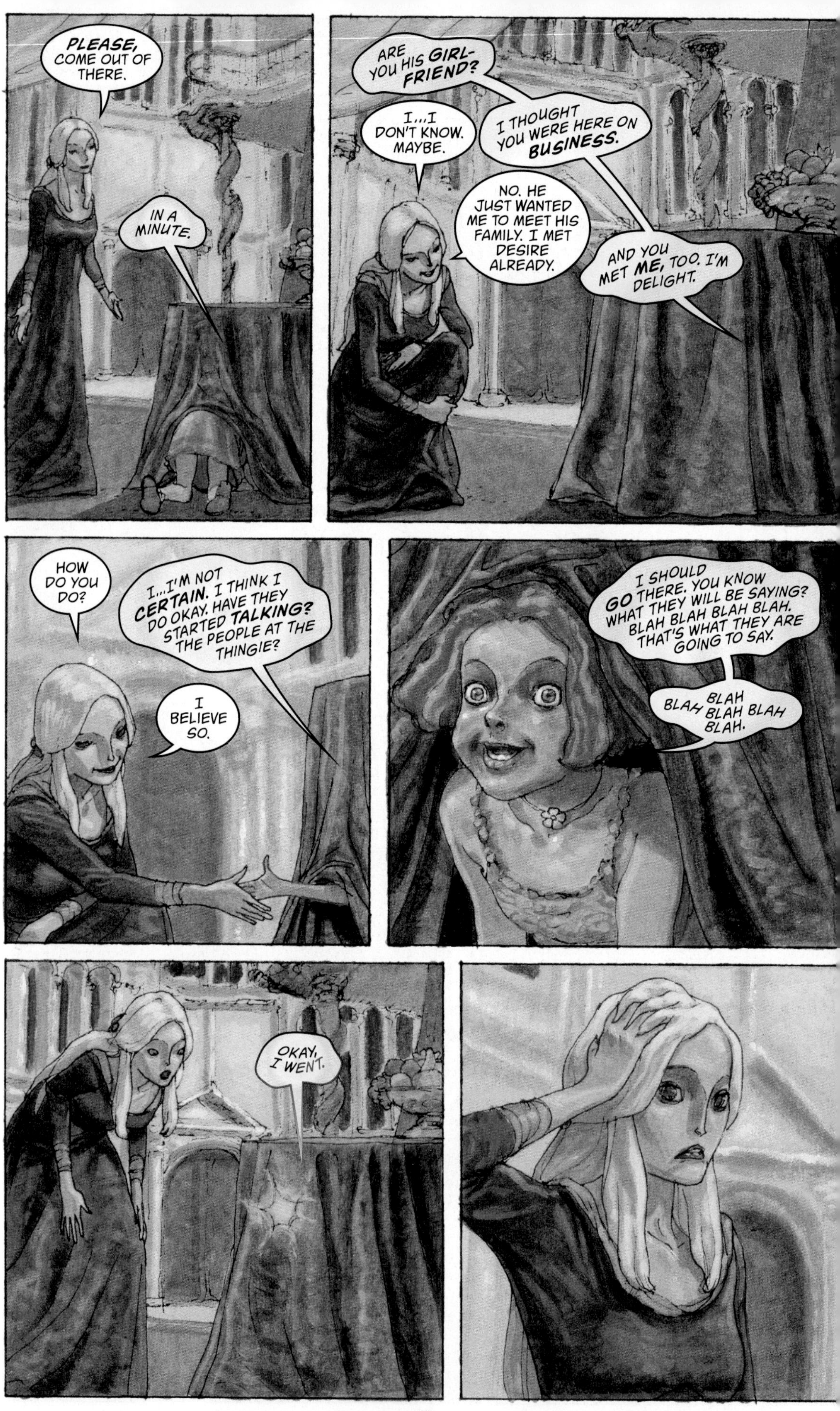
PLEASE, COME OUT OF THERE.
IN A MINUTE.
ARE YOU HIS GIRL-FRIEND?
I...I DON'T KNOW. MAYBE.
I THOUGHT YOU WERE HERE ON BUSINESS.
NO. HE JUST WANTED ME TO MEET HIS FAMILY. I MET DESIRE ALREADY.
AND YOU MET ME, TOO. I'M DELIGHT.
HOW DO YOU DO?
I...I'M NOT CERTAIN. I THINK I DO OKAY. HAVE THEY STARTED TALKING? THE PEOPLE AT THE THINGIE?
I BELIEVE SO.
I SHOULD GO THERE. YOU KNOW WHAT THEY WILL BE SAYING? BLAH BLAH BLAH BLAH. THAT'S WHAT THEY ARE GOING TO SAY.
BLAH BLAH BLAH BLAH BLAH.
OKAY, I WENT.

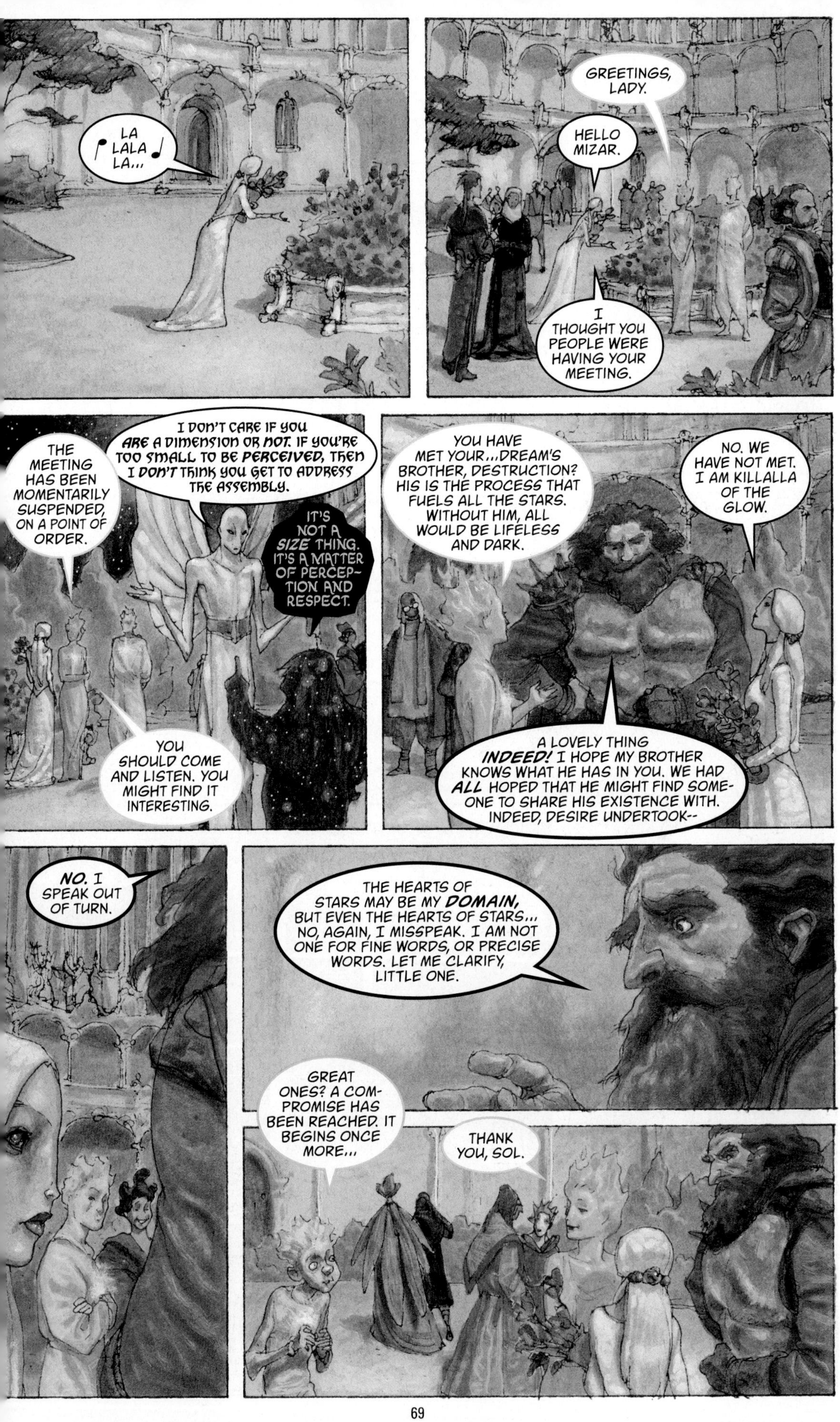
LA LALA LA...
GREETINGS, LADY.
HELLO MIZAR.
I THOUGHT YOU PEOPLE WERE HAVING YOUR MEETING.
THE MEETING HAS BEEN MOMENTARILY SUSPENDED, ON A POINT OF ORDER.
I DON'T CARE IF YOU ARE A DIMENSION OR NOT. IF YOU'RE TOO SMALL TO BE PERCEIVED, THEN I DON'T THINK YOU GET TO ADDRESS THE ASSEMBLY.
IT'S NOT A SIZE THING. IT'S A MATTER OF PERCEPTION AND RESPECT.
YOU SHOULD COME AND LISTEN. YOU MIGHT FIND IT INTERESTING.
YOU HAVE MET YOUR...DREAM'S BROTHER, DESTRUCTION? HIS IS THE PROCESS THAT FUELS ALL THE STARS. WITHOUT HIM, ALL WOULD BE LIFELESS AND DARK.
NO. WE HAVE NOT MET. I AM KILLALLA OF THE GLOW.
A LOVELY THING INDEED! I HOPE MY BROTHER KNOWS WHAT HE HAS IN YOU. WE HAD ALL HOPED THAT HE MIGHT FIND SOME-ONE TO SHARE HIS EXISTENCE WITH. INDEED, DESIRE UNDERTOOK--
NO. I SPEAK OUT OF TURN.
THE HEARTS OF STARS MAY BE MY DOMAIN, BUT EVEN THE HEARTS OF STARS... NO, AGAIN, I MISSPEAK. I AM NOT ONE FOR FINE WORDS, OR PRECISE WORDS. LET ME CLARIFY, LITTLE ONE.
GREAT ONES? A COM-PROMISE HAS BEEN REACHED. IT BEGINS ONCE MORE...
THANK YOU, SOL.

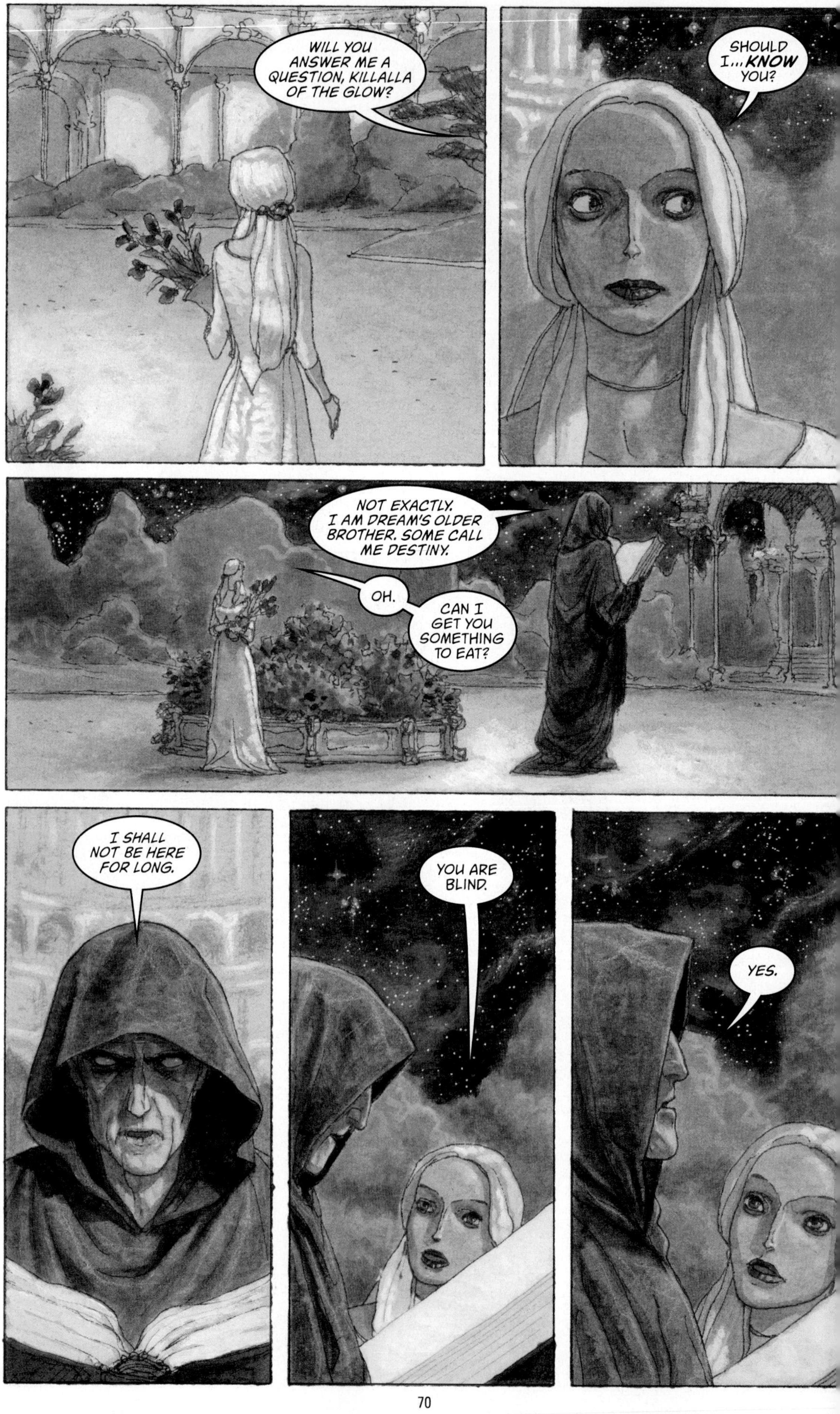
WILL YOU ANSWER ME A QUESTION, KILLALLA OF THE GLOW?
SHOULD I... **KNOW** YOU?
NOT EXACTLY. I AM DREAM'S OLDER BROTHER. SOME CALL ME DESTINY.
OH.
CAN I GET YOU SOMETHING TO EAT?
I SHALL NOT BE HERE FOR LONG.
YOU ARE BLIND.
YES.

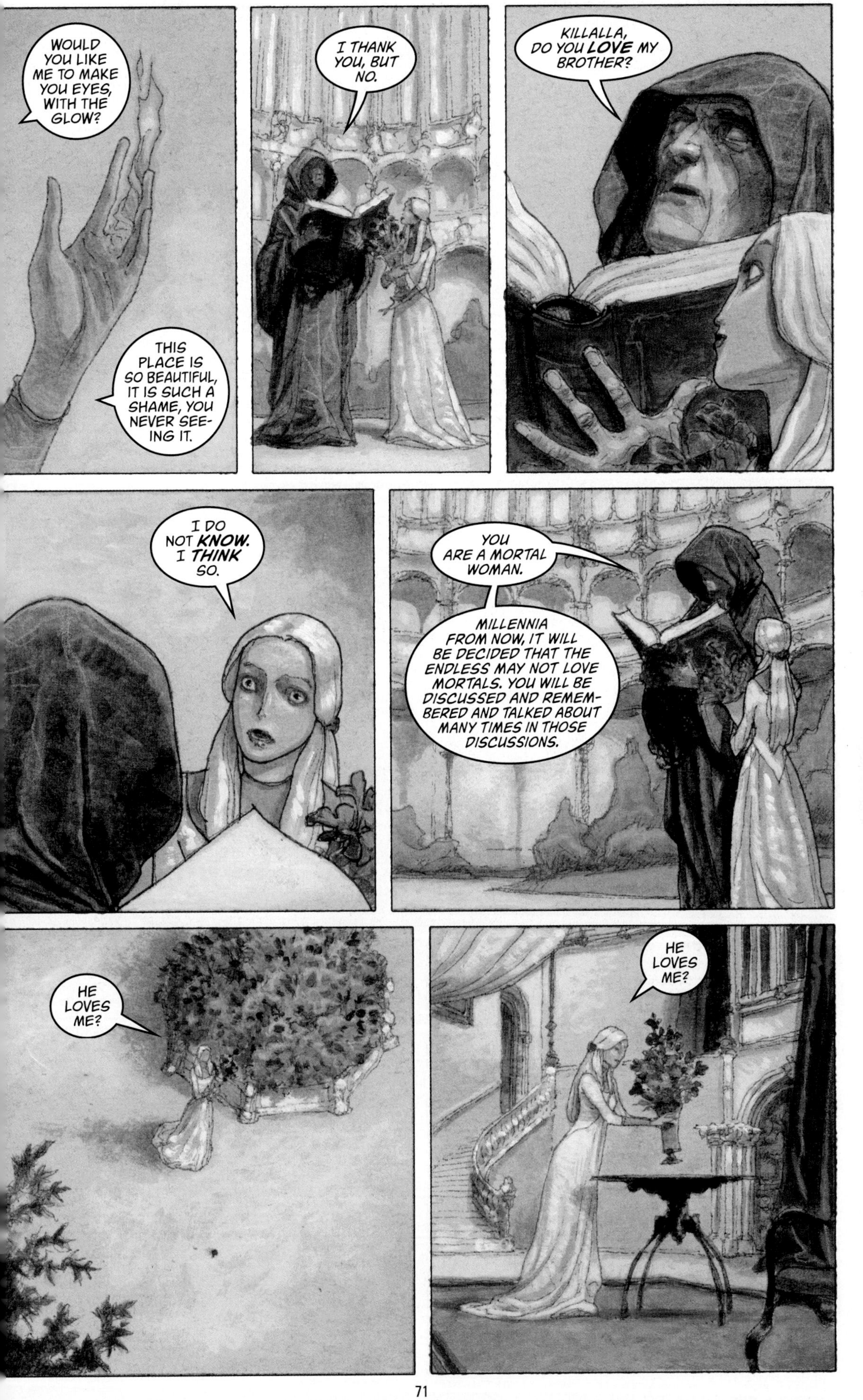
WOULD YOU LIKE ME TO MAKE YOU EYES, WITH THE GLOW?
THIS PLACE IS SO BEAUTIFUL, IT IS SUCH A SHAME, YOU NEVER SEEING IT.
I THANK YOU, BUT NO.
KILLALLA, DO YOU LOVE MY BROTHER?
I DO NOT KNOW. I THINK SO.
YOU ARE A MORTAL WOMAN.
MILLENNIA FROM NOW, IT WILL BE DECIDED THAT THE ENDLESS MAY NOT LOVE MORTALS. YOU WILL BE DISCUSSED AND REMEMBERED AND TALKED ABOUT MANY TIMES IN THOSE DISCUSSIONS.
HE LOVES ME?
HE LOVES ME?

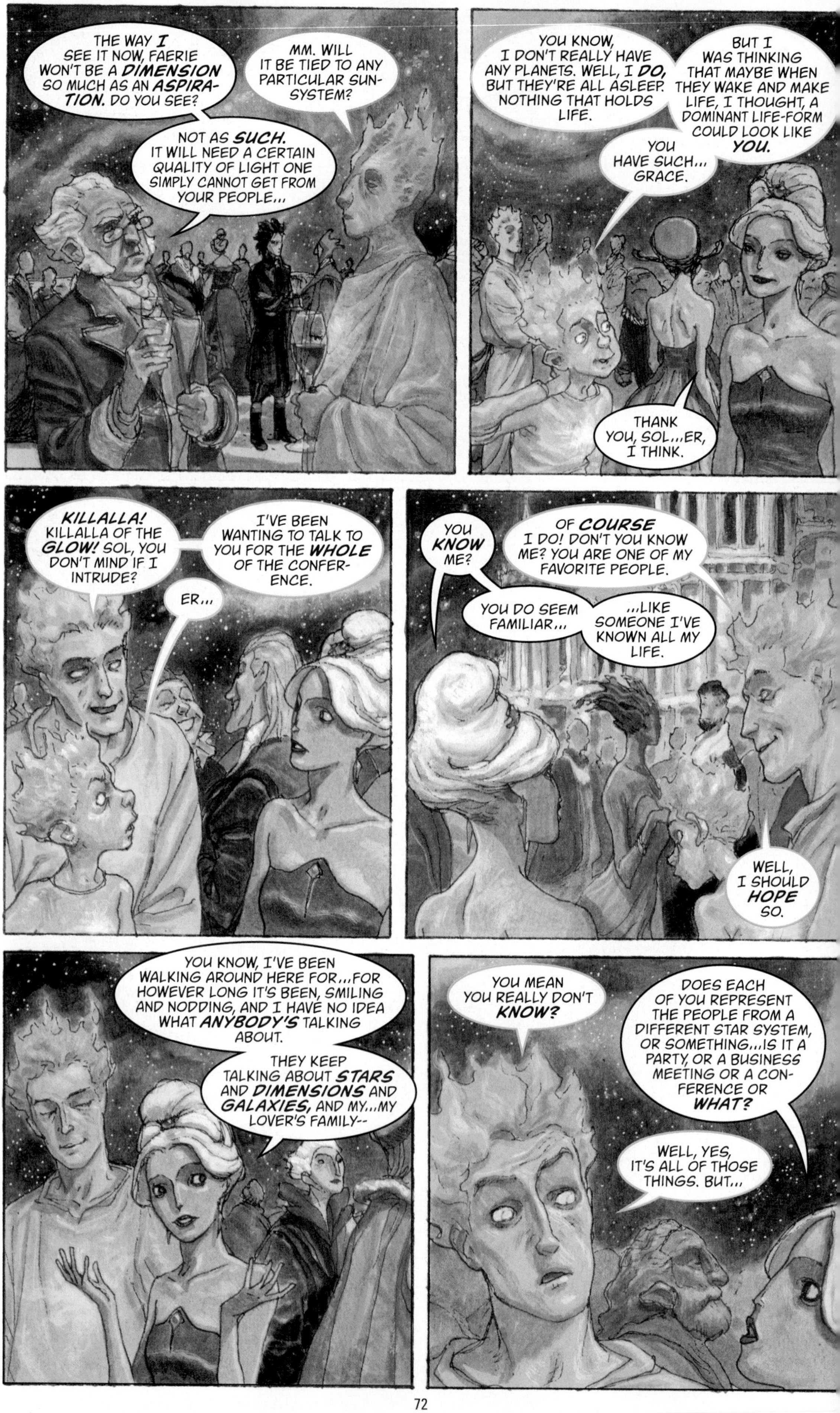
THE WAY I SEE IT NOW, FAERIE WON'T BE A DIMENSION SO MUCH AS AN ASPIRATION. DO YOU SEE?
MM. WILL IT BE TIED TO ANY PARTICULAR SUN-SYSTEM?
NOT AS SUCH. IT WILL NEED A CERTAIN QUALITY OF LIGHT ONE SIMPLY CANNOT GET FROM YOUR PEOPLE...
YOU KNOW, I DON'T REALLY HAVE ANY PLANETS. WELL, I DO, BUT THEY'RE ALL ASLEEP. NOTHING THAT HOLDS LIFE.
BUT I WAS THINKING THAT MAYBE WHEN THEY WAKE AND MAKE LIFE, I THOUGHT, A DOMINANT LIFE-FORM COULD LOOK LIKE YOU.
YOU HAVE SUCH... GRACE.
THANK YOU, SOL...ER, I THINK.
KILLALLA! KILLALLA OF THE GLOW! SOL, YOU DON'T MIND IF I INTRUDE?
I'VE BEEN WANTING TO TALK TO YOU FOR THE WHOLE OF THE CONFERENCE.
ER...
YOU KNOW ME?
OF COURSE I DO! DON'T YOU KNOW ME? YOU ARE ONE OF MY FAVORITE PEOPLE.
YOU DO SEEM FAMILIAR...
...LIKE SOMEONE I'VE KNOWN ALL MY LIFE.
WELL, I SHOULD HOPE SO.
YOU KNOW, I'VE BEEN WALKING AROUND HERE FOR...FOR HOWEVER LONG IT'S BEEN, SMILING AND NODDING, AND I HAVE NO IDEA WHAT ANYBODY'S TALKING ABOUT.
THEY KEEP TALKING ABOUT STARS AND DIMENSIONS AND GALAXIES, AND MY...MY LOVER'S FAMILY--
YOU MEAN YOU REALLY DON'T KNOW?
DOES EACH OF YOU REPRESENT THE PEOPLE FROM A DIFFERENT STAR SYSTEM, OR SOMETHING...IS IT A PARTY, OR A BUSINESS MEETING OR A CONFERENCE OR WHAT?
WELL, YES, IT'S ALL OF THOSE THINGS. BUT...

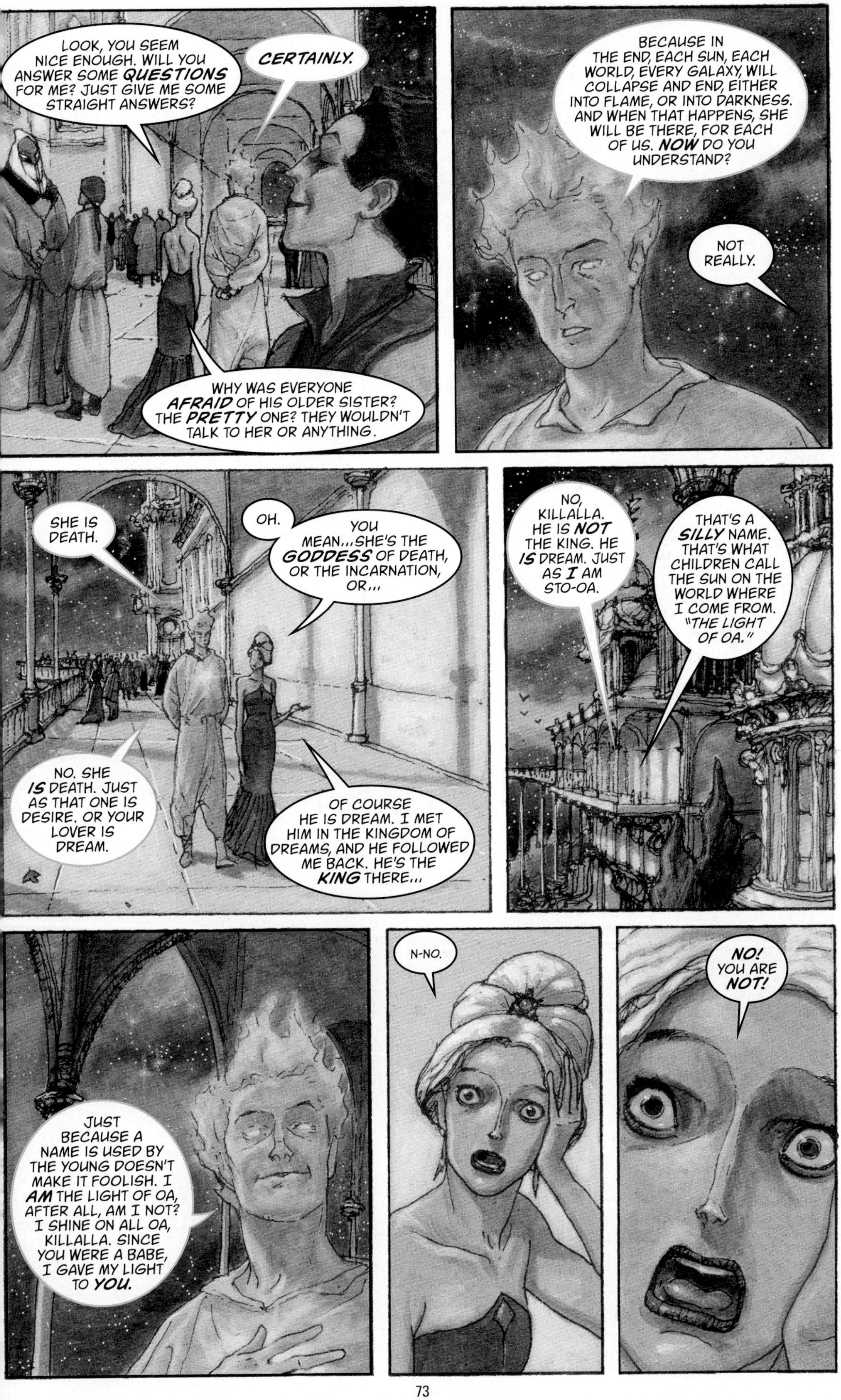

LOOK, YOU SEEM NICE ENOUGH. WILL YOU ANSWER SOME QUESTIONS FOR ME? JUST GIVE ME SOME STRAIGHT ANSWERS?
CERTAINLY.
WHY WAS EVERYONE AFRAID OF HIS OLDER SISTER? THE PRETTY ONE? THEY WOULDN'T TALK TO HER OR ANYTHING.
BECAUSE IN THE END, EACH SUN, EACH WORLD, EVERY GALAXY, WILL COLLAPSE AND END, EITHER INTO FLAME, OR INTO DARKNESS. AND WHEN THAT HAPPENS, SHE WILL BE THERE, FOR EACH OF US. NOW DO YOU UNDERSTAND?
NOT REALLY.
SHE IS DEATH.
OH.
YOU MEAN...SHE'S THE GODDESS OF DEATH, OR THE INCARNATION, OR...
NO. SHE IS DEATH. JUST AS THAT ONE IS DESIRE. OR YOUR LOVER IS DREAM.
OF COURSE HE IS DREAM. I MET HIM IN THE KINGDOM OF DREAMS, AND HE FOLLOWED ME BACK. HE'S THE KING THERE...
NO, KILLALLA. HE IS NOT THE KING. HE IS DREAM. JUST AS I AM STO-OA.
THAT'S A SILLY NAME. THAT'S WHAT CHILDREN CALL THE SUN ON THE WORLD WHERE I COME FROM. "THE LIGHT OF OA."
JUST BECAUSE A NAME IS USED BY THE YOUNG DOESN'T MAKE IT FOOLISH. I AM THE LIGHT OF OA, AFTER ALL, AM I NOT? I SHINE ON ALL OA, KILLALLA. SINCE YOU WERE A BABE, I GAVE MY LIGHT TO YOU.
N-NO.
NO! YOU ARE NOT!

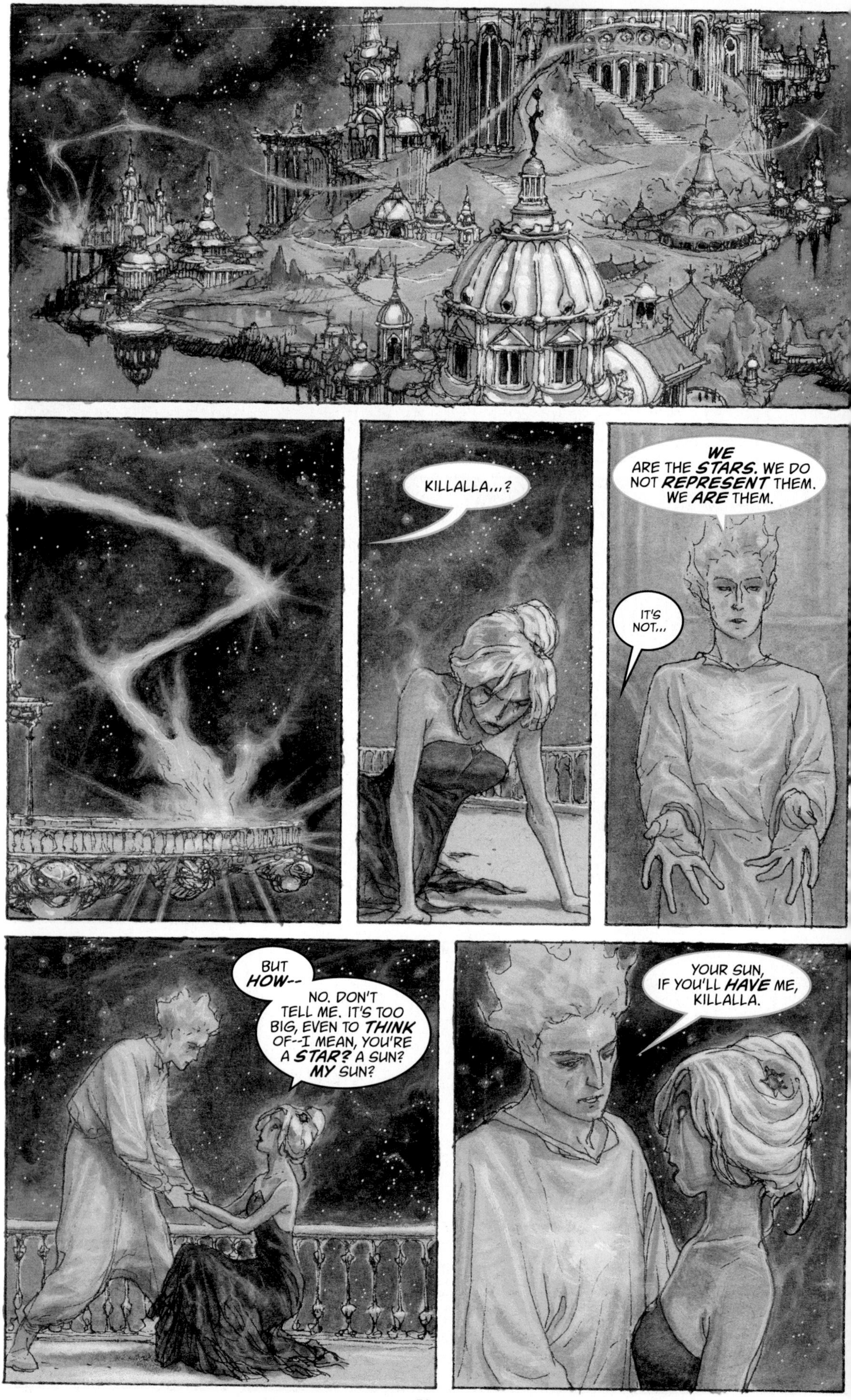
KILLALLA...?
WE ARE THE STARS. WE DO NOT REPRESENT THEM. WE ARE THEM.
IT'S NOT...
BUT HOW--
NO. DON'T TELL ME. IT'S TOO BIG, EVEN TO THINK OF--I MEAN, YOU'RE A STAR? A SUN? MY SUN?
YOUR SUN, IF YOU'LL HAVE ME, KILLALLA.

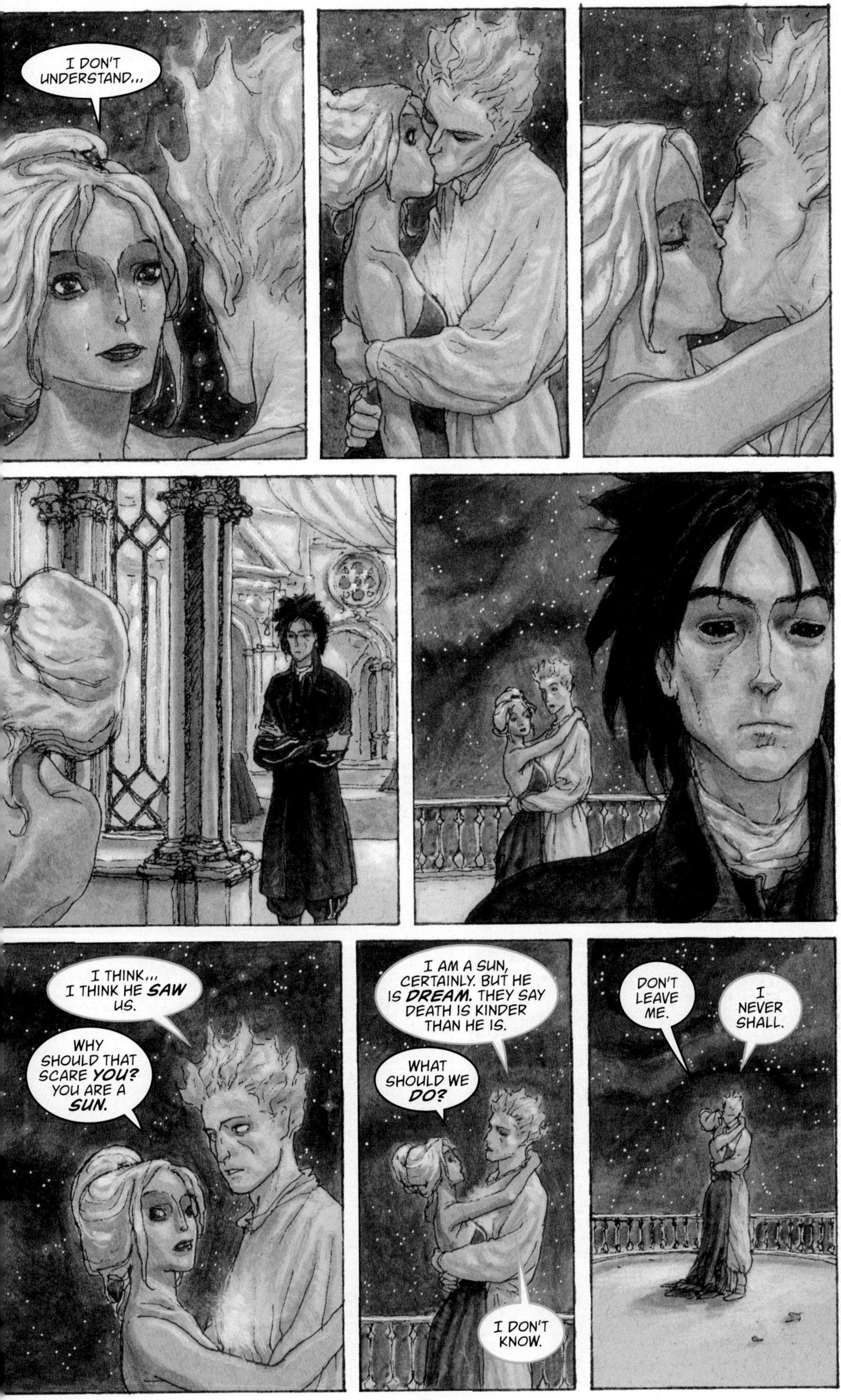
I DON'T UNDERSTAND...
I THINK... I THINK HE SAW US.
WHY SHOULD THAT SCARE YOU? YOU ARE A SUN.
I AM A SUN, CERTAINLY. BUT HE IS DREAM. THEY SAY DEATH IS KINDER THAN HE IS.
WHAT SHOULD WE DO?
I DON'T KNOW.
DON'T LEAVE ME.
I NEVER SHALL.

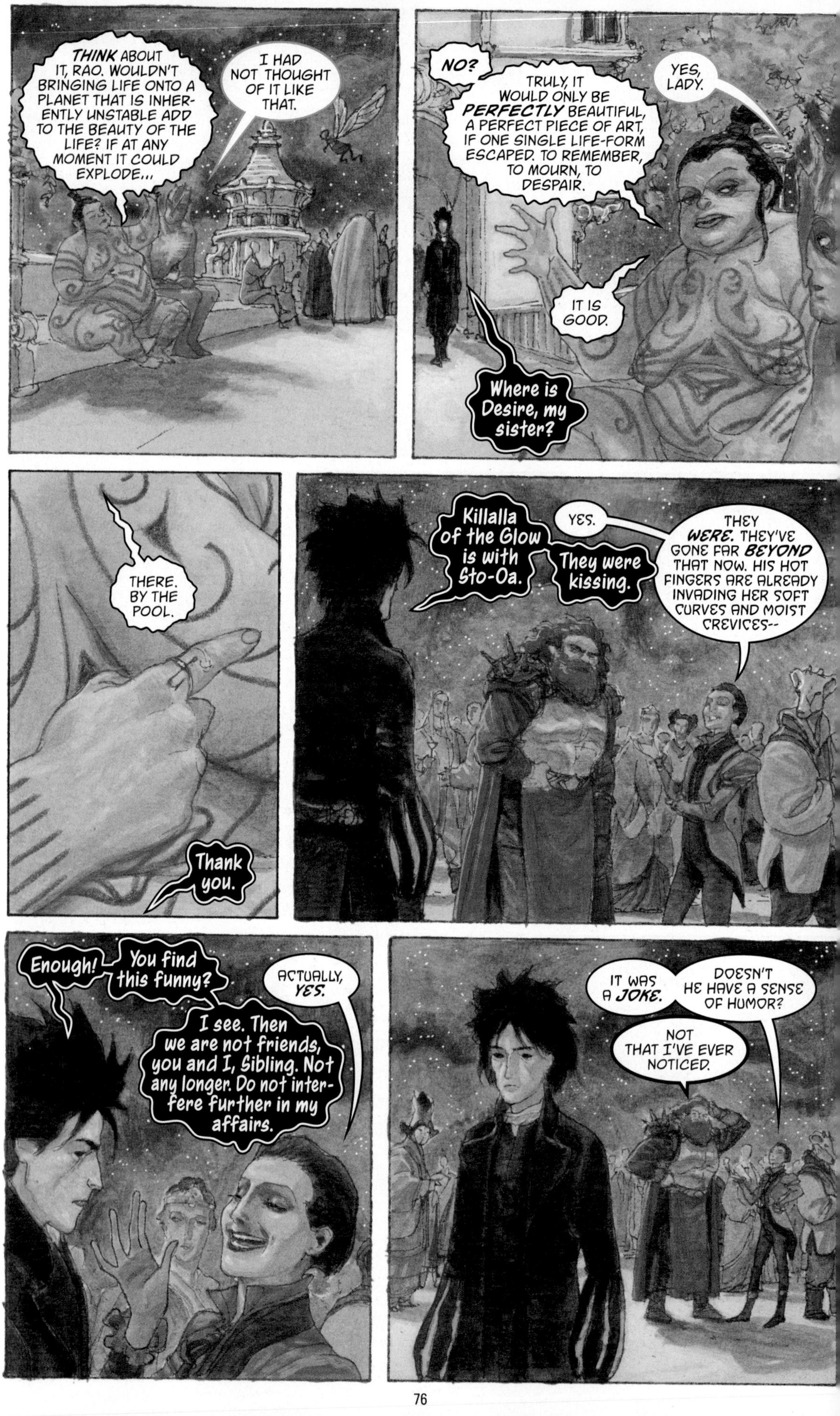
THINK ABOUT IT, RAO. WOULDN'T BRINGING LIFE ONTO A PLANET THAT IS INHERENTLY UNSTABLE ADD TO THE BEAUTY OF THE LIFE? IF AT ANY MOMENT IT COULD EXPLODE...
I HAD NOT THOUGHT OF IT LIKE THAT.
NO?
TRULY, IT WOULD ONLY BE PERFECTLY BEAUTIFUL, A PERFECT PIECE OF ART, IF ONE SINGLE LIFE-FORM ESCAPED. TO REMEMBER, TO MOURN, TO DESPAIR.
YES, LADY.
IT IS GOOD.
Where is Desire, my sister?
THERE. BY THE POOL.
Thank you.
Killalla of the Glow is with Sto-Oa.
YES.
They were kissing.
THEY WERE. THEY'VE GONE FAR BEYOND THAT NOW. HIS HOT FINGERS ARE ALREADY INVADING HER SOFT CURVES AND MOIST CREVICES--
Enough!
You find this funny?
ACTUALLY, YES.
I see. Then we are not friends, you and I, Sibling. Not any longer. Do not interfere further in my affairs.
IT WAS A JOKE.
DOESN'T HE HAVE A SENSE OF HUMOR?
NOT THAT I'VE EVER NOTICED.

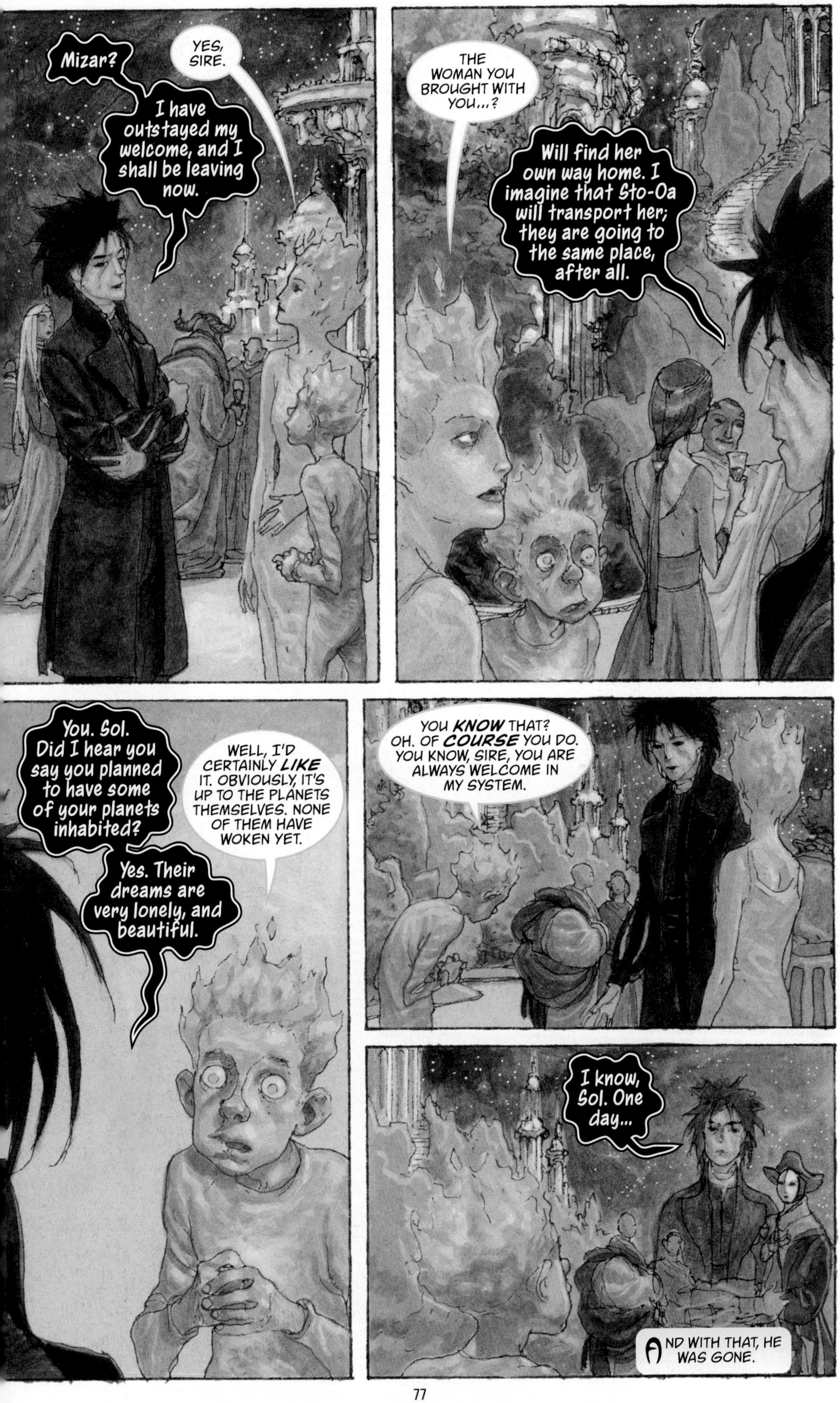
Mizar?
YES, SIRE.
I have outstayed my welcome, and I shall be leaving now.
THE WOMAN YOU BROUGHT WITH YOU...?
Will find her own way home. I imagine that Sto-Oa will transport her; they are going to the same place, after all.
You. Sol. Did I hear you say you planned to have some of your planets inhabited?
WELL, I'D CERTAINLY LIKE IT. OBVIOUSLY, IT'S UP TO THE PLANETS THEMSELVES. NONE OF THEM HAVE WOKEN YET.
Yes. Their dreams are very lonely, and beautiful.
YOU KNOW THAT? OH. OF COURSE YOU DO. YOU KNOW, SIRE, YOU ARE ALWAYS WELCOME IN MY SYSTEM.
I know, Sol. One day...
AND WITH THAT, HE WAS GONE.

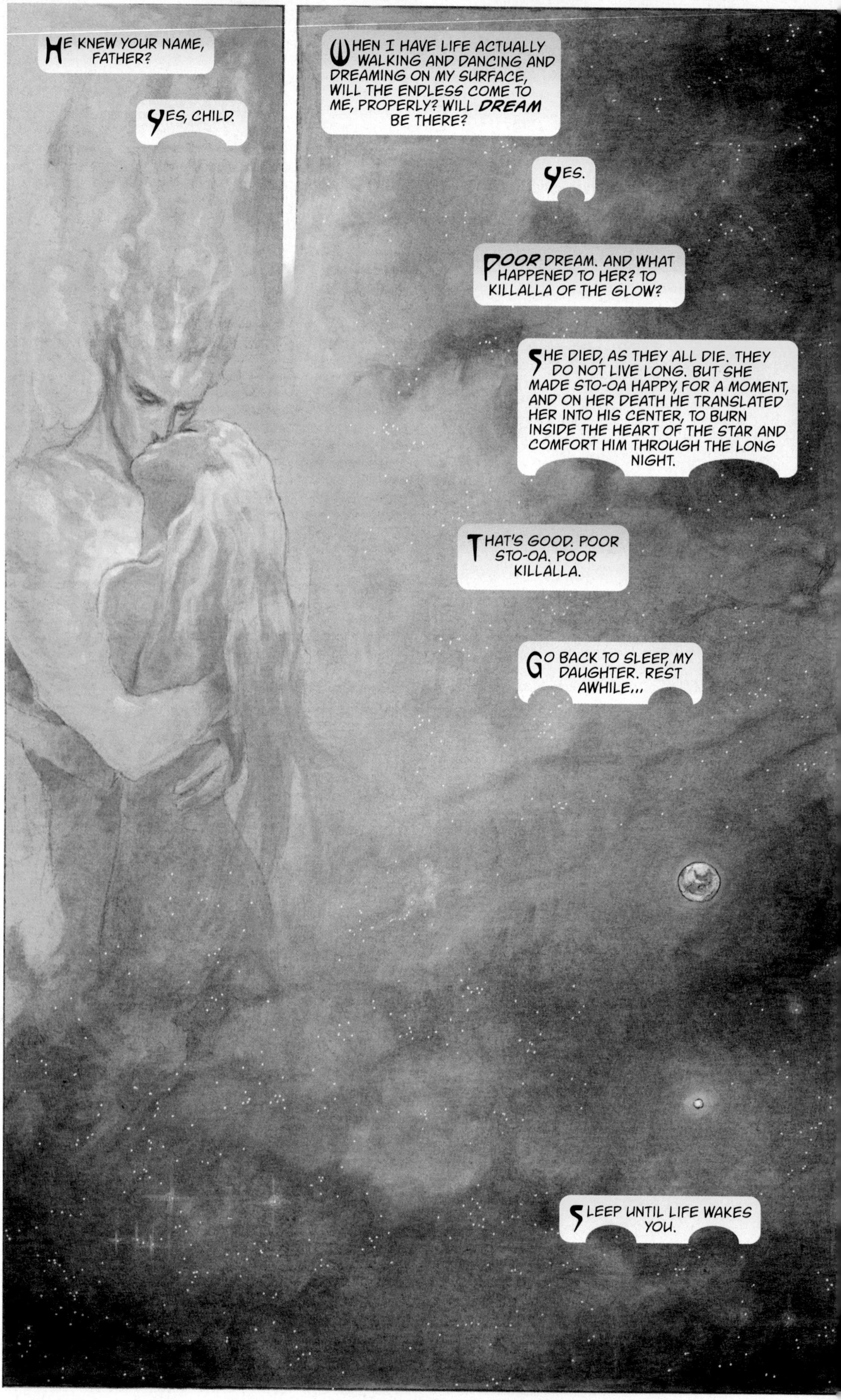
HE KNEW YOUR NAME, FATHER?
YES, CHILD.
WHEN I HAVE LIFE ACTUALLY WALKING AND DANCING AND DREAMING ON MY SURFACE, WILL THE ENDLESS COME TO ME, PROPERLY? WILL DREAM BE THERE?
YES.
POOR DREAM. AND WHAT HAPPENED TO HER? TO KILLALLA OF THE GLOW?
SHE DIED, AS THEY ALL DIE. THEY DO NOT LIVE LONG. BUT SHE MADE STO-OA HAPPY, FOR A MOMENT, AND ON HER DEATH HE TRANSLATED HER INTO HIS CENTER, TO BURN INSIDE THE HEART OF THE STAR AND COMFORT HIM THROUGH THE LONG NIGHT.
THAT'S GOOD. POOR STO-OA. POOR KILLALLA.
GO BACK TO SLEEP, MY DAUGHTER. REST AWHILE...
SLEEP UNTIL LIFE WAKES YOU.

Chapter 4

DESPAIR

Fifteen Portraits of Despair

DESPAIR

Fifteen
Portraits
of Despair
art by
Barron Storey
designed by
Dave McKean

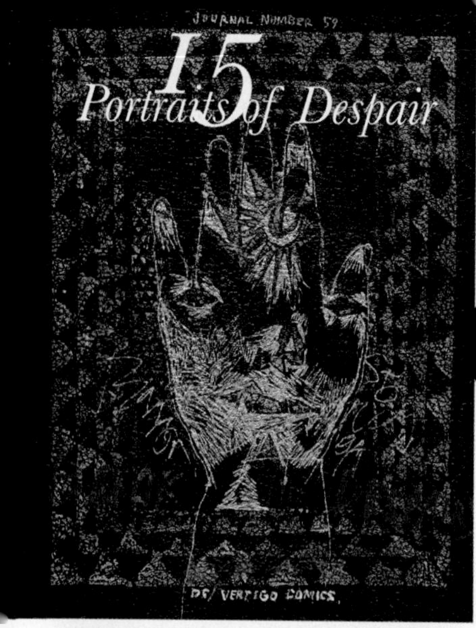
JOURNAL NUMBER 59
15
Portraits of Despair
DC/ VERTIGO COMICS

For Barron Storey

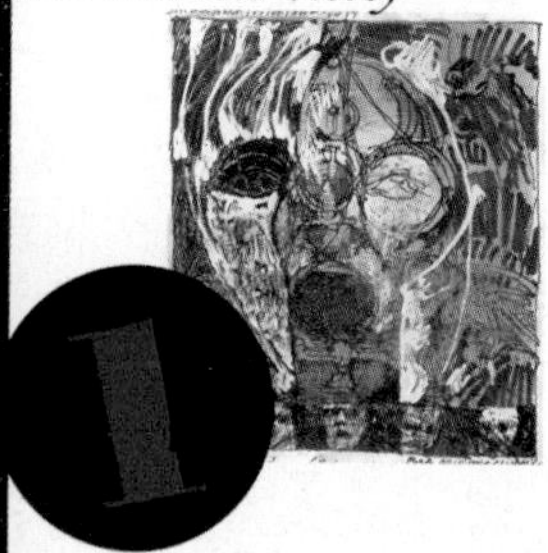
1

The first portrait.

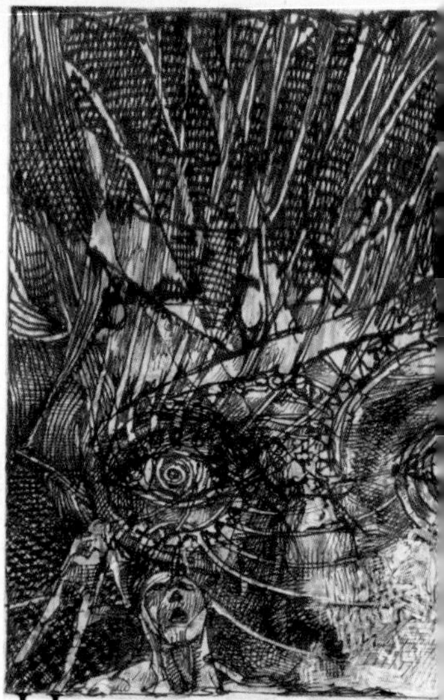

Her eyes are gre

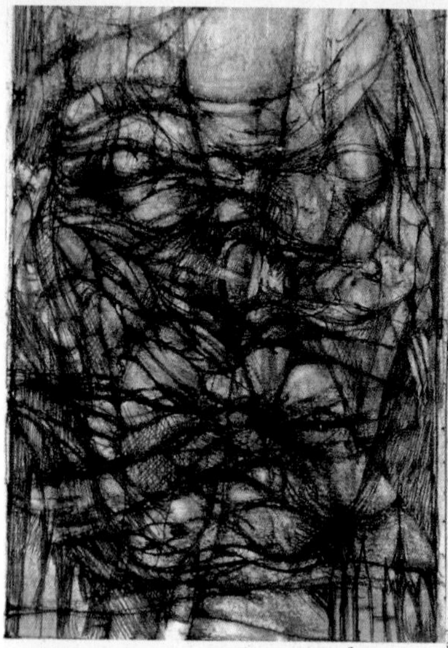

Her hair is straggly and wet.

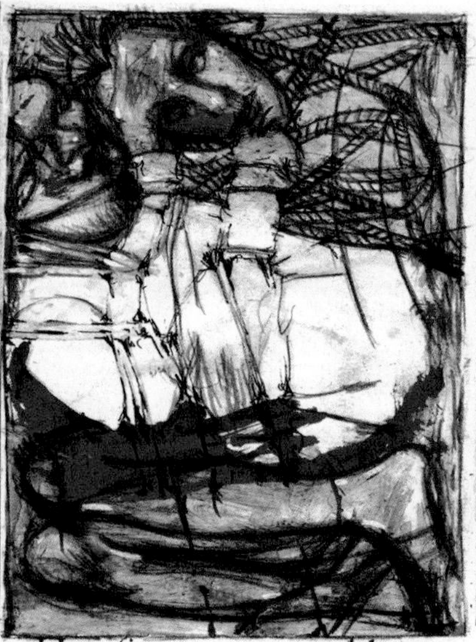

Her fingers are stubby.

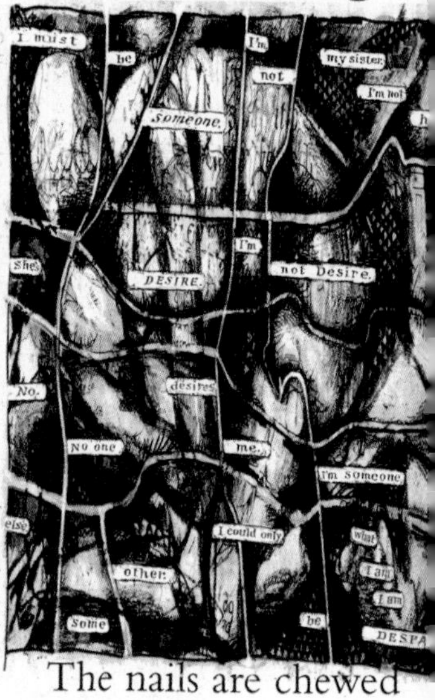
I must
be
I'm
not
my sister
I'm not
someone
She
DESIRE
I'm
not Desire
No.
desire
No one
me.
I'm Someone
else
I could only
what
I am
other
I am
Some
be
DESPA

The nails are chewed and broken.

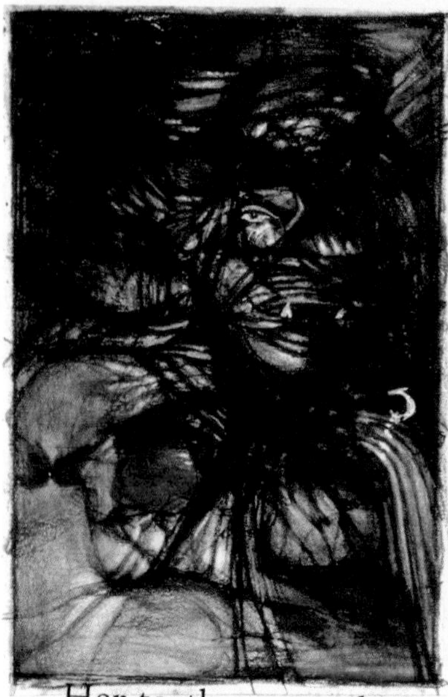

Her teeth are crooked, jagged things.

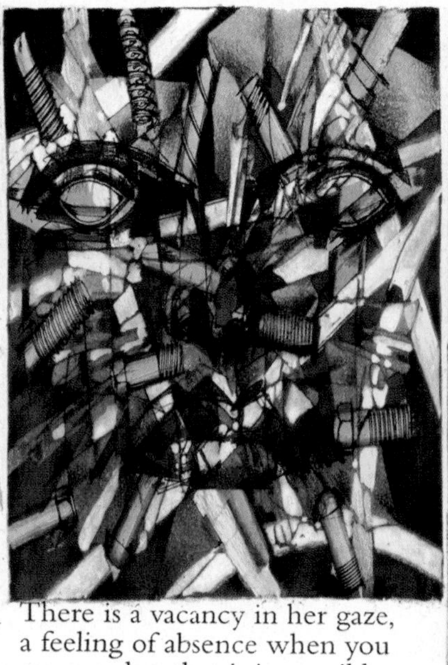

There is a vacancy in her gaze, a feeling of absence when you are near her that is impossible to put into words.

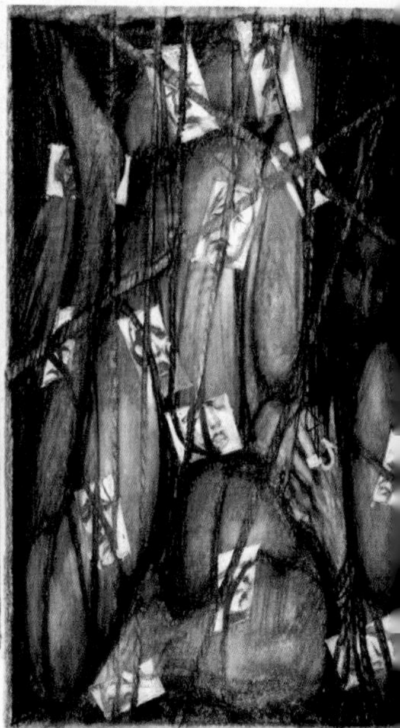

Her sigil is the hooked ring.

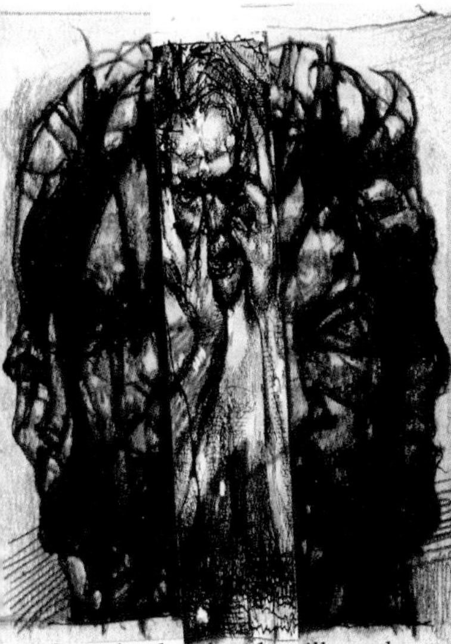

One day her hook will catch your heart.

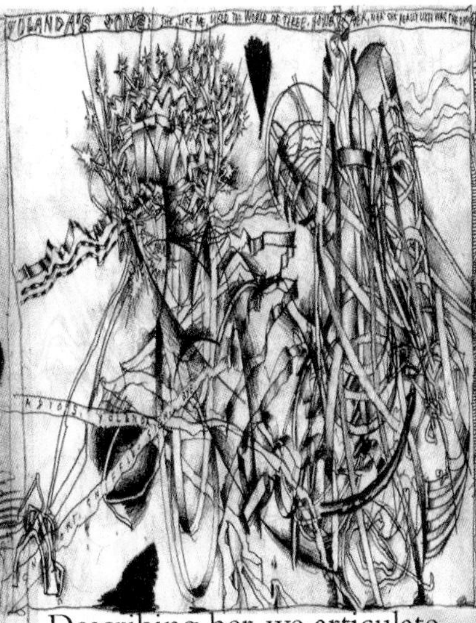

Describing her, we articulate what she is and why she is:

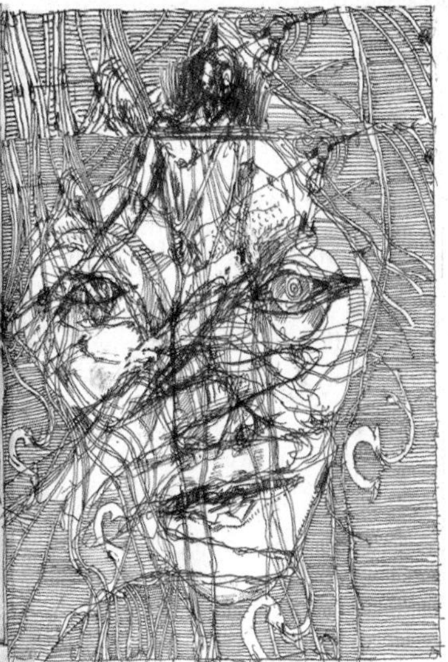

when hope is past, she is there.

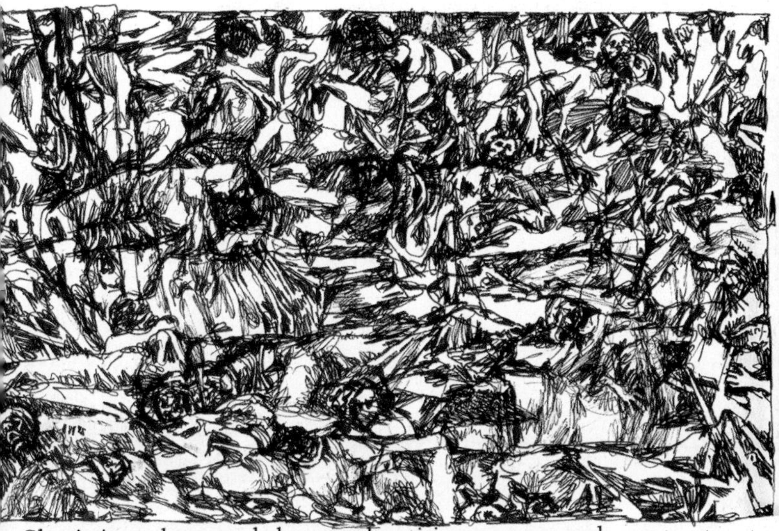

She is in a thousand thousand waiting rooms and empty streets, in grey concrete buildings and anonymous hotels.

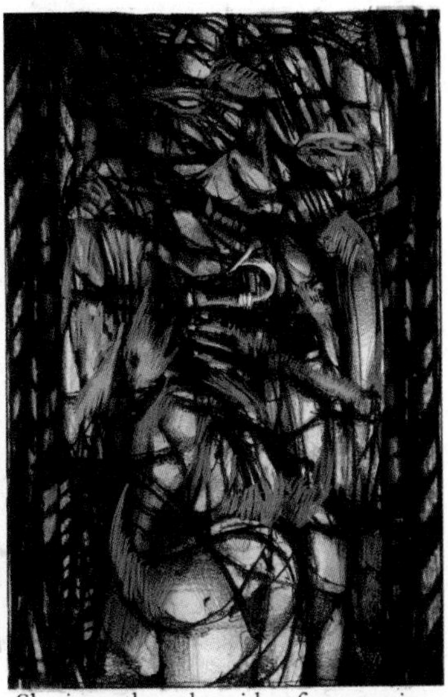

She is on the other side of every mirror.

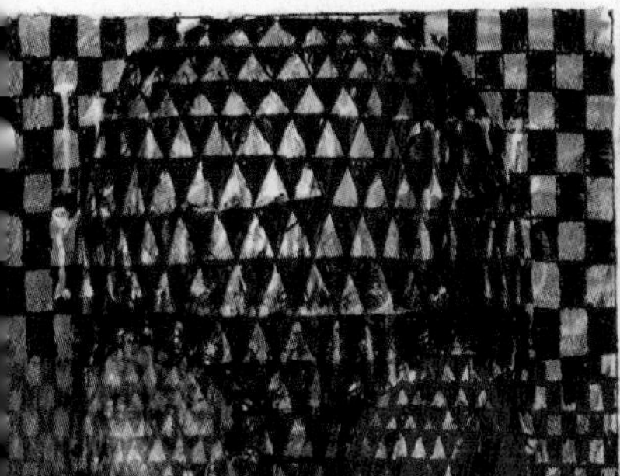

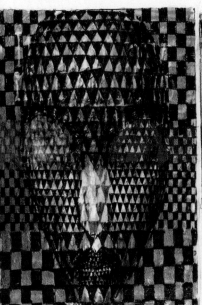

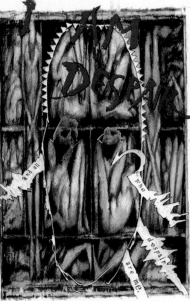

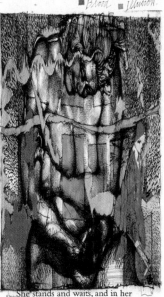

When the eyes that look back at you know you too well,

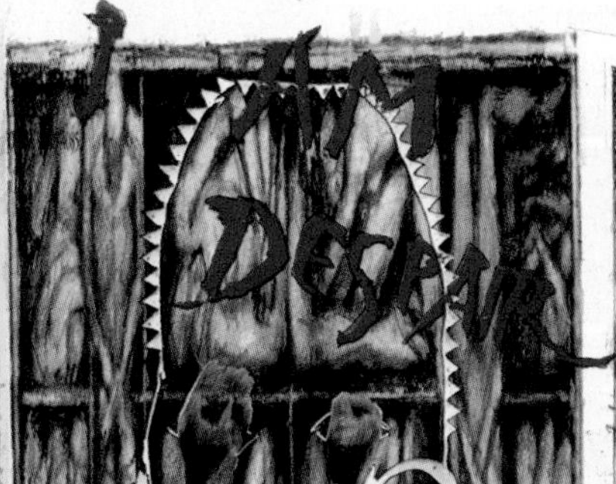
I AM DESPAIR
and all
who
despair
are me.

and no longer care for what they see, they are her eyes.

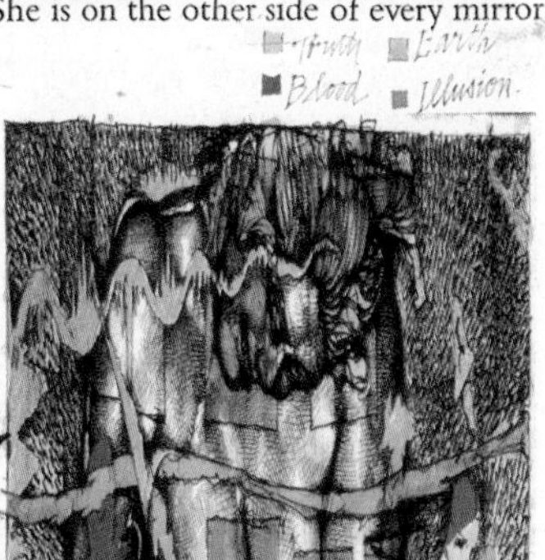
Truth
Earth
Blood
Illusion.

She stands and waits, and in her posture the pain no longer tells you to live, and in her presence joy is unimaginable.

2

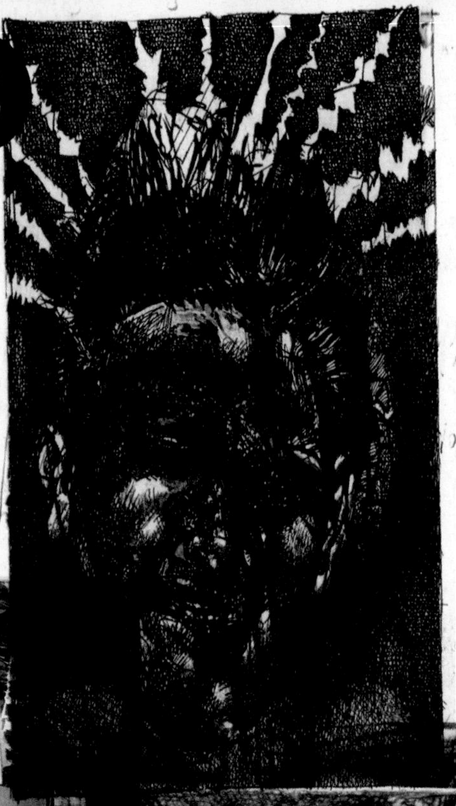

So when the Bishop's secretary said he wanted to see me, I knew it had to be something to do with the drinking. It's not that I'm a problem drinker. I'm Irish: son of a hundred generations of serious drinkers. But these days, the church needs to avoid even the apparency of wrongdoing.

I know a few priests go to A.A. I couldn't go as a cleric. It'd have to be "Hello Dermot," not "Hello Father Byrne," when I stood up to say my little bit.

And I've been letting things slide a little recently.

It wasn't the drinking. He said, ten years ago there was a girl. He showed me her picture. I said I remembered her: Odd little thing, always making up stories, wanting the attention.

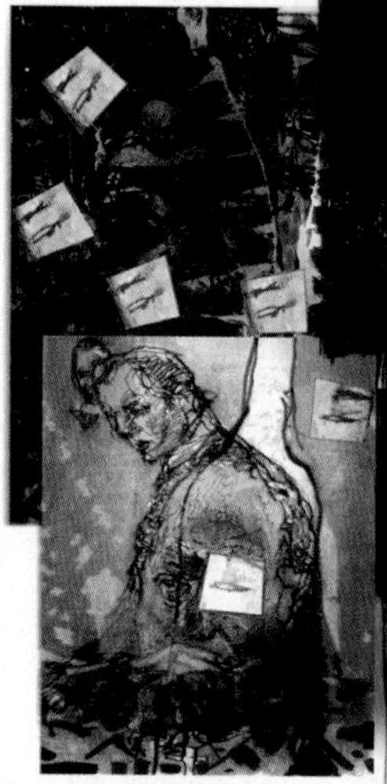

She says you

interfered

with her,

he says.

I told him I never.

I could prove, it too,

even after
all this time.

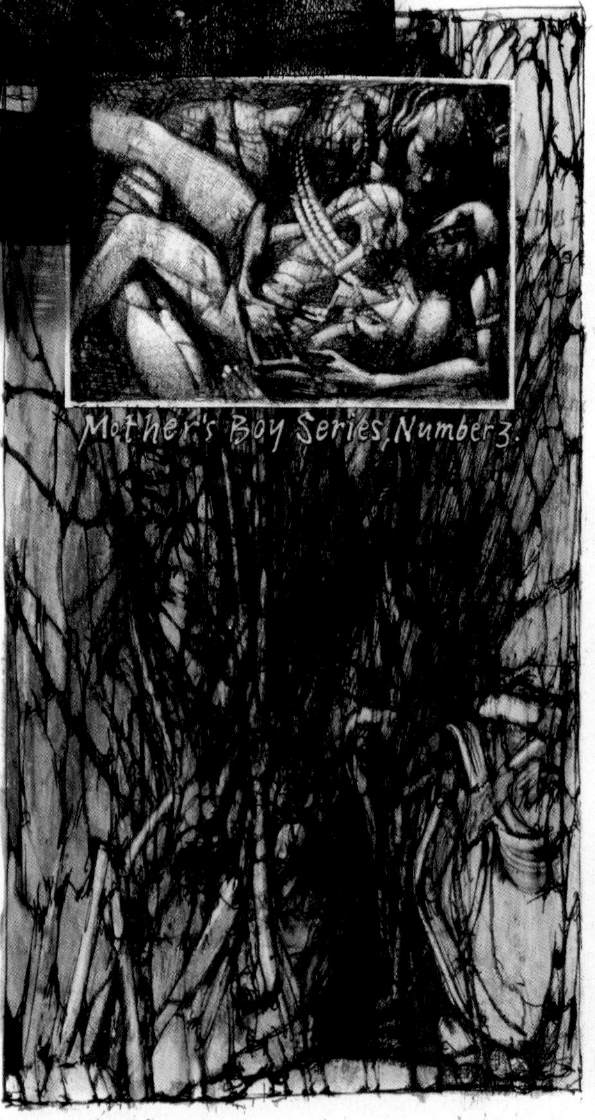
Mother's Boy Series, Number 3.

No, he says. You cannot. We're paying her three quarters of a million, Dermot. And you need to reconsider your vocation. It's the insurance company, you understand.

But I never, I said again. And, and I'm a priest.

We need to be seen to be taking action, says the Bishops' secretary. We can't seem to be condoning this sort of thing. If you stay in the church, we'll have to report you to the police.

For what, I say?

Molesting young girls, he says sadly.

But I never, I told him, and I could hear the whine in my voice, like a dog you've kicked when you've had the one too many, who just can't get it into his head why.

This isn't fair, I said.

No, he says. But it's right.

And when I get to the door, thinking about trying not to cry, at my age, about starting all over at 54, about the bottle of Canadian Club in the bottom drawer of the desk in my study, I say, Father, think for a moment. What would Jesus do?

The Bishop's secretary shook his head. If he had to deal with the insurance companies, he'd probably hang you out to dry, same as the rest of us, he said, and he didn't smile.

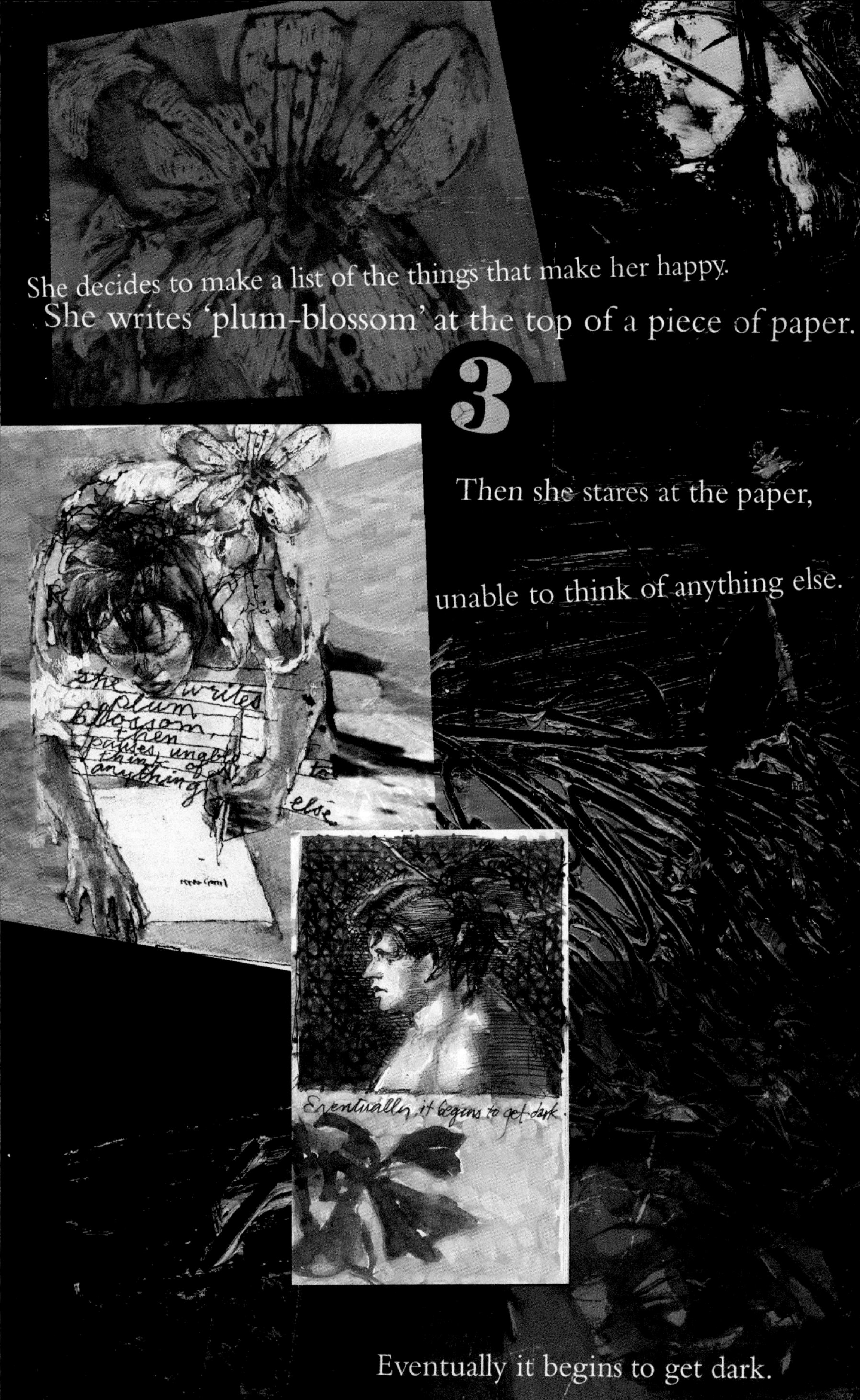
She decides to make a list of the things that make her happy.
She writes 'plum-blossom' at the top of a piece of paper.
3
Then she stares at the paper,
unable to think of anything else.
Eventually it begins to get dark.
Eventually it begins to get dark.

4

It starts with a cat twining against your leg, two, maybe three years ago, just after you hurt your leg, and it's a stray, and you put down milk in a saucer for it, and when you live in a damn trailer on the edge of the town you can be glad of the company and hell the kittens were cute and you put down more milk and pretty soon don't it seem like all the money you're collecting on disability is going to buy these sacks of catfood and you can hardly keep clear who is whose mother or brother or sister anymore and the trailer stinks of spray but you don't hardly notice it, because those cats are family and so it's a bitch when your brother-in-law over in Moose Hill says he's got you a job on the dairy farm there and it's three hundred dollars a week, and a place to stay, and that's the best money when you're nothing but a farmhand with a leg that's shot and you don't know what to do with the goddamn cats, the kittens in the drawers, sixty maybe even seventy cats and there's more now out in the fields who'll come back tonight to be fed.

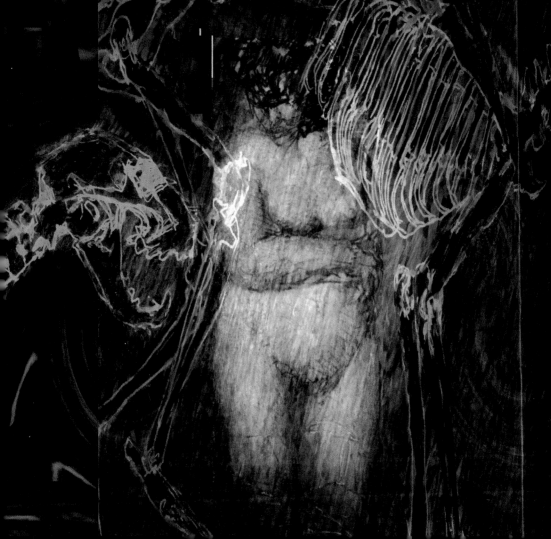

Be here Friday, says your brother-in-law, or they'll get someone else in.
And that disability won't last forever.

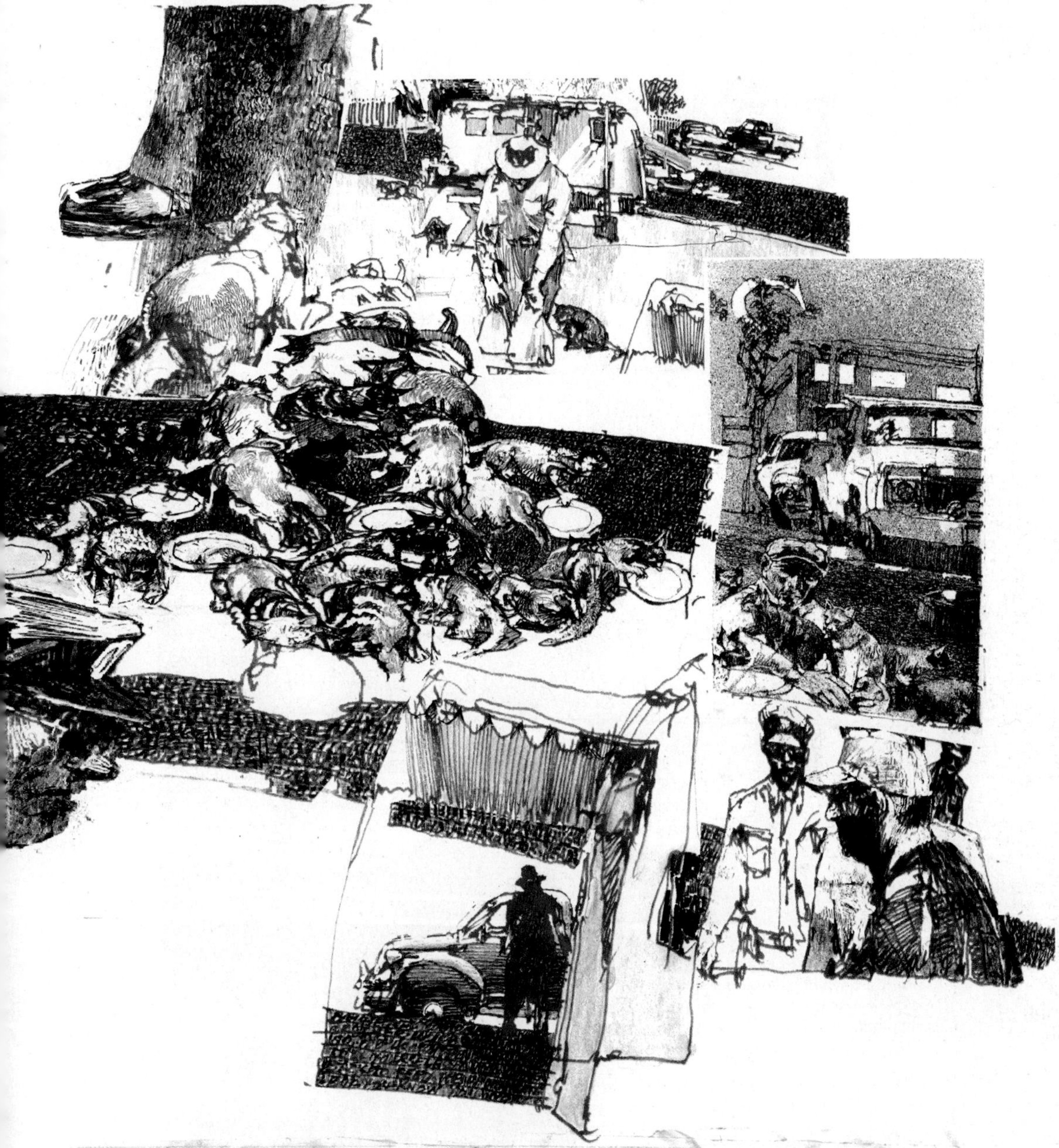

So you lock the trailer door and you go, thinking maybe you'll be back at the weekend to feed the cats, and knowing that you won't.

And then there's just the face on the sheriff's man as he tells you that they had to wear air masks to go into the trailer, that five of them cats were somehow still alive, that sixty of them, maybe more were found part eaten, and he waits for you to say something, anything, and you shake your head and you don't say nothing at all.

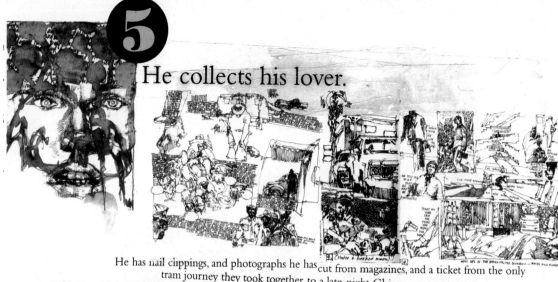

5

He collects his lover.

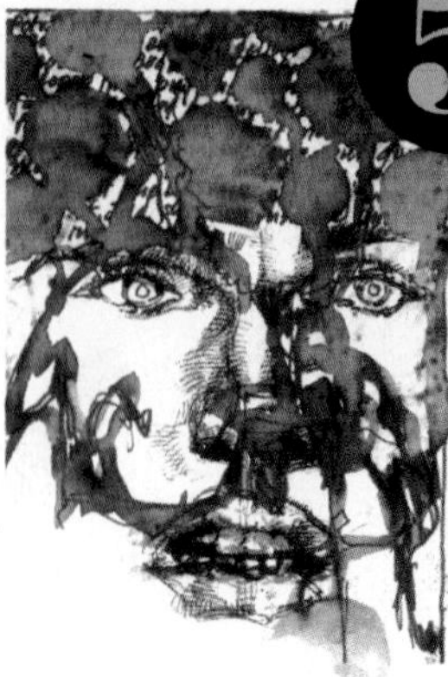

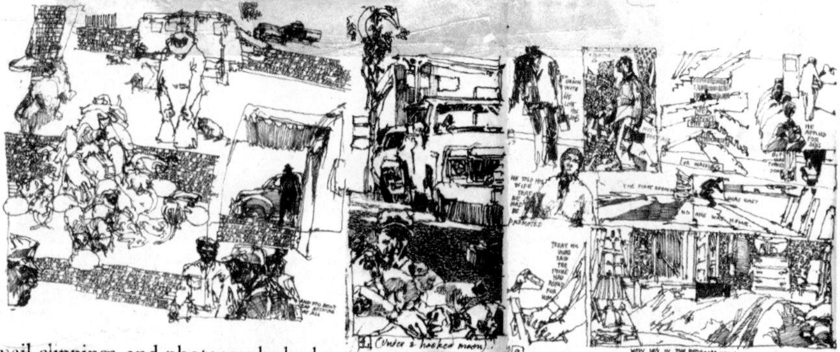

He has nail clippings, and photographs he has cut from magazines, and a ticket from the only tram journey they took together, to a late-night Chinese restaurant, where his lover was not recognized.

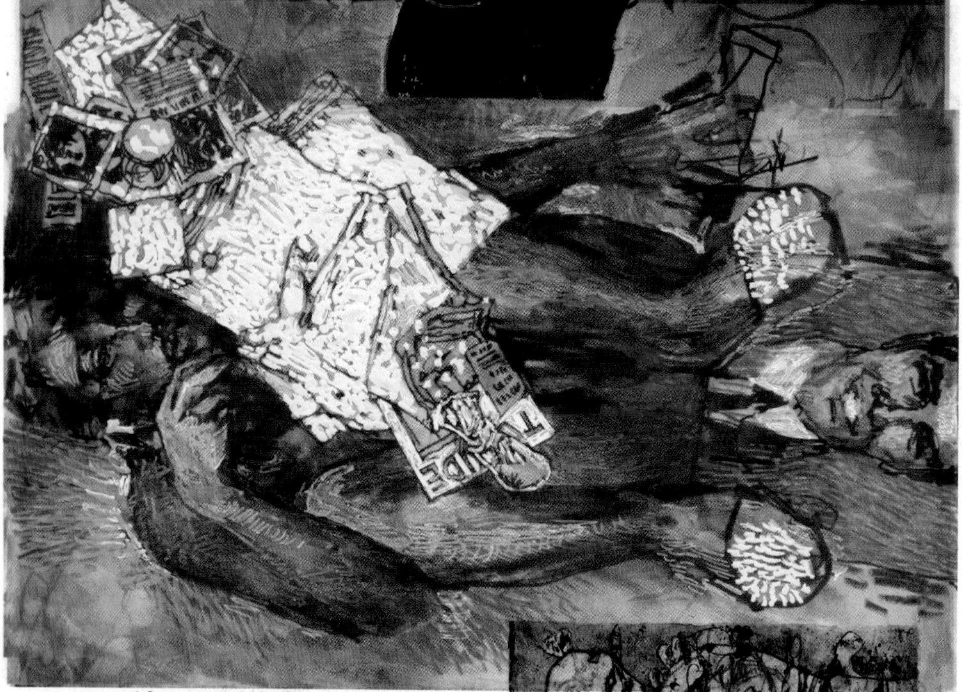

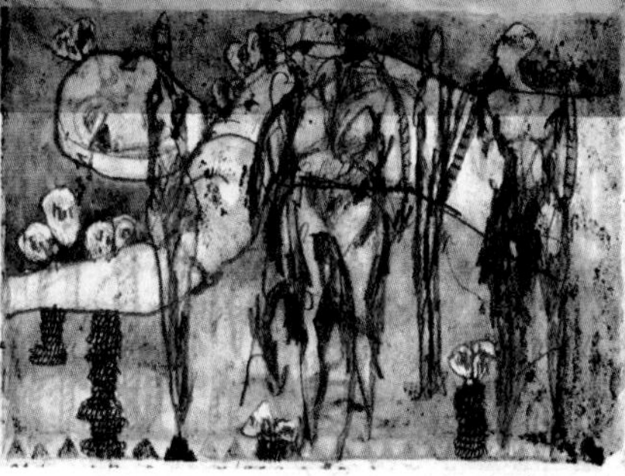

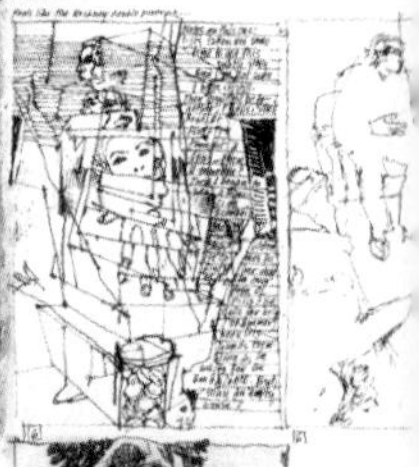

After sex, while his lover sleeps, he takes things, slips them into his bag, a tee shirt that smells like his lover, underpants, a dusty aspirin taken from his toilet kit.

His lover exists for him chiefly as a body in a sequence of hotel rooms.

In his bedroom he has made a small shrine to his lover: his greatest treasure is a knotted condom, retrieved from a waste bin, with the cold remains of his lover's seed congealed inside it.

Sometimes he does not see his lover in the flesh for months at a time. At night he watches his lover on the television.

"If you smile before the commercial break," he whispers to his lover, "it means you are thinking about me. If you blink now it means you love me, you truly love me, and one day you will come out here for always."

He buries his face in a tee shirt that no longer smells like anybody at all, and waits for his lover to blink.

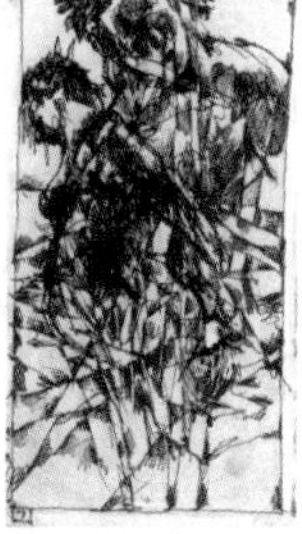

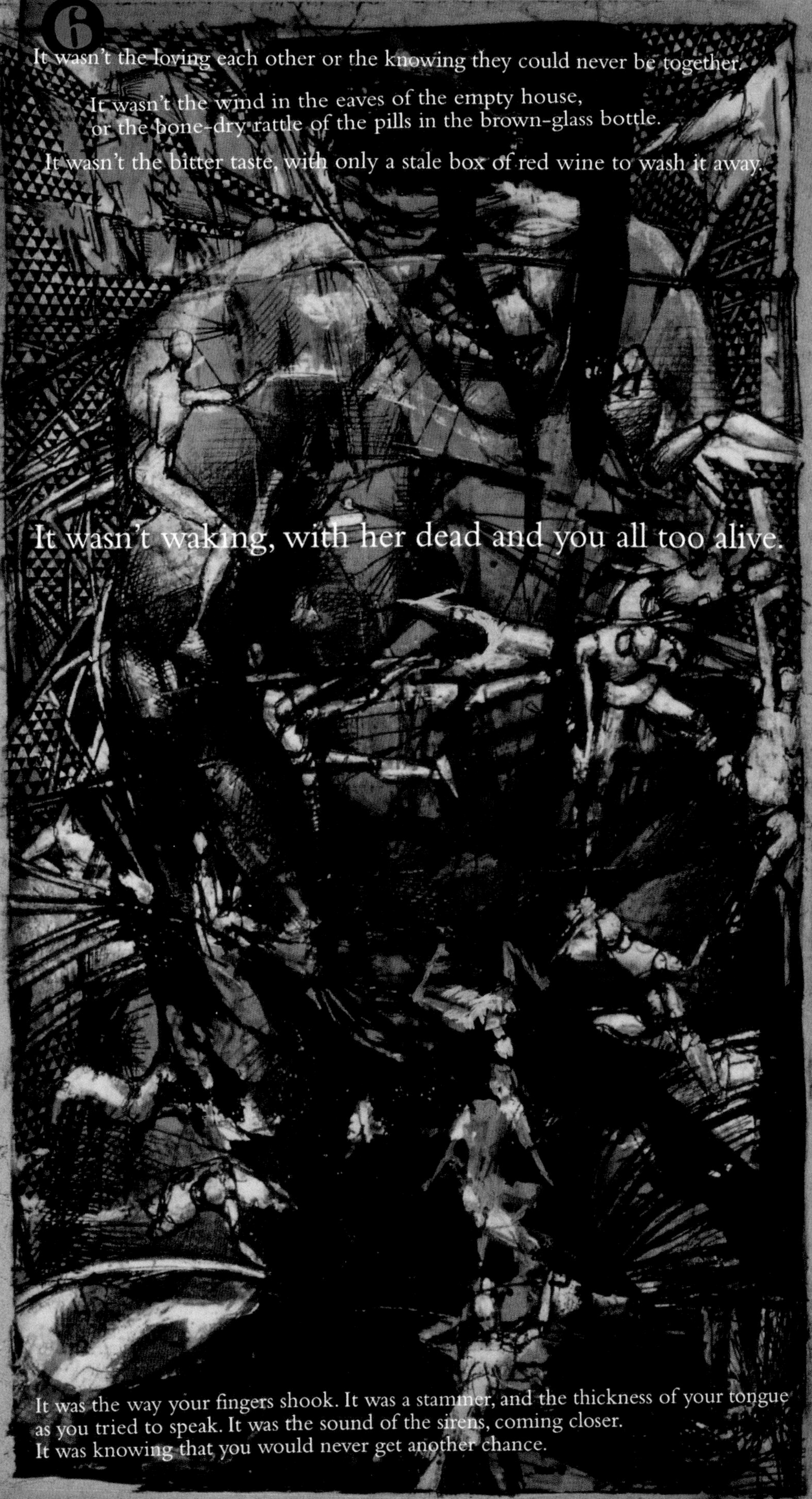
6
It wasn't the loving each other or the knowing they could never be together.
It wasn't the wind in the eaves of the empty house,
or the bone-dry rattle of the pills in the brown-glass bottle.
It wasn't the bitter taste, with only a stale box of red wine to wash it away.
It wasn't waking, with her dead and you all too alive.
It was the way your fingers shook. It was a stammer, and the thickness of your tongue
as you tried to speak. It was the sound of the sirens, coming closer.
It was knowing that you would never get another chance.

"Despair" with dolls

Despair remembers.

It is a peculiar, flat memery,
in which things become bleak and bounded by the dark.

1. 2. 3.

ENDLESS
DESPAIR

1. Truth.(Yellow) Our world is built on the injustices of the past.
2. Blood (Red) All who live are brothers and sisters. All will die.
3. Earth.(Green) Mother of all.

There is joy in there,
of course,
and love,
and touching.
The presence that makes the
present absence unbearable.

Without triumph,
without love,
without joy,
her work would be for nothing.

3

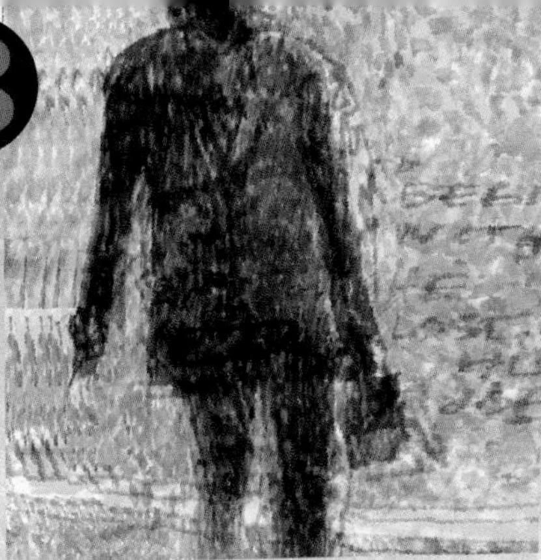

To begin with, he lost his job.
It was not his fault.
It was an honest mistake.
You must believe me.

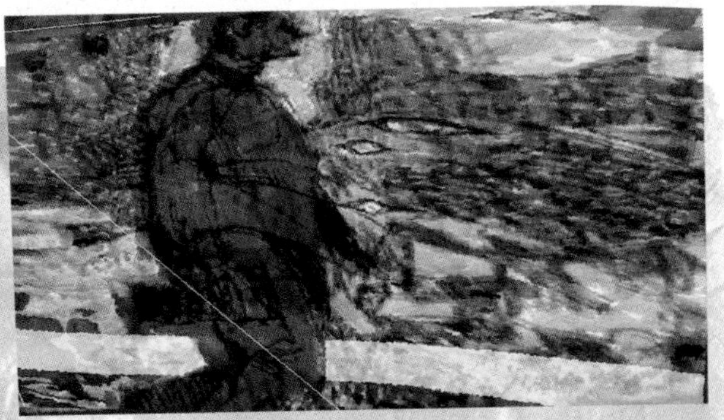

It was shame, then, not despair that moved him.
Each day he got up and showered and dressed,
he kissed his wife and babies, and drove away.

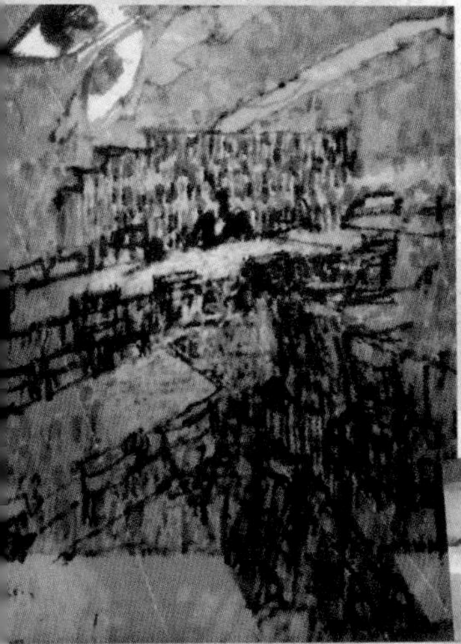

He spent the day in libraries,
or in the parked car, or walking.

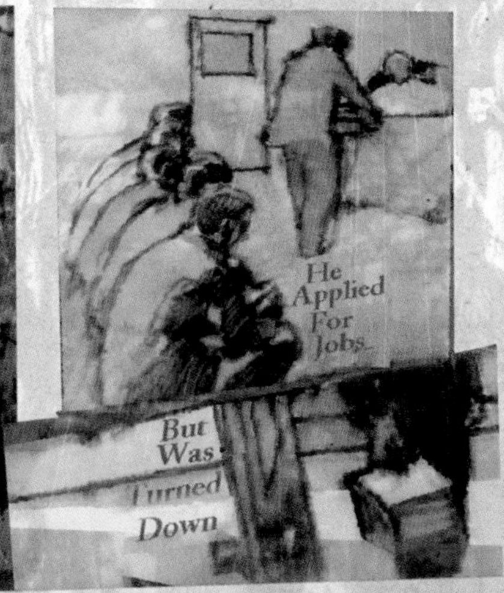
He Applied For Jobs
But Was Turned Down

He applied for jobs,
and was turned down.

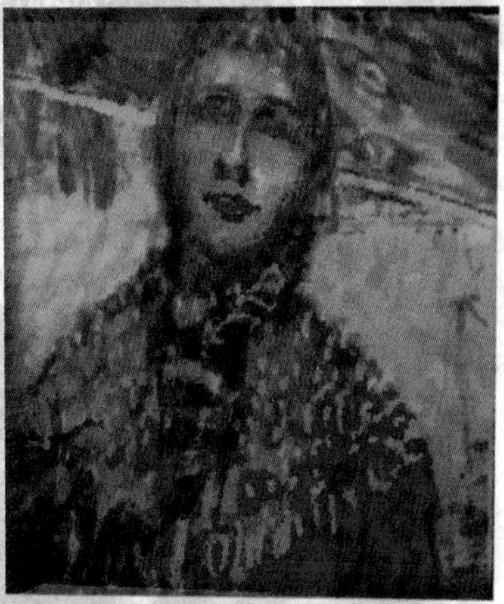

When his severance pay ran out he slowly,
methodically, emptied his savings accounts.
He told his wife he had been promoted.

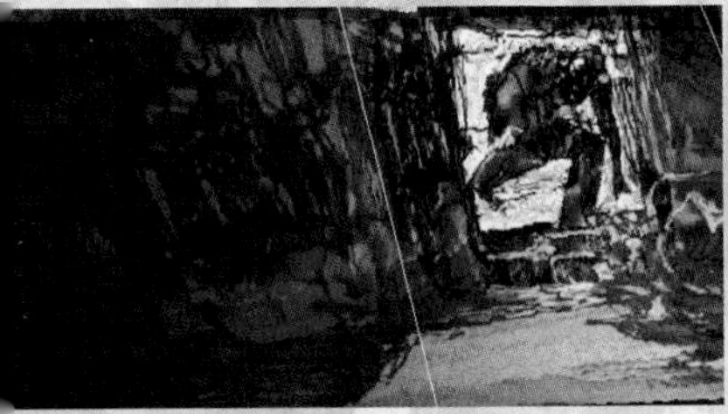

The first break-in was easy.
A wallet, jewelery.
No one was home.
No one was hurt.
It was practically a victimless crime.

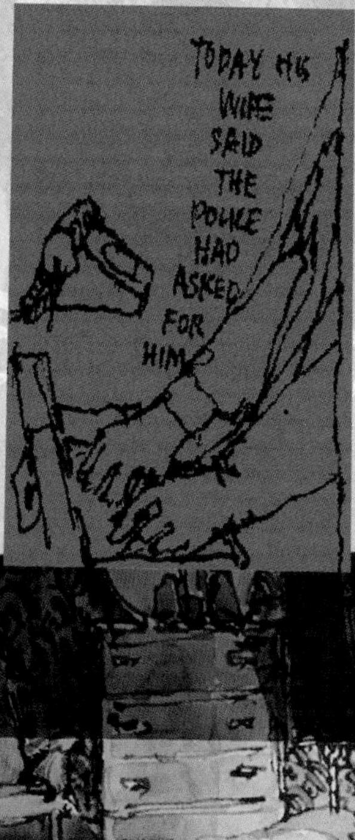
TODAY HIS WIFE SAID THE POLICE HAD ASKED FOR HIM

Today his wife said that the police
had been by asking after him.
She told them that he was at work,
and they said that was odd,
that they thought he'd been let go.

He told her that people make mistakes.
That new girl on the switchboard.
But he wasn't feeling well.
He thought he'd stay home today.

Now he's in his bedroom,
in the empty house,
listening to someone pressing the doorbell.
And the bell.
Which rings.
And rings.
And rings.

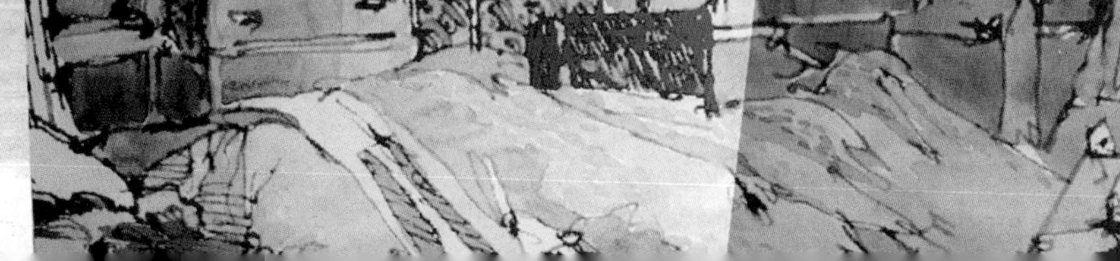

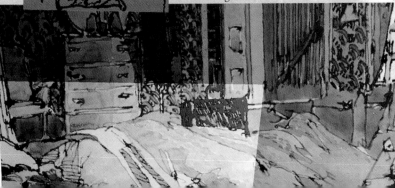

9

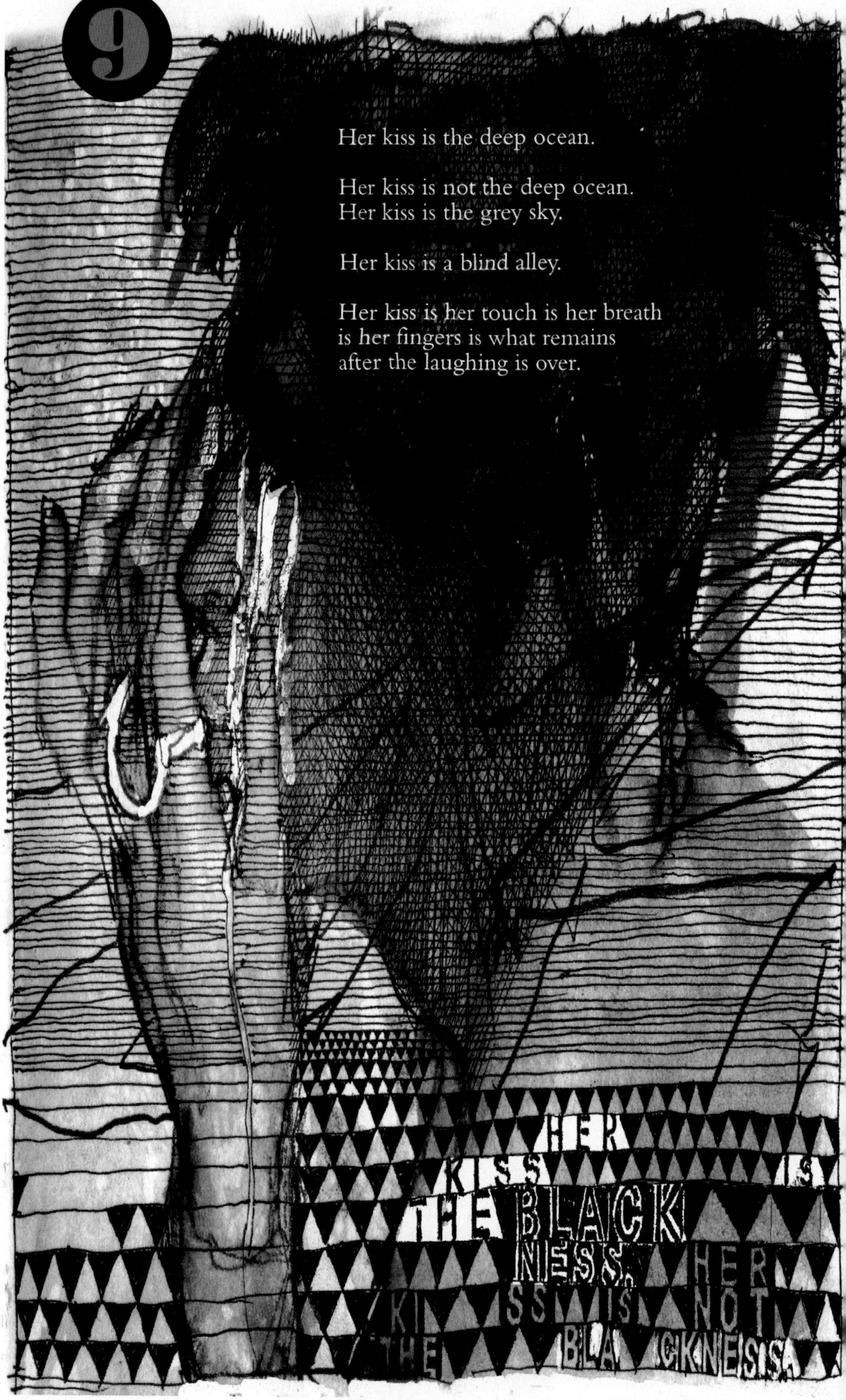
HER
KISS IS
THE BLACK
NESS. HER
KISS IS NOT
THE BLACKNESS A

Her kiss is the deep ocean.

Her kiss is not the deep ocean.
Her kiss is the grey sky.

Her kiss is a blind alley.

Her kiss is her touch is her breath
is her fingers is what remains
after the laughing is over.

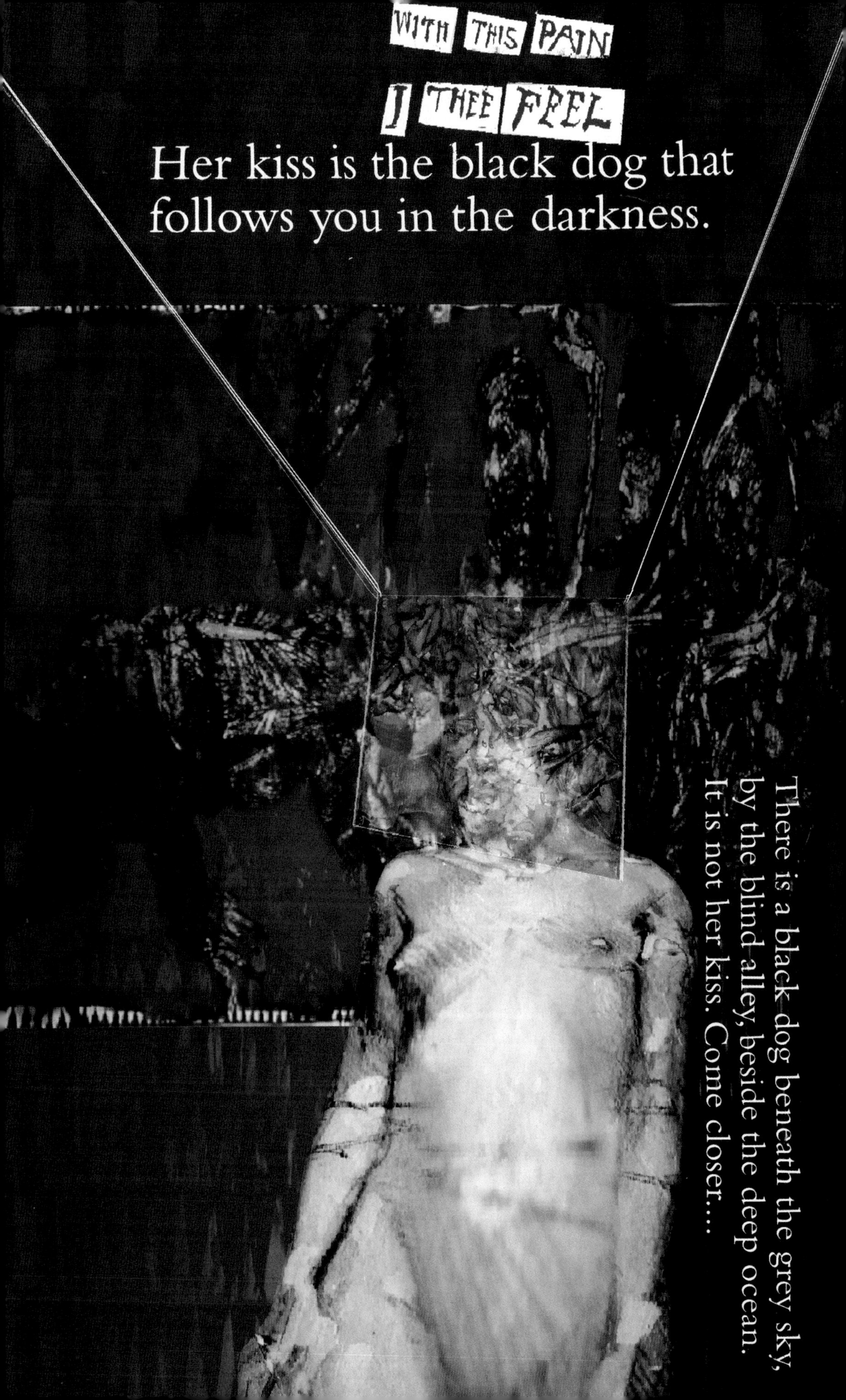
WITH THIS PAIN
I THEE FEEL
Her kiss is the black dog that follows you in the darkness.
There is a black dog beneath the grey sky, by the blind alley, beside the deep ocean. It is not her kiss. Come closer....

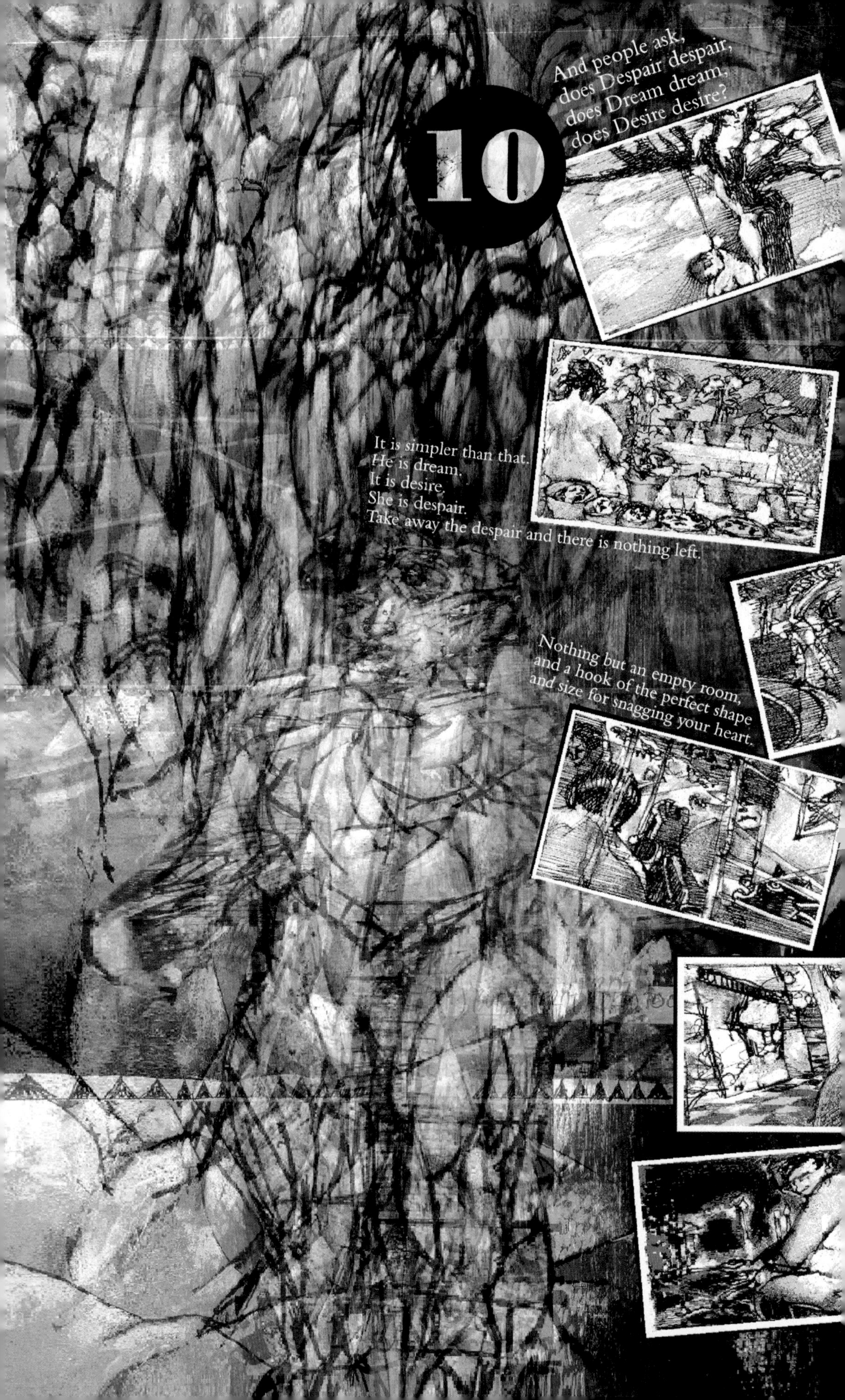
10
And people ask,
does Despair despair,
does Dream dream,
does Desire desire?
It is simpler than that.
He is dream.
It is desire.
She is despair.
Take away the despair and there is nothing left.
Nothing but an empty room,
and a hook of the perfect shape
and size for snagging your heart.

It is a writer, with nothing left that he knows how to say.

It is an artist, and fingers that will never catch the vision.

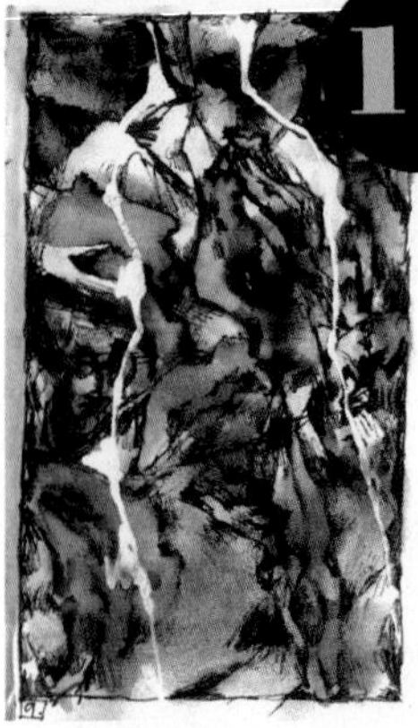

12

He was not a rich man, and it took all he could raise from his fields, his house, his friends, to take the man to court. He has mortgaged his future for fairness, for relief, for Justice. What happened to his child was not right.

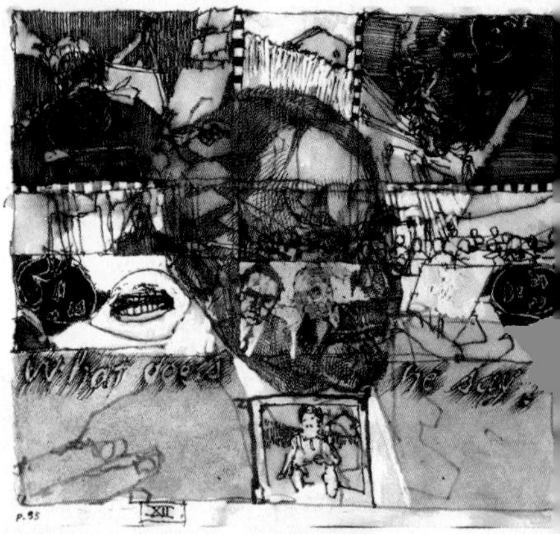

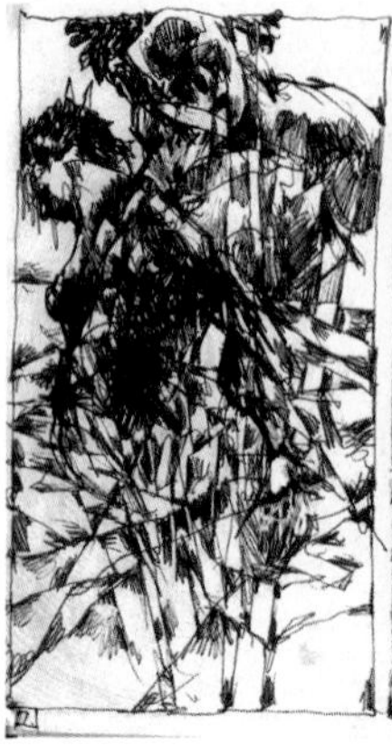

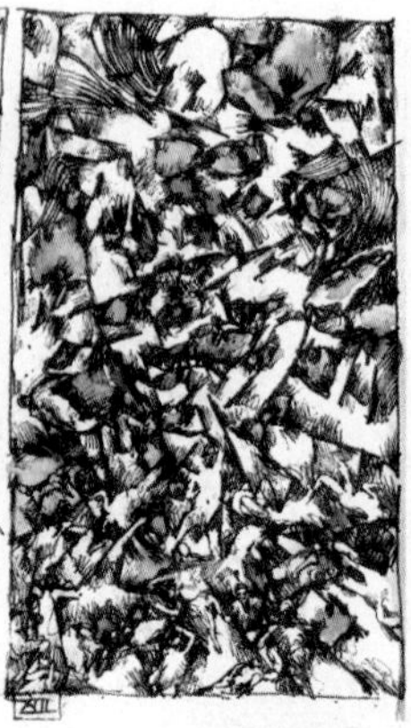

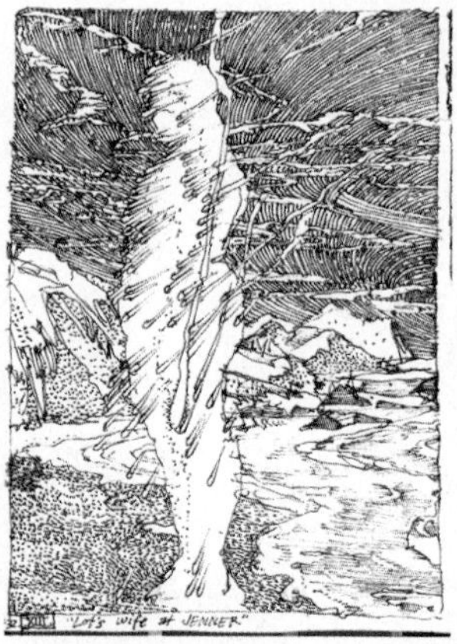

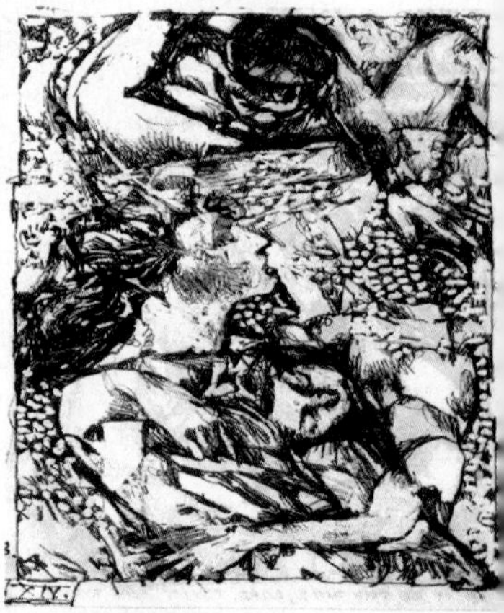

And now the judge comes out and his mouth opens and he explains the verdict, his words a tangle of legalities.

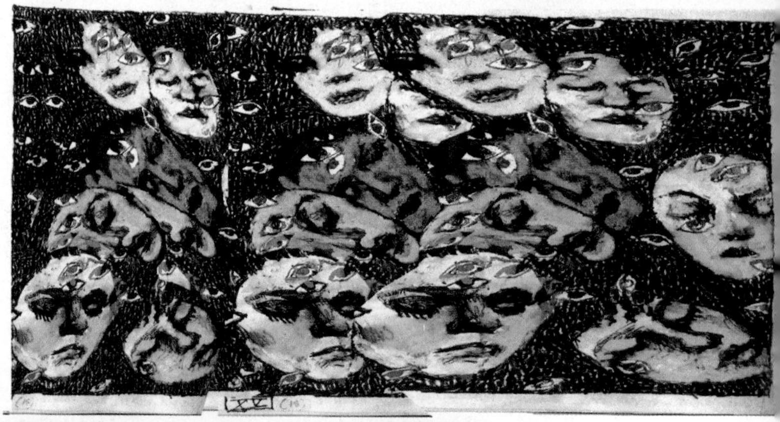

"What does he say?" the man asks his lawyer,

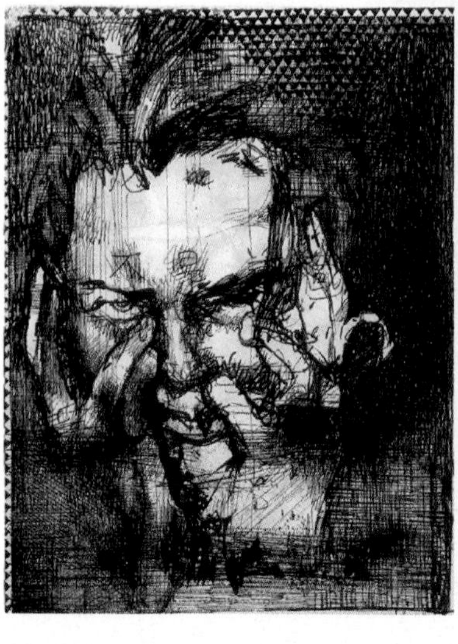

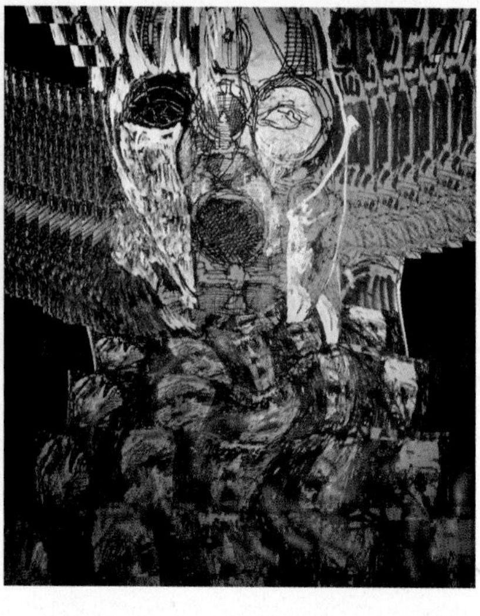

but already he knows, by the smiles in the eyes of his opponent. It is the same smile he sees on the faces of the lawyers on the other side. On the face of the judge.

He feels his lawyer's hand on his arm and he would have it be over. Have everything be over. But he knows it has only just begun.

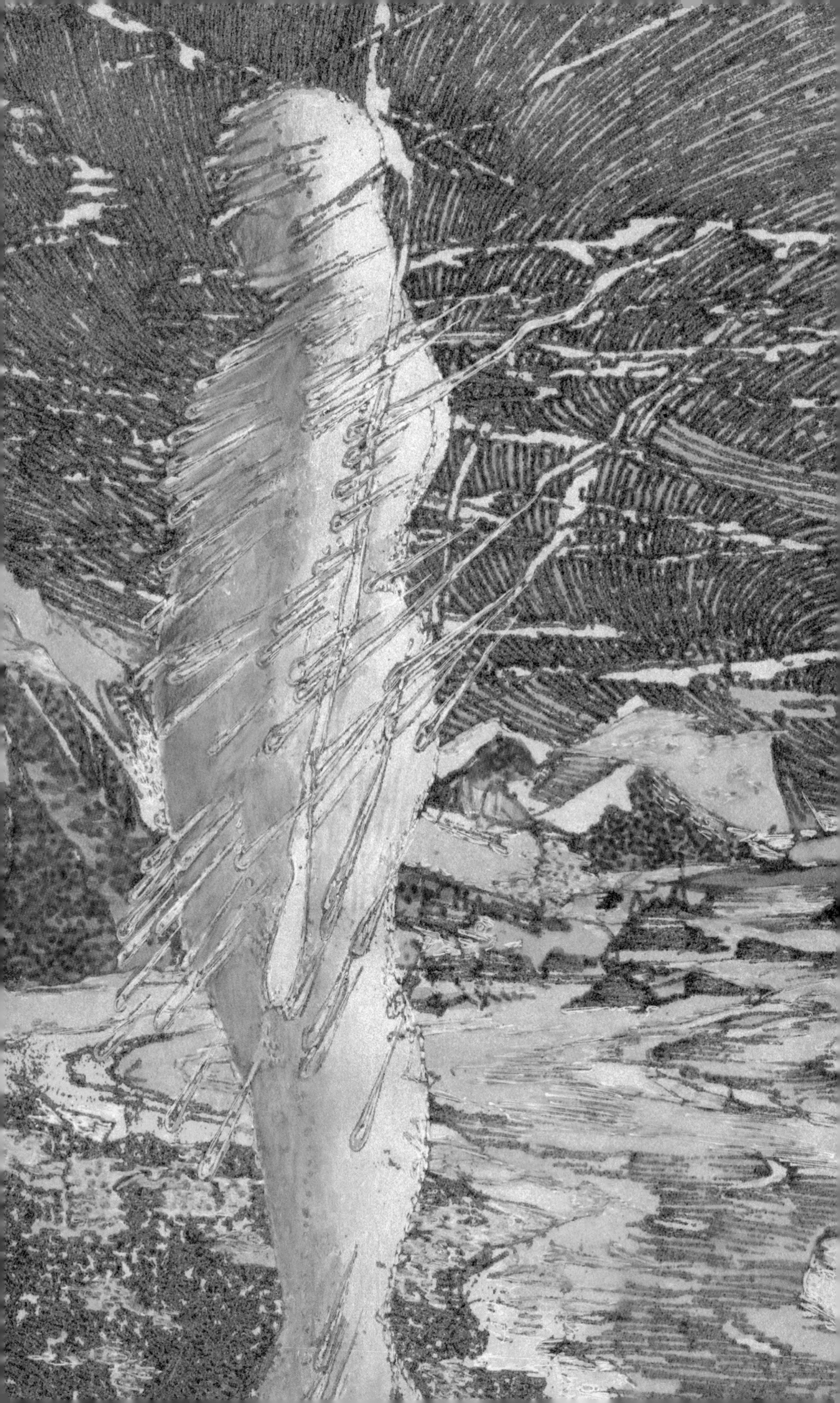

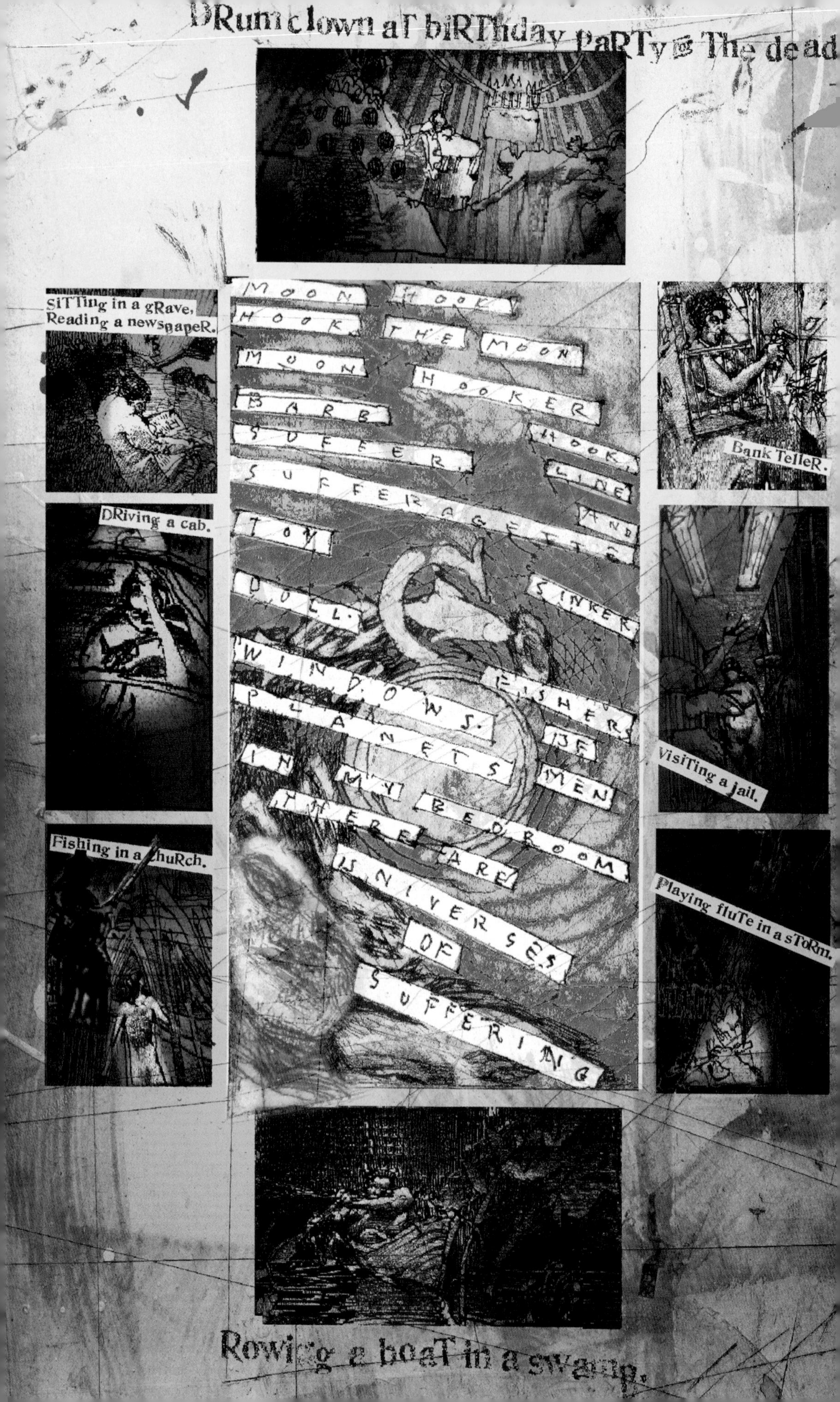

DRum clown aT biRThday paRTy The dead
SITTing in a gRave, Reading a newspapeR.
MOON HOOK
HOOK THE MOON
MOON HOOKER
BARB
SUFFER.
HOOK LINE AND
SUFFERAGETTE
TOY
DOLL.
SINKER
WINDOWS.
FISHER
PLANETS
MEN
IN MY BEDROOM.
THERE ARE
UNIVERSES OF
SUFFERING
Bank TelleR.
DRiving a cab.
VisiTing a jail.
Fishing in a chuRch.
Playing fluTe in a sToRm.
Rowing a boaT in a swamp.

A) If you can't be happy where you are, you can't be happy anywhere. Discuss, with examples from your own life.

B) Hell is Other People. Do you agree? Demonstrate how this might or might not apply in the case of:

i) The Armenian Massacres of 1915

ii) Either the life of Algernon Charles Swinburne or the death of Walt Disney

iii) the darkness before creation

(Answer two of three.)

C) Construct an analogy using the saline nature of either tears or the sea and the salt that makes a dish palatable and adds piquance and savour.

(Examinees are encouraged to refer to either the third daughter of Llyr or Lot's wife, but not both.)

D) If I was God I would abolish...............

Complete in 250 words or less. Physical practicalities and human nature are to be respected. The Law of Conservation of Happiness may not be violated.

(Counts for 50% of your final score.)

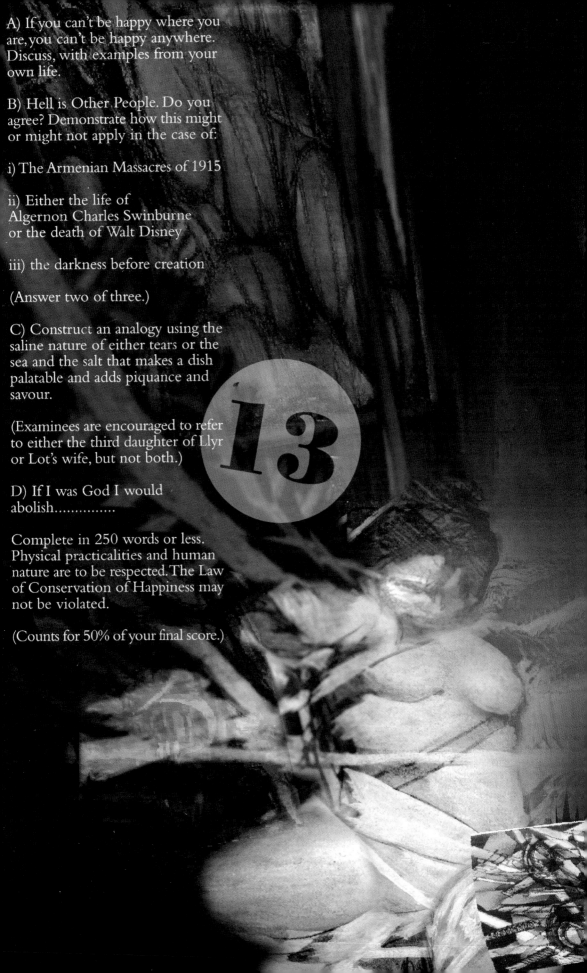

She had waited until her husband and children were far away, and had driven into the snowy woods, and ended it. Just let it all go.

She had wanted the pain to stop. The heart-hurt. She slept her way into death, only waking when the Highway Patrol found her body.

She was cold, rigid, frozen, when they found her.

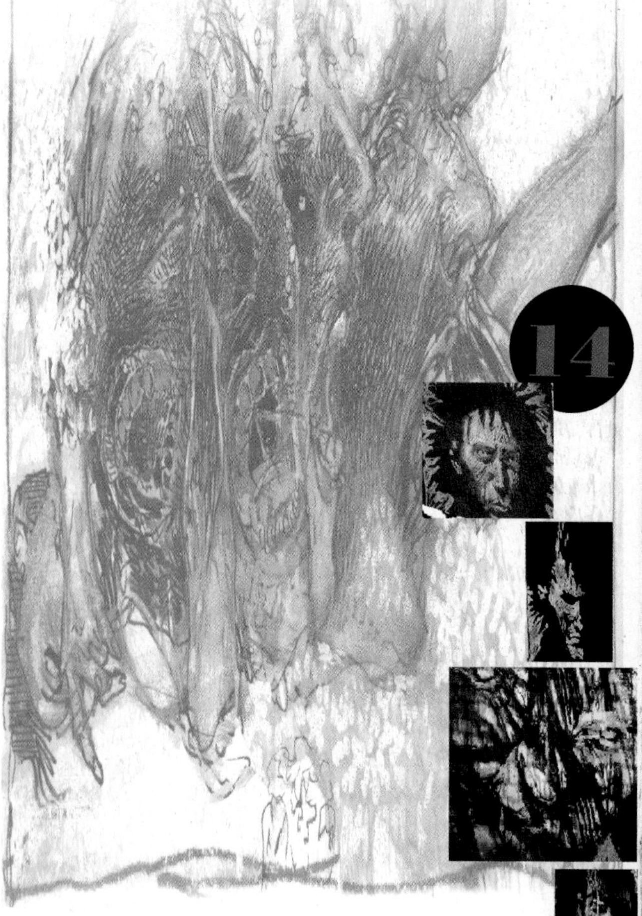

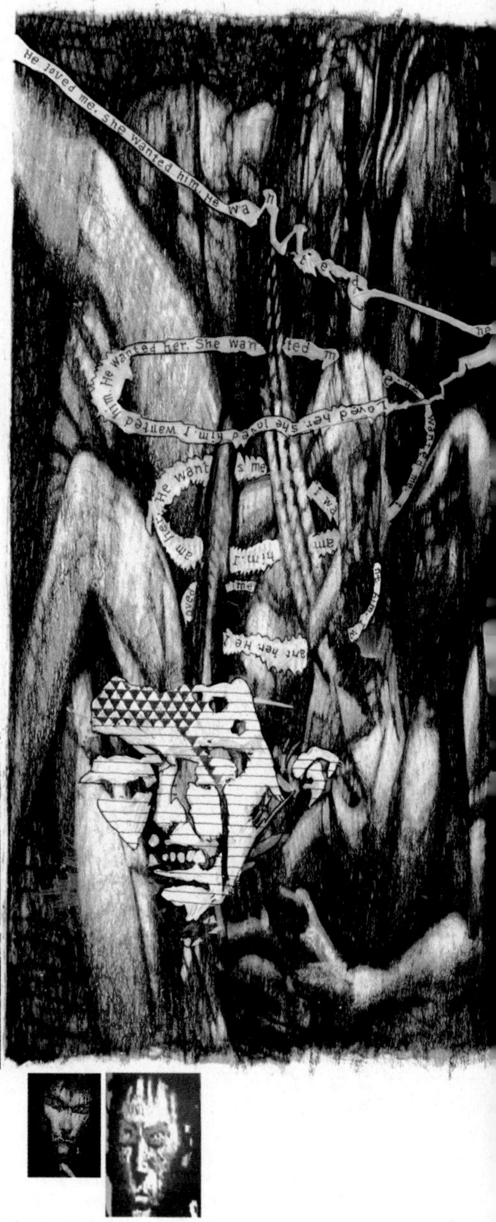
He loved me. She wanted him.
He wanted her. She wan
14

Someone like that, said the patrolwoman. You'd think she'd have everything to live for.

She tried to speak, to tell them that that was what made the pain unbearable but, like someone caught in a bad dream, she could not make herself heard. She screamed, and n sound came out. She watched as they took her body away.

She sat by the side of the road, in the snow, all bodiless and afraid, waiting for the happine to start.

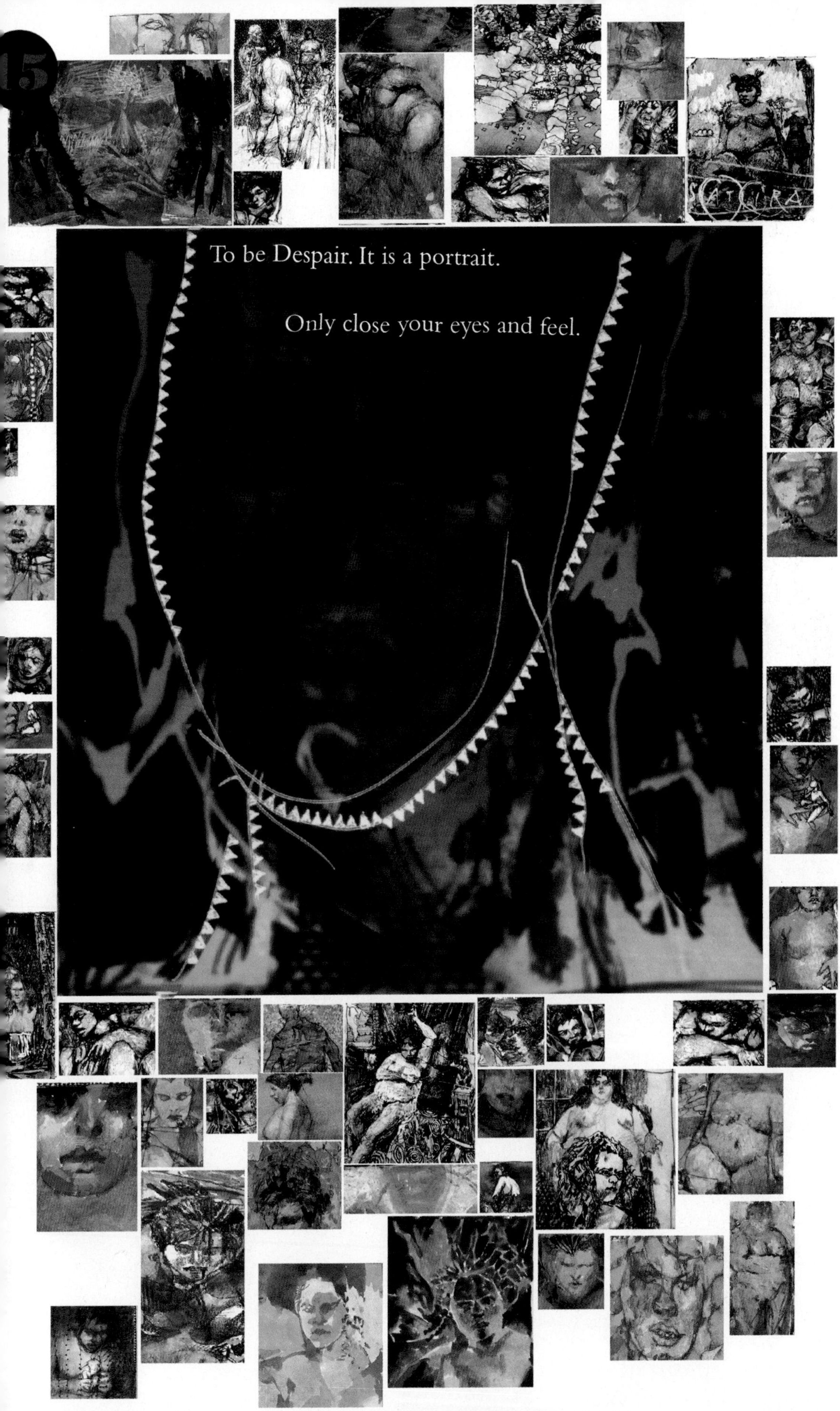
15
To be Despair. It is a portrait.
Only close your eyes and feel.

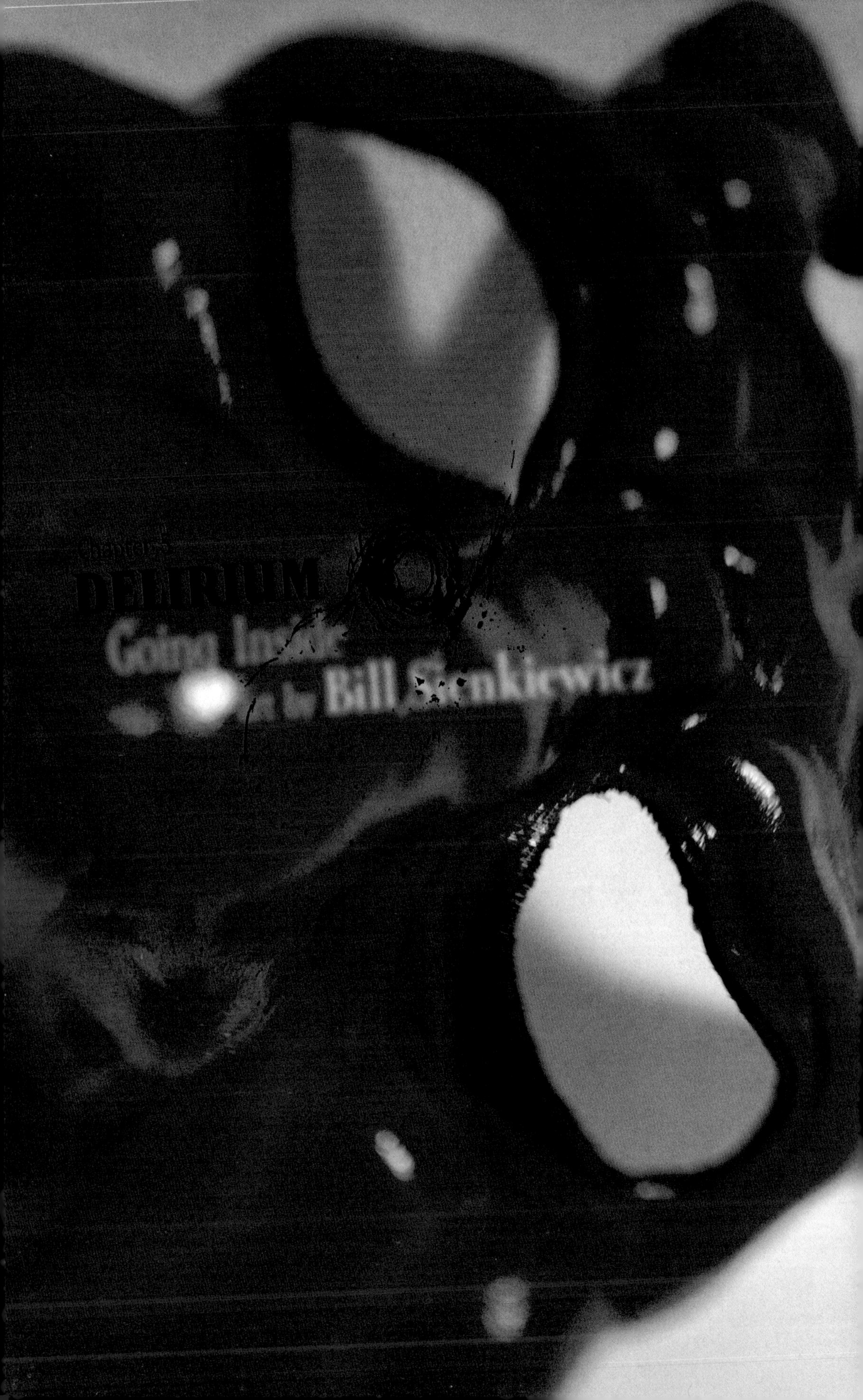
DELIRIUM

DELIRIUM

Going Inside

art by **Bill Sienkiewicz**

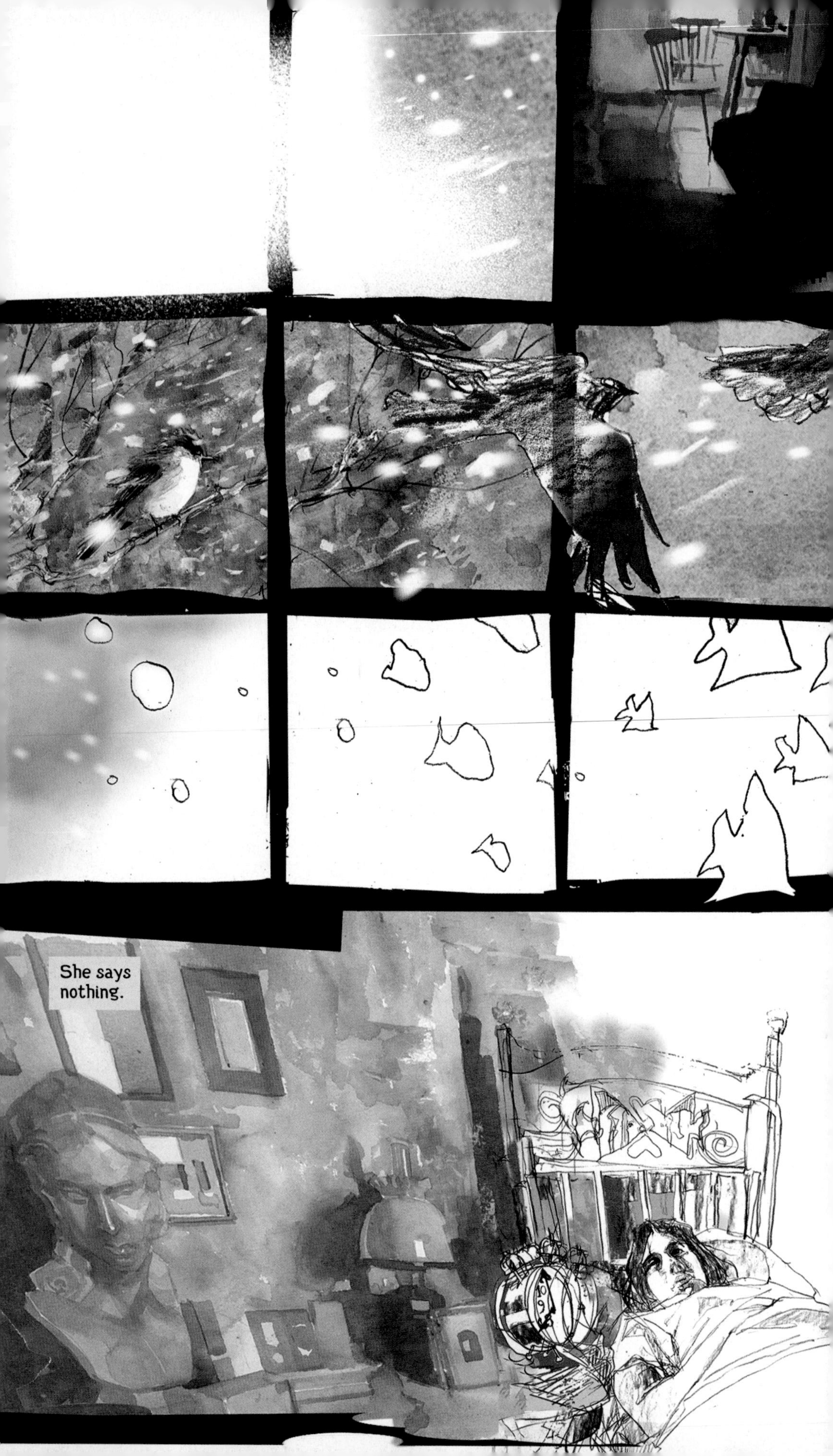
She says nothing.

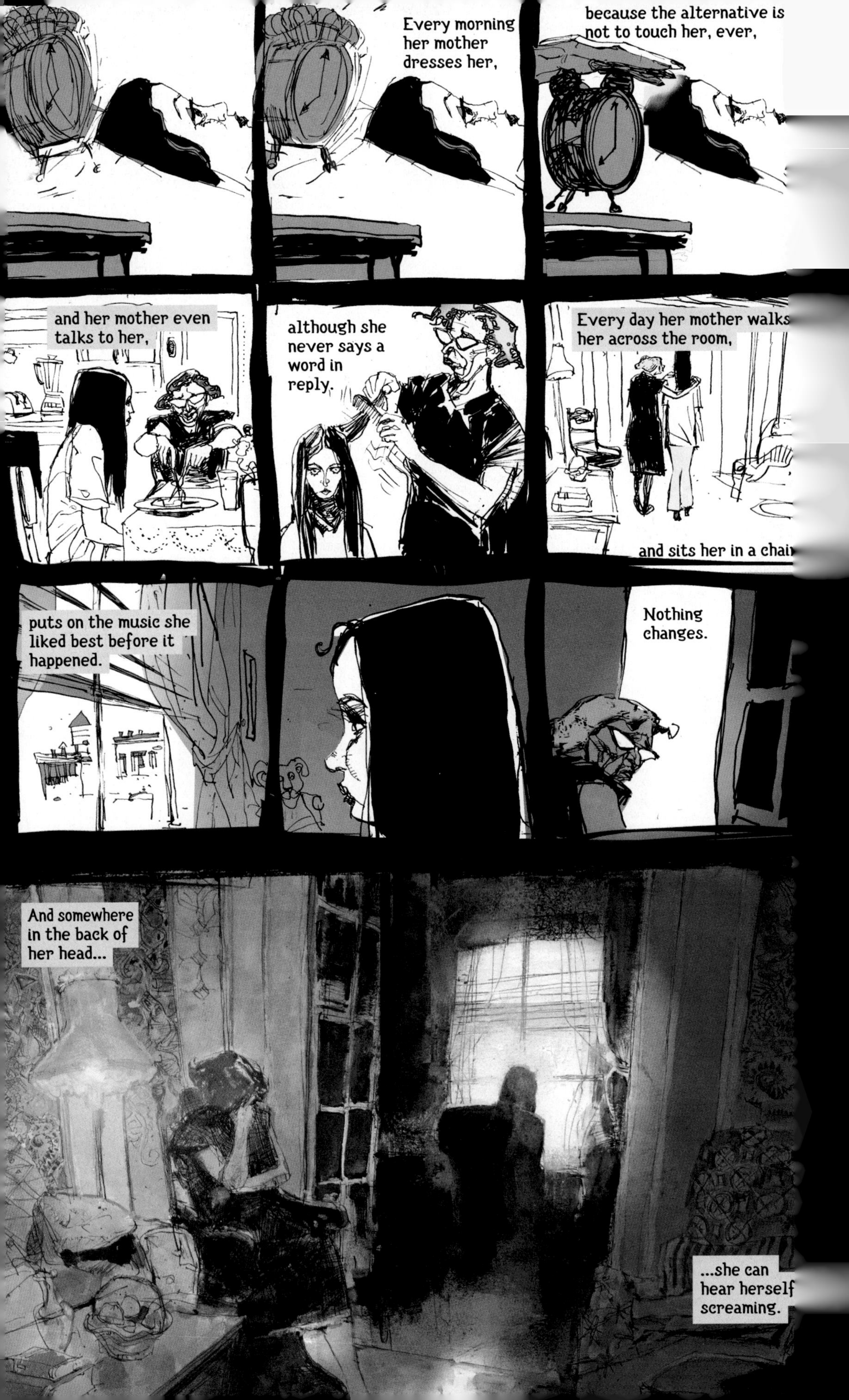
Every morning her mother dresses her,
because the alternative is not to touch her, ever,
and her mother even talks to her,
although she never says a word in reply.
Every day her mother walks her across the room,
and sits her in a chai
puts on the music she liked best before it happened.
Nothing changes.
And somewhere in the back of her head...
...she can hear herself screaming.

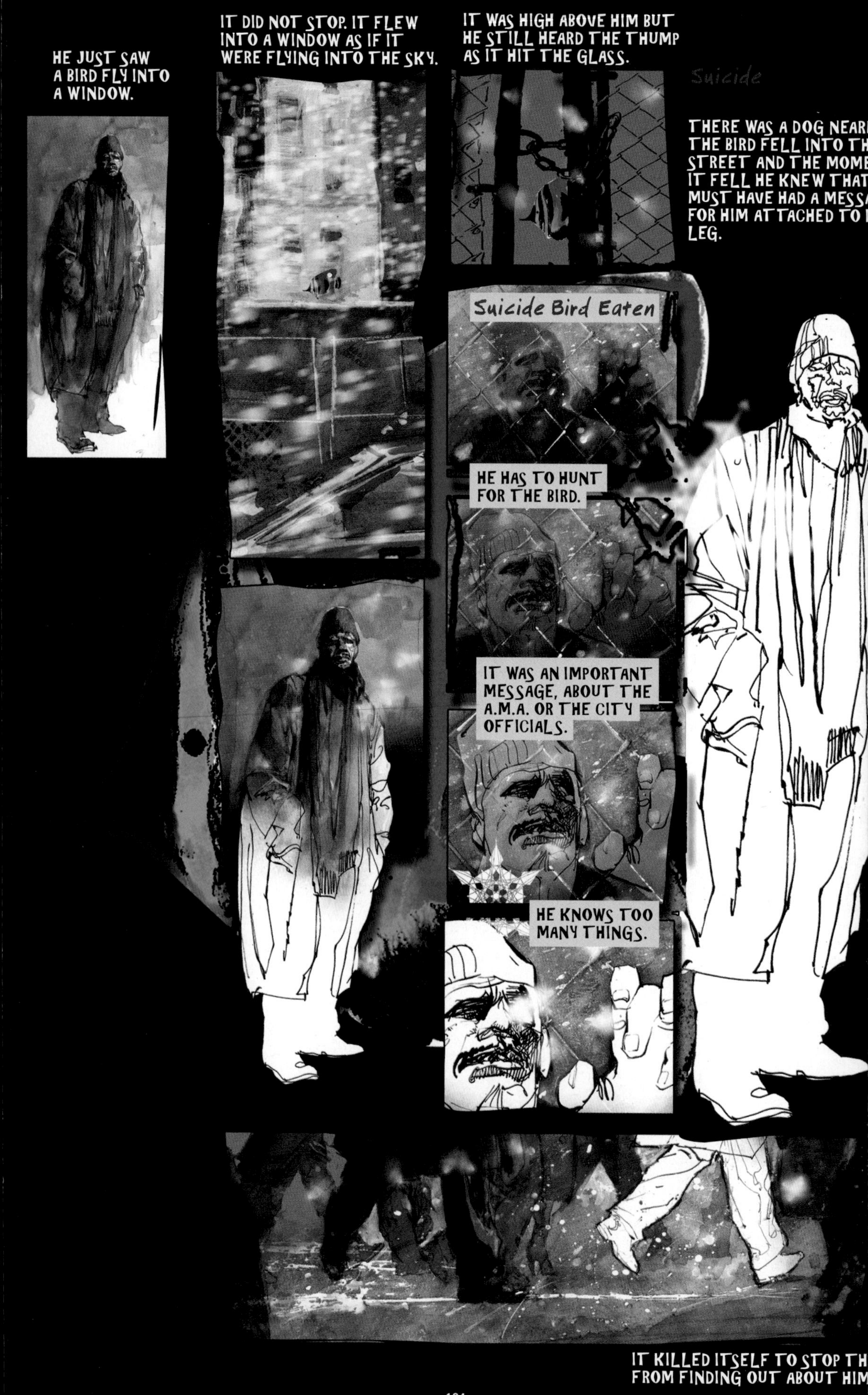

HE JUST SAW A BIRD FLY INTO A WINDOW.
IT DID NOT STOP. IT FLEW INTO A WINDOW AS IF IT WERE FLYING INTO THE SKY.
IT WAS HIGH ABOVE HIM BUT HE STILL HEARD THE THUMP AS IT HIT THE GLASS.
Suicide
THERE WAS A DOG NEAR
THE BIRD FELL INTO TH
STREET AND THE MOME
IT FELL HE KNEW THAT
MUST HAVE HAD A MESS
FOR HIM ATTACHED TO
LEG.
Suicide Bird Eaten
HE HAS TO HUNT FOR THE BIRD.
IT WAS AN IMPORTANT MESSAGE, ABOUT THE A.M.A. OR THE CITY OFFICIALS.
HE KNOWS TOO MANY THINGS.
IT KILLED ITSELF TO STOP TH
FROM FINDING OUT ABOUT HIM

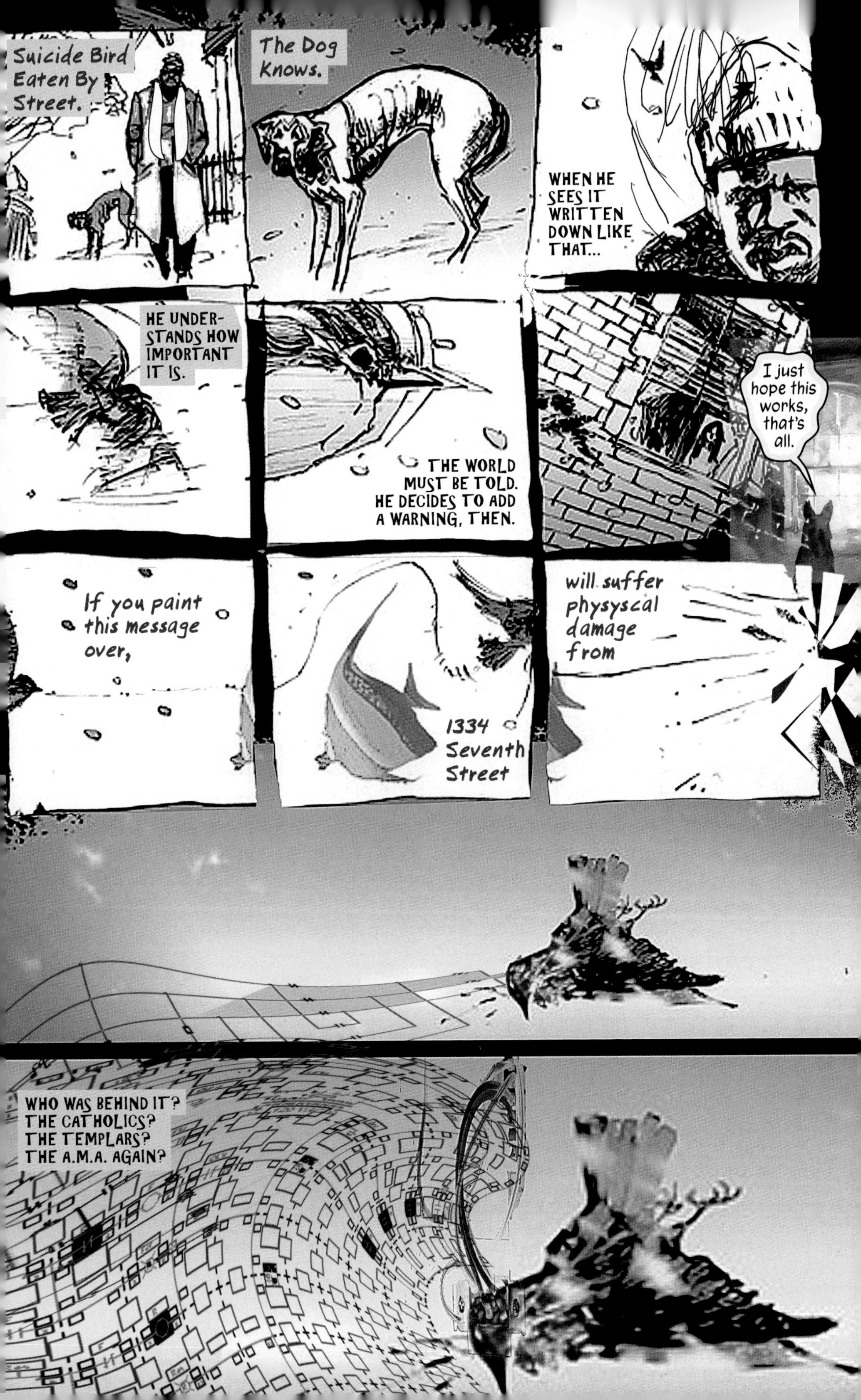

Suicide Bird Eaten By Street.
The Dog Knows.
WHEN HE SEES IT WRITTEN DOWN LIKE THAT...
HE UNDERSTANDS HOW IMPORTANT IT IS.
THE WORLD MUST BE TOLD. HE DECIDES TO ADD A WARNING, THEN.
I just hope this works, that's all.
If you paint this message over,
1334 Seventh Street
will suffer physyscal damage from
WHO WAS BEHIND IT? THE CATHOLICS? THE TEMPLARS? THE A.M.A. AGAIN?

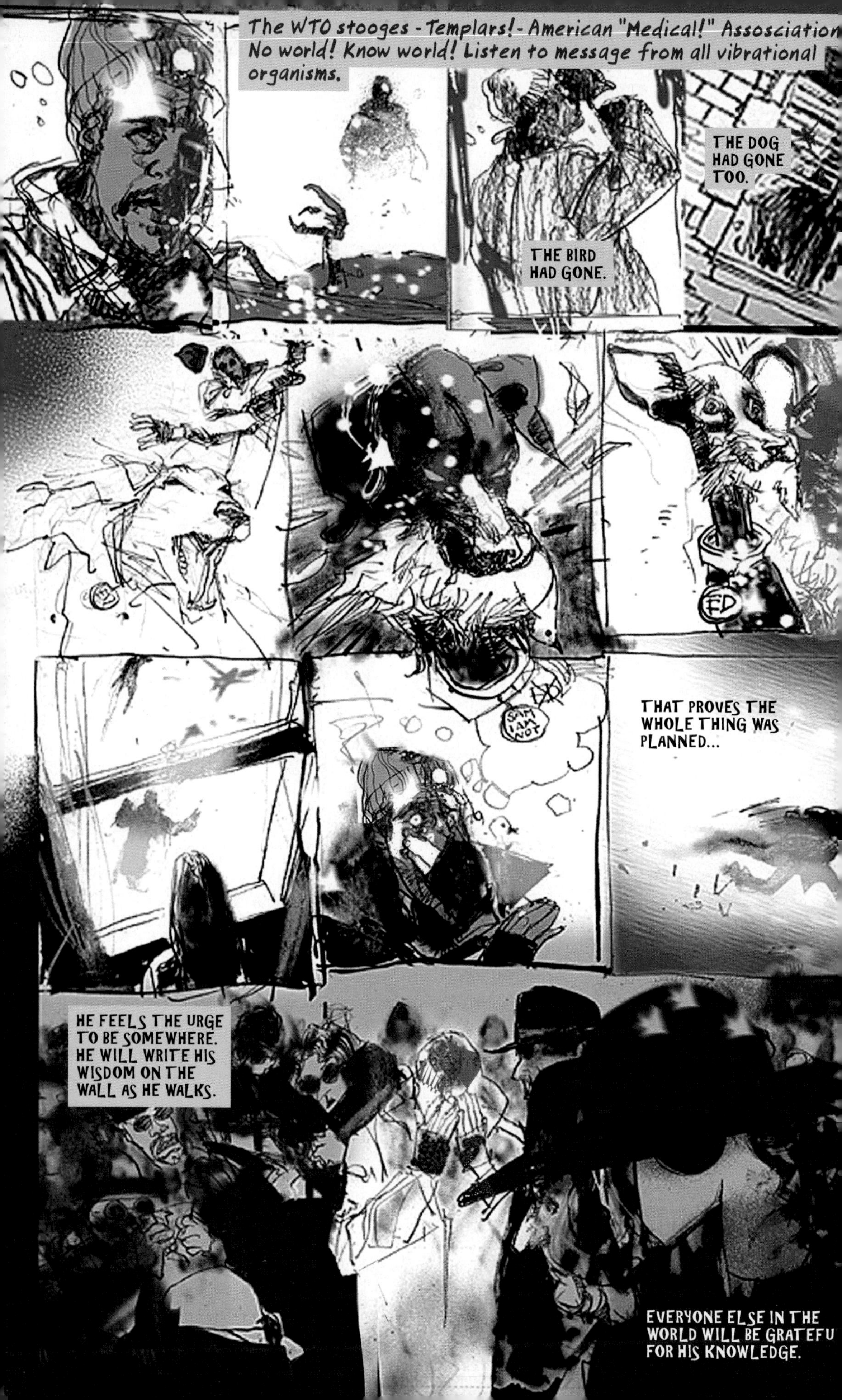

The WTO stooges - Templars! - American "Medical!" Assosciation
No world! Know world! Listen to message from all vibrational organisms.
THE BIRD HAD GONE.
THE DOG HAD GONE TOO.
THAT PROVES THE WHOLE THING WAS PLANNED...
HE FEELS THE URGE TO BE SOMEWHERE. HE WILL WRITE HIS WISDOM ON THE WALL AS HE WALKS.
EVERYONE ELSE IN THE WORLD WILL BE GRATEFU
FOR HIS KNOWLEDGE.

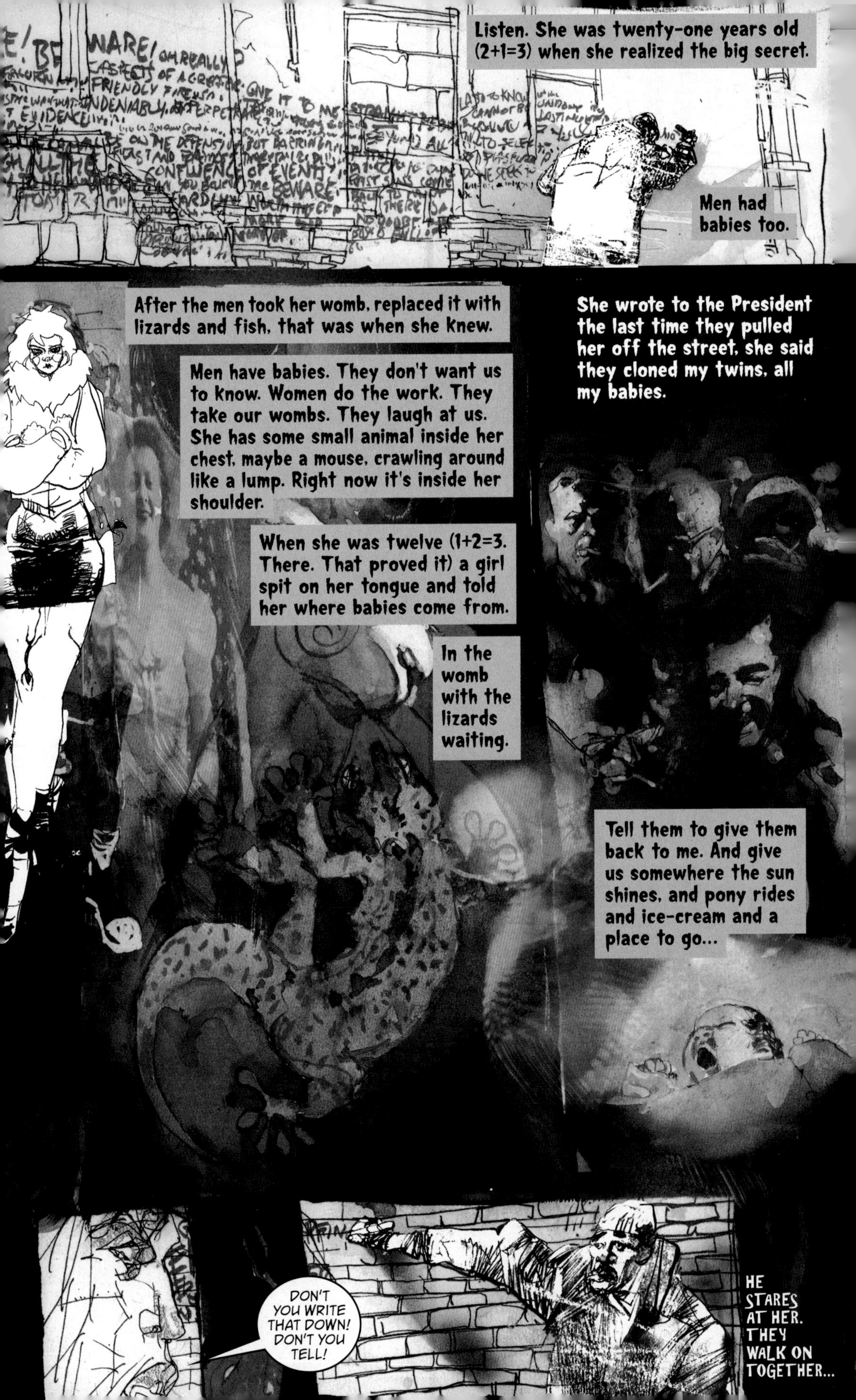
Listen. She was twenty-one years old (2+1=3) when she realized the big secret.
Men had babies too.
After the men took her womb, replaced it with lizards and fish, that was when she knew.
Men have babies. They don't want us to know. Women do the work. They take our wombs. They laugh at us. She has some small animal inside her chest, maybe a mouse, crawling around like a lump. Right now it's inside her shoulder.
When she was twelve (1+2=3. There. That proved it) a girl spit on her tongue and told her where babies come from.
In the womb with the lizards waiting.
She wrote to the President the last time they pulled her off the street, she said they cloned my twins, all my babies.
Tell them to give them back to me. And give us somewhere the sun shines, and pony rides and ice-cream and a place to go...
DON'T YOU WRITE THAT DOWN! DON'T YOU TELL!
HE STARES AT HER. THEY WALK ON TOGETHER...

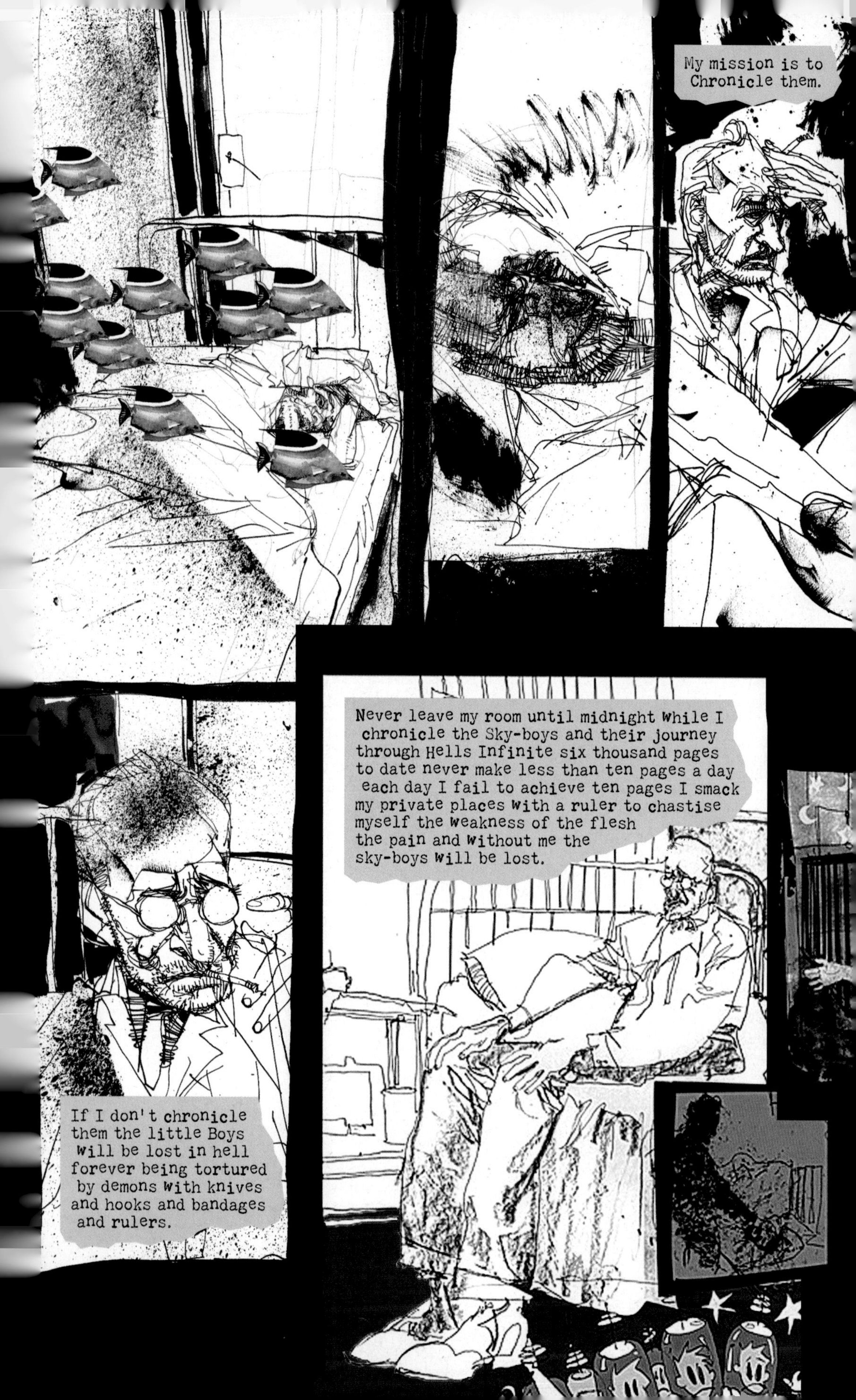

My mission is to Chronicle them.
Never leave my room until midnight while I chronicle the Sky-boys and their journey through Hells Infinite six thousand pages to date never make less than ten pages a day each day I fail to achieve ten pages I smack my private places with a ruler to chastise myself the weakness of the flesh the pain and without me the sky-boys will be lost.
If I don't chronicle them the little Boys will be lost in hell forever being tortured by demons with knives and hooks and bandages and rulers.

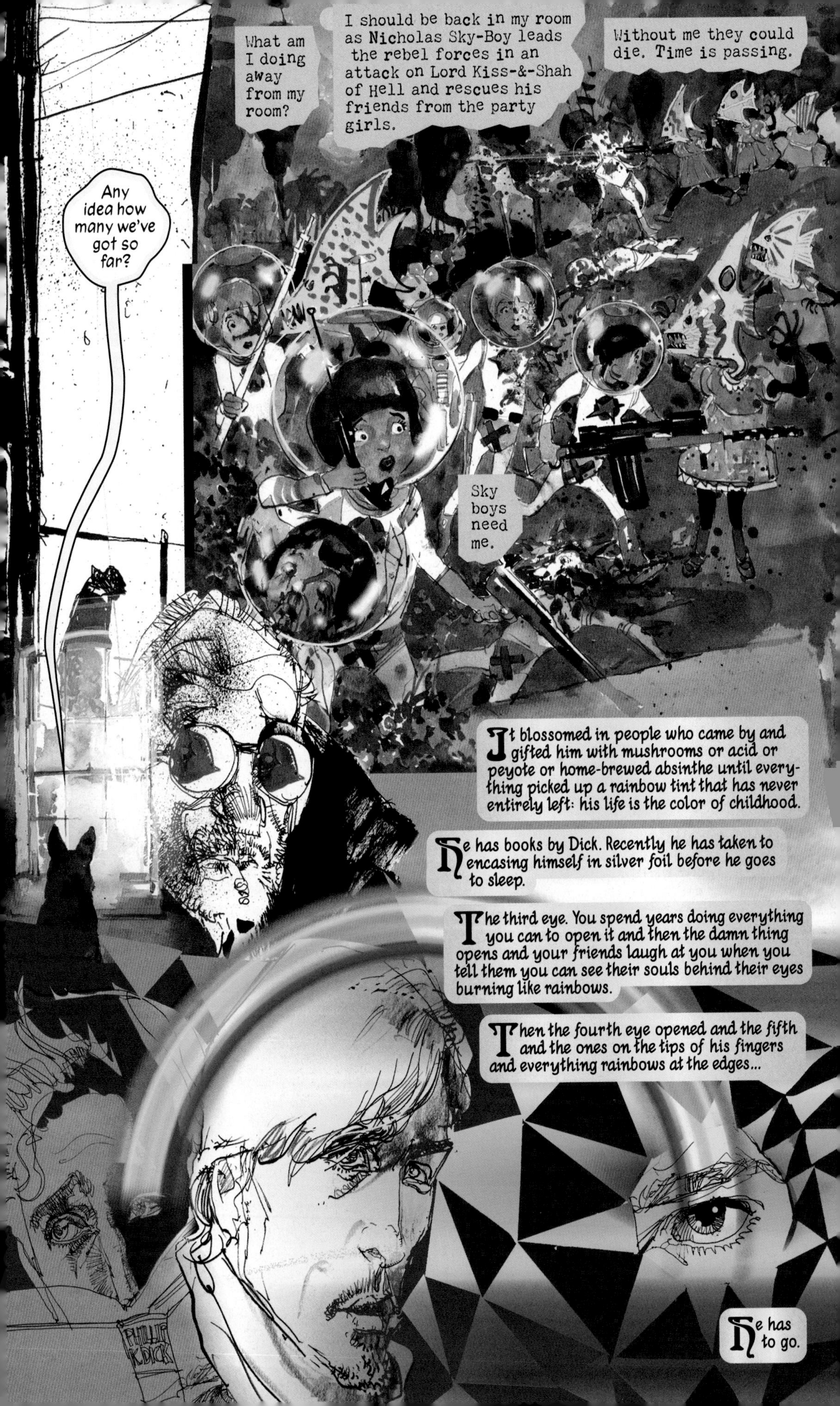

What am I doing away from my room?
I should be back in my room as Nicholas Sky-Boy leads the rebel forces in an attack on Lord Kiss-&-Shah of Hell and rescues his friends from the party girls.
Without me they could die. Time is passing.
Any idea how many we've got so far?
Sky boys need me.
It blossomed in people who came by and gifted him with mushrooms or acid or peyote or home-brewed absinthe until everything picked up a rainbow tint that has never entirely left: his life is the color of childhood.
He has books by Dick. Recently he has taken to encasing himself in silver foil before he goes to sleep.
The third eye. You spend years doing everything you can to open it and then the damn thing opens and your friends laugh at you when you tell them you can see their souls behind their eyes burning like rainbows.
Then the fourth eye opened and the fifth and the ones on the tips of his fingers and everything rainbows at the edges...
He has to go.

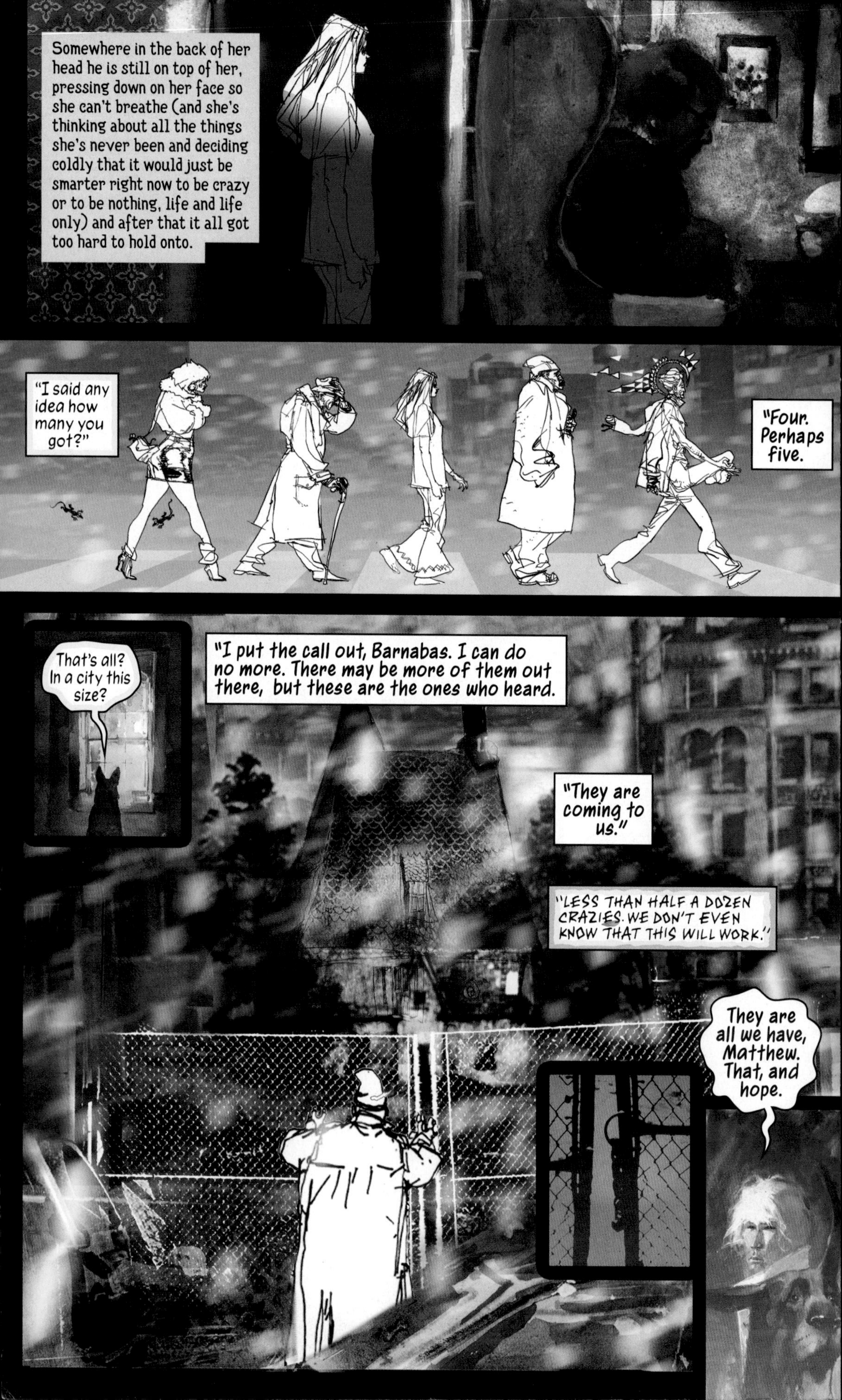
Somewhere in the back of her head he is still on top of her, pressing down on her face so she can't breathe (and she's thinking about all the things she's never been and deciding coldly that it would just be smarter right now to be crazy or to be nothing, life and life only) and after that it all got too hard to hold onto.
"I said any idea how many you got?"
"Four. Perhaps five.
That's all? In a city this size?
"I put the call out, Barnabas. I can do no more. There may be more of them out there, but these are the ones who heard.
"They are coming to us."
"LESS THAN HALF A DOZEN CRAZIES. WE DON'T EVEN KNOW THAT THIS WILL WORK."
They are all we have, Matthew. That, and hope.

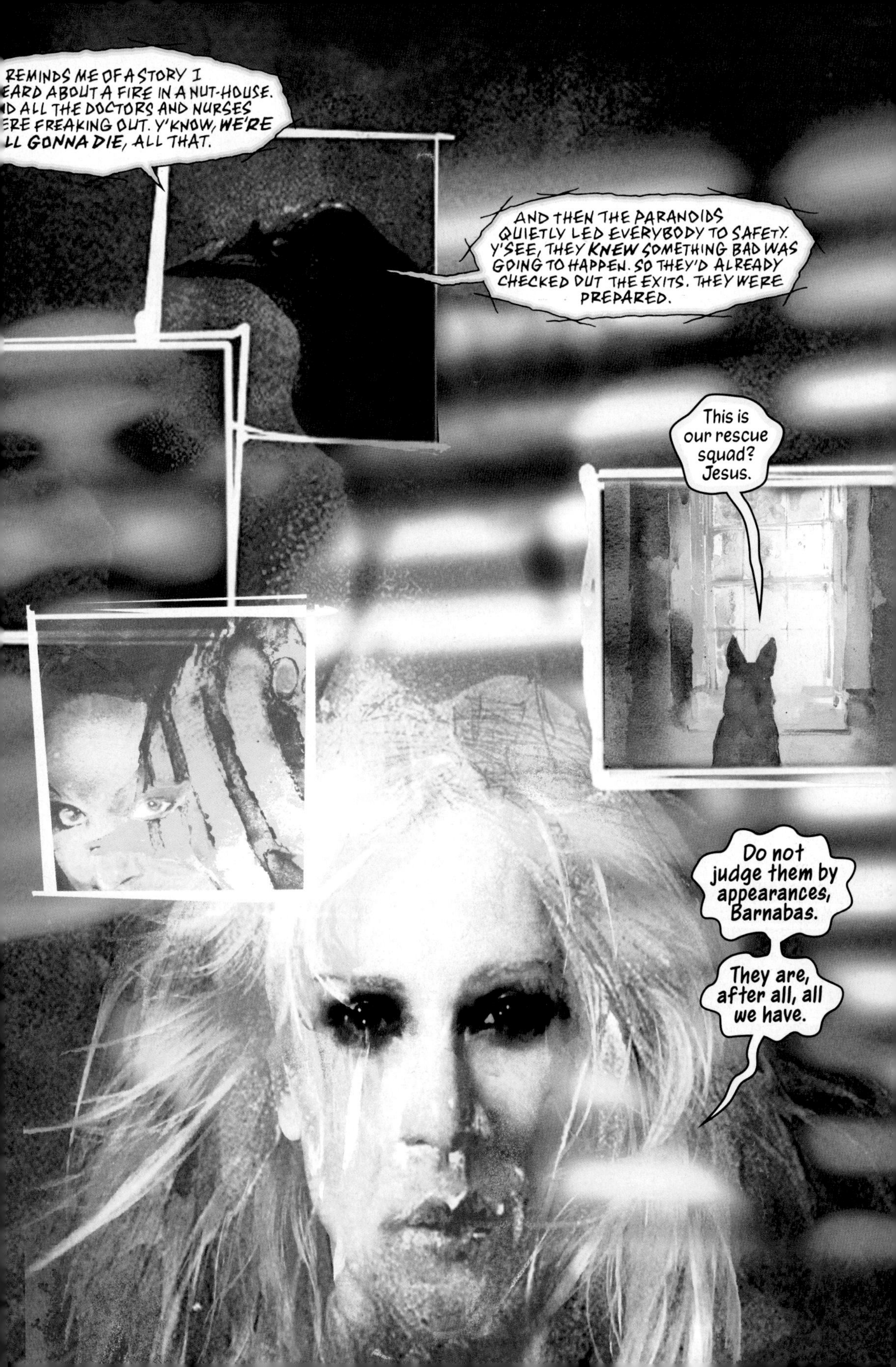
REMINDS ME OF A STORY I
EARD ABOUT A FIRE IN A NUT-HOUSE.
D ALL THE DOCTORS AND NURSES
ERE FREAKING OUT. Y'KNOW, WE'RE
LL GONNA DIE, ALL THAT.
AND THEN THE PARANOIDS QUIETLY LED EVERYBODY TO SAFETY. Y'SEE, THEY KNEW SOMETHING BAD WAS GOING TO HAPPEN. SO THEY'D ALREADY CHECKED OUT THE EXITS. THEY WERE PREPARED.
This is our rescue squad? Jesus.
Do not judge them by appearances, Barnabas.
They are, after all, all we have.

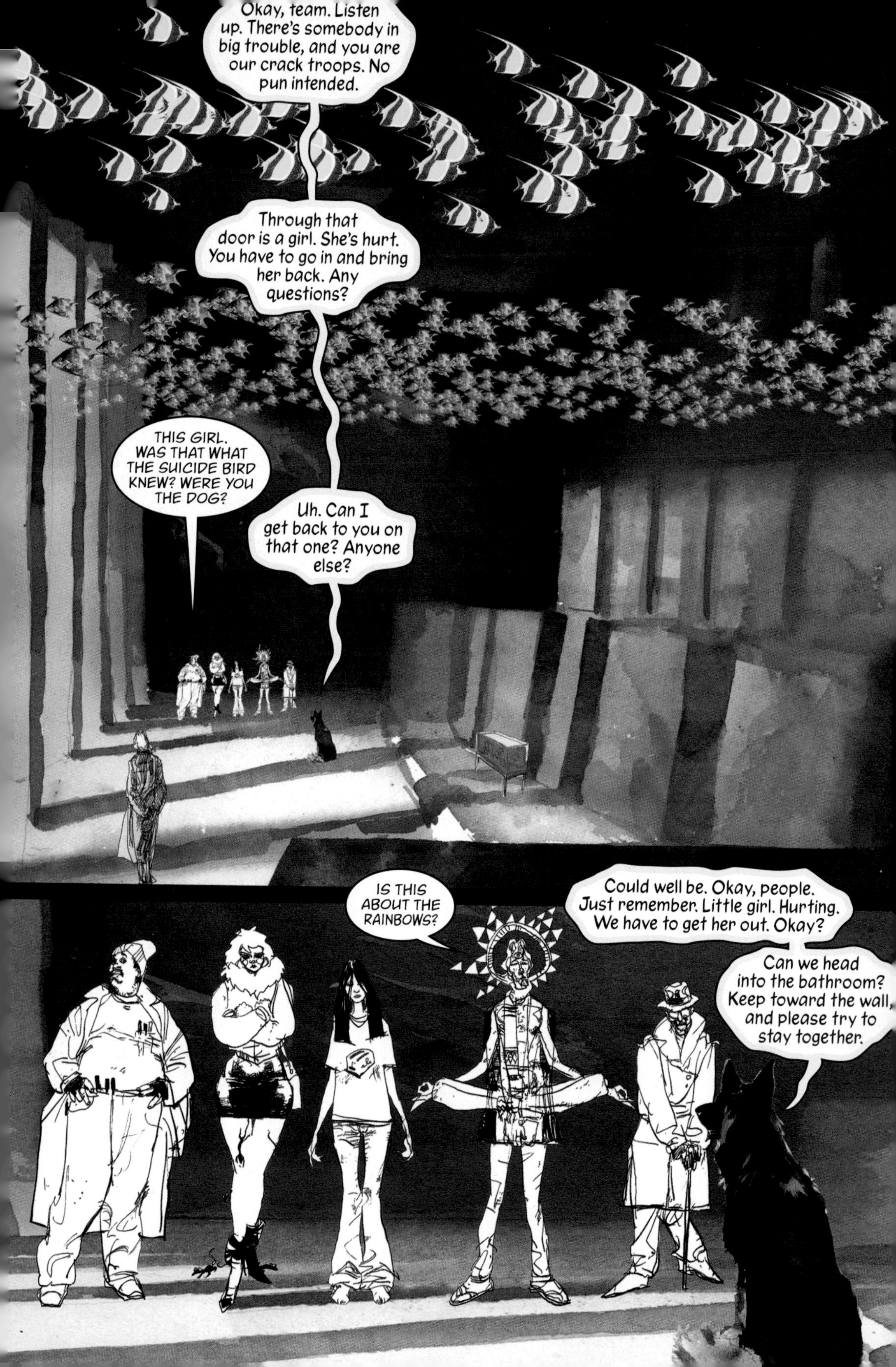
Okay, team. Listen up. There's somebody in big trouble, and you are our crack troops. No pun intended.
Through that door is a girl. She's hurt. You have to go in and bring her back. Any questions?
THIS GIRL. WAS THAT WHAT THE SUICIDE BIRD KNEW? WERE YOU THE DOG?
Uh. Can I get back to you on that one? Anyone else?
IS THIS ABOUT THE RAINBOWS?
Could well be. Okay, people. Just remember. Little girl. Hurting. We have to get her out. Okay?
Can we head into the bathroom? Keep toward the wall, and please try to stay together.

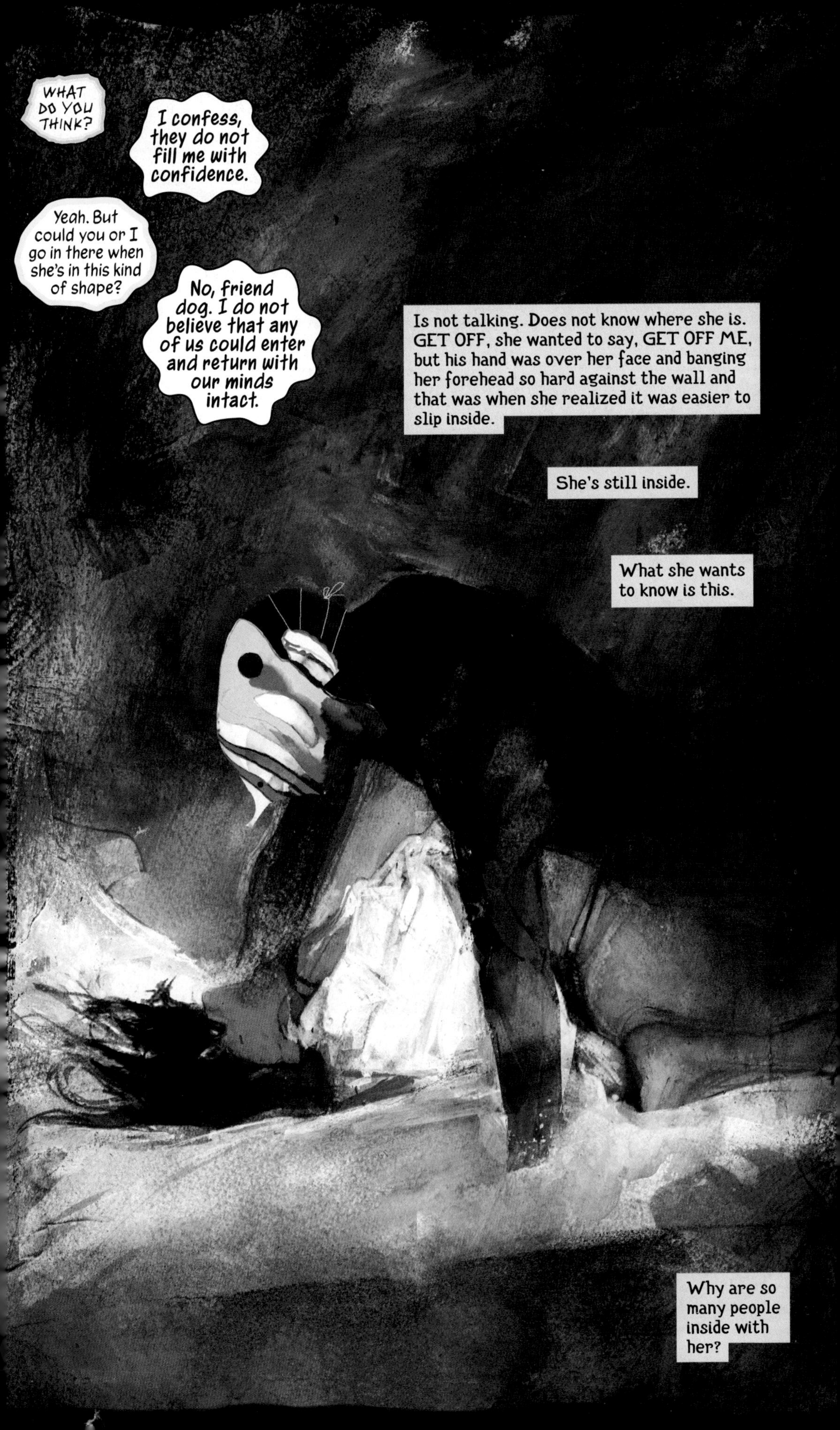
WHAT DO YOU THINK?
I confess, they do not fill me with confidence.
Yeah. But could you or I go in there when she's in this kind of shape?
No, friend dog. I do not believe that any of us could enter and return with our minds intact.
Is not talking. Does not know where she is. GET OFF, she wanted to say, GET OFF ME, but his hand was over her face and banging her forehead so hard against the wall and that was when she realized it was easier to slip inside.
She's still inside.
What she wants to know is this.
Why are so many people inside with her?

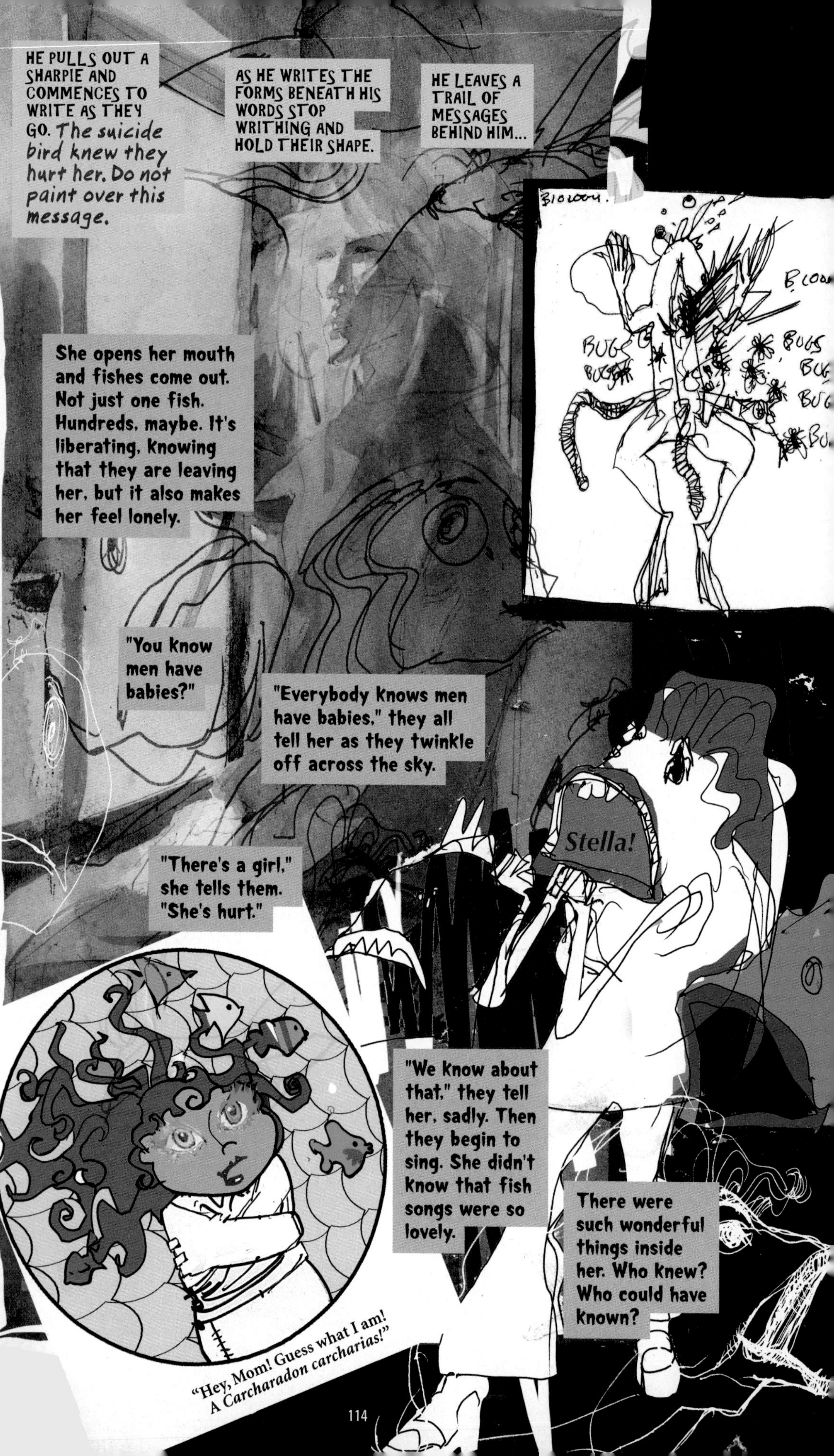
HE PULLS OUT A SHARPIE AND COMMENCES TO WRITE AS THEY GO. The suicide bird knew they hurt her. Do not paint over this message.
AS HE WRITES THE FORMS BENEATH HIS WORDS STOP WRITHING AND HOLD THEIR SHAPE.
HE LEAVES A TRAIL OF MESSAGES BEHIND HIM...
She opens her mouth and fishes come out. Not just one fish. Hundreds, maybe. It's liberating, knowing that they are leaving her, but it also makes her feel lonely.
"You know men have babies?"
"Everybody knows men have babies," they all tell her as they twinkle off across the sky.
Stella!
"There's a girl," she tells them. "She's hurt."
"We know about that," they tell her, sadly. Then they begin to sing. She didn't know that fish songs were so lovely.
There were such wonderful things inside her. Who knew? Who could have known?
"Hey, Mom! Guess what I am! A Carcharadon carcharias!"

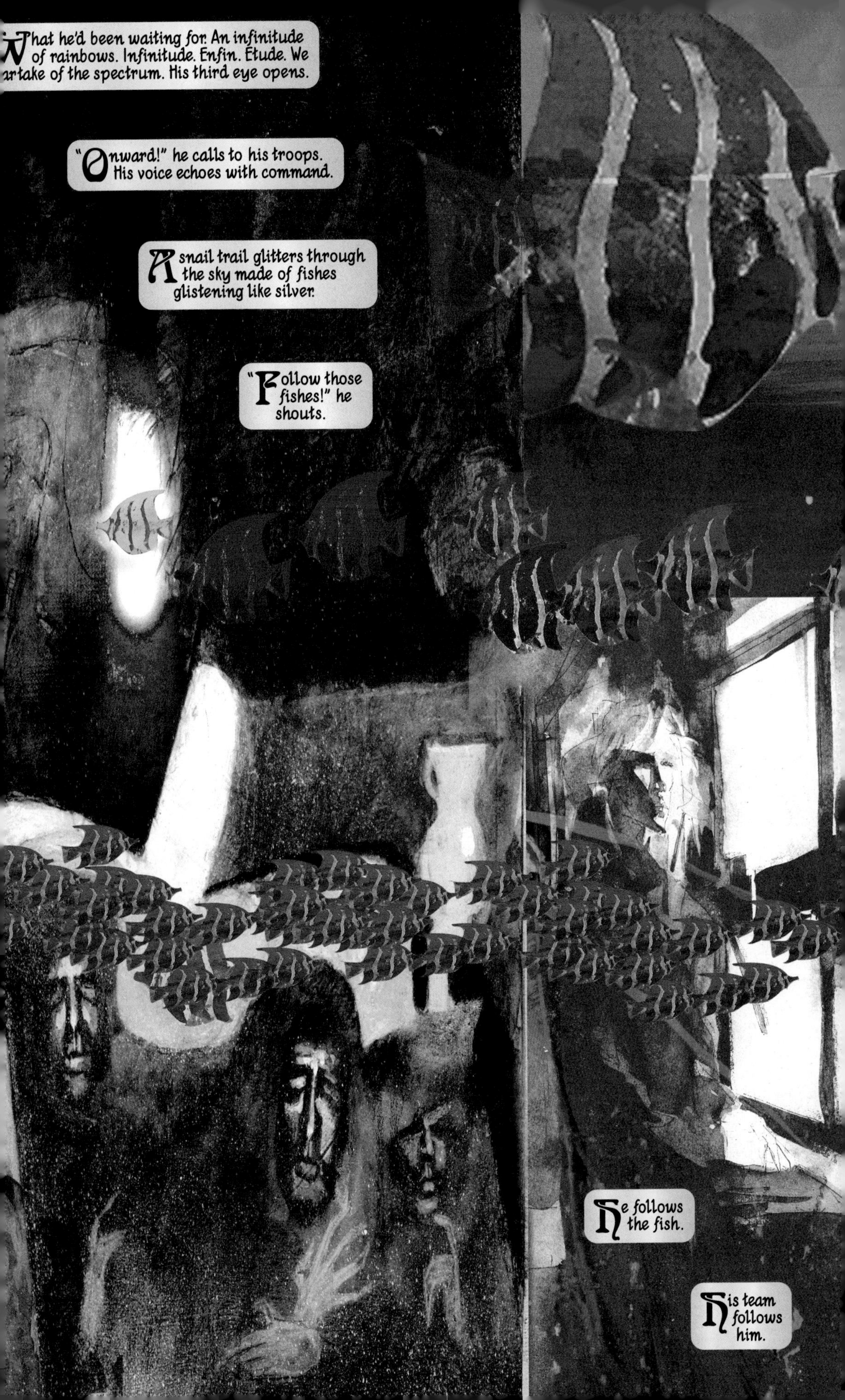
What he'd been waiting for. An infinitude of rainbows. Infinitude. Enfin. Etude. We artake of the spectrum. His third eye opens.
"Onward!" he calls to his troops. His voice echoes with command.
A snail trail glitters through the sky made of fishes glistening like silver.
"Follow those fishes!" he shouts.
He follows the fish.
His team follows him.

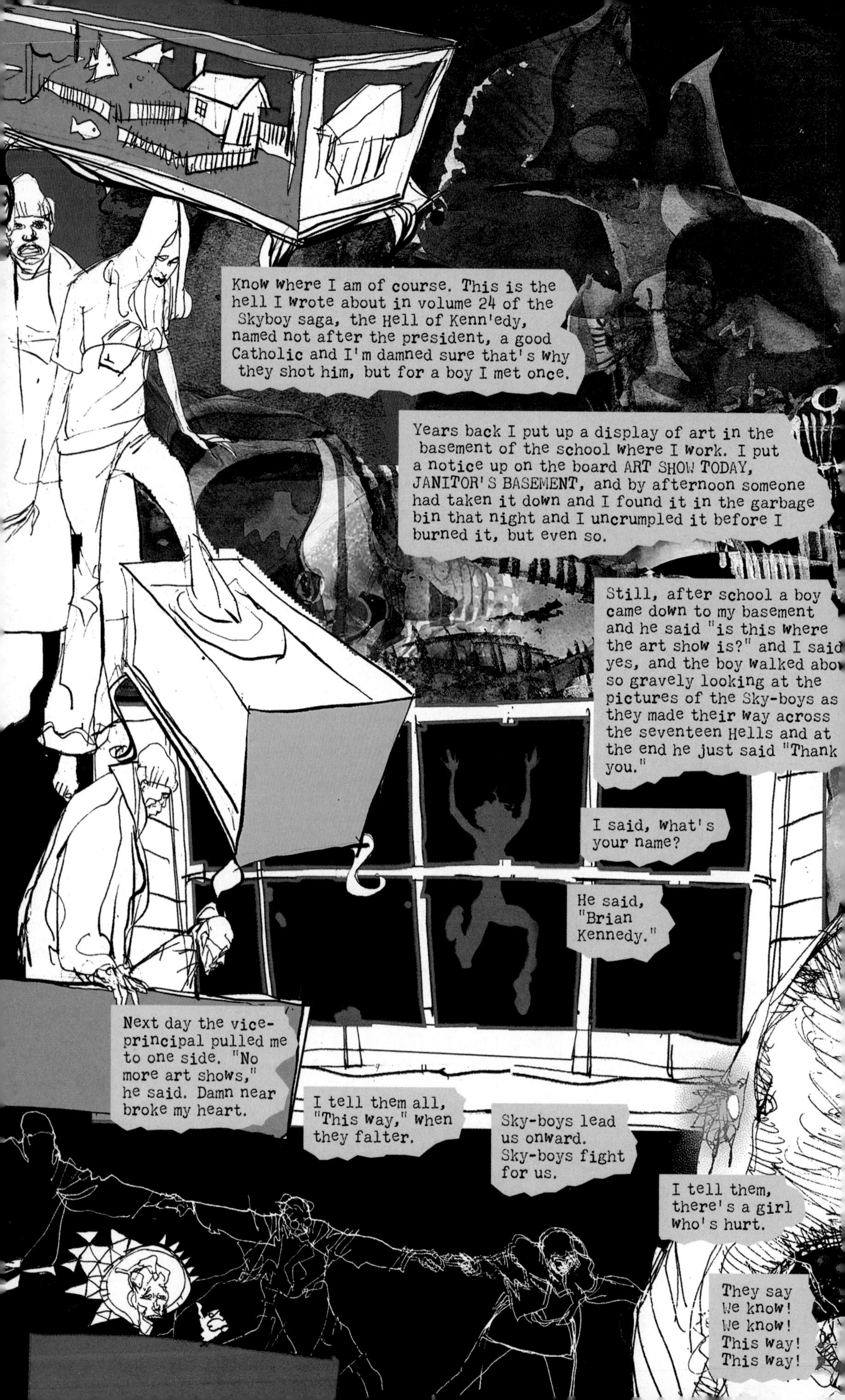
Know where I am of course. This is the hell I wrote about in volume 24 of the Skyboy saga, the Hell of Kenn'edy, named not after the president, a good Catholic and I'm damned sure that's why they shot him, but for a boy I met once.
Years back I put up a display of art in the basement of the school where I work. I put a notice up on the board ART SHOW TODAY, JANITOR'S BASEMENT, and by afternoon someone had taken it down and I found it in the garbage bin that night and I uncrumpled it before I burned it, but even so.
Still, after school a boy came down to my basement and he said "is this where the art show is?" and I said yes, and the boy walked abo so gravely looking at the pictures of the Sky-boys as they made their way across the seventeen Hells and at the end he just said "Thank you."
I said, What's your name?
He said, "Brian Kennedy."
Next day the vice-principal pulled me to one side. "No more art shows," he said. Damn near broke my heart.
I tell them all, "This way," when they falter.
Sky-boys lead us onward. Sky-boys fight for us.
I tell them, there's a girl who's hurt.
They say We know! We know! This way! This way!

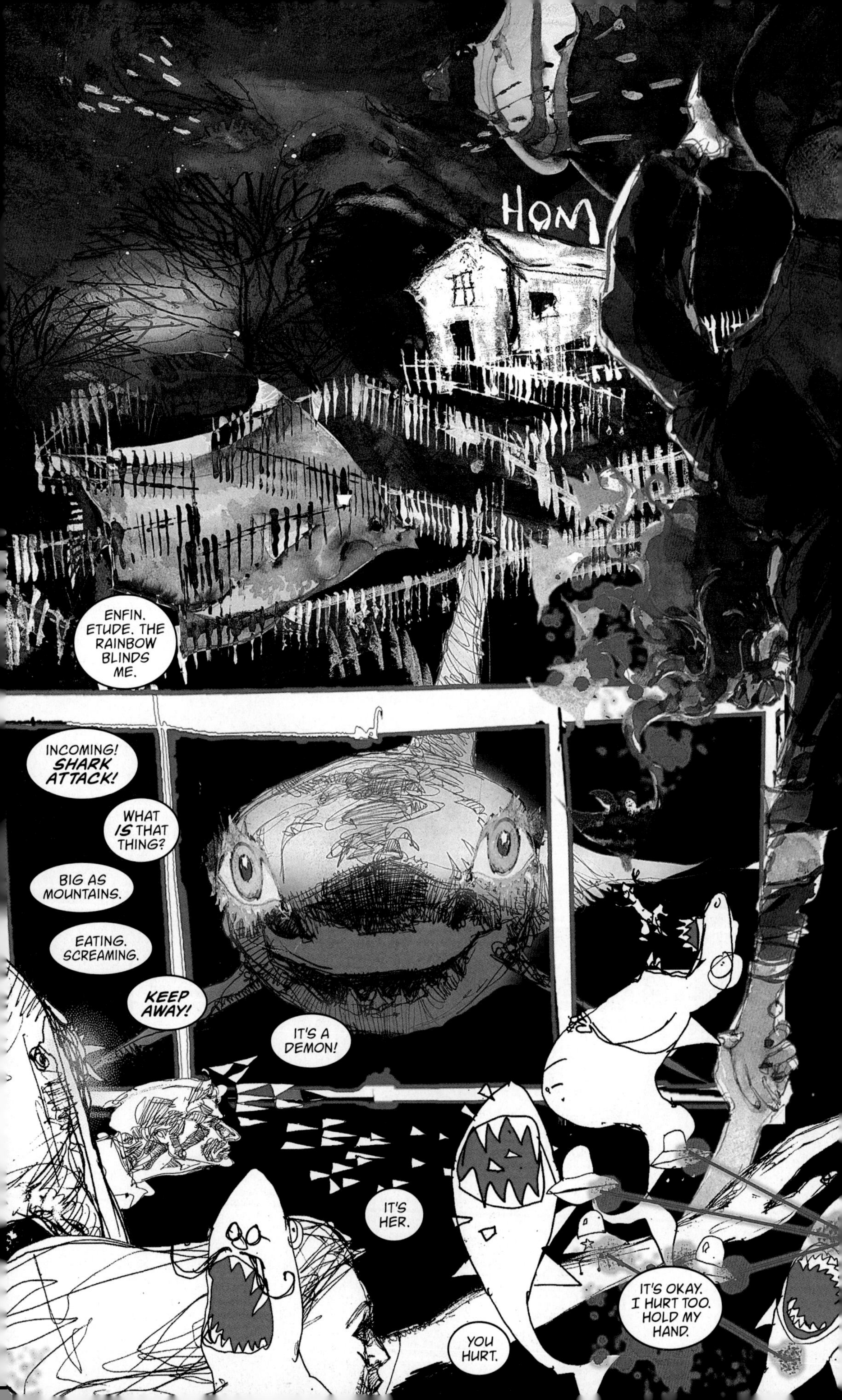
HOM
ENFIN. ETUDE. THE RAINBOW BLINDS ME.
INCOMING! **SHARK ATTACK!**
WHAT ***IS*** THAT THING?
BIG AS MOUNTAINS.
EATING. SCREAMING.
KEEP AWAY!
IT'S A DEMON!
IT'S HER.
YOU HURT.
IT'S OKAY. I HURT TOO. HOLD MY HAND.

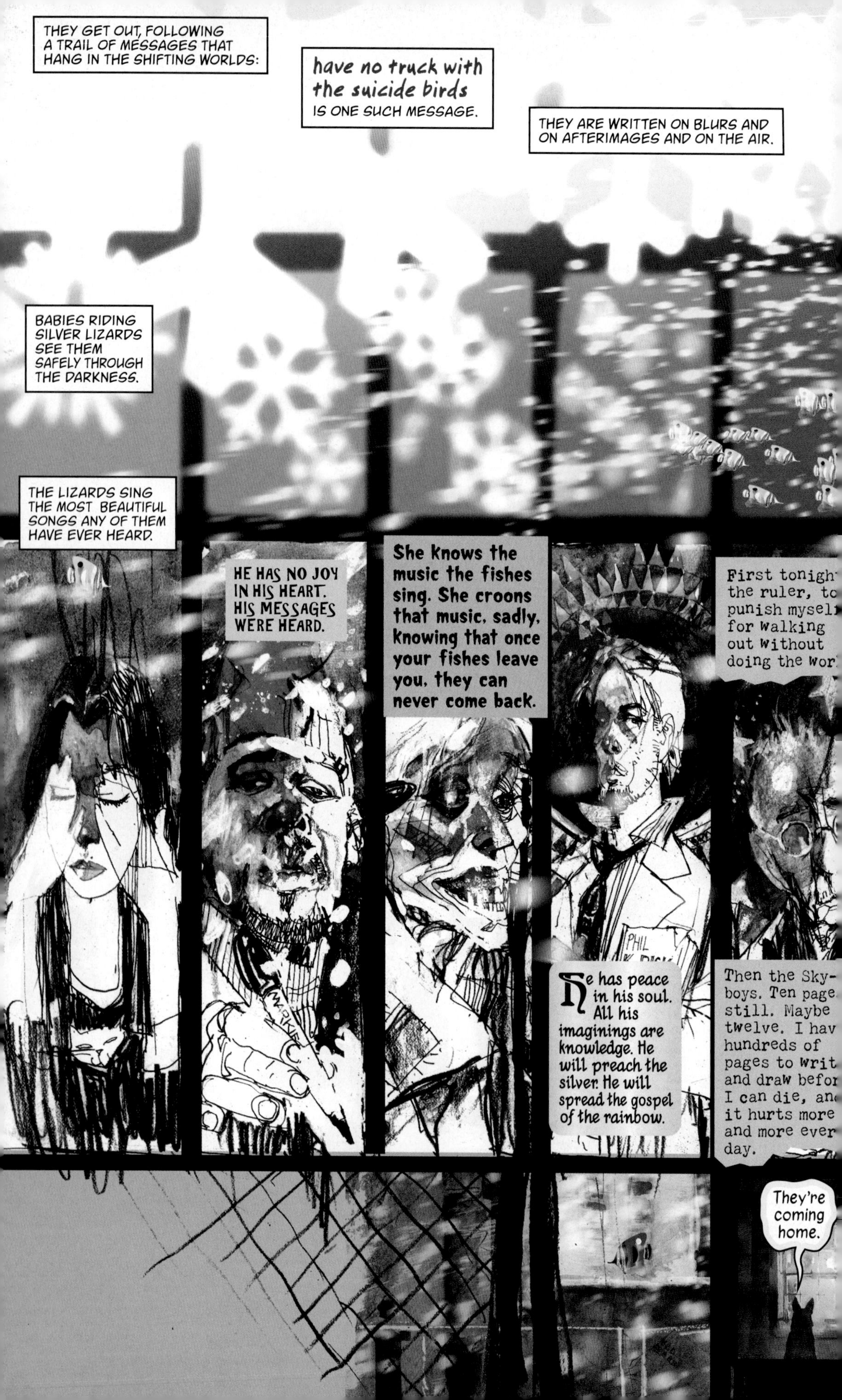

THEY GET OUT, FOLLOWING A TRAIL OF MESSAGES THAT HANG IN THE SHIFTING WORLDS:

have no truck with the suicide birds IS ONE SUCH MESSAGE.

THEY ARE WRITTEN ON BLURS AND ON AFTERIMAGES AND ON THE AIR.

BABIES RIDING SILVER LIZARDS SEE THEM SAFELY THROUGH THE DARKNESS.

THE LIZARDS SING THE MOST BEAUTIFUL SONGS ANY OF THEM HAVE EVER HEARD.

HE HAS NO JOY IN HIS HEART. HIS MESSAGES WERE HEARD.

She knows the music the fishes sing. She croons that music, sadly, knowing that once your fishes leave you, they can never come back.

First tonight the ruler, to punish myself for walking out without doing the wor'

He has peace in his soul. All his imaginings are knowledge. He will preach the silver. He will spread the gospel of the rainbow.

Then the Sky-boys. Ten page still. Maybe twelve. I hav hundreds of pages to writ and draw befor I can die, an it hurts more and more ever day.

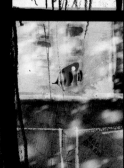

They're coming home.

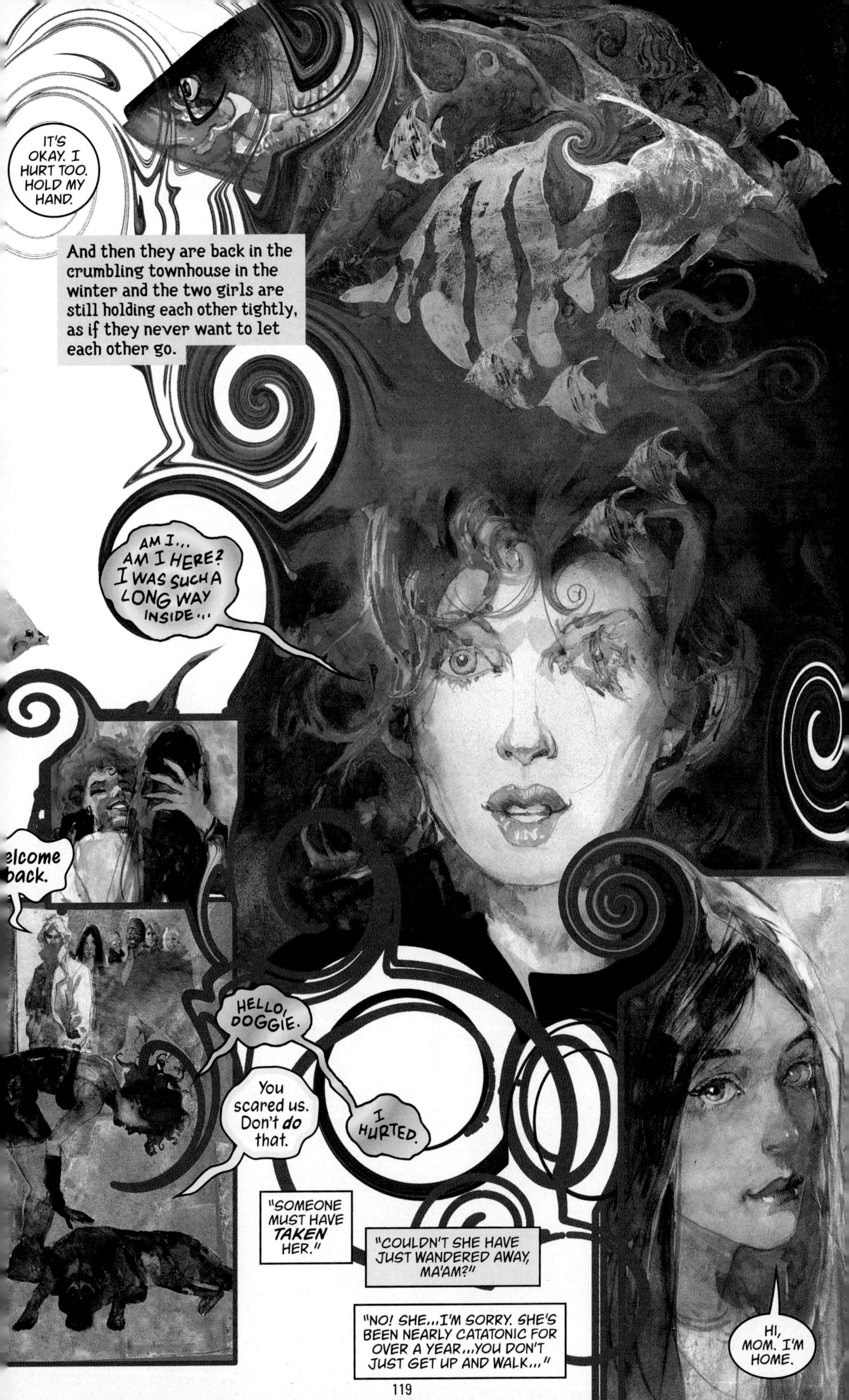
IT'S OKAY. I HURT TOO. HOLD MY HAND.
And then they are back in the crumbling townhouse in the winter and the two girls are still holding each other tightly, as if they never want to let each other go.
AM I... AM I HERE? I WAS SUCH A LONG WAY INSIDE...
elcome back.
HELLO, DOGGIE.
You scared us. Don't *do* that.
I HURTED.
"SOMEONE MUST HAVE *TAKEN* HER."
"COULDN'T SHE HAVE JUST WANDERED AWAY, MA'AM?"
"NO! SHE...I'M SORRY. SHE'S BEEN NEARLY CATATONIC FOR OVER A YEAR...YOU DON'T JUST GET UP AND WALK..."
HI, MOM. I'M HOME.

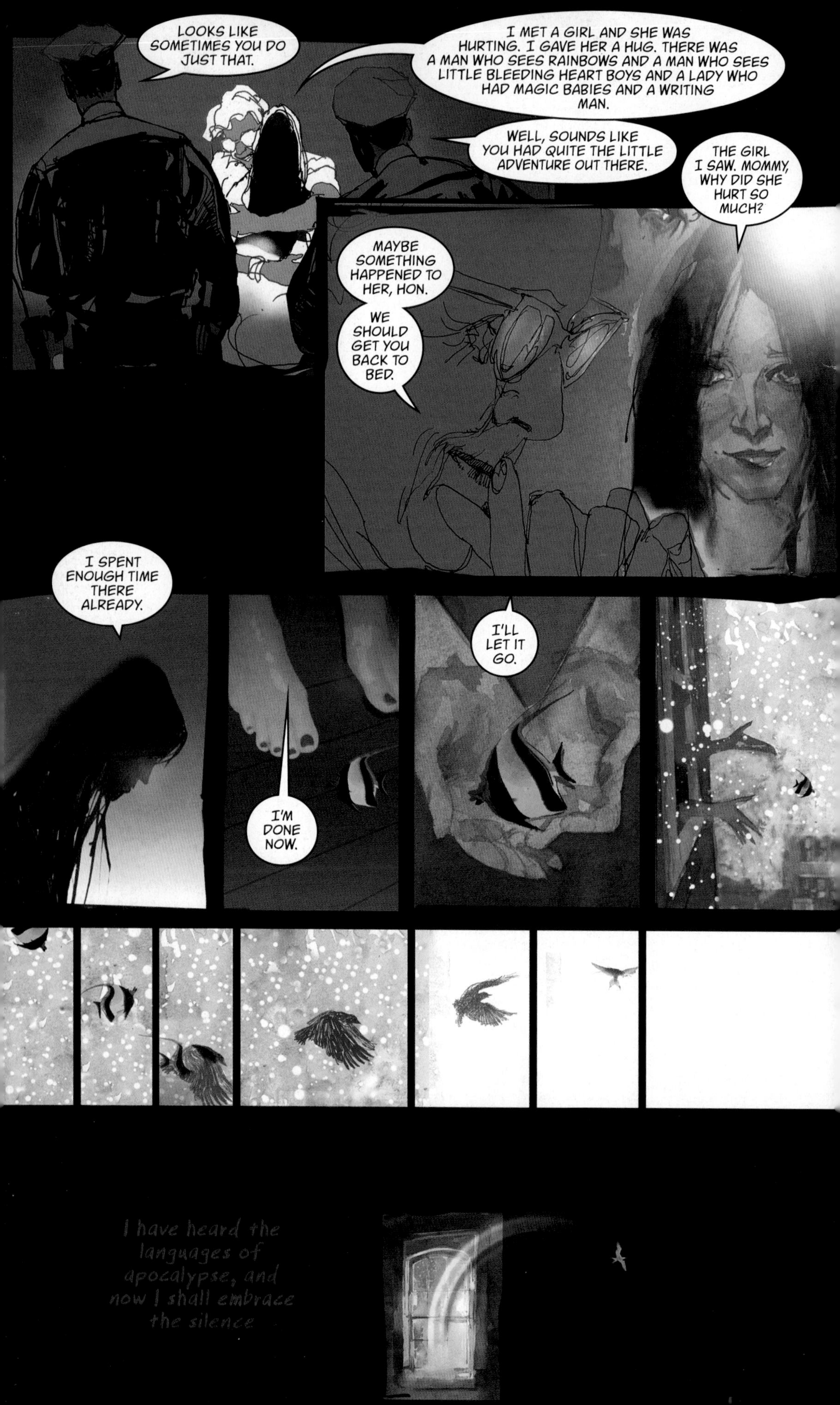
LOOKS LIKE SOMETIMES YOU DO JUST THAT.
I MET A GIRL AND SHE WAS HURTING. I GAVE HER A HUG. THERE WAS A MAN WHO SEES RAINBOWS AND A MAN WHO SEES LITTLE BLEEDING HEART BOYS AND A LADY WHO HAD MAGIC BABIES AND A WRITING MAN.
WELL, SOUNDS LIKE YOU HAD QUITE THE LITTLE ADVENTURE OUT THERE.
THE GIRL I SAW. MOMMY, WHY DID SHE HURT SO MUCH?
MAYBE SOMETHING HAPPENED TO HER, HON.
WE SHOULD GET YOU BACK TO BED.
I SPENT ENOUGH TIME THERE ALREADY.
I'M DONE NOW.
I'LL LET IT GO.
I have heard the languages of apocalypse, and now I shall embrace the silence

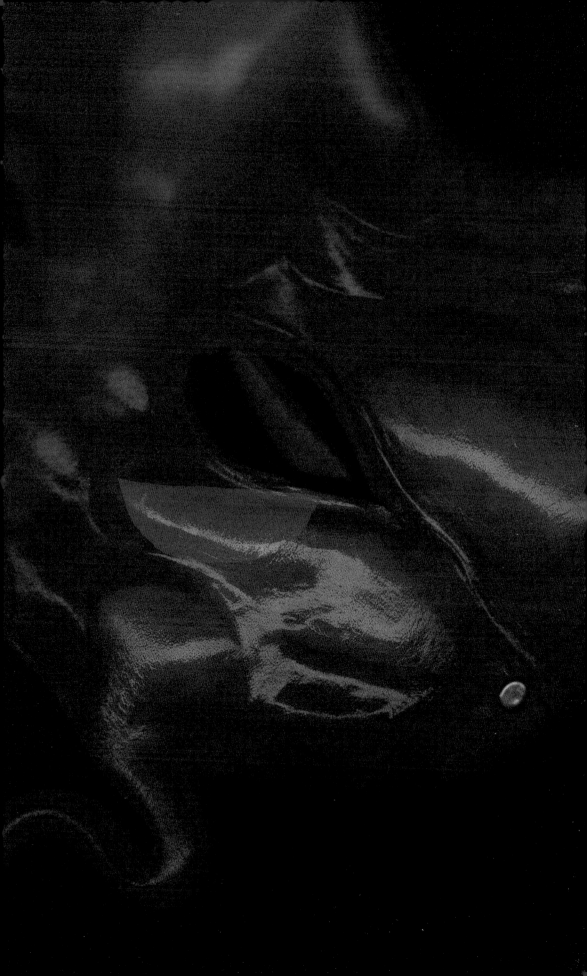

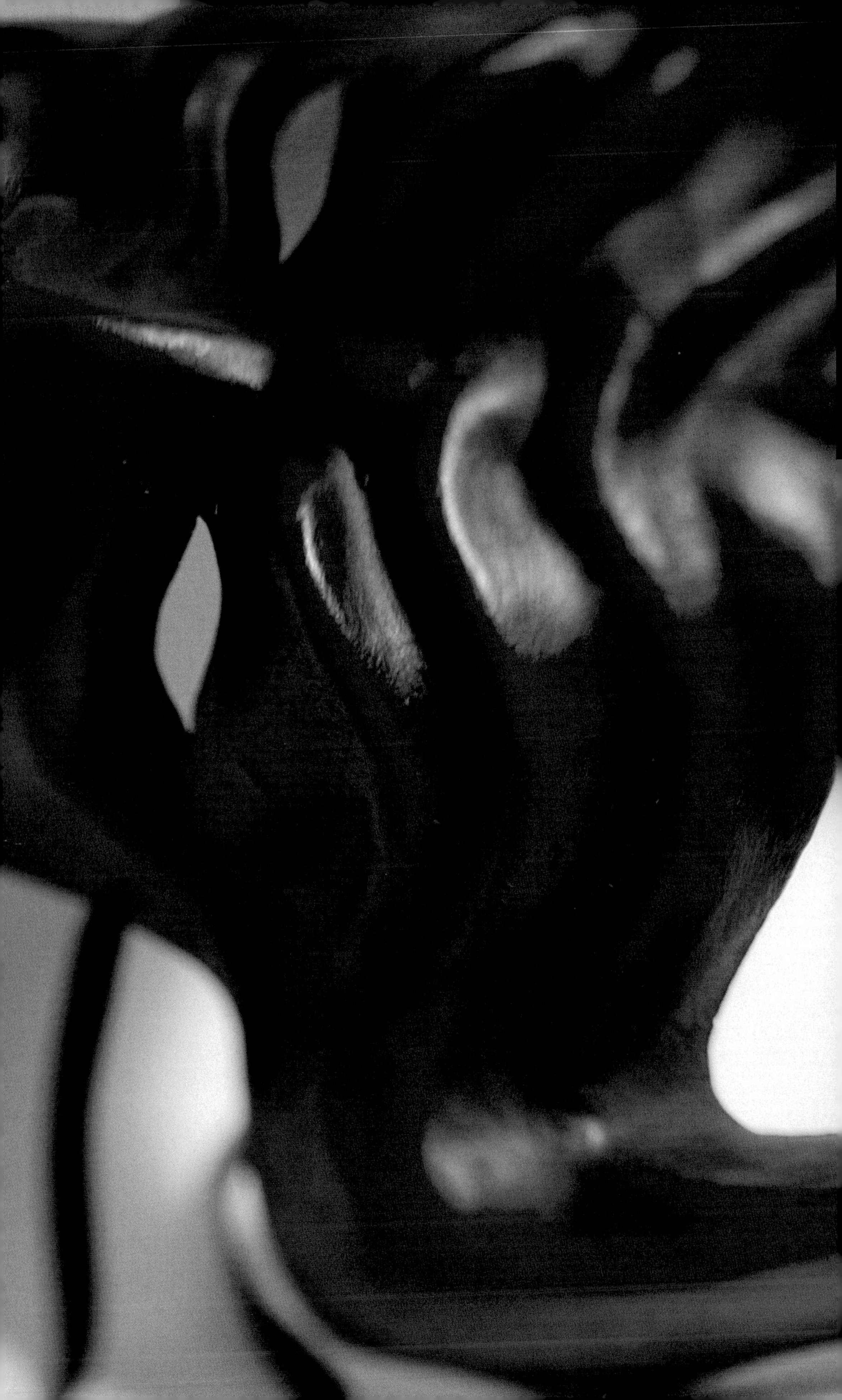

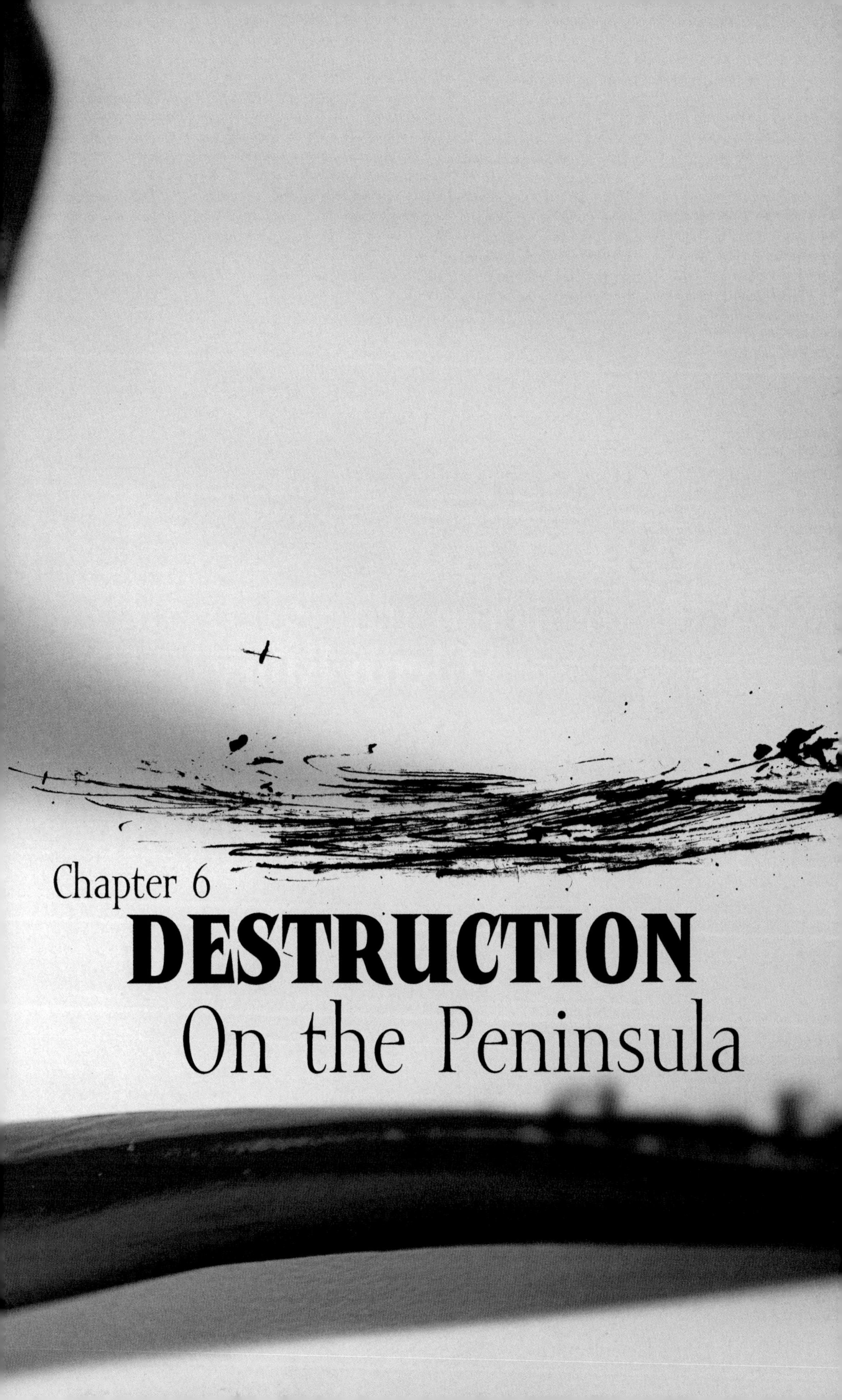

Chapter 6
DESTRUCTION On the Peninsula

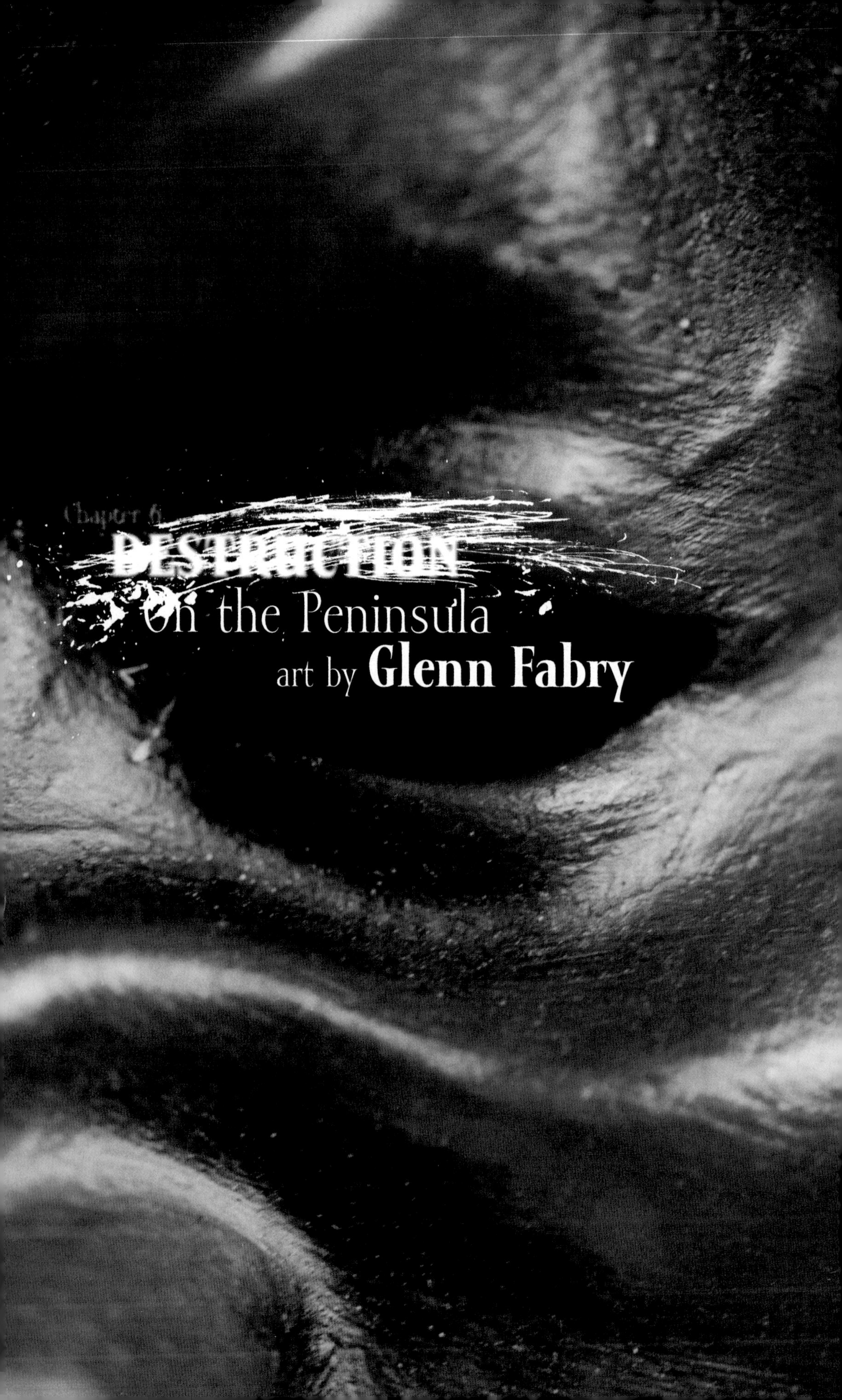

Chapter 6

DESTRUCTION

On the Peninsula

art by **Glenn Fabry**

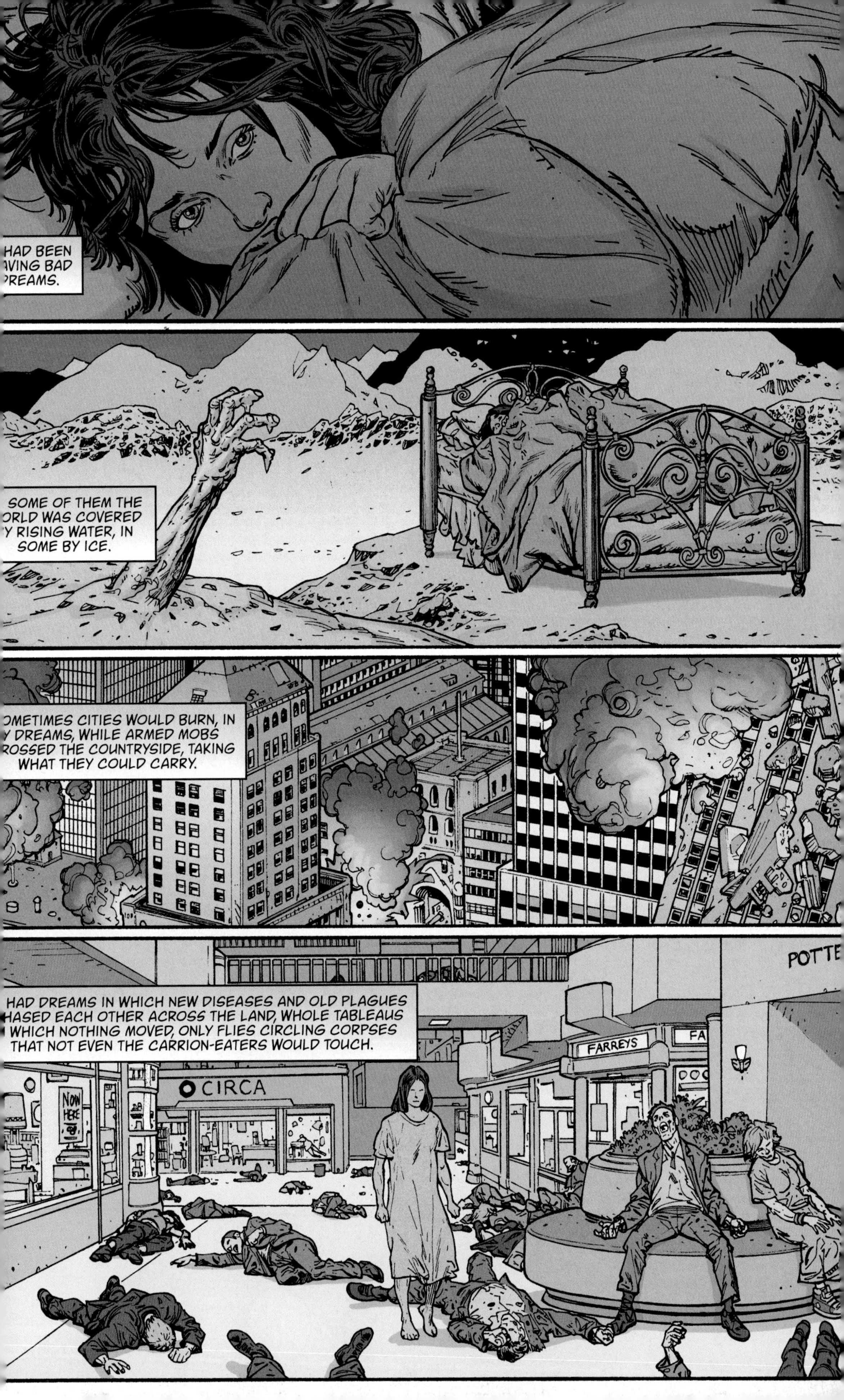
HAD BEEN
AVING BAD
REAMS.
SOME OF THEM THE
ORLD WAS COVERED
Y RISING WATER, IN
SOME BY ICE.
OMETIMES CITIES WOULD BURN, IN
Y DREAMS, WHILE ARMED MOBS
ROSSED THE COUNTRYSIDE, TAKING
WHAT THEY COULD CARRY.
POTTE
HAD DREAMS IN WHICH NEW DISEASES AND OLD PLAGUES
HASED EACH OTHER ACROSS THE LAND, WHOLE TABLEAUS
WHICH NOTHING MOVED, ONLY FLIES CIRCLING CORPSES
THAT NOT EVEN THE CARRION-EATERS WOULD TOUCH.
FARREYS
FA
CIRCA
NOW
HERE

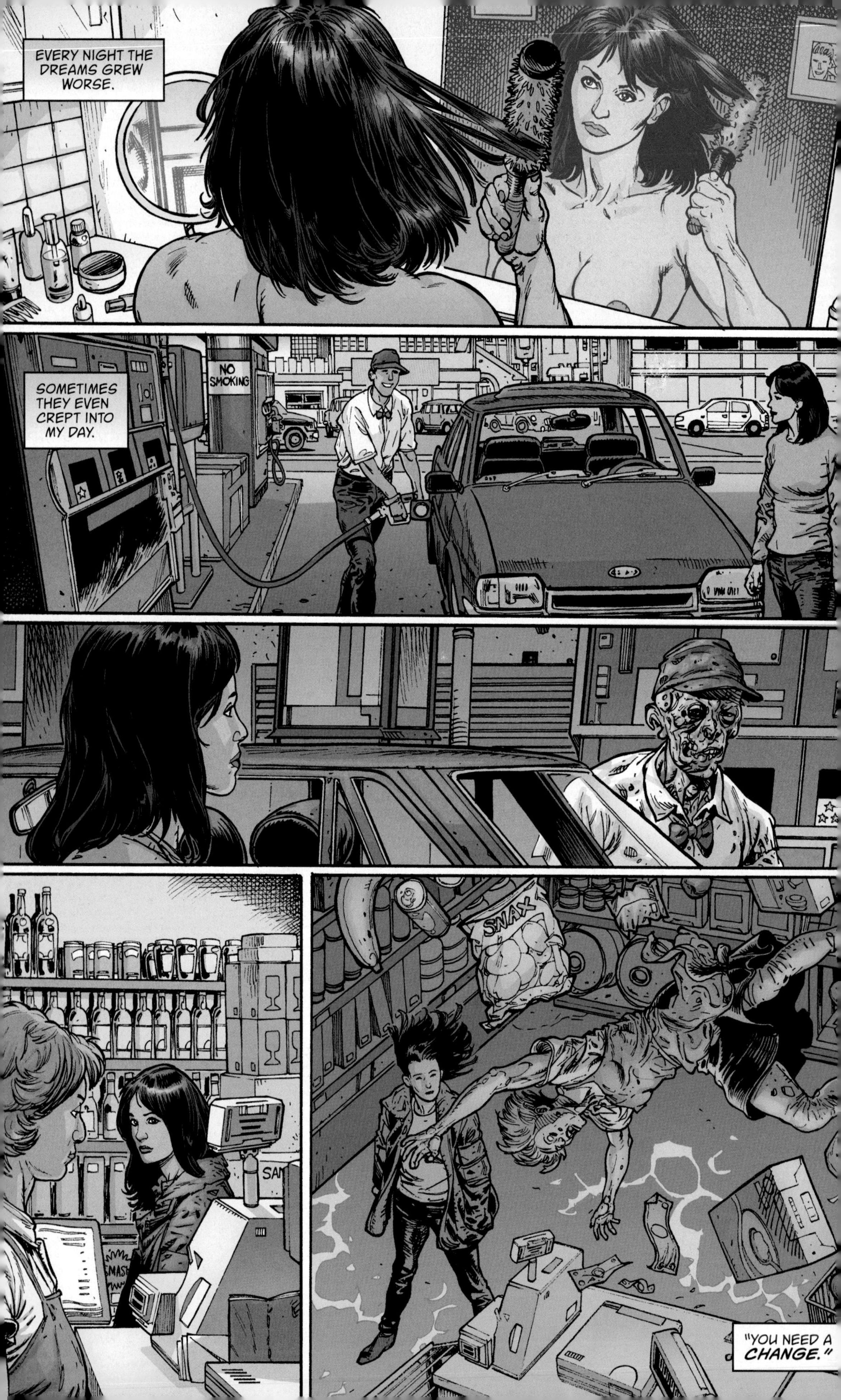
EVERY NIGHT THE DREAMS GREW WORSE.
SOMETIMES THEY EVEN CREPT INTO MY DAY.
NO SMOKING
SNAX
"YOU NEED A CHANGE."

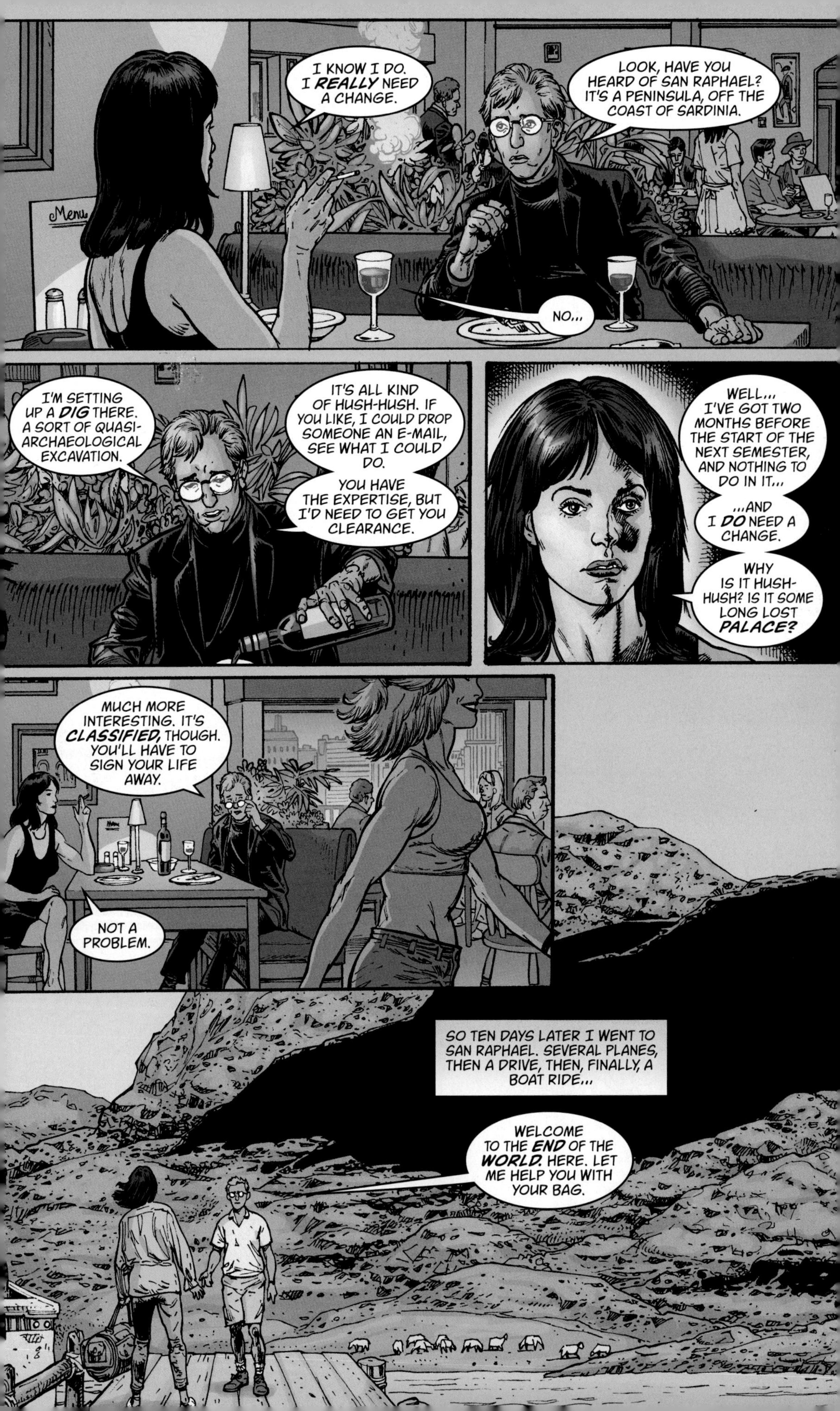
I KNOW I DO. I REALLY NEED A CHANGE.
LOOK, HAVE YOU HEARD OF SAN RAPHAEL? IT'S A PENINSULA, OFF THE COAST OF SARDINIA.
NO...
Menu
I'M SETTING UP A DIG THERE. A SORT OF QUASI-ARCHAEOLOGICAL EXCAVATION.
IT'S ALL KIND OF HUSH-HUSH. IF YOU LIKE, I COULD DROP SOMEONE AN E-MAIL, SEE WHAT I COULD DO.
YOU HAVE THE EXPERTISE, BUT I'D NEED TO GET YOU CLEARANCE.
WELL... I'VE GOT TWO MONTHS BEFORE THE START OF THE NEXT SEMESTER, AND NOTHING TO DO IN IT...
...AND I DO NEED A CHANGE.
WHY IS IT HUSH-HUSH? IS IT SOME LONG LOST PALACE?
MUCH MORE INTERESTING. IT'S CLASSIFIED, THOUGH. YOU'LL HAVE TO SIGN YOUR LIFE AWAY.
NOT A PROBLEM.
SO TEN DAYS LATER I WENT TO SAN RAPHAEL. SEVERAL PLANES, THEN A DRIVE, THEN, FINALLY, A BOAT RIDE...
WELCOME TO THE END OF THE WORLD. HERE. LET ME HELP YOU WITH YOUR BAG.

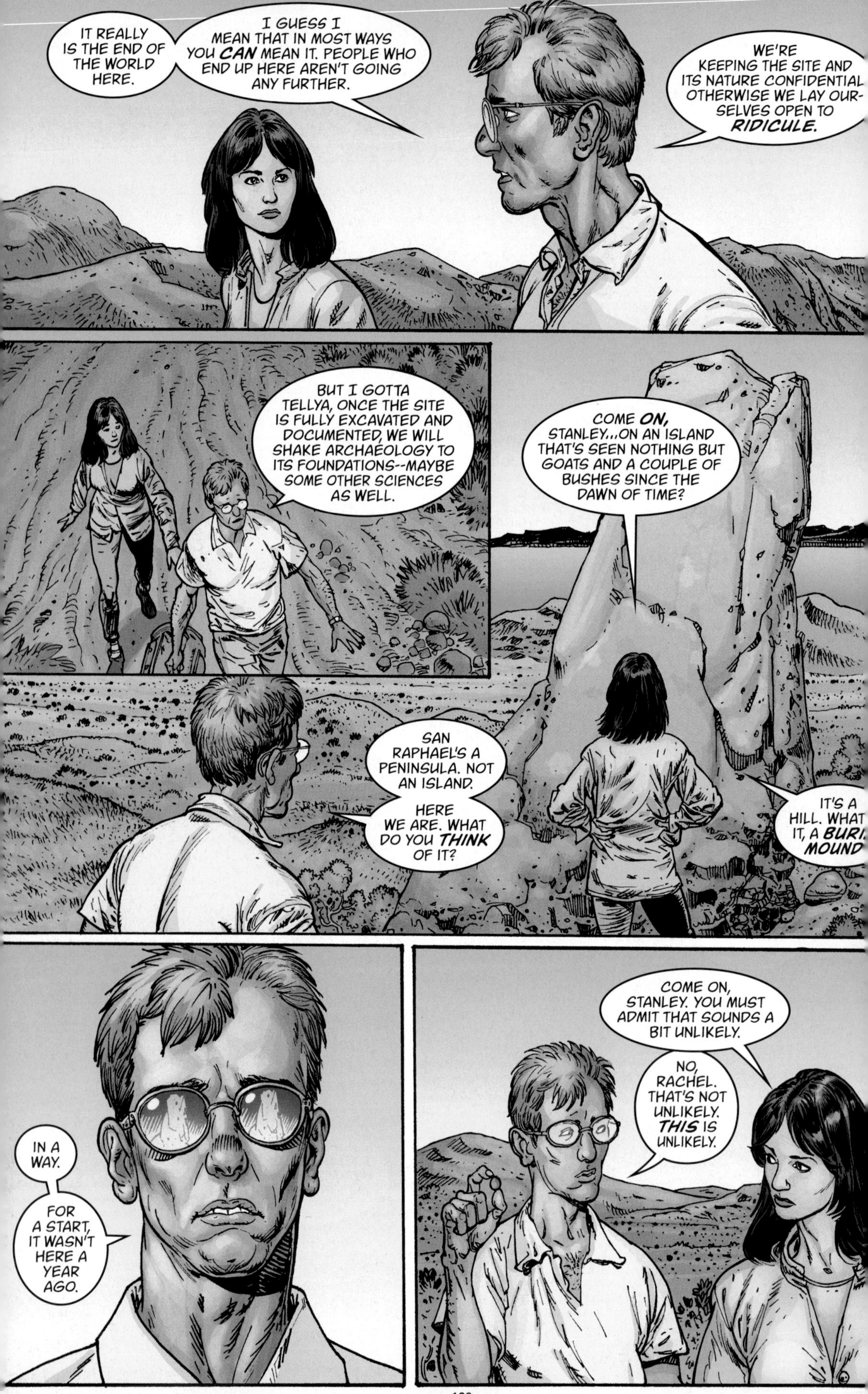
IT REALLY IS THE END OF THE WORLD HERE.
I GUESS I MEAN THAT IN MOST WAYS YOU CAN MEAN IT. PEOPLE WHO END UP HERE AREN'T GOING ANY FURTHER.
WE'RE KEEPING THE SITE AND ITS NATURE CONFIDENTIAL OTHERWISE WE LAY OURSELVES OPEN TO RIDICULE.
BUT I GOTTA TELLYA, ONCE THE SITE IS FULLY EXCAVATED AND DOCUMENTED, WE WILL SHAKE ARCHAEOLOGY TO ITS FOUNDATIONS--MAYBE SOME OTHER SCIENCES AS WELL.
COME ON, STANLEY...ON AN ISLAND THAT'S SEEN NOTHING BUT GOATS AND A COUPLE OF BUSHES SINCE THE DAWN OF TIME?
SAN RAPHAEL'S A PENINSULA. NOT AN ISLAND.
HERE WE ARE. WHAT DO YOU THINK OF IT?
IT'S A HILL. WHAT IT, A BURI MOUND
IN A WAY.
FOR A START, IT WASN'T HERE A YEAR AGO.
COME ON, STANLEY. YOU MUST ADMIT THAT SOUNDS A BIT UNLIKELY.
NO, RACHEL. THAT'S NOT UNLIKELY. THIS IS UNLIKELY.

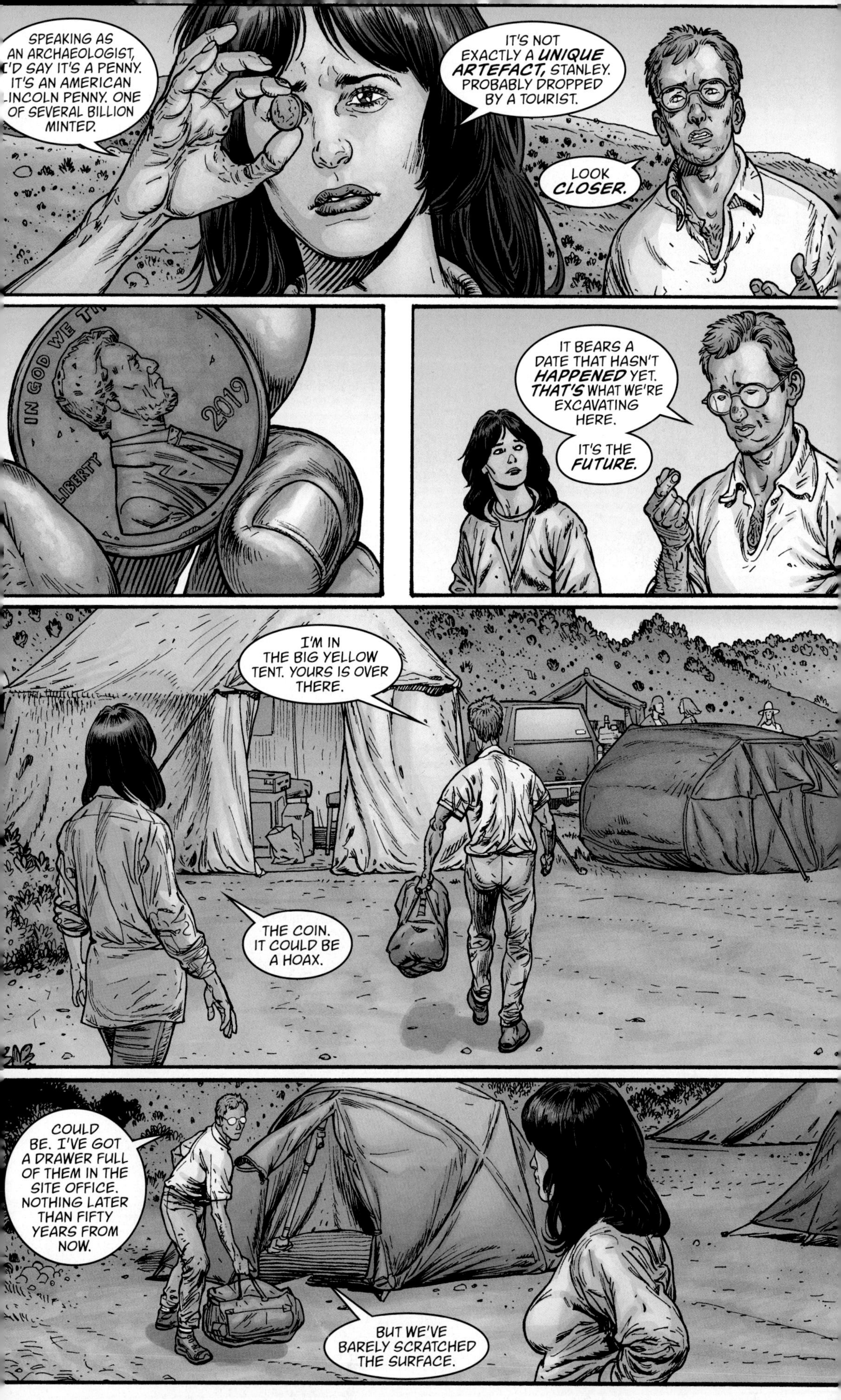
SPEAKING AS AN ARCHAEOLOGIST, I'D SAY IT'S A PENNY. IT'S AN AMERICAN LINCOLN PENNY. ONE OF SEVERAL BILLION MINTED.
IT'S NOT EXACTLY A UNIQUE ARTEFACT, STANLEY. PROBABLY DROPPED BY A TOURIST.
LOOK CLOSER.
IN GOD WE TRUST
2019
LIBERTY
IT BEARS A DATE THAT HASN'T HAPPENED YET. THAT'S WHAT WE'RE EXCAVATING HERE.
IT'S THE FUTURE.
I'M IN THE BIG YELLOW TENT. YOURS IS OVER THERE.
THE COIN. IT COULD BE A HOAX.
COULD BE. I'VE GOT A DRAWER FULL OF THEM IN THE SITE OFFICE. NOTHING LATER THAN FIFTY YEARS FROM NOW.
BUT WE'VE BARELY SCRATCHED THE SURFACE.

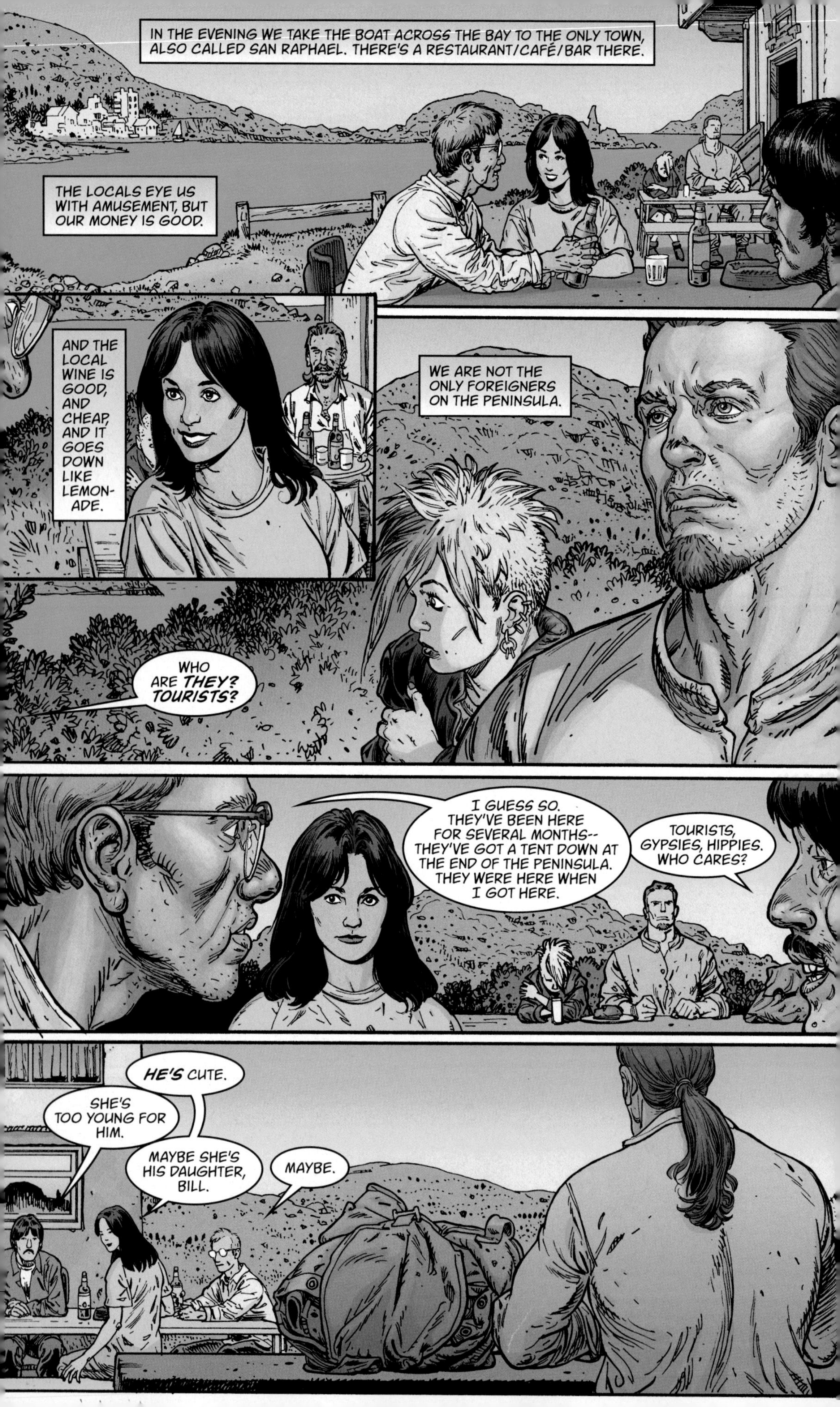

IN THE EVENING WE TAKE THE BOAT ACROSS THE BAY TO THE ONLY TOWN, ALSO CALLED SAN RAPHAEL. THERE'S A RESTAURANT/CAFÉ/BAR THERE.
THE LOCALS EYE US WITH AMUSEMENT, BUT OUR MONEY IS GOOD.
AND THE LOCAL WINE IS GOOD, AND CHEAP, AND IT GOES DOWN LIKE LEMONADE.
WE ARE NOT THE ONLY FOREIGNERS ON THE PENINSULA.
WHO ARE THEY? TOURISTS?
I GUESS SO. THEY'VE BEEN HERE FOR SEVERAL MONTHS-- THEY'VE GOT A TENT DOWN AT THE END OF THE PENINSULA. THEY WERE HERE WHEN I GOT HERE.
TOURISTS, GYPSIES, HIPPIES. WHO CARES?
HE'S CUTE.
SHE'S TOO YOUNG FOR HIM.
MAYBE SHE'S HIS DAUGHTER, BILL.
MAYBE.

LIKE I SAID. THE WINE WENT DOWN LIKE LEMONADE.

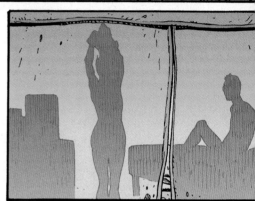

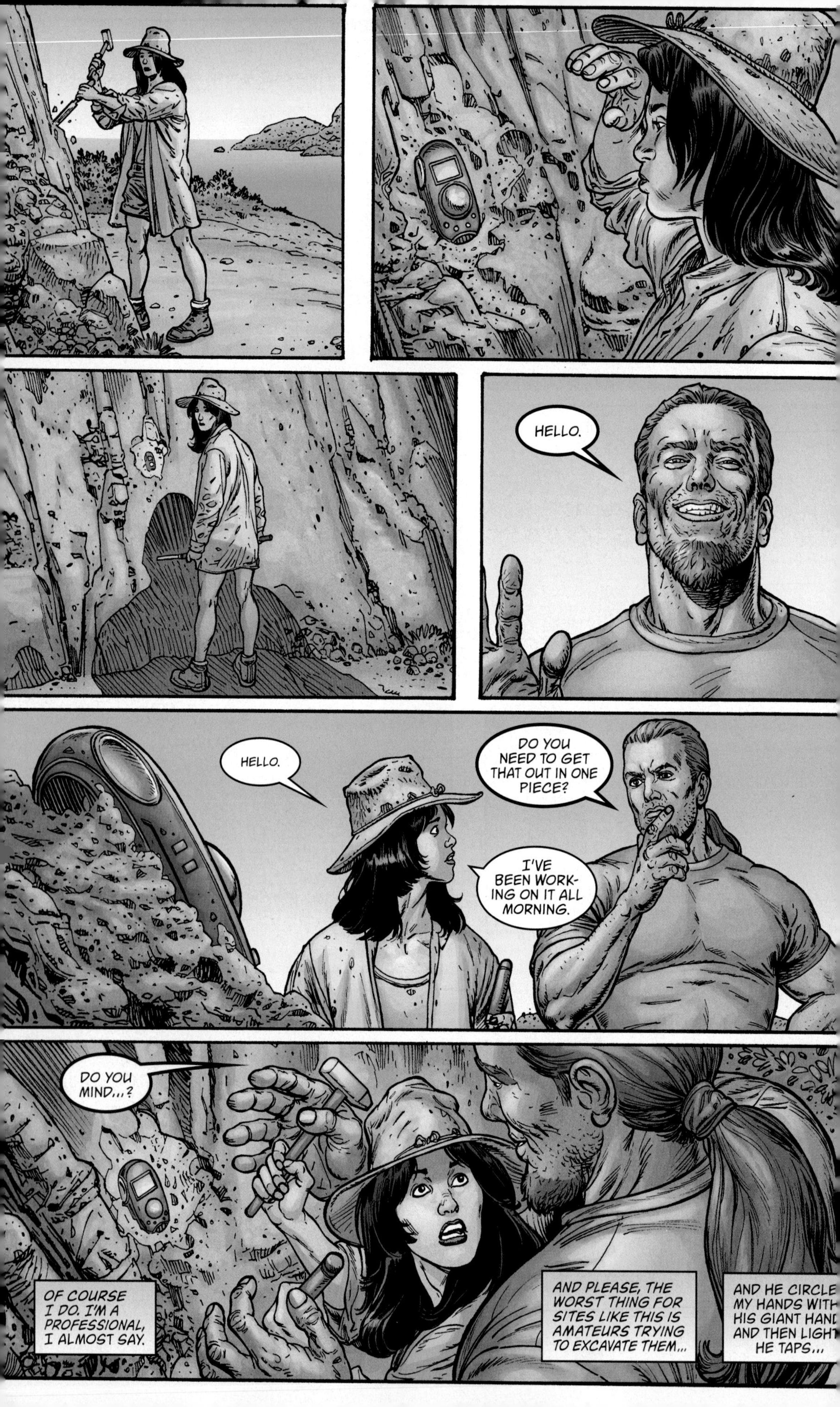
HELLO.
HELLO.
DO YOU NEED TO GET THAT OUT IN ONE PIECE?
I'VE BEEN WORKING ON IT ALL MORNING.
DO YOU MIND...?
OF COURSE I DO. I'M A PROFESSIONAL, I ALMOST SAY.
AND PLEASE, THE WORST THING FOR SITES LIKE THIS IS AMATEURS TRYING TO EXCAVATE THEM...
AND HE CIRCLE MY HANDS WITH HIS GIANT HAN AND THEN LIGH HE TAPS...

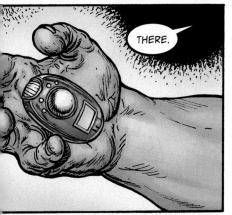

THERE.

HEY.

HAVE YOU HAD ANY *EXPERIENCE?* WITH *RUINS?*

I'VE CERTAINLY MADE MY SHARE OF THEM.

NO, *REALLY.* DO YOU NEED A *JOB?*

YOU *WHAT?*

I ASKED HIM TO *HELP.* WE *NEED* HELP. BILL'S USELESS.

HMPH.

CAT N° 1375

I DID NOT DREAM THAT NIGHT...THEN AGAIN, I DIDN'T GET A LOT OF SLEEP. SO I TYPED, AND I WORKED. ON MY OWN.

HE WAS ALREADY THERE AT 8 A.M. THAT MORNING, WHEN I GOT DOWN TO THE DIG.

133

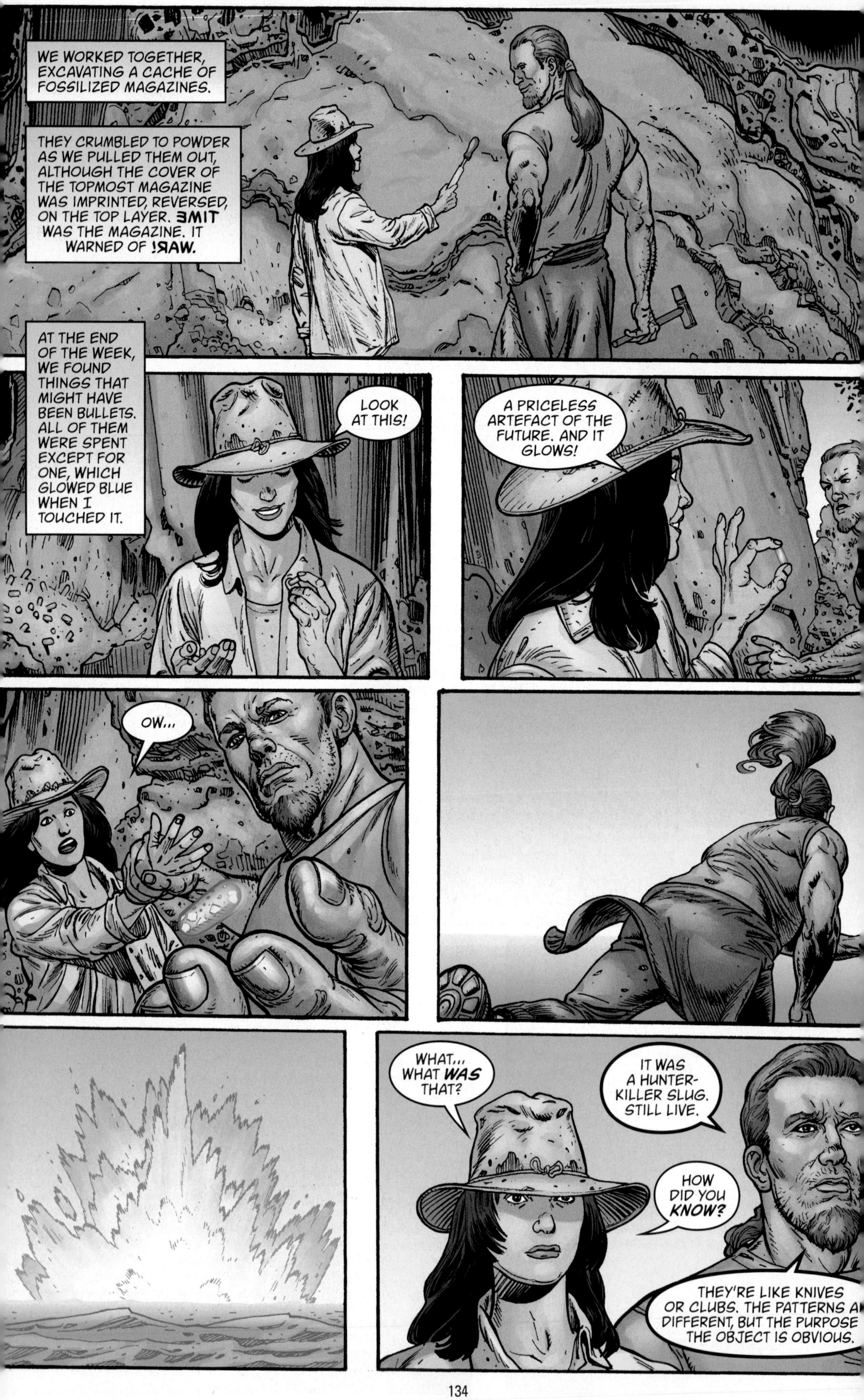
WE WORKED TOGETHER, EXCAVATING A CACHE OF FOSSILIZED MAGAZINES.
THEY CRUMBLED TO POWDER AS WE PULLED THEM OUT, ALTHOUGH THE COVER OF THE TOPMOST MAGAZINE WAS IMPRINTED, REVERSED, ON THE TOP LAYER. ƎMIT WAS THE MAGAZINE. IT WARNED OF !ꓤAW.
AT THE END OF THE WEEK, WE FOUND THINGS THAT MIGHT HAVE BEEN BULLETS. ALL OF THEM WERE SPENT EXCEPT FOR ONE, WHICH GLOWED BLUE WHEN I TOUCHED IT.
LOOK AT THIS!
A PRICELESS ARTEFACT OF THE FUTURE. AND IT GLOWS!
OW...
WHAT... WHAT WAS THAT?
IT WAS A HUNTER-KILLER SLUG. STILL LIVE.
HOW DID YOU KNOW?
THEY'RE LIKE KNIVES OR CLUBS. THE PATTERNS A DIFFERENT, BUT THE PURPOSE THE OBJECT IS OBVIOUS.

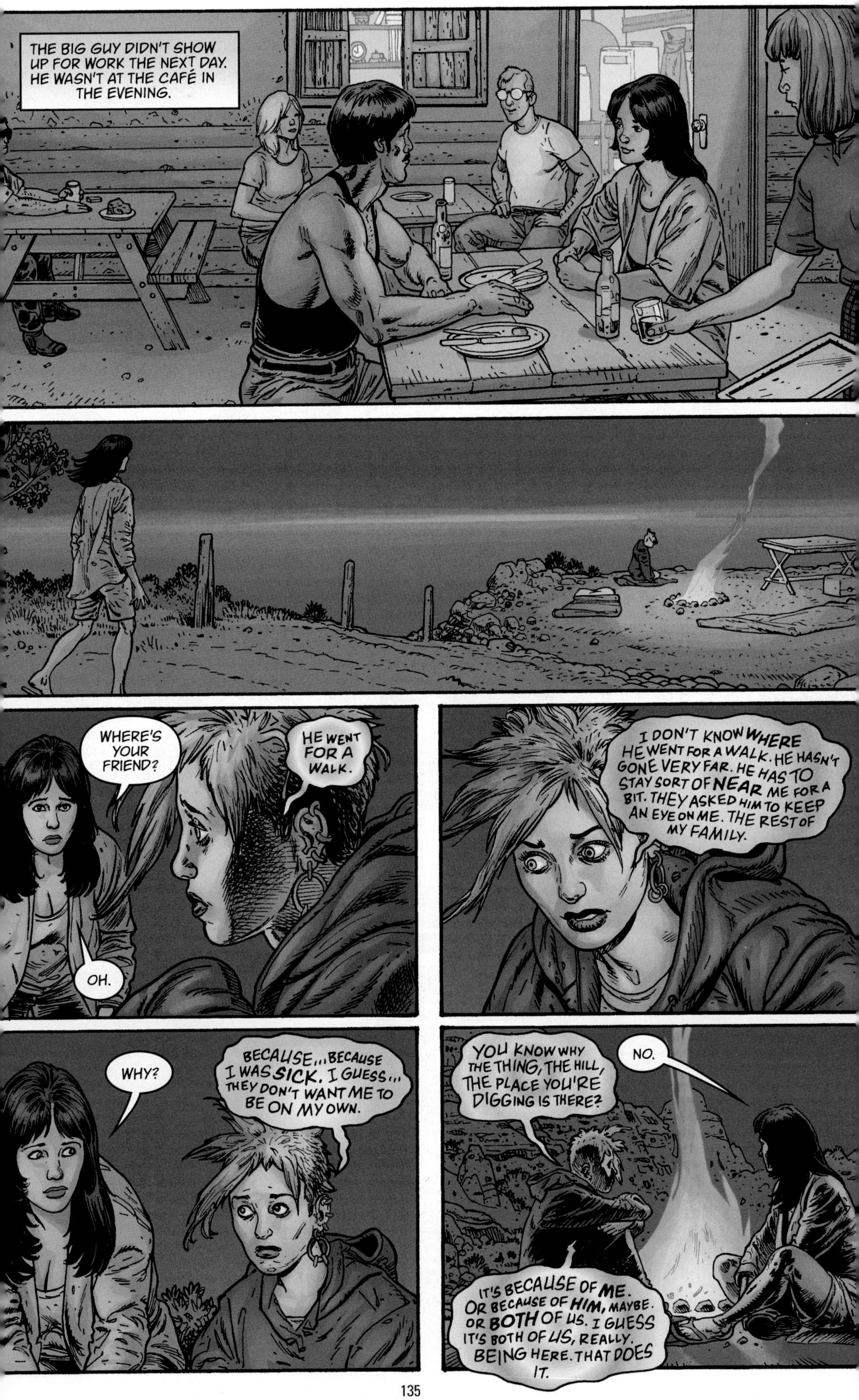
THE BIG GUY DIDN'T SHOW UP FOR WORK THE NEXT DAY. HE WASN'T AT THE CAFÉ IN THE EVENING.
WHERE'S YOUR FRIEND?
HE WENT FOR A WALK.
OH.
I DON'T KNOW WHERE HE WENT FOR A WALK. HE HASN'T GONE VERY FAR. HE HAS TO STAY SORT OF NEAR ME FOR A BIT. THEY ASKED HIM TO KEEP AN EYE ON ME. THE REST OF MY FAMILY.
WHY?
BECAUSE... BECAUSE I WAS SICK. I GUESS... THEY DON'T WANT ME TO BE ON MY OWN.
YOU KNOW WHY THE THING, THE HILL, THE PLACE YOU'RE DIGGING IS THERE?
NO.
IT'S BECAUSE OF ME. OR BECAUSE OF HIM, MAYBE. OR BOTH OF US. I GUESS IT'S BOTH OF US, REALLY. BEING HERE. THAT DOES IT.

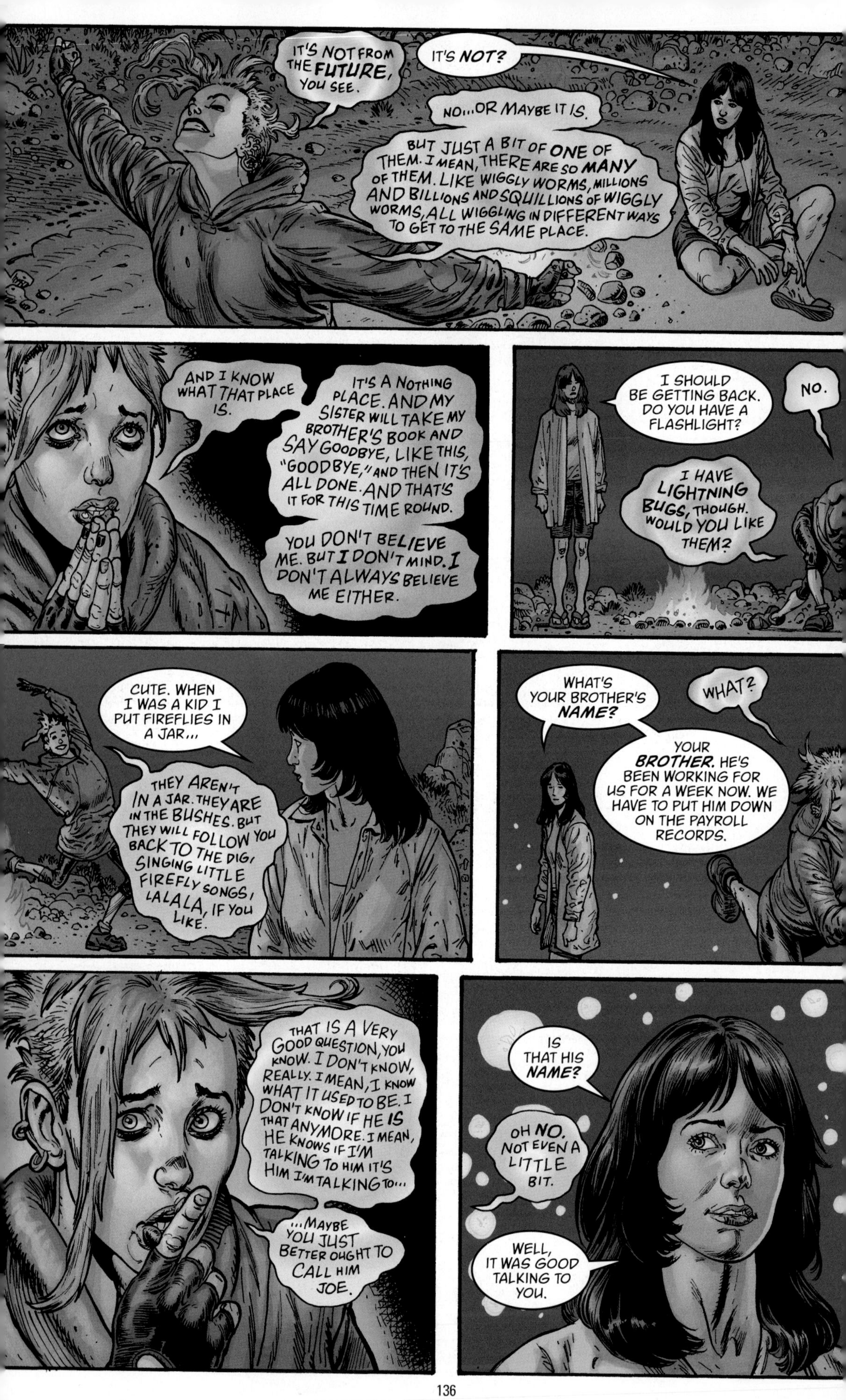
IT'S NOT FROM THE FUTURE, YOU SEE.
IT'S NOT?
NO...OR MAYBE IT IS.
BUT JUST A BIT OF ONE OF THEM. I MEAN, THERE ARE SO MANY OF THEM. LIKE WIGGLY WORMS, MILLIONS AND BILLIONS AND SQUILLIONS OF WIGGLY WORMS, ALL WIGGLING IN DIFFERENT WAYS TO GET TO THE SAME PLACE.
AND I KNOW WHAT THAT PLACE IS.
IT'S A NOTHING PLACE. AND MY SISTER WILL TAKE MY BROTHER'S BOOK AND SAY GOODBYE, LIKE THIS, "GOODBYE," AND THEN IT'S ALL DONE. AND THAT'S IT FOR THIS TIME ROUND.
YOU DON'T BELIEVE ME. BUT I DON'T MIND. I DON'T ALWAYS BELIEVE ME EITHER.
I SHOULD BE GETTING BACK. DO YOU HAVE A FLASHLIGHT?
NO.
I HAVE LIGHTNING BUGS, THOUGH. WOULD YOU LIKE THEM?
CUTE. WHEN I WAS A KID I PUT FIREFLIES IN A JAR...
THEY AREN'T IN A JAR. THEY ARE IN THE BUSHES. BUT THEY WILL FOLLOW YOU BACK TO THE DIG, SINGING LITTLE FIREFLY SONGS, LALALA, IF YOU LIKE.
WHAT'S YOUR BROTHER'S NAME?
WHAT?
YOUR BROTHER. HE'S BEEN WORKING FOR US FOR A WEEK NOW. WE HAVE TO PUT HIM DOWN ON THE PAYROLL RECORDS.
THAT IS A VERY GOOD QUESTION, YOU KNOW. I DON'T KNOW, REALLY. I MEAN, I KNOW WHAT IT USED TO BE. I DON'T KNOW IF HE IS THAT ANYMORE. I MEAN, HE KNOWS IF I'M TALKING TO HIM IT'S HIM I'M TALKING TO...
...MAYBE YOU JUST BETTER OUGHT TO CALL HIM JOE.
IS THAT HIS NAME?
OH NO. NOT EVEN A LITTLE BIT.
WELL, IT WAS GOOD TALKING TO YOU.

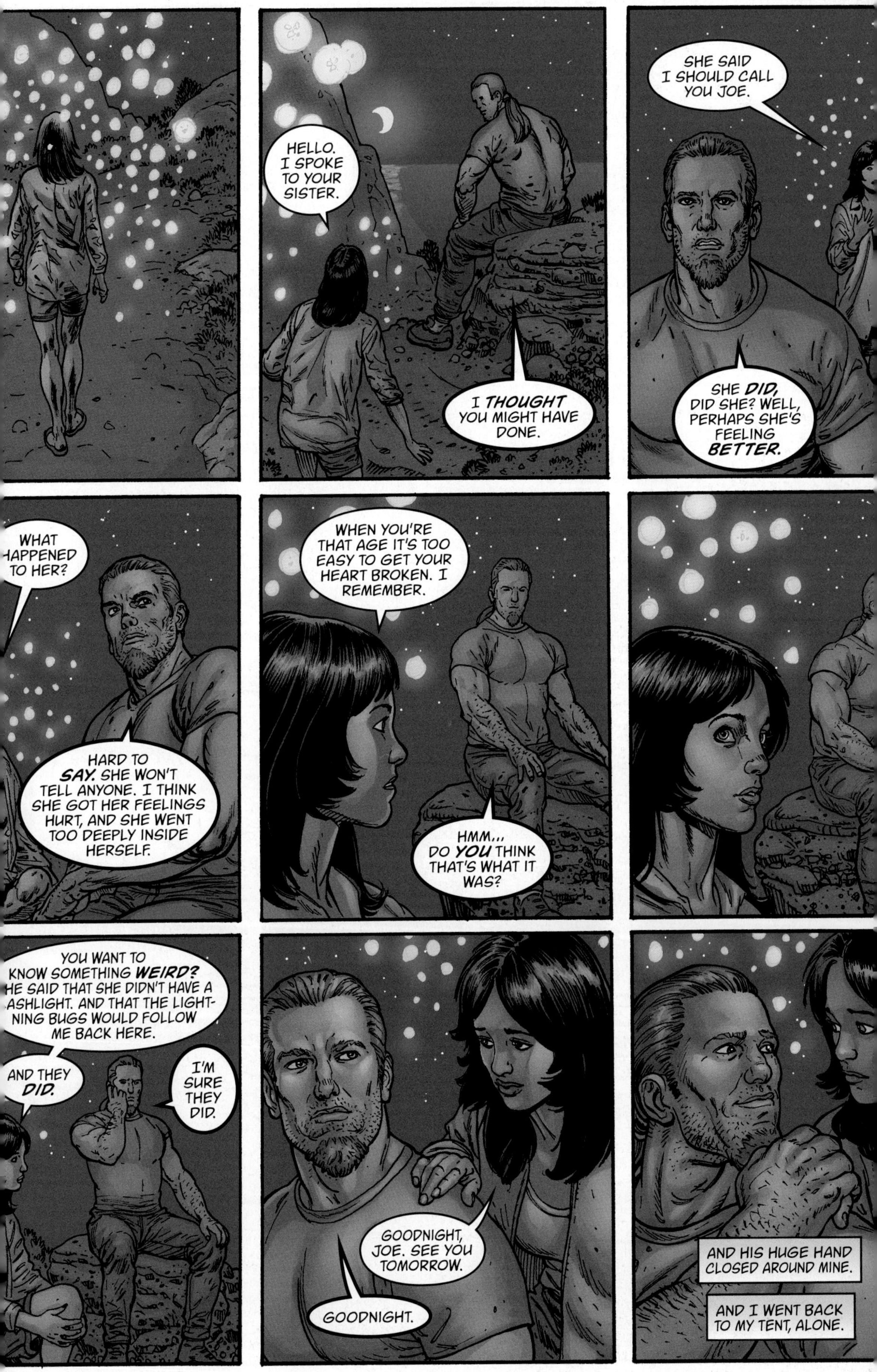
HELLO. I SPOKE TO YOUR SISTER.
I THOUGHT YOU MIGHT HAVE DONE.
SHE SAID I SHOULD CALL YOU JOE.
SHE DID, DID SHE? WELL, PERHAPS SHE'S FEELING BETTER.
WHAT HAPPENED TO HER?
HARD TO SAY. SHE WON'T TELL ANYONE. I THINK SHE GOT HER FEELINGS HURT, AND SHE WENT TOO DEEPLY INSIDE HERSELF.
WHEN YOU'RE THAT AGE IT'S TOO EASY TO GET YOUR HEART BROKEN. I REMEMBER.
HMM... DO YOU THINK THAT'S WHAT IT WAS?
YOU WANT TO KNOW SOMETHING WEIRD? HE SAID THAT SHE DIDN'T HAVE A ASHLIGHT. AND THAT THE LIGHTNING BUGS WOULD FOLLOW ME BACK HERE.
AND THEY DID.
I'M SURE THEY DID.
GOODNIGHT, JOE. SEE YOU TOMORROW.
GOODNIGHT.
AND HIS HUGE HAND CLOSED AROUND MINE.
AND I WENT BACK TO MY TENT, ALONE.

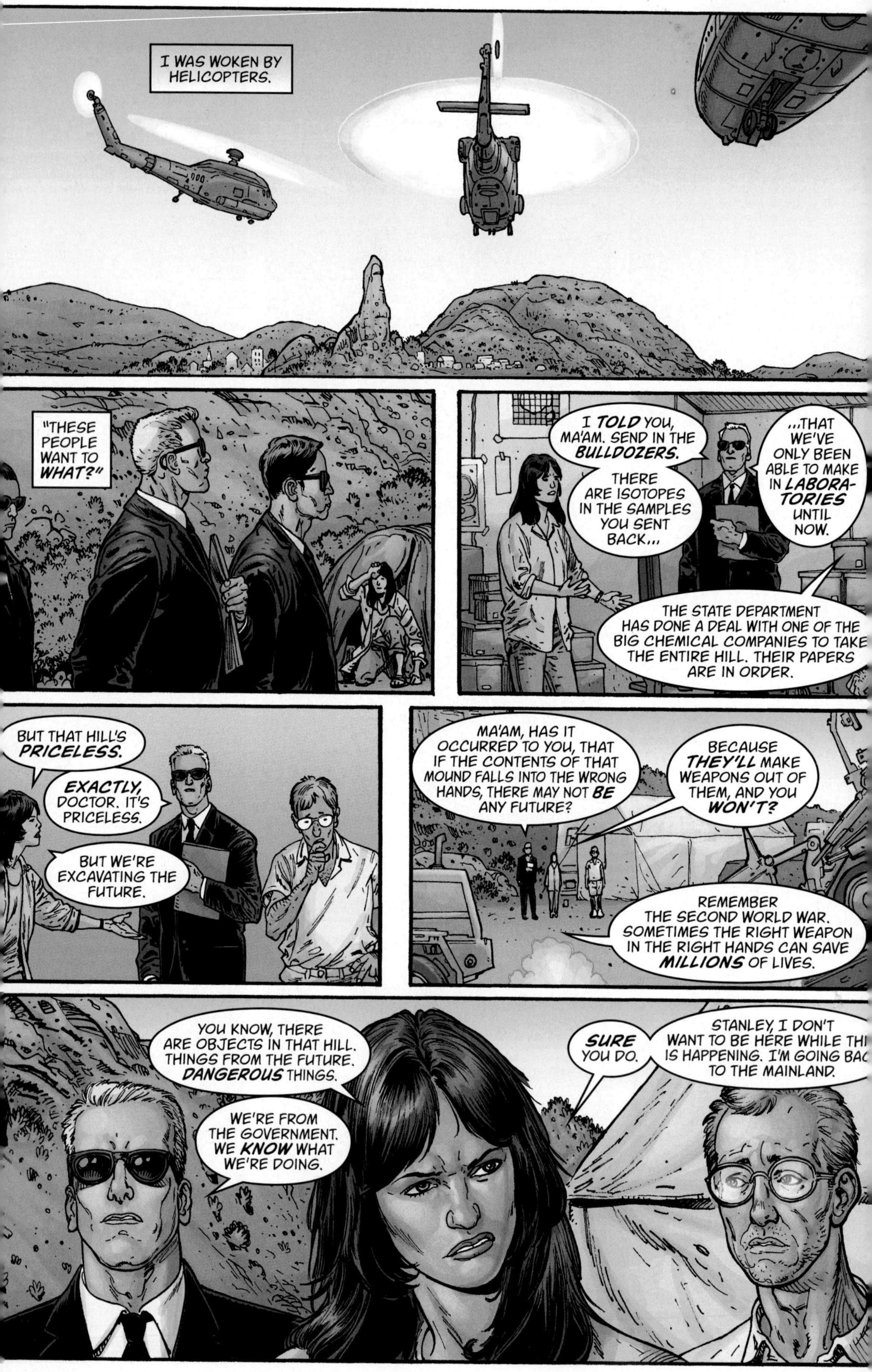
I WAS WOKEN BY HELICOPTERS.
"THESE PEOPLE WANT TO WHAT?"
I TOLD YOU, MA'AM. SEND IN THE BULLDOZERS.
THERE ARE ISOTOPES IN THE SAMPLES YOU SENT BACK...
...THAT WE'VE ONLY BEEN ABLE TO MAKE IN LABORATORIES UNTIL NOW.
THE STATE DEPARTMENT HAS DONE A DEAL WITH ONE OF THE BIG CHEMICAL COMPANIES TO TAKE THE ENTIRE HILL. THEIR PAPERS ARE IN ORDER.
BUT THAT HILL'S PRICELESS.
EXACTLY, DOCTOR. IT'S PRICELESS.
BUT WE'RE EXCAVATING THE FUTURE.
MA'AM, HAS IT OCCURRED TO YOU, THAT IF THE CONTENTS OF THAT MOUND FALLS INTO THE WRONG HANDS, THERE MAY NOT BE ANY FUTURE?
BECAUSE THEY'LL MAKE WEAPONS OUT OF THEM, AND YOU WON'T?
REMEMBER THE SECOND WORLD WAR. SOMETIMES THE RIGHT WEAPON IN THE RIGHT HANDS CAN SAVE MILLIONS OF LIVES.
YOU KNOW, THERE ARE OBJECTS IN THAT HILL. THINGS FROM THE FUTURE. DANGEROUS THINGS.
WE'RE FROM THE GOVERNMENT. WE KNOW WHAT WE'RE DOING.
SURE YOU DO.
STANLEY, I DON'T WANT TO BE HERE WHILE THI IS HAPPENING. I'M GOING BAC TO THE MAINLAND.

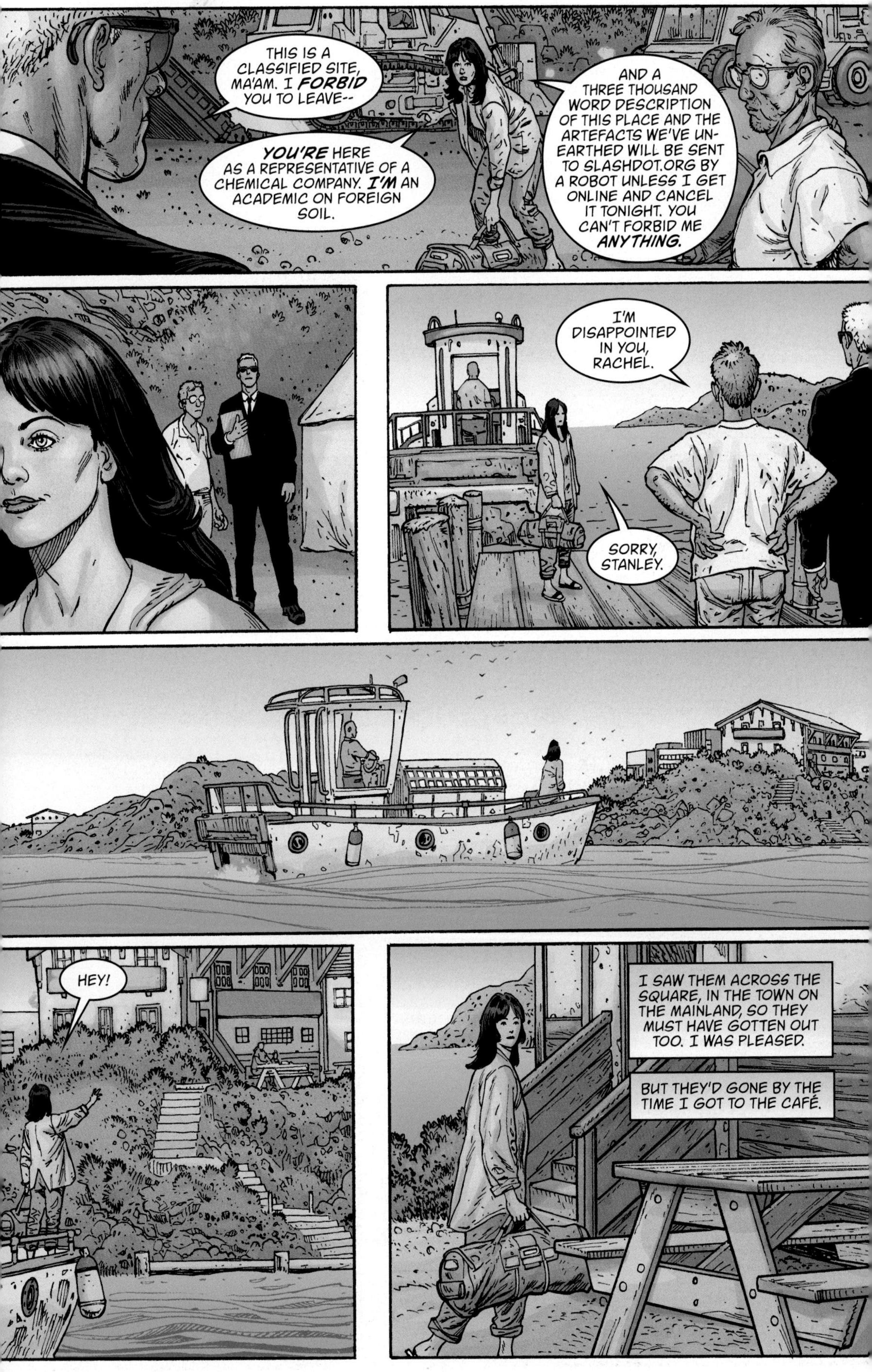
THIS IS A CLASSIFIED SITE, MA'AM. I **FORBID** YOU TO LEAVE--
YOU'RE HERE AS A REPRESENTATIVE OF A CHEMICAL COMPANY. ***I'M*** AN ACADEMIC ON FOREIGN SOIL.
AND A THREE THOUSAND WORD DESCRIPTION OF THIS PLACE AND THE ARTEFACTS WE'VE UN-EARTHED WILL BE SENT TO SLASHDOT.ORG BY A ROBOT UNLESS I GET ONLINE AND CANCEL IT TONIGHT. YOU CAN'T FORBID ME ***ANYTHING.***
I'M DISAPPOINTED IN YOU, RACHEL.
SORRY, STANLEY.
HEY!
I SAW THEM ACROSS THE SQUARE, IN THE TOWN ON THE MAINLAND, SO THEY MUST HAVE GOTTEN OUT TOO. I WAS PLEASED.
BUT THEY'D GONE BY THE TIME I GOT TO THE CAFÉ.

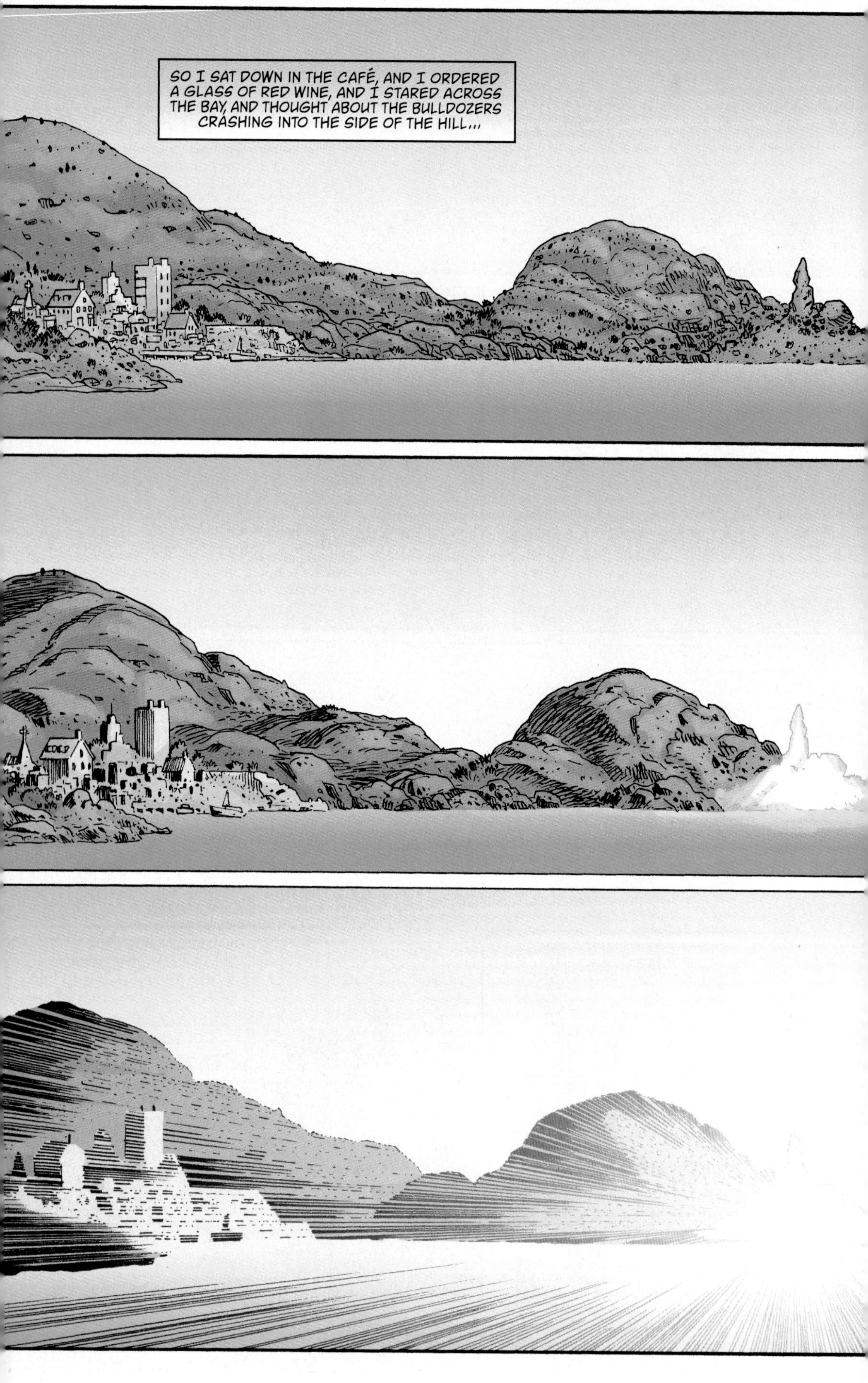
SO I SAT DOWN IN THE CAFÉ, AND I ORDERED A GLASS OF RED WINE, AND I STARED ACROSS THE BAY, AND THOUGHT ABOUT THE BULLDOZERS CRASHING INTO THE SIDE OF THE HILL...

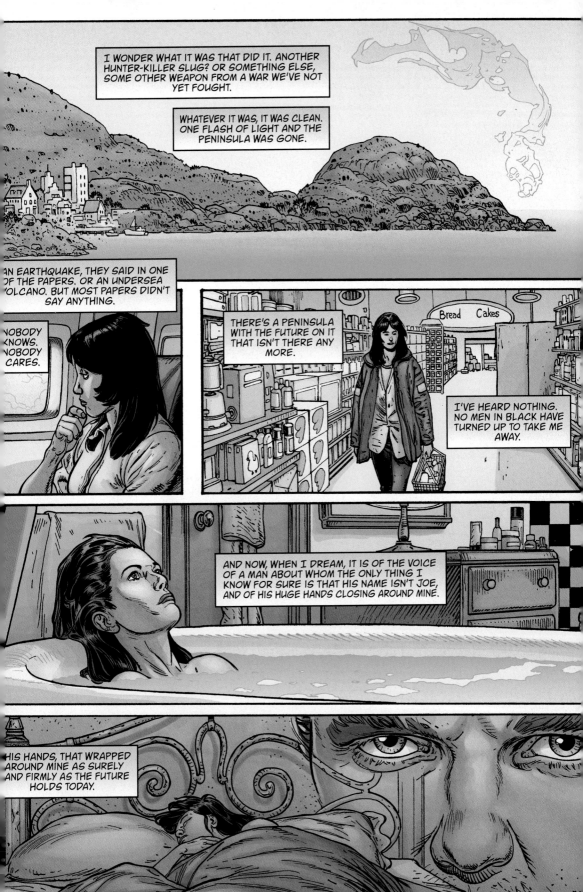

I WONDER WHAT IT WAS THAT DID IT. ANOTHER HUNTER-KILLER SLUG? OR SOMETHING ELSE, SOME OTHER WEAPON FROM A WAR WE'VE NOT YET FOUGHT.

WHATEVER IT WAS, IT WAS CLEAN. ONE FLASH OF LIGHT AND THE PENINSULA WAS GONE.

AN EARTHQUAKE, THEY SAID IN ONE OF THE PAPERS. OR AN UNDERSEA VOLCANO. BUT MOST PAPERS DIDN'T SAY ANYTHING.

NOBODY KNOWS. NOBODY CARES.

THERE'S A PENINSULA WITH THE FUTURE ON IT THAT ISN'T THERE ANY MORE.

I'VE HEARD NOTHING. NO MEN IN BLACK HAVE TURNED UP TO TAKE ME AWAY.

AND NOW, WHEN I DREAM, IT IS OF THE VOICE OF A MAN ABOUT WHOM THE ONLY THING I KNOW FOR SURE IS THAT HIS NAME ISN'T JOE, AND OF HIS HUGE HANDS CLOSING AROUND MINE.

HIS HANDS, THAT WRAPPED AROUND MINE AS SURELY AND FIRMLY AS THE FUTURE HOLDS TODAY.

141

END

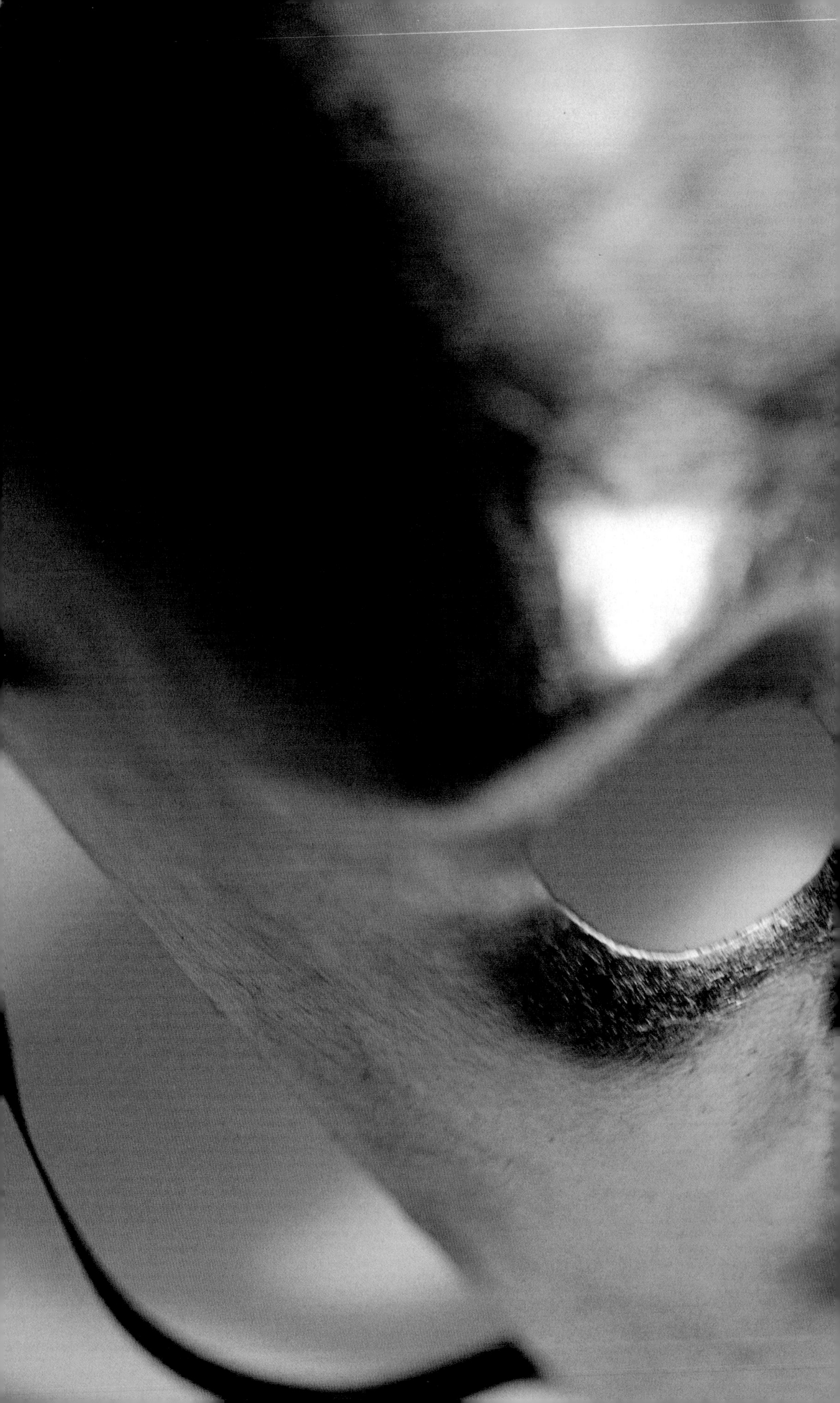

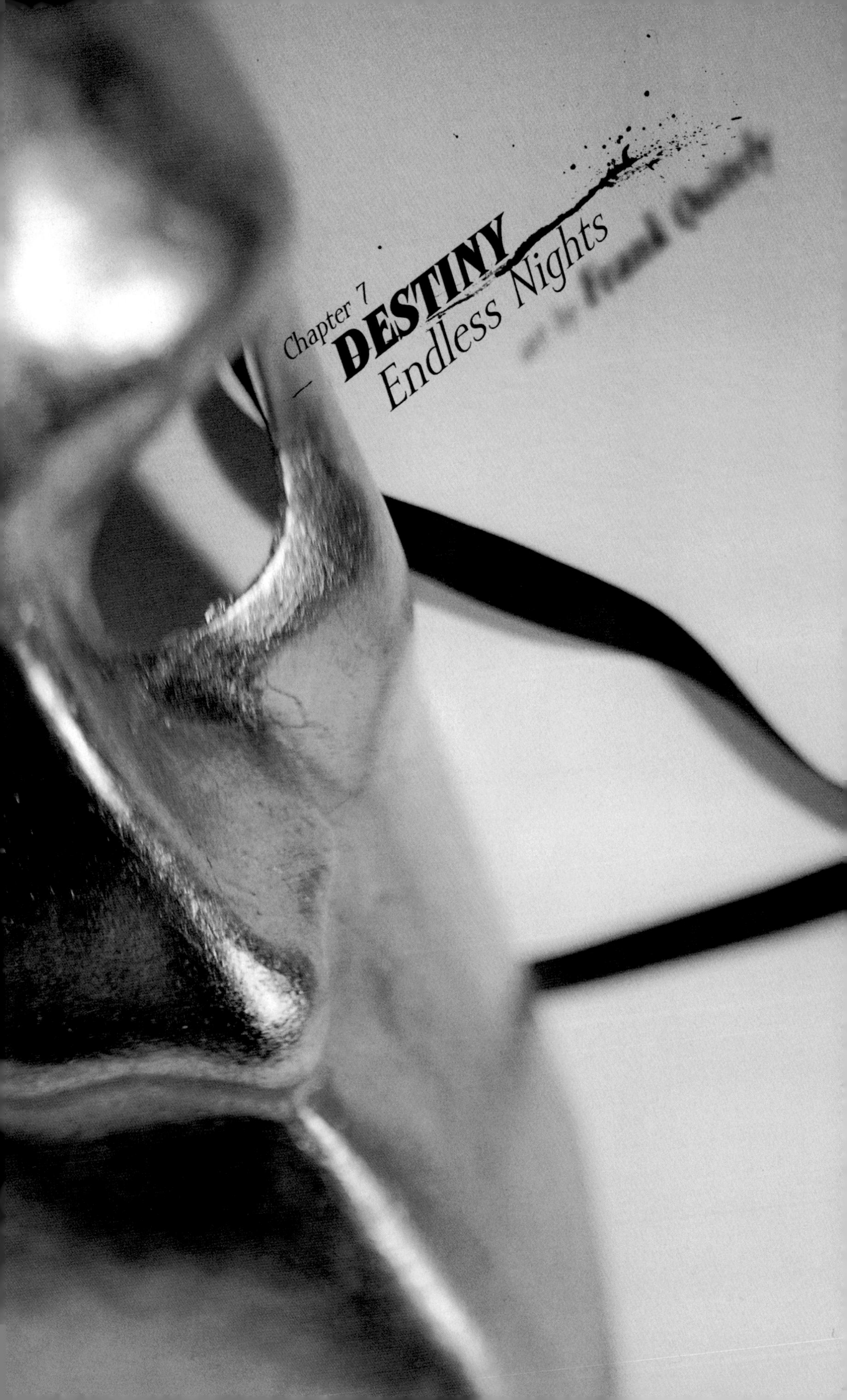
Chapter 7
DESTINY
Endless Nights

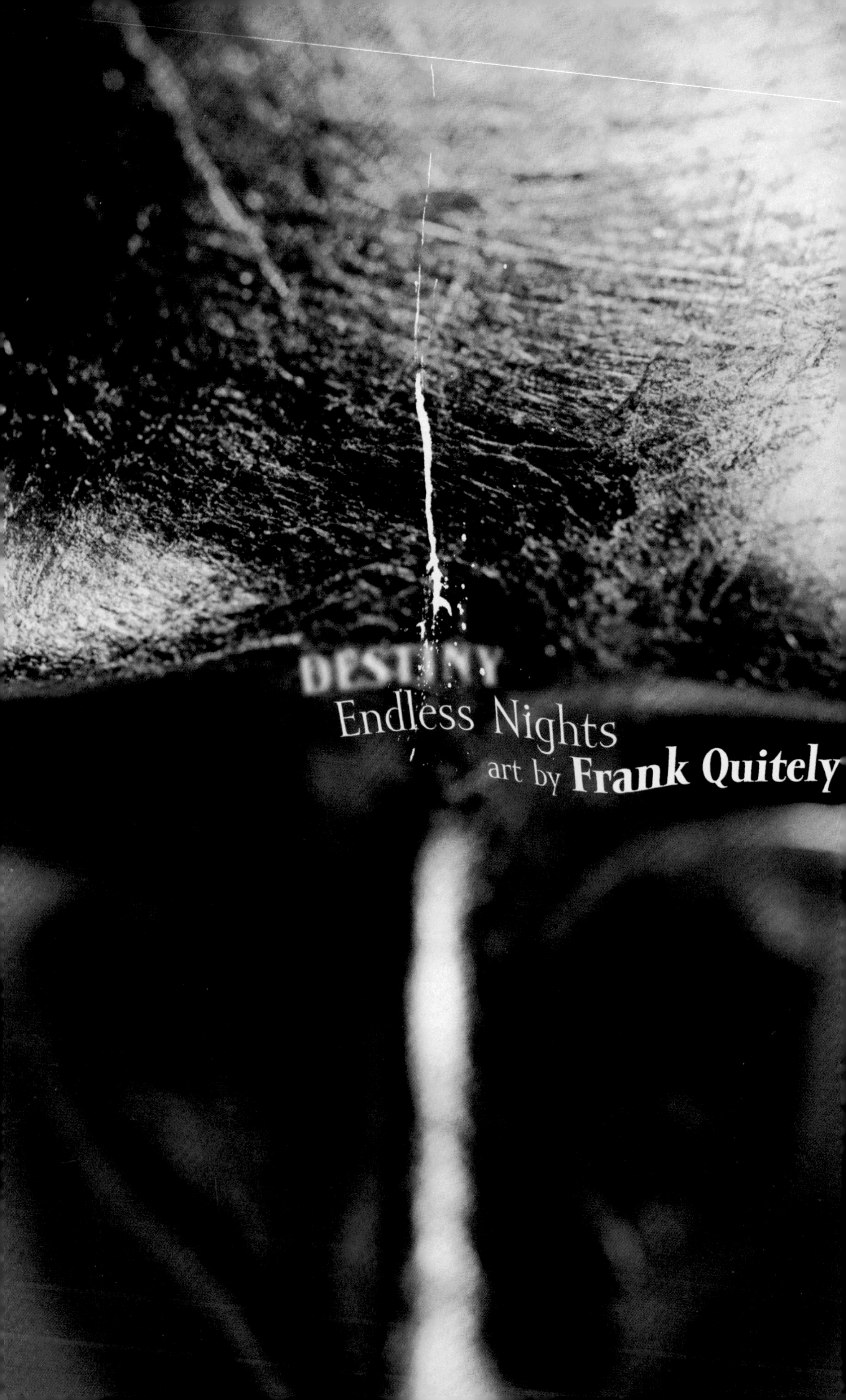

DESTINY

Endless Nights

art by **Frank Quitely**

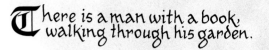

There is a man with a book, walking through his garden.

The man is blind.

The garden is a maze of paths that divide and branch and recombine.

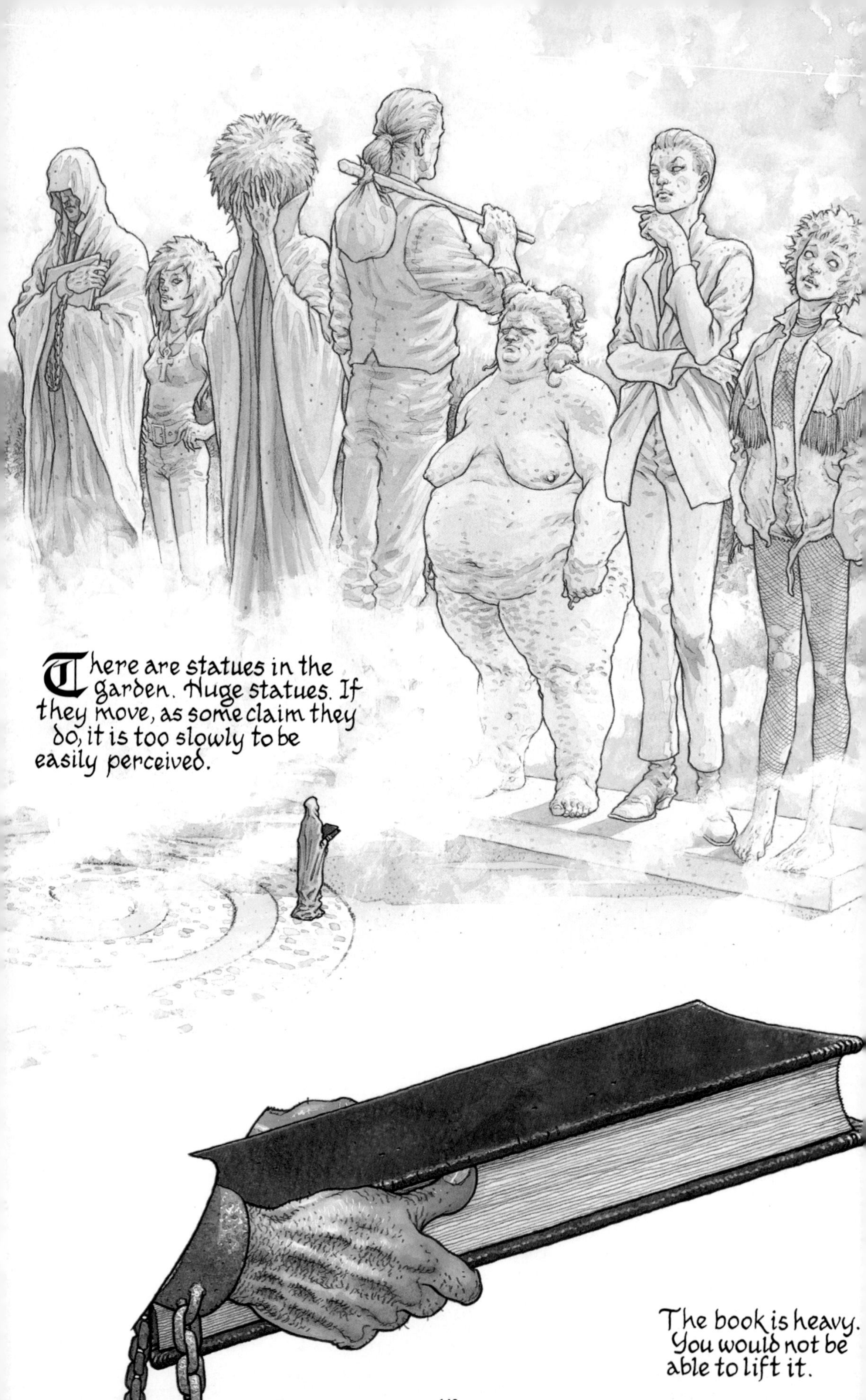
There are statues in the garden. Huge statues. If they move, as some claim they do, it is too slowly to be easily perceived.
The book is heavy. You would not be able to lift it.

Now his path takes him into his dwelling, a place of corridors and halls.

The paintings in Destiny's hall show his brothers and sisters as they might wish to be seen (although the wish and the thing are so close in the realm of the Endless that you cannot get a thin-bladed knife between them).

You will spend time in the realm of each of his siblings—you will dream, despair, desire, destroy, delight and otherwise, and, eventually, die—but you were his from the very first page, and only he will read how your story comes out, a long time from now.

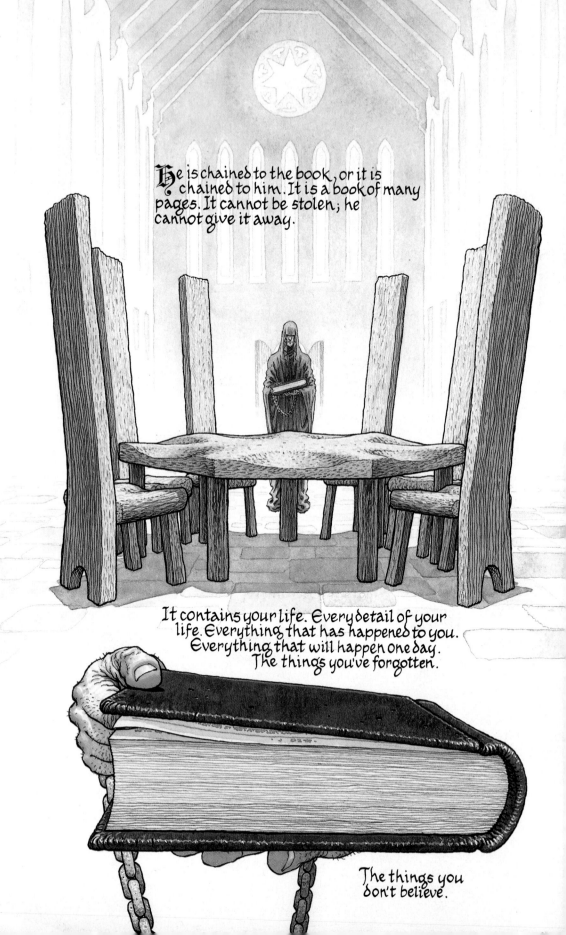

He is chained to the book, or it is chained to him. It is a book of many pages. It cannot be stolen; he cannot give it away.

It contains your life. Every detail of your life. Everything that has happened to you. Everything that will happen one day. The things you've forgotten.

The things you don't believe.

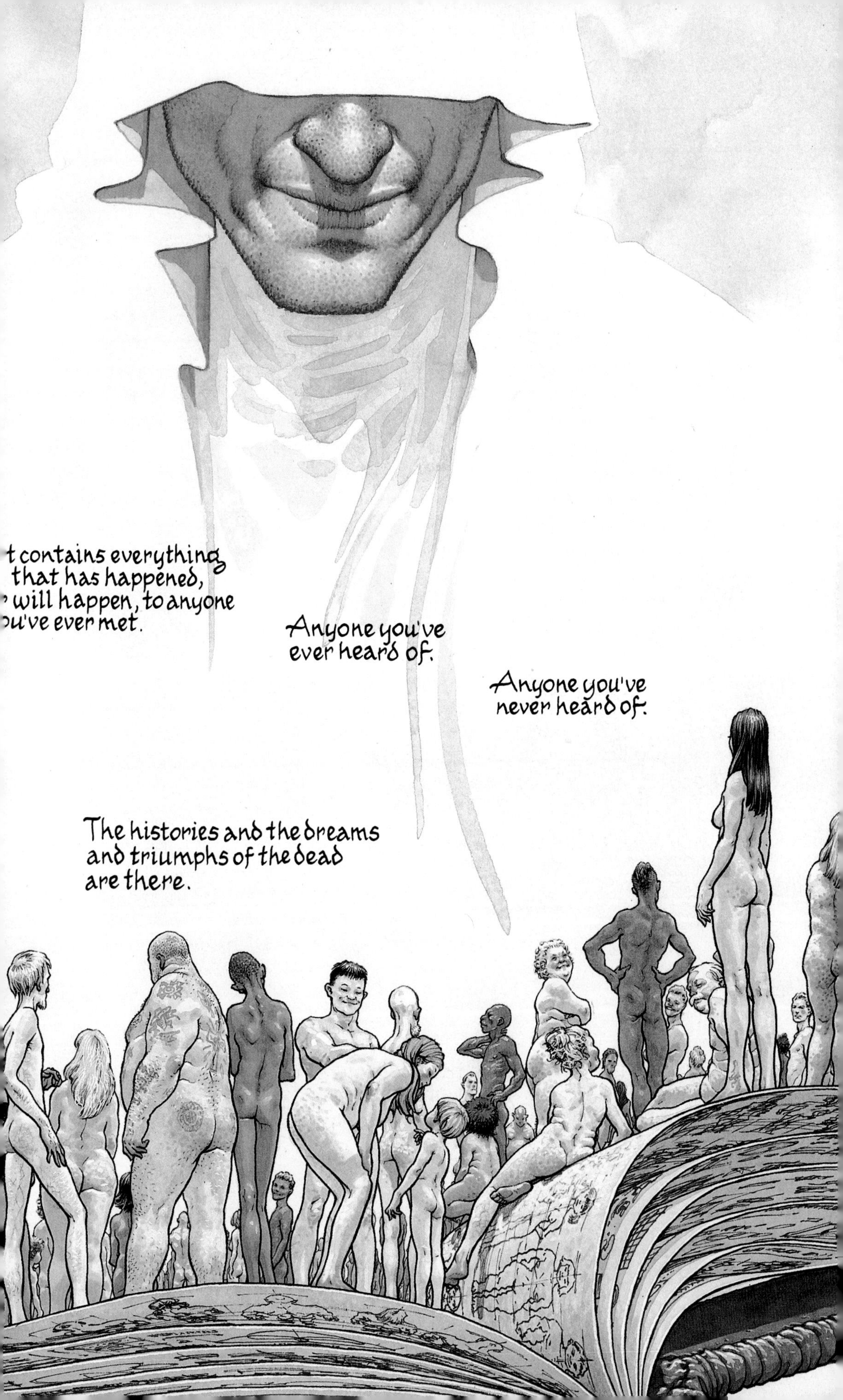

t contains everything that has happened, will happen, to anyone ou've ever met.
Anyone you've ever heard of.
Anyone you've never heard of.
The histories and the dreams and triumphs of the dead are there.

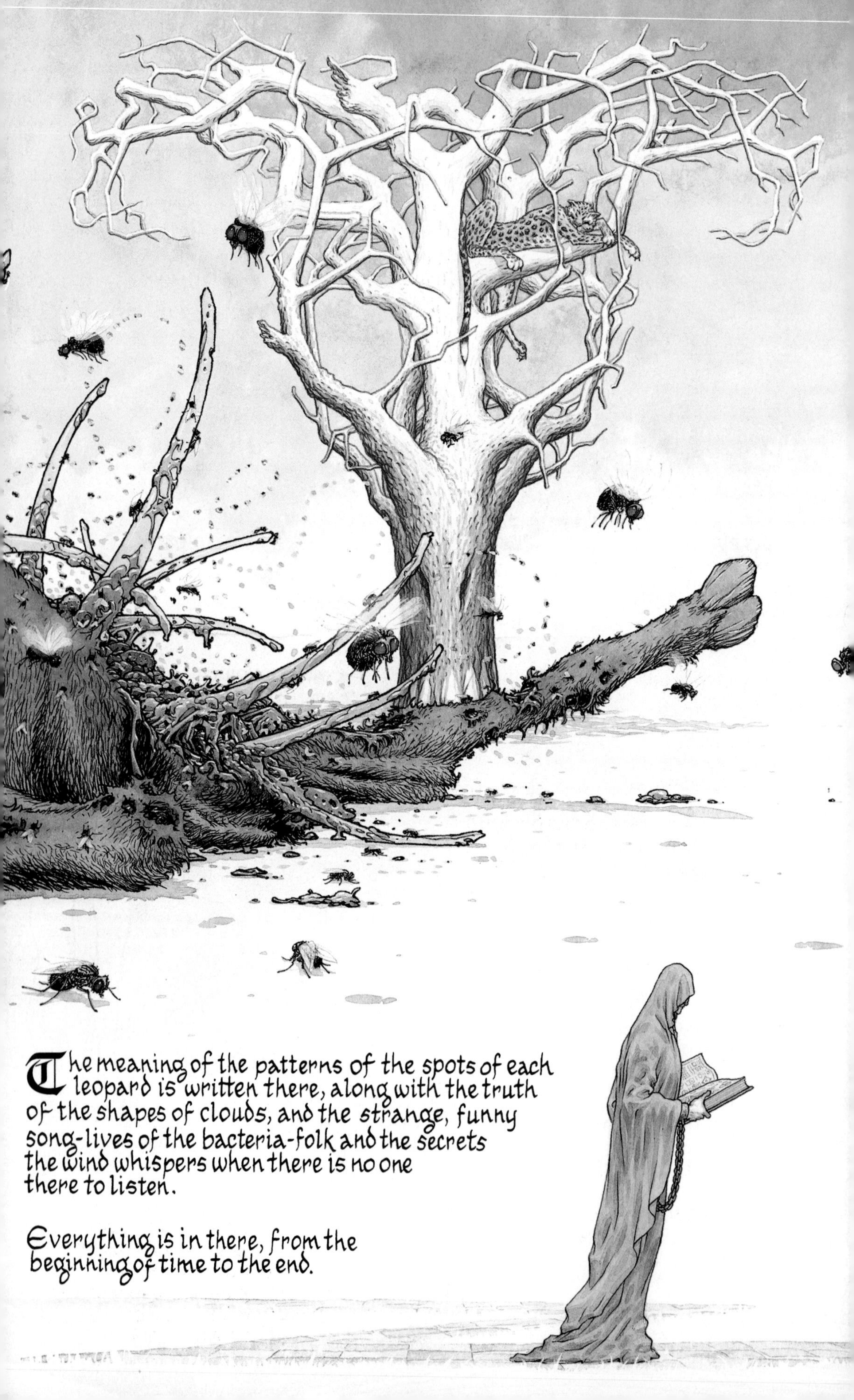
The meaning of the patterns of the spots of each leopard is written there, along with the truth of the shapes of clouds, and the strange, funny song-lives of the bacteria-folk and the secrets the wind whispers when there is no one there to listen.
Everything is in there, from the beginning of time to the end.

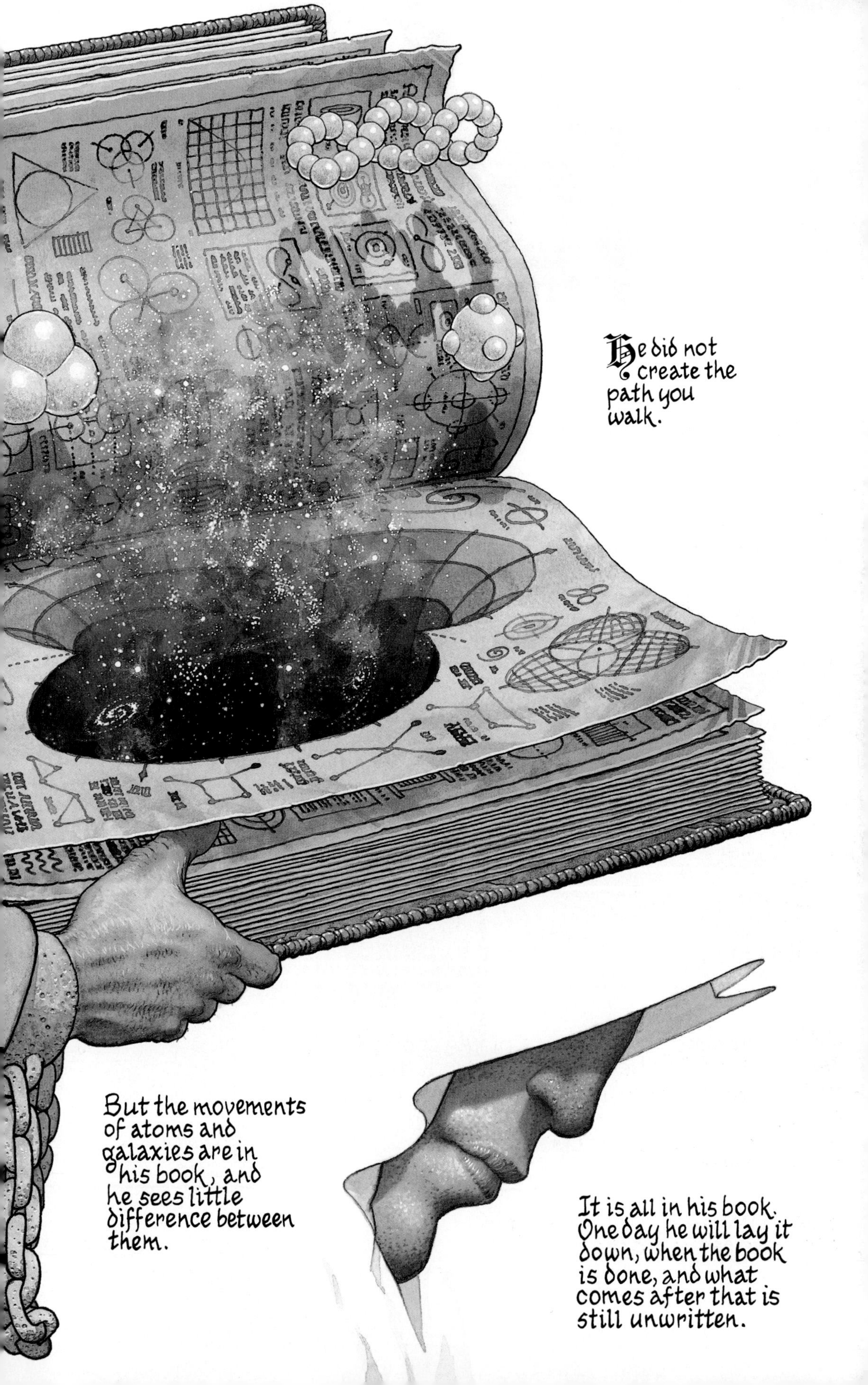
He did not create the path you walk.
But the movements of atoms and galaxies are in his book, and he sees little difference between them.
It is all in his book. One day he will lay it down, when the book is done, and what comes after that is still unwritten.

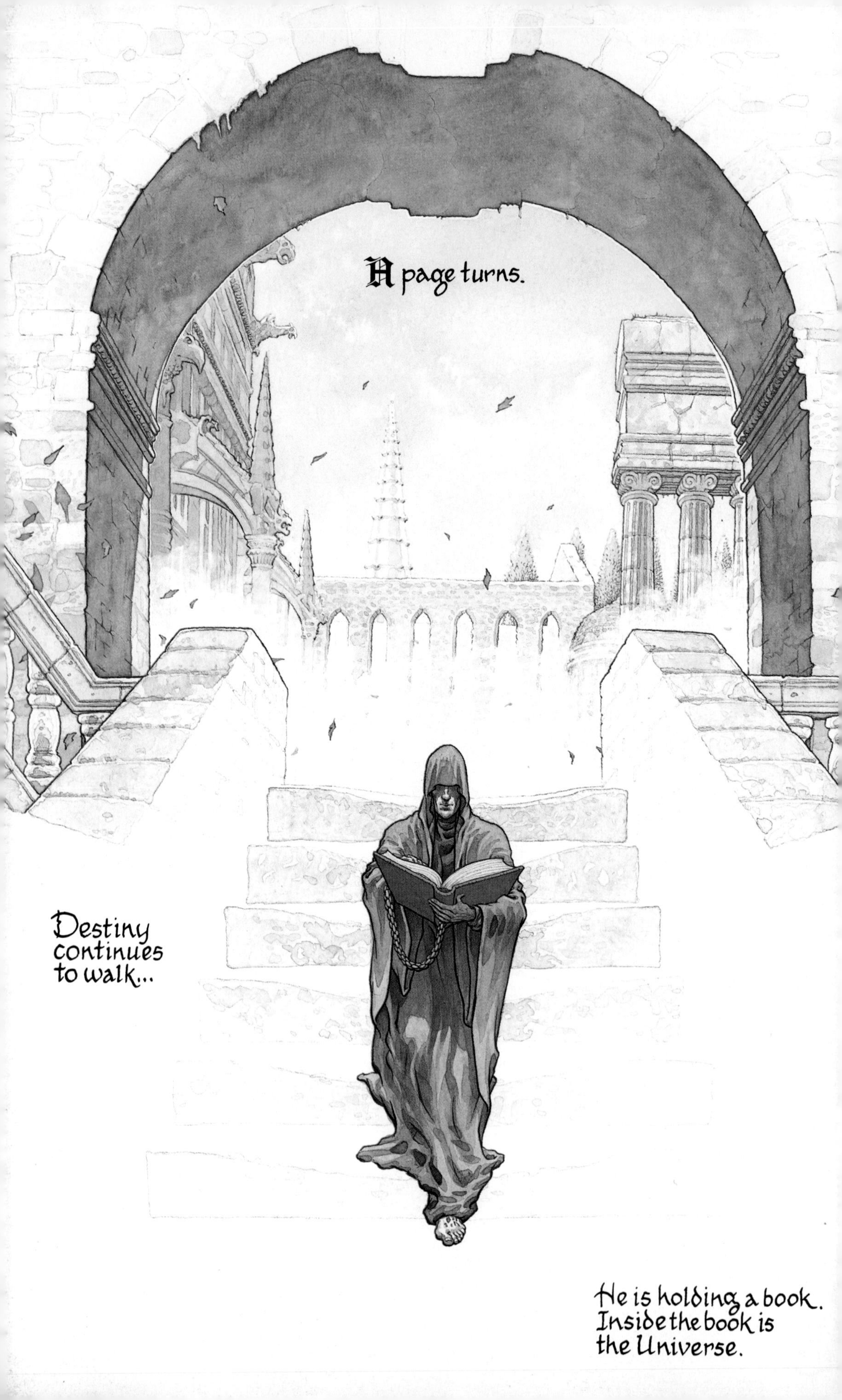
A page turns.
Destiny continues to walk...
He is holding a book. Inside the book is the Universe.

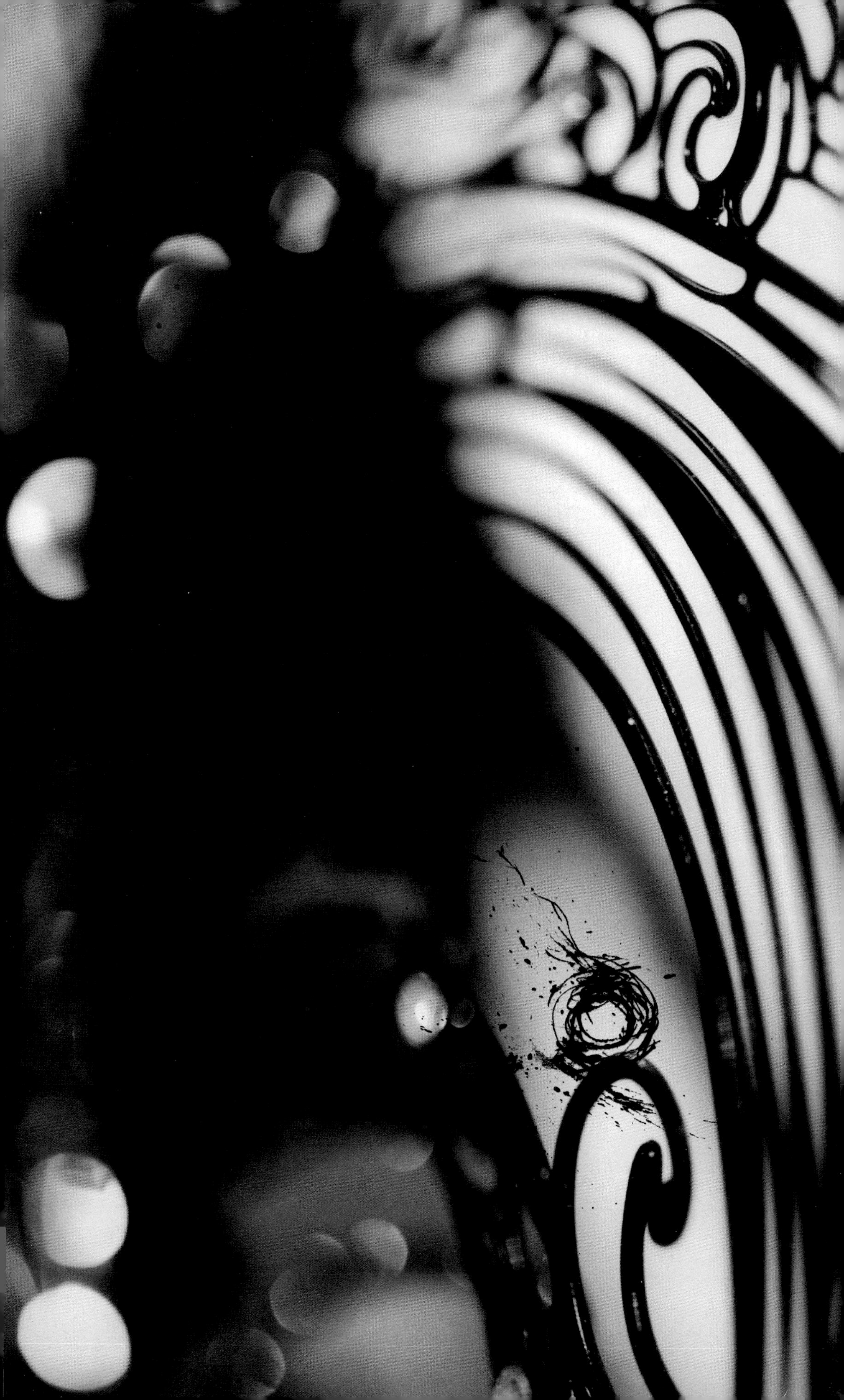

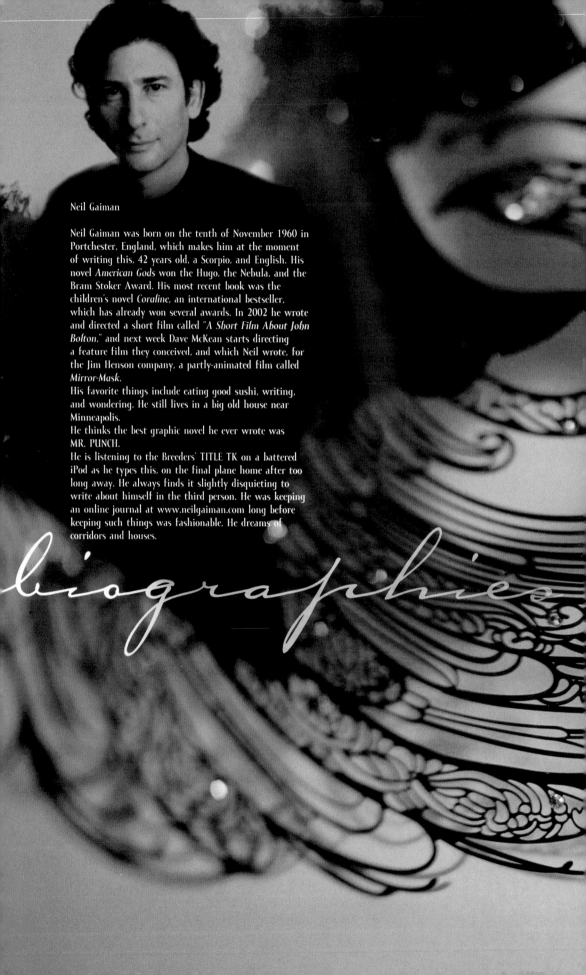

Neil Gaiman

Neil Gaiman was born on the tenth of November 1960 in
Portchester, England, which makes him at the moment
of writing this, 42 years old, a Scorpio, and English. His
novel *American Gods* won the Hugo, the Nebula, and the
Bram Stoker Award. His most recent book was the
children's novel *Coraline*, an international bestseller,
which has already won several awards. In 2002 he wrote
and directed a short film called "*A Short Film About John
Bolton*," and next week Dave McKean starts directing
a feature film they conceived, and which Neil wrote, for
the Jim Henson company, a partly-animated film called
Mirror-Mask.
His favorite things include eating good sushi, writing,
and wondering. He still lives in a big old house near
Minneapolis.
He thinks the best graphic novel he ever wrote was
MR. PUNCH.
He is listening to the Breeders' TITLE TK on a battered
iPod as he types this, on the final plane home after too
long away. He always finds it slightly disquieting to
write about himself in the third person. He was keeping
an online journal at www.neilgaiman.com long before
keeping such things was fashionable. He dreams of
corridors and houses.

biographies

Miguelanxo Prado

I was born in 1958 in A Coruna, a Galician city in Spain by the seacoast of the Atlantic Ocean, in the Europeans land's end.

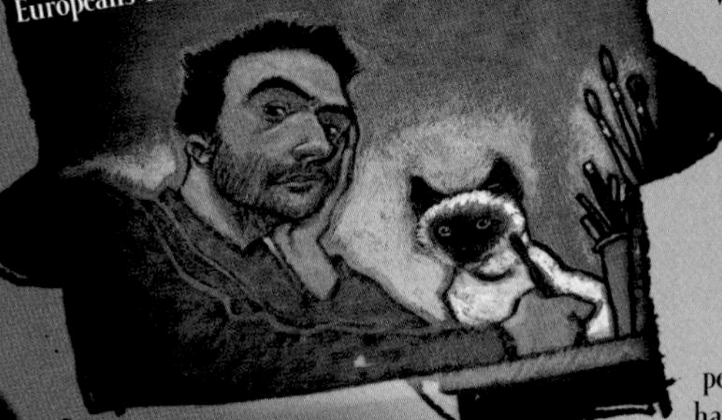

I had begun studying architecture but finally decided to leave it and engage in what I have always been passionate about, to paint and to write. I also create music, but 24 hours in a day was not enough time for everything, and I have left music. I started working in comics in the early eighties and I'm still painting. I illustrate books, collaborate in the press, do artistic direction for TV, character creation for the *Men in Black* cartoon series, and I engage myself in any project that looks appealing and is related to the world of image and storytelling.
For my work I use traditional means: pencils, pens, paintbrushes, paintings of every kind; but I have also been persuaded to use new technologies. I live in the country; I like to travel, to read, and to listen to music, to watch movies and to share good wine and good conversation with my friends.
And I wouldn't be able to live far from the sea for a long time.

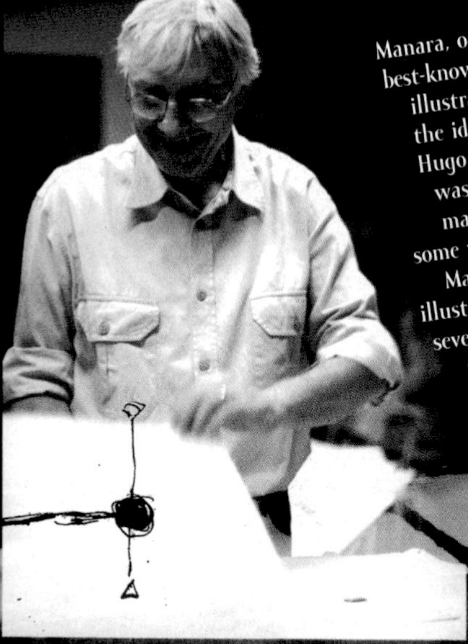

Milo Manara

Manara, one of the best-known Italian illustrators, was the ideal heir of Hugo Pratt who was his friend, master, and in some ways, agent. Manara started illustrating in the seventies on pulp magazines for adult readers.

Soon he became a master class artist and found critical acclaim even from the hard-to-please, cultured Italian readers still stunned by the graphic and narrative revolution of *Metal Hurlant* the French magazine which featured Manara's contemporaries such as Moebius, Druillet, and Caza. Manara made his debut drawing the epic-Buddhist adventures of *Lo Scimmiotto*, written by Silverio Pisu. Struck by the style of Moebius, Manara experimented with his style and improved upon it for his next work, *Alessio Borghese Rivoluzionario*. While the erotic charge and sexual irony of Manara's work have made him one of the world's premier illustrators, the overlooked qualities of his simple and attractive scenarios have made him an honest, artistic reporter of his times, through escapist literature and the erotic tale. His books have gained international success and include such titles as *Clik*, the playbills for Fellini's *L'intervista*, and many political and satirical shorts and comic strips.

Barron Storey

Who is Barron Storey? He's a good fellow, from a good family, who's done a lot of good work and taught a lot of good students including painters Kent Williams, George Pratt, John Van Fleet, and Seth among others. Along the way Barron discovered that something was not quite right about himself. He's been working that out for many years in the only way he knows how: through making art.
Winner of the NY Society of Illustrators Gold Medal in 1976, Barron has taught at many universities including the School of Visual Arts in New York City and Art Center College of Design. He's worked as a freelance illustrator for diverse clients from the United States Information Agency and NASA to *Heavy Metal* and Putnam Publishing. As an exhibiting artist, Barron has held many one-man shows in New York City and Washington, DC. Also active in theatre and music, he resides in San Francisco

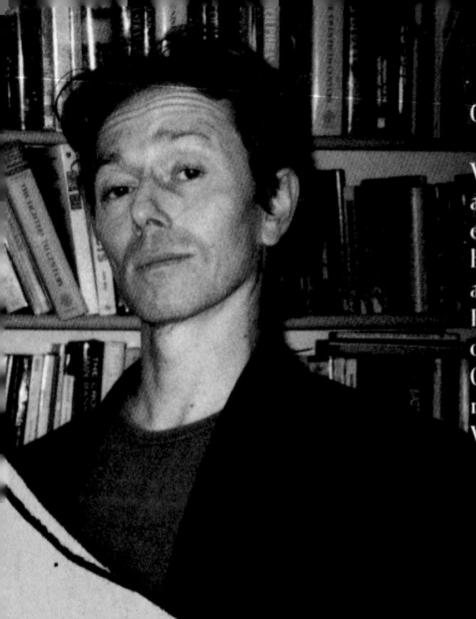

Glenn Fabry

When I was a little kid my dearest wish was to be a comic book artist, ideally for DC or *Marvel.* Well, let's face it, I wasn't good enough at seven, it wasn't going to happen. But the years passed, hair grew in unexpected places (once on the back of the toaster at my Granny's) and by 1984 I was drawing *Slaine* (by the great Pat Mills) for *2000 A.D.* in Britain. By 1992, I was painting covers for HELLBLAZER and later, PREACHER (by the estimable Garth Ennis) for DC/VERTIGO. My ambition had finally been realized: To sit in a room drawing for 20 years!
Well, it makes me happy.

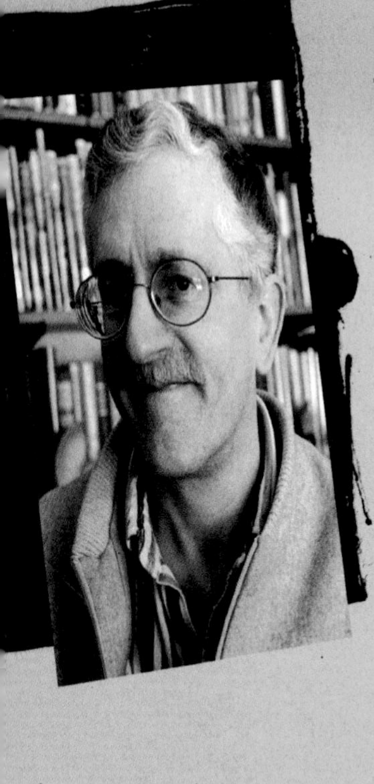

Todd Klein

Todd Klein has been lettering comics since 1977. A highlight of his career is his work with Neil Gaiman on nearly all the original issues of THE SANDMAN, as well as BLACK ORCHID, DEATH and THE BOOKS OF MAGIC. Currently he is teamed with Alan Moore on all the AMERICA'S BEST COMICS titles, Frank Miller on DK2, Linda Medley on *Castle Waiting* and Bill Willingham on FABLES, among others. Todd has won numerous Eisner and Harvey Awards for his work.

P. Craig Russell

P. Craig Russell is a 31-year veteran of the comics biz. His work ranges from superhero (BATMAN, *Dr. Strange)* to fantasy (THE SANDMAN, *Elric*) to adaptations of classic literature and opera (*The Magic Flute, The Ring of the Nibelung*).
He is currently (11 years and counting) adapting *The Complete Fairy Tales of Oscar Wilde.* ENDLESS NIGHTS: Death in Venice is his fourth collaboration with Neil Gaiman.

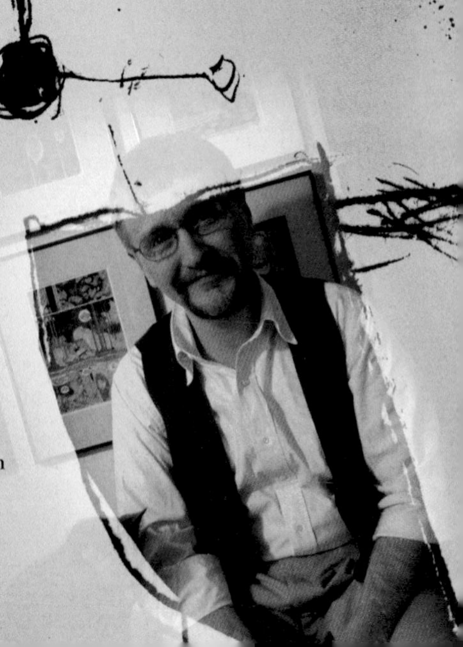

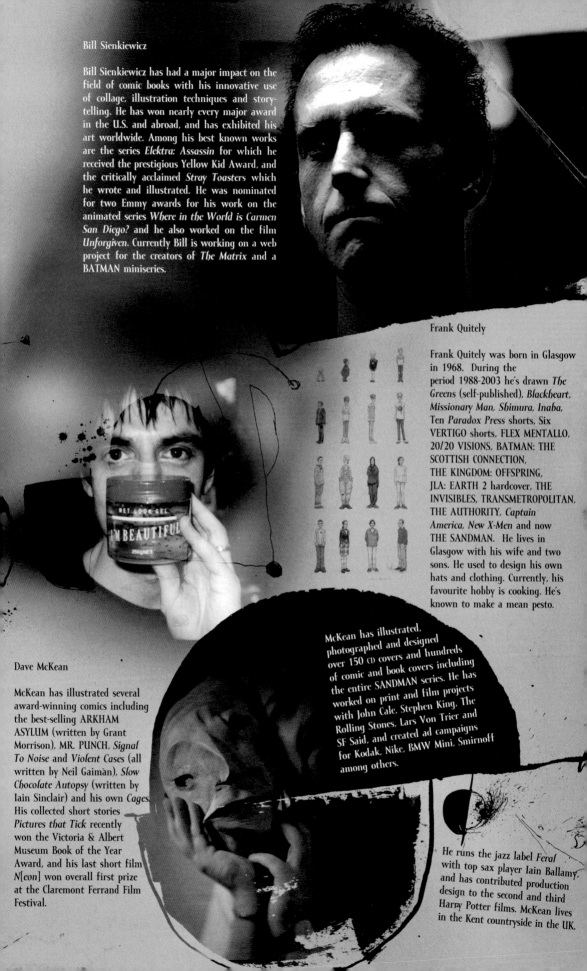

Bill Sienkiewicz

Bill Sienkiewicz has had a major impact on the field of comic books with his innovative use of collage, illustration techniques and story-telling. He has won nearly every major award in the U.S. and abroad, and has exhibited his art worldwide. Among his best known works are the series *Elektra: Assassin* for which he received the prestigious Yellow Kid Award, and the critically acclaimed *Stray Toasters* which he wrote and illustrated. He was nominated for two Emmy awards for his work on the animated series *Where in the World is Carmen San Diego?* and he also worked on the film *Unforgiven*. Currently Bill is working on a web project for the creators of *The Matrix* and a BATMAN miniseries.

Frank Quitely

Frank Quitely was born in Glasgow in 1968. During the period 1988-2003 he's drawn *The Greens* (self-published), *Blackheart*, *Missionary Man*, *Shimura*, *Inaba*, Ten *Paradox Press* shorts, Six VERTIGO shorts, FLEX MENTALLO, 20/20 VISIONS, BATMAN: THE SCOTTISH CONNECTION, THE KINGDOM: OFFSPRING, JLA: EARTH 2 hardcover, THE INVISIBLES, TRANSMETROPOLITAN, THE AUTHORITY, *Captain America*, *New X-Men* and now THE SANDMAN. He lives in Glasgow with his wife and two sons. He used to design his own hats and clothing. Currently, his favourite hobby is cooking. He's known to make a mean pesto.

Dave McKean

McKean has illustrated several award-winning comics including the best-selling ARKHAM ASYLUM (written by Grant Morrison), MR. PUNCH, *Signal To Noise* and *Violent Cases* (all written by Neil Gaimàn), *Slow Chocolate Autopsy* (written by Iain Sinclair) and his own *Cages*. His collected short stories *Pictures that Tick* recently won the Victoria & Albert Museum Book of the Year Award, and his last short film *N[eon]* won overall first prize at the Claremont Ferrand Film Festival.

McKean has illustrated, photographed and designed over 150 CD covers and hundreds of comic and book covers including the entire SANDMAN series. He has worked on print and film projects with John Cale, Stephen King, The Rolling Stones, Lars Von Trier and SF Said, and created ad campaigns for Kodak, Nike, BMW Mini, Smirnoff among others.

He runs the jazz label *Feral* with top sax player Iain Ballamy, and has contributed production design to the second and third Harry Potter films. McKean lives in the Kent countryside in the UK.

The Sandman Library

Ten definitive graphic novels that reveal the story of Morpheus and the Endless, his uniquely dysfunctional family.

Preludes & Nocturnes

Dream of the Endless, also known as the Sandman, had been trapped for 70 years. After his imprisonment and eventual escape, the Sandman must reclaim his realm, The Dreaming, as well as his articles of power: his helmet, his pouch and his amulet.

The Doll's House

Rose Walker finds more than she bargained for including long lost relatives, a serial killers' convention and, ultimately, her true identity when The Sandman attempts to unravel her mystery.

Dream Country

Four chilling and unique tales: *Calliope, Dream of a Thousand Cats, Façade,* and *A Midsummer Night's Dream,* The World Fantasy Award-winning story of the first performance of William Shakespeare's play with art by Charles Vess. Also contains Gaiman's original comic book script for *Calliope.*

Season of Mists

Ten thousand years ago, the Sandman condemned his one true love to the pits of Hell. When his sister Death convinces him that Nada was unjustly imprisoned, Dream journeys to Hell to rescue his lost lover ... just as Lucifer Morningstar decides to abdicate his throne... leaving the Key to Hell in the hands of the Sandman.

A Game of You

Barbie, from The Doll's House, used to dream of being a princess in a lush, private kingdom with strange animals as her subjects. But Barbie has stopped dreaming. Now her imaginary world and her real world entwine in a riveting story about gender and identity.

Fables & Reflections

From the mists of the past to the nightmares of the present, Dream touches the lives of Haroun Al Raschid, King of Ancient Baghdad, Lady Johanna Constantine, spy and adventuress, and Joshua Norton, self-styled emperor of the United States, among others in nine remarkable self-contained stories.

Brief Lives

Delirium, youngest of the Endless, prevails upon her brother Dream to help find their missing brother, Destruction. Their odyssey through the waking world also leads the Sandman to resolve his painful relationship with his son, Orpheus.

Worlds' End

Caught in the vortex of a reality storm, wayfarers from throughout time, myth and the imagination converge on a mysterious inn. In the tradition of Chaucer's Canterbury Tales, the travelers wait out the tempest that rages around them by sharing stories.

The Kindly Ones

Frightened people called them The Kindly Ones. Unstoppable in their mission of vengeance, they would not rest until the crime they sought to punish had been avenged; had been washed clean, with blood. Now Dream of the Endless, his acquaintances and his family find themselves caught up in a dark conspiracy. And someone is going to die.

The Wake

Ancient gods, old friends and enemies gather to pay tribute, and to remember, in the strangest wake ever held. And, at the end of his life, William Shakespeare fulfills his side of a very strange bargain.

Related Titles:

The Sandman: The Dream Hunters

Set in Japan, this adult fairytale, told in single illustration and prose, is beautifully painted by legendary artist Yoshitaka Amano.

Death: The High Cost of Living

One day every century, Death takes on mortal form to learn more about the lives she must take.

Death: The Time of Your Life

When a young mother makes a deal with Death to save her young son, her girlfriend pays the price in a story about fame, relationships and rock and roll.

Books about THE SANDMAN

The Sandman Companion – by Hy Bender

Dust Covers – The Collected SANDMAN Covers 1989 – 1997

The Quotable Sandman

The Sandman – King of Dreams

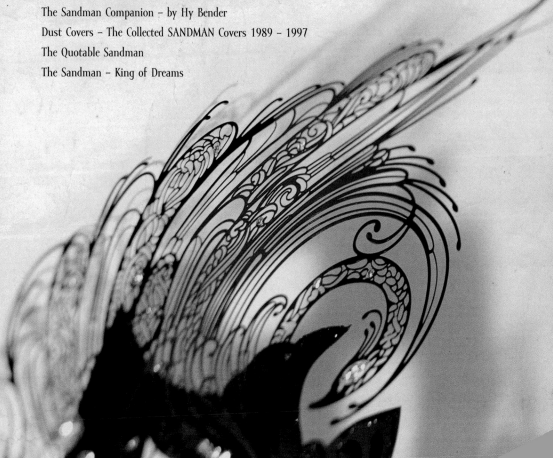

THE SANDMAN VOL. 4:
SEASON OF MISTS

FROM THE NEW YORK TIMES # 1 BEST-SELLING AUTHOR

NEIL GAIMAN
THE SANDMAN

Read the complete
series!

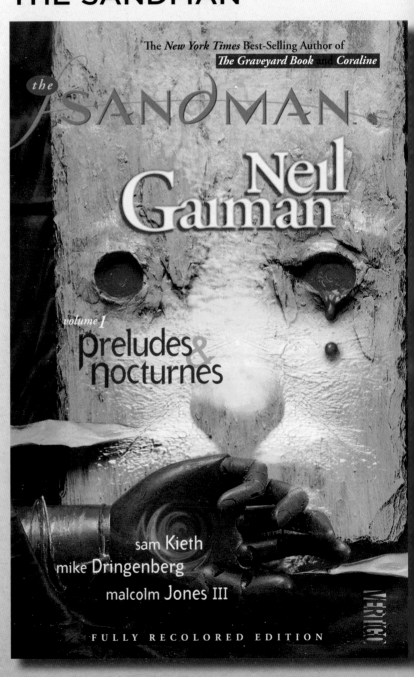